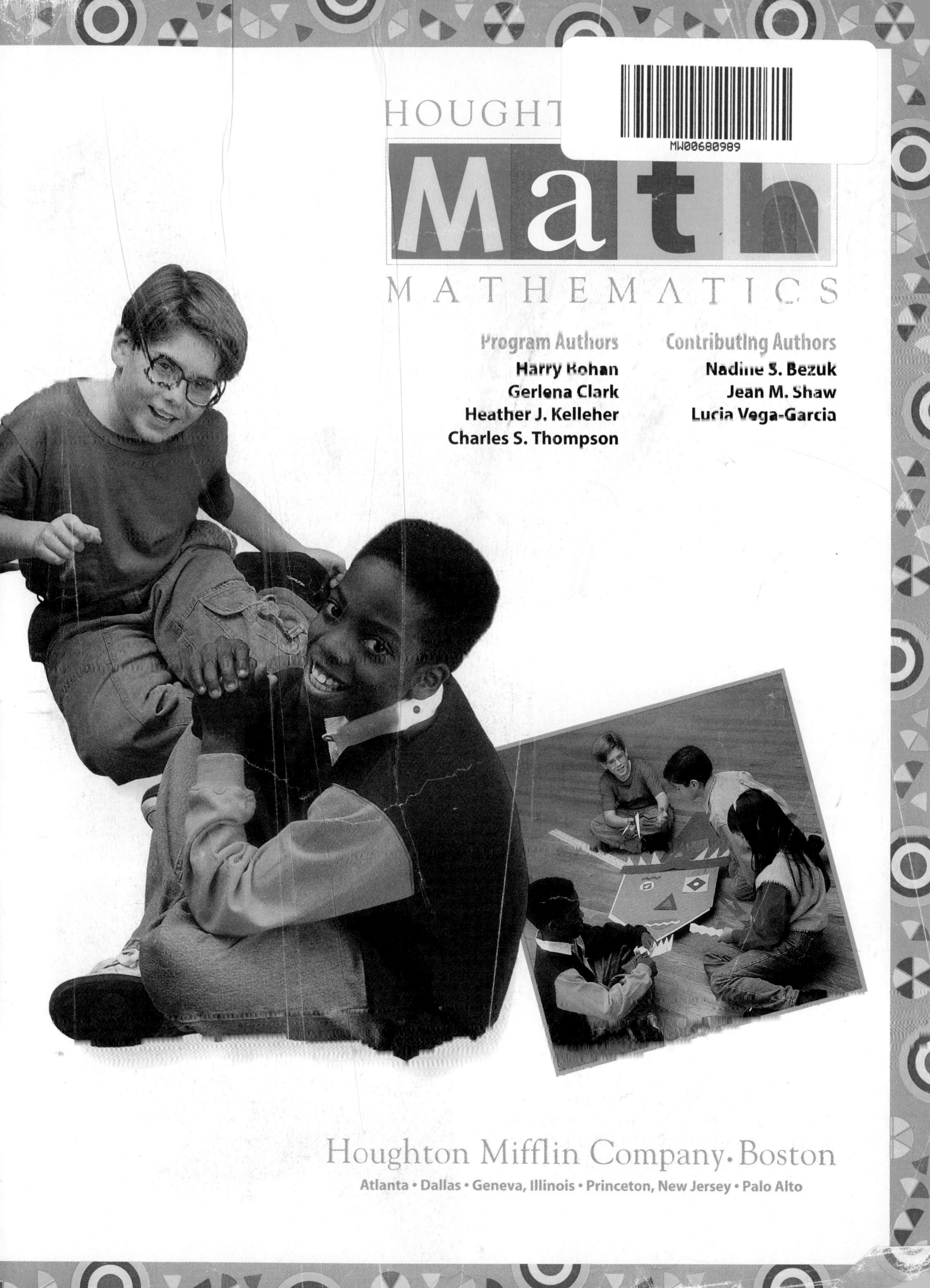

HOUGHT[illegible]

# Math

MATHEMATICS


Program Authors
Harry Bohan
Gerlena Clark
Heather J. Kelleher
Charles S. Thompson

Contributing Authors
Nadine S. Bezuk
Jean M. Shaw
Lucia Vega-Garcia





Houghton Mifflin Company • Boston

Atlanta • Dallas • Geneva, Illinois • Princeton, New Jersey • Palo Alto

# Authors and Contributors

**Nadine S. Bezuk**
Associate Professor of Mathematics Education
San Diego State University
San Diego, CA

*Contributing Author, Developer of Concept and Materials for* Math to Go

**Harry Bohan**
Professor of Mathematics Education
Sam Houston State University
Huntsville, TX

*Program Author, Developer of Philosophy and Grades 3-6*

**Gerlena Clark**
Los Angeles County Mathematics Consultant
Los Angeles, CA

*Program Author, Developer of Philosophy and Teacher Training Materials*

**Heather J. Kelleher**
Former Classroom Teacher and Doctoral Student
University of British Columbia
Vancouver, BC, Canada

*Program Author, Developer of Philosophy and Grades 1–2*

**Jean M. Shaw**
Professor of Elementary Education
University of Mississippi
University, MS

*Contributing Author, Developer of Kindergarten Level*

**Charles S. Thompson**
Professor of Education
University of Louisville
Louisville, KY

*Program Author, Developer of Philosophy and Grades 3–6*

**Lucia Vega-Garcia**
Bilingual Education Director
Santa Clara County Office of Education
San Jose, CA

*Contributing Author, Developer of Teacher Support for Students Acquiring English*

## Acknowledgments

Grateful acknowledgment is made for the use of the following material: **36** From *Counting on Frank*, by Rod Clement. U.S. edition copyright © 1991 by Gareth Stevens Children's Books.
*—Continued on page 462*



*Developed and produced by* Ligature

Printed in the U.S.A. ISBN: 0-395-67911-7
23456789-VH-98 97 96 95 94

## Specialists

**Brenda Gentry-Norton**
Research Associate
Program for Complex Instruction
Stanford University
Palo Alto, CA
*Consultant for Assessment Philosophy and Materials*

**Brenda Glen**
Classroom Teacher
Balderas Elementary School
Fresno, CA
*Field Test Coordinator and Developer of Teacher's Edition Notes, Grades 5–6*

**Joan L. Hopkins**
Classroom Teacher
Escondido Elementary School
Palo Alto, CA
*Field Test Coordinator and Developer of Teacher's Edition Notes, Grades K–2*

**Betty Iehl**
Educational Consultant
San Gabriel, CA
*Developer of Teacher's Edition Notes, Grades 4 and 6*

**National Center to Improve the Tools of Educators**
Douglas Carnine, Director
Edward Kameenui, Associate Director
University of Oregon
Eugene, OR
*Developer of Alternate Strategies Materials, Grades 2–6*

**Mary Anne O'Neal**
Educational Consultant
Carson, CA
*Developer of Teacher's Edition Notes, Grades 3 and 5*

**Annie Podesto**
Staff Development Specialist
Stockton Unified School District
Stockton, CA
*Consultant for Assessment Philosophy and Materials*

**Sally Y. Wong**
Title VII Adviser
Los Angeles Unified School District
Los Angeles, CA
*Developer of Teacher's Edition Notes, Grades 3–6*

## Field Test Teachers

### Kindergarten Modules

**Traci Assad,** Fall River Summer School Program, Fall River, MA • **Susanne Burke,** Holmes School, Dorchester, MA • **Leland Clarke,** Holmes School, Dorchester, MA • **Beverly Letendre,** Fall River Summer School Program, Fall River, MA • **Sarah Outten,** Slade Regional Catholic School, Glen Burnie, MD • **Debbie L. Rea,** Escondido School, Stanford, CA • **Pat Robinson,** Escondido School, Stanford, CA

### Grade 1 Modules

**Robin Crawley,** Holmes School Dorchester, MA • **Suraya Driscoll,** River Heights School, East Grand Forks, MN • **Nancy Matthews,** Douglas School, Douglas, MA • **Mary Miller,** Holmes School, Dorchester, MA • **Johanna Roses,** Baker School, Chestnut Hill, MA • **Elaine Kuritani Tsumura,** Marrama School, Denver, CO

### Grade 2 Modules

**Najwa Abdul-Tawwab,** Holmes School, Dorchester, MA • **Mary Jane Brown,** Forwood School, Wilmington, DE • **Joan L. Hopkins,** Escondido School, Stanford, CA • **Dorene Odom,** Holmes School, Dorchester, MA • **Ida R. Wellington,** Washington School, Oakland, CA

### Grade 3 Modules

**Robin Burstein,** Greenwood School, Des Moines, IA • **Joanne Castelano,** Slade Regional Catholic School, Glen Burnie, MD • **Diane Rezek Fator,** Emerson School, Berwyn, IL • **Linda Griffiths,** Kennedy School, San Diego, CA • **Michele Hilbing,** Slade Regional Catholic School, Glen Burnie, MD • **Sharnell Jackson** Decatur School, Chicago, IL • **Janet M. Laws,** Lombardy School, Wilmington, DE • **Patricia Y. Lynch,** Lombardy School, Wilmington, DE • **Efraín Meléndez,** Dacotah Street School, Los Angeles, CA • **Doris Miles,** Sandburg School, Wheaton, IL • **Ricki Raymond,** Piper School, Berwyn, IL • **Deb Schantzen,** River Heights School, East Grand Forks, MN • **Bonnie Schindler,** Kennedy School, San Diego, CA • **Theresa Sievers,** Komensky School, Berwyn, IL • **Kimberly Bassett Whitehead,** Lombardy School, Wilmington, DE

### Grade 4 Modules

**Lynda Alexander,** St. Elizabeth School, Chicago, IL • **Betty Coleman,** Parkman School, Chicago, IL • **Karen DeRon-Head,** Armour School, Chicago, IL • **Keith Libert,** Escondido School, Stanford, CA • **Joe Montoya,** Horace Mann School, Rapid City, SD • **Robert Poncé,** Niños Heroes School, Chicago, IL

### Grade 5 Modules

**Lynnise H. Akinkunle-Gool,** Niños Heroes School, Chicago, IL • **Doris Buffo,** Balderas School, Fresno, CA • **Ronni K. Cohen,** Burnett School, Wilmington, DE • **Valerie De George,** Greeley School, Chicago, IL • **Brenda Glen,** Balderas School, Fresno, CA • **Brenda Leigh,** River Heights School, East Grand Forks, MN • **Cynthia L. Lew,** Madison School, Pomona, CA • **Lisa Palacios,** Pleasant Hill School, Carol Stream, IL • **Kathryn Peecher,** Revere School, Chicago, IL • **Cindy Sardo,** Burnett School, Wilmington, DE • **Henry A. Simmons,** Balderas School, Fresno, CA • **Delorise Singley,** Oakwood Windsor School, Aiken, SC • **Cecilia Maria Vasquez,** Balderas School, Fresno, CA • **Michelle Wilson,** Jefferson School, Fresno, CA

### Grade 6 Modules

**Dorothy Cooper Jones,** Banneker Achievement Center, Gary, IN • **Albert Martinez,** Marianna Avenue School, Los Angeles, CA • **Sharon Oechsel,** Hiawatha School, Berwyn, IL • **Christopher G. Reising,** Kennedy School, San Diego, CA • **Lee Wirth,** Pershing School, Berwyn, IL

## Reviewers

**Kathryn A. Alexander,** Macon Middle School, Brunswick, GA (Grade 6 modules) • **Sherry Bailey,** Richland School District #2, Columbia, SC (Grade 5 modules) • **Elisheva Bellomore,** Scarborough School District, Scarborough, ME (Grade 5 modules) • **Sharon L. Cannon,** Myrtle Beach Middle School, Myrtle Beach, SC (Grade 6 modules) • **Cleo Charging,** White Shield School, Roseglen, ND (Grade K modules) • **Judy C. Curtis,** Colfax School, Denver, CO (Grade 3 modules) • **Myra S. Dietz,** Carroll School #46, Rochester, NY (Grade 6 modules) • **W. L. Duncker,** Midland School District, Midland, TX (Grade 5 modules) • **Donna Marie Falat,** Longfellow School, Bridgeport, CT (Grade 2 modules) • **Linda Gojak,** Hawken School, Lyndhurst, OH (Grade 6 modules) • **Annette D. Ham,** Waltersville School, Bridgeport, CT (Grade 5 modules) • **Feliciano Mendoza,** Miles Avenue School, Huntington Park, CA (Grades 5 and 6 modules) • **Kenneth Millett,** Department of Mathematics, University of California, Santa Barbara, CA (Grade 6 modules) • **Rita Nappi,** Read School, Bridgeport, CT (Grade 4 modules) • **Mahesh Sharma,** Cambridge College, Cambridge, MA (Grades K and 6 modules) • **Patricia E. Smith,** Crosswell School, Easley, SC (Grades 3 and 4 modules) • **Bonnie Townzen,** Lubin School, Sacramento, CA (Grade 1 modules) • **Angelia W. Whiting,** Beardsley School, Bridgeport, CT (Grade 1 modules) • **Pamela Yoka,** Covedale School, Cincinnati, OH (Grade K modules)

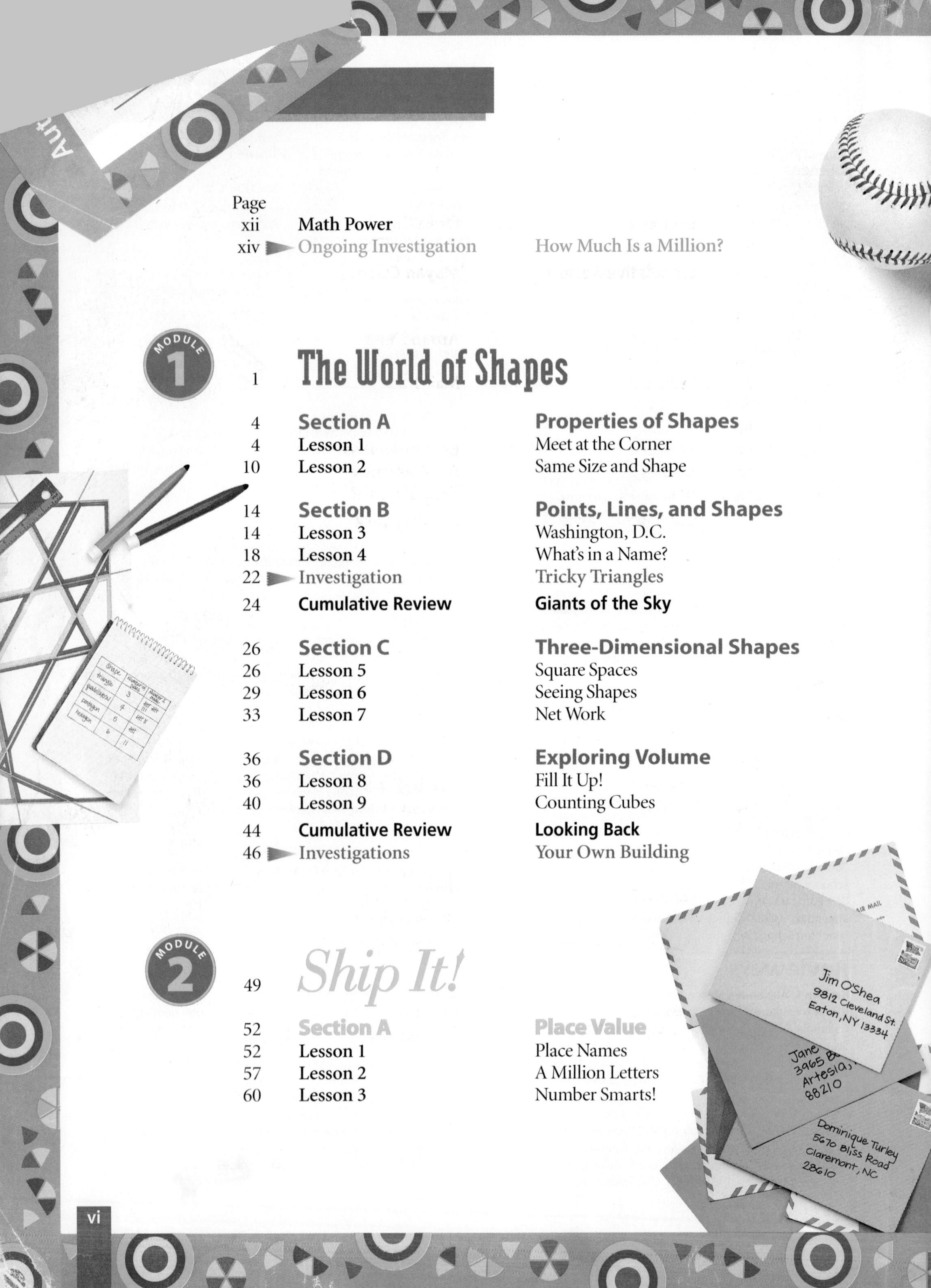




Jim O'Shea
9812 Cleveland St.
Eaton, NY 13334
Dominique Turley
5670 Bliss Road
Claremont, NC
28610

Contents

MODULE
3

Penelope Gorgo
7684 Blossom Ave.
Tallapoosa, GA
30176

José Alfaro
7653 Thayer Rd.
San Geronimo, CA
94963

MODULE 4

# 193 Discovering Treasure

# 241 Decimals in My World

## Contents

MODULE
8




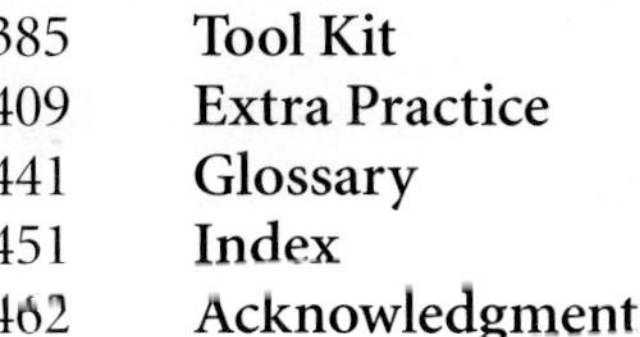

JULY in Mayport, Florida
JULY in Portland, Oregon
Portland, Oregon

# Math Power

The goal of this book is to help you build your **math power.** Math power means being able to understand and use math.

Learning to think mathematically and developing your skills as a problem solver are important parts of building math power.

By communicating about math, you can make your thinking clearer and find connections between new math ideas and the math you already know.

**As your math power grows,** you'll use math more and more in your daily life. Math power can help you in shopping, planning activities, or working on your favorite hobby.

Math power can also help people in their jobs. Whatever job you may have one day, you can be pretty sure that it will involve math. Discuss with your class some ways that pilots or nurses or construction workers use math in their work.

*These students are showing some keys to math power. When you see one of these keys in your book, you will know that the question or activity below it can help you build math power.*

Ongoing Investigation

# How Much Is a Million?

This is the first of many investigations you'll find in this book. But what is an investigation, anyway? An investigation is an open-ended problem. That means it may not have just one right answer. In fact, an investigation can lead to many answers and even to other questions.

An investigation also takes time. Some take hours or days. Others take a week or more. This one is called an ongoing investigation—you'll work on it all year.

## 1 First Thoughts

**This year, your class will investigate how much a million is. Your goal will be to collect a million pieces of something by the end of the year. What items can you count or measure in millions? Start a list.**

## 2 So Many Choices . . .

**Working with your group, make a plan for what your class should collect this year. You'll want to think about questions like these:**

- Can everyone in the class easily get the item?
- Does the item come in one standard size?
- About how much space will it take to store a million of the item?
- What will you do with your collection at the end of the year? Can you recycle it or donate it to some group?

**Record your ideas.**

| | Easy to get? | Standard size? | Storage space? | Recyclable? |
|---|---|---|---|---|
| buttons | | | | |
| canceled stamps | | | | |
| paper clips | | | | |
| | | | | |
| | | | | |
| | | | | |

## 3 Plan Ahead

**You'll also need to think about how to manage your collection as it grows.**

- Where will you store it?
- What size containers will you need?
- How will you know when you have a million?
- What kind of record-keeping system will you use?

**Now write your plan.**

## Keep In Mind

Be sure to do the following things in your plan:

- ☐ State clearly what items you considered and which your group thinks is best.
- ☐ Support your choice with words, numbers—even a chart or graph.
- ☐ Answer important questions about size and storage.
- ☐ Plan for problems you might have in collecting your chosen item.

### 4 Get Going

After your class decides what to collect, make a class plan. Figure out how to get started, and assign jobs to individuals or groups. By the end of the year, you'll have a good idea of a million.

### Computer Option

You may want to use a spreadsheet program to track your collection as it grows. You could even print out a line graph to predict when you'll reach your goal.

Investigate! Investigate! Investigate! Investigate! Investigate! Investigate! Investigate! Investigate! Investigate! Investigate! Investigate! Investigate! Investigate!

# Investigations Preview

You will learn to describe and compare different types of shapes. This will help you design tricky triangles and even trickier buildings.

**Tricky Triangles** (pages 22–23)

How many different kinds of triangles can you make? Plan a way to find as many kinds of triangles as possible.

**Your Own Building** (pages 46–48)

How are shapes used in buildings? Use what you know about shapes to design your own building.

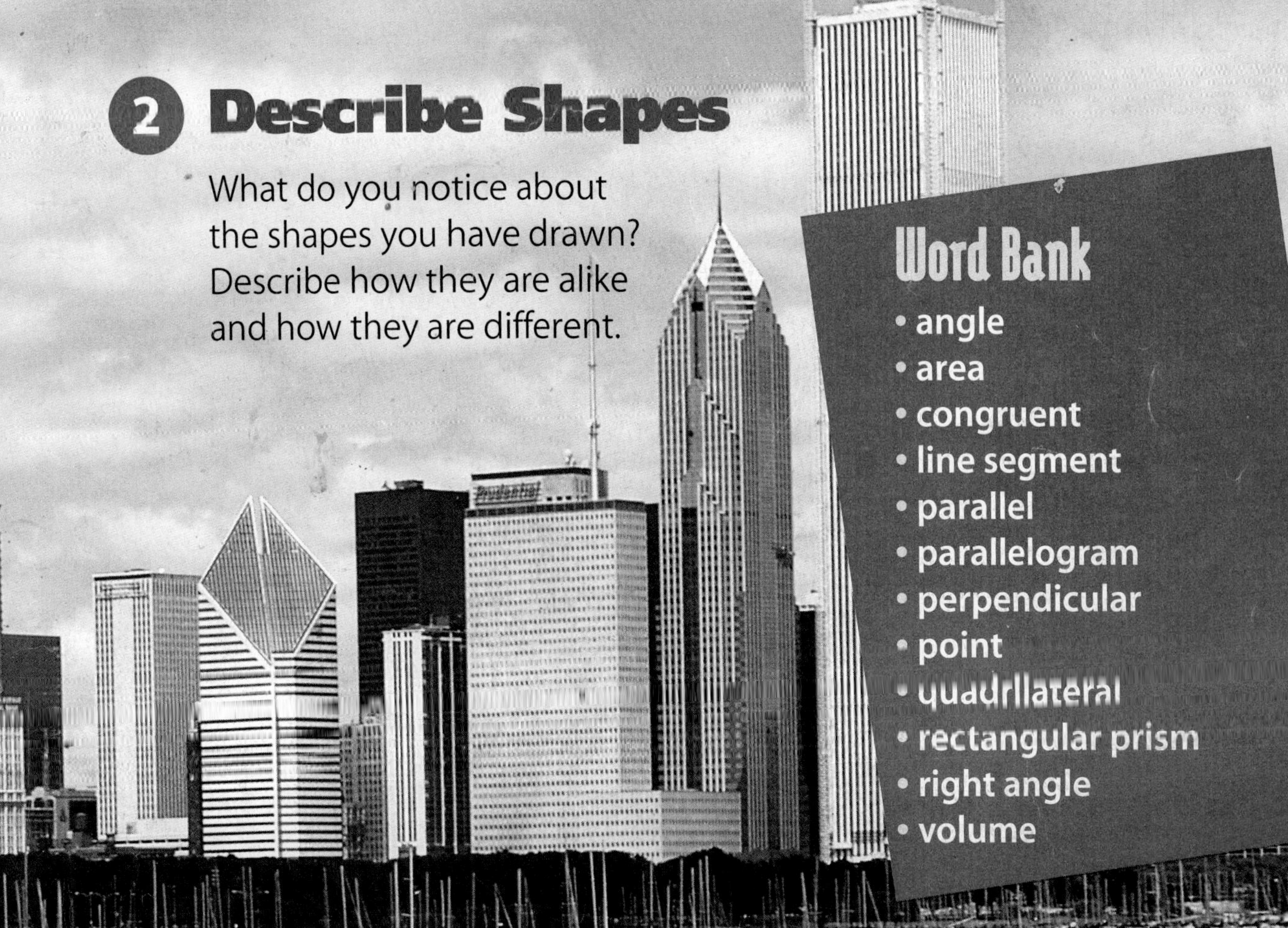

## 2 Describe Shapes

What do you notice about the shapes you have drawn? Describe how they are alike and how they are different.

### Word Bank

- angle
- area
- congruent
- line segment
- parallel
- parallelogram
- perpendicular
- point
- quadrilateral
- rectangular prism
- right angle
- volume

## Properties of Shapes

# Meet at the Corner

## ACTIVITY 1 Streets and Corners

**With Your Class** Explore the map and answer these questions.

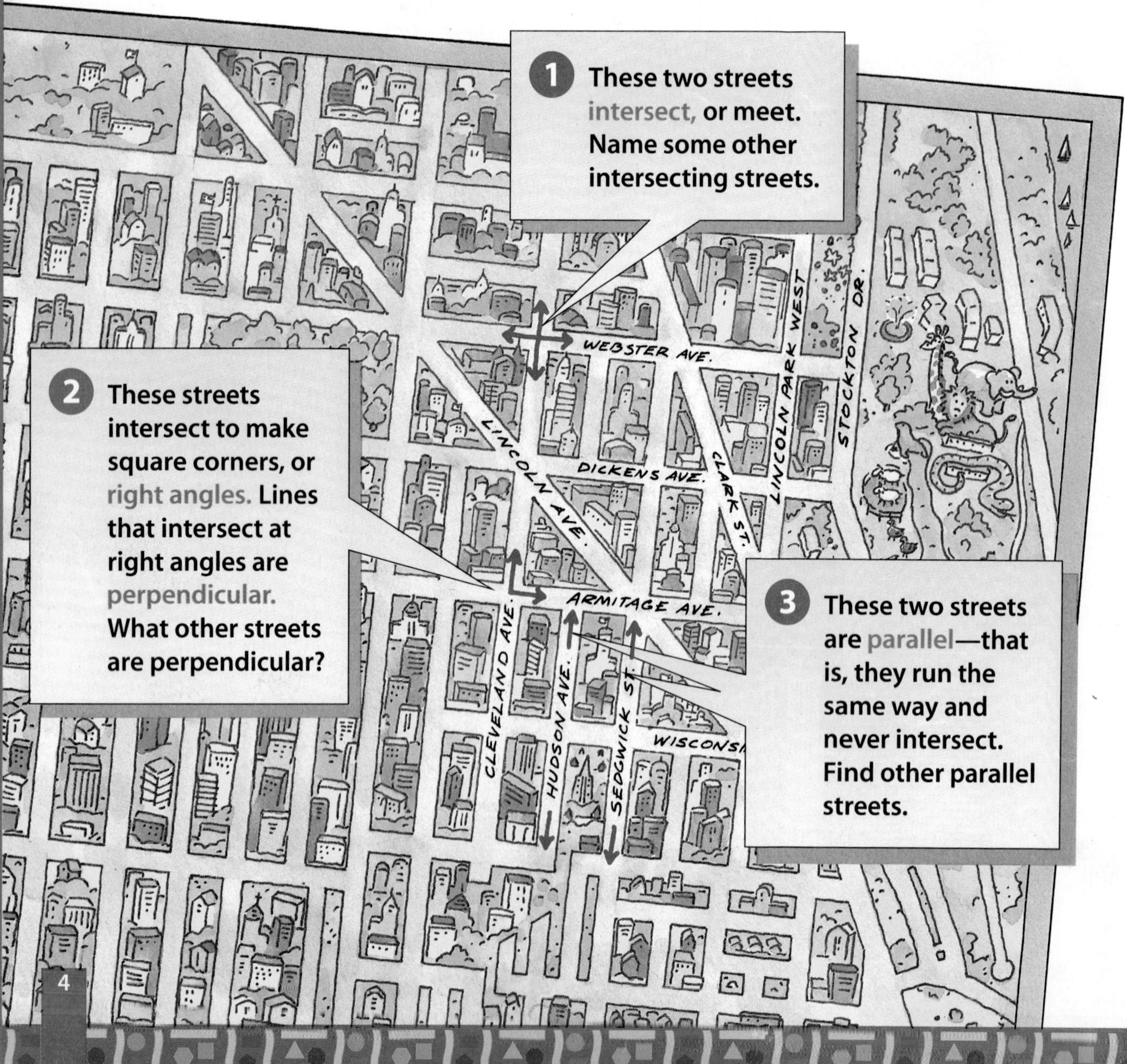

**1** These two streets intersect, or meet. Name some other intersecting streets.

**2** These streets intersect to make square corners, or right angles. Lines that intersect at right angles are perpendicular. What other streets are perpendicular?

**3** These two streets are parallel—that is, they run the same way and never intersect. Find other parallel streets.

WEBSTER AVE.
LINCOLN AVE.
DICKENS AVE.
CLARK ST.
LINCOLN PARK WEST
STOCKTON DR.
ARMITAGE AVE.
CLEVELAND AVE.
HUDSON AVE.
SEDGWICK ST.
WISCONSI

## ACTIVITY 2 Shape Sketches

**On Your Own** Intersecting lines can make shapes. What kinds of shapes can you make just by drawing straight lines?

### What You'll Need

- *ruler*
- *colored pencils or markers*

*You can do this activity on the computer if you have a drawing program.*

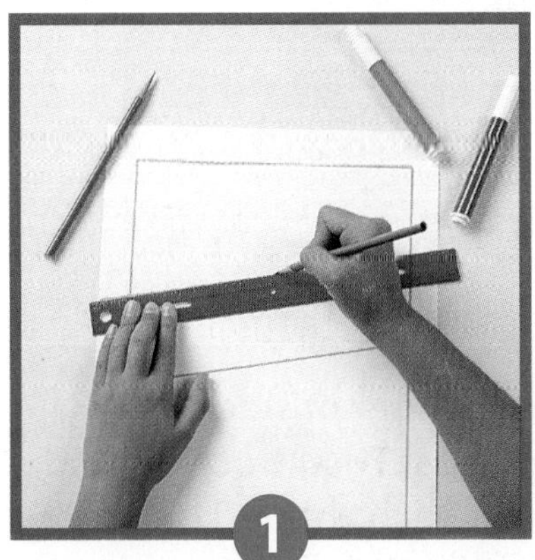

**1** **Draw a border around your paper. Then draw two parallel lines across the page.**

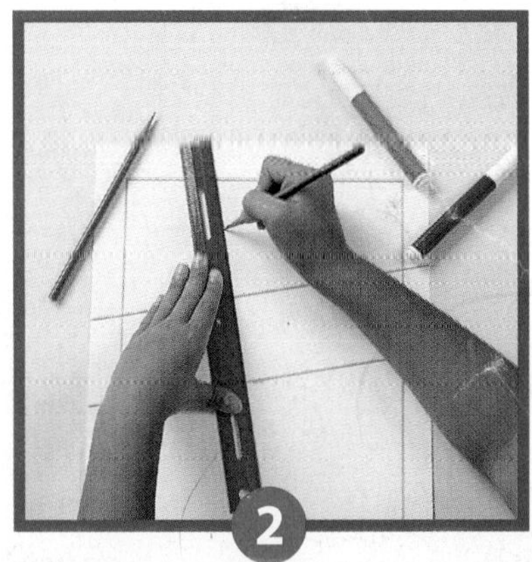

**2** **Draw a straight line through the parallel lines to make perpendicular lines.**

**3** **Draw five more straight lines across the page. Make sure you have many intersecting lines.**

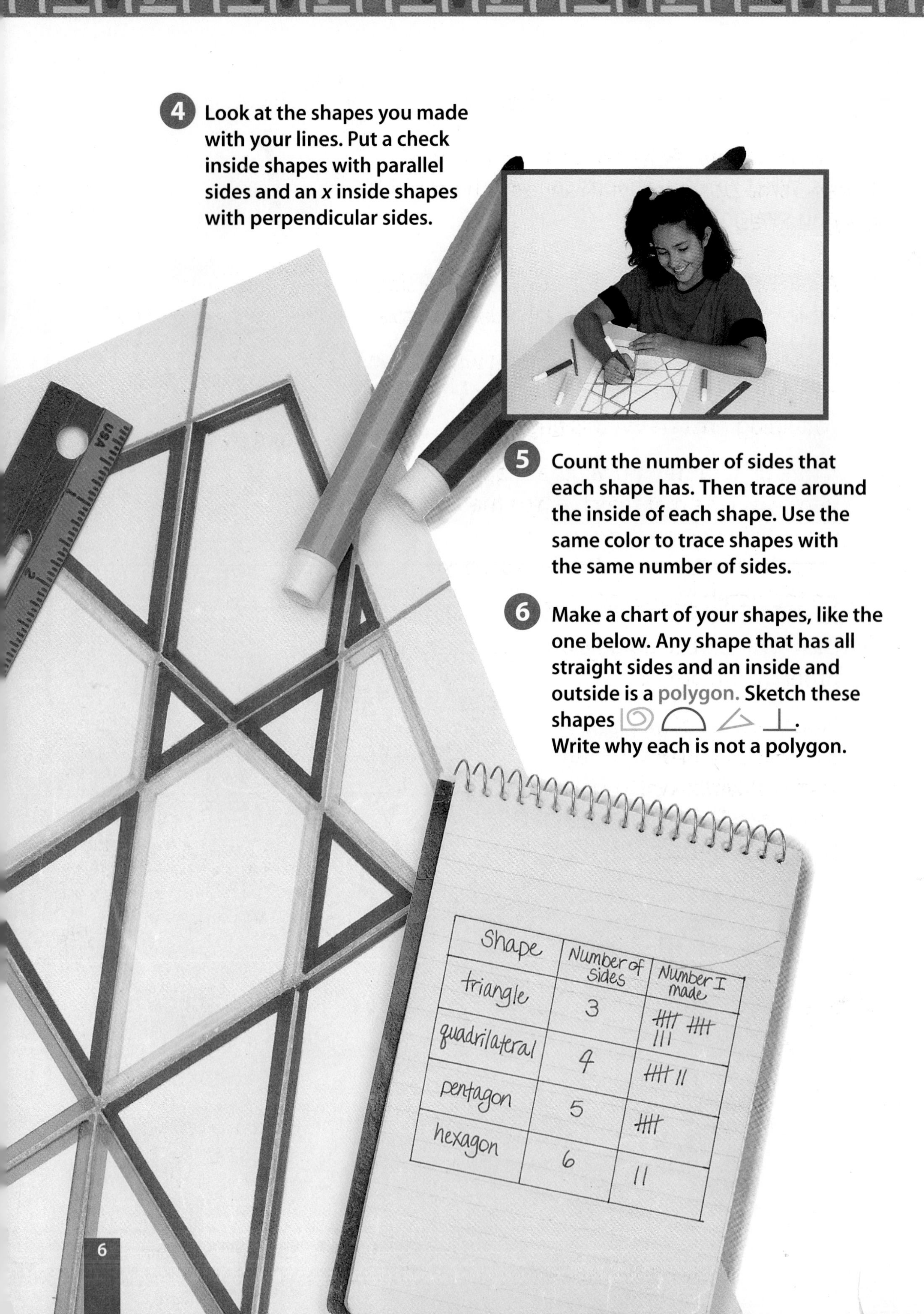


**4** Look at the shapes you made with your lines. Put a check inside shapes with parallel sides and an *x* inside shapes with perpendicular sides.

**5** Count the number of sides that each shape has. Then trace around the inside of each shape. Use the same color to trace shapes with the same number of sides.

**6** Make a chart of your shapes, like the one below. Any shape that has all straight sides and an inside and outside is a **polygon.** Sketch these shapes. Write why each is not a polygon.

## ACTIVITY 3 Four-sided Shapes

**On Your Own** Polygons come in many shapes. Some polygons with four sides have special names.

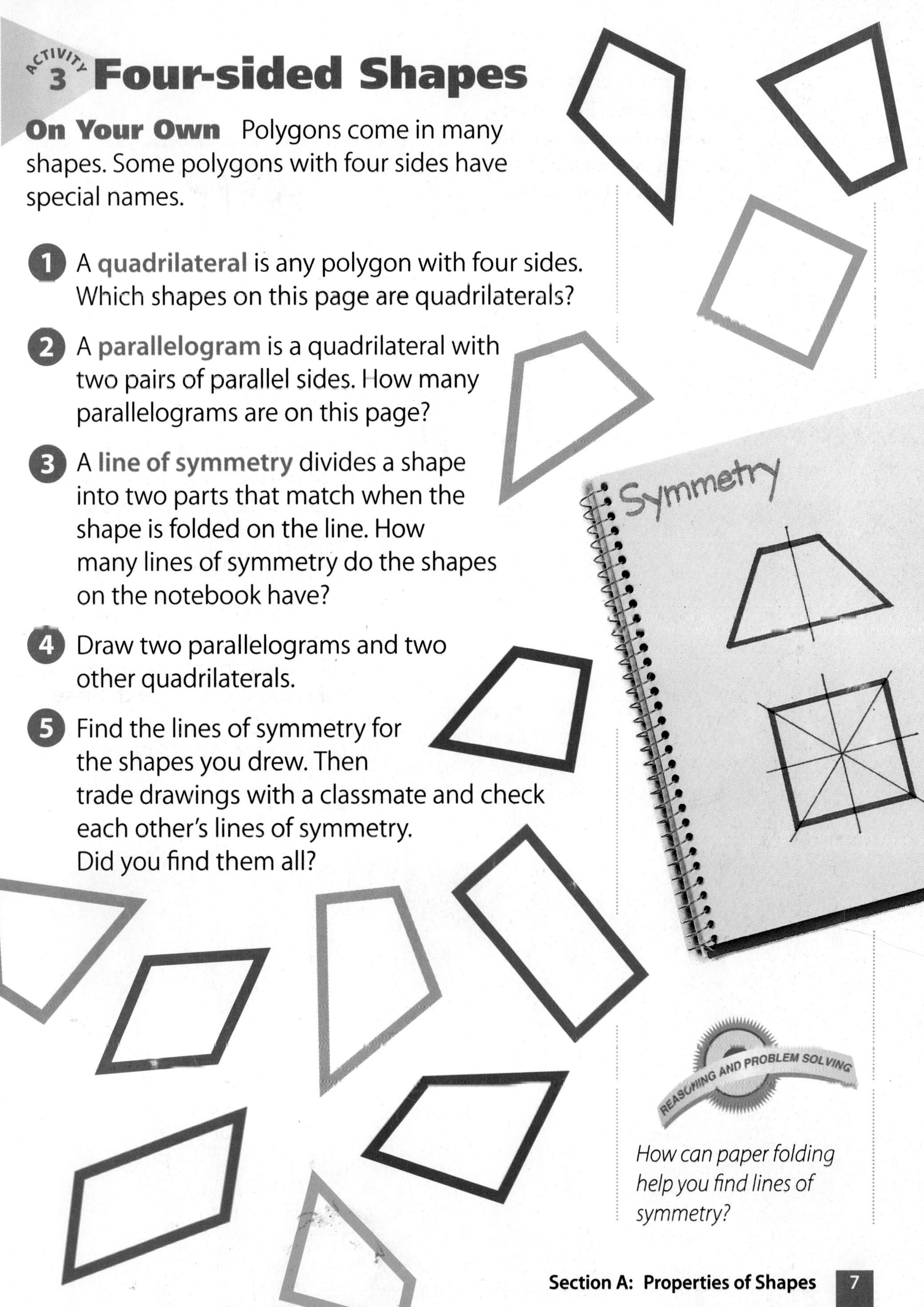


1. A **quadrilateral** is any polygon with four sides. Which shapes on this page are quadrilaterals?
2. A **parallelogram** is a quadrilateral with two pairs of parallel sides. How many parallelograms are on this page?
3. A **line of symmetry** divides a shape into two parts that match when the shape is folded on the line. How many lines of symmetry do the shapes on the notebook have?
4. Draw two parallelograms and two other quadrilaterals.
5. Find the lines of symmetry for the shapes you drew. Then trade drawings with a classmate and check each other's lines of symmetry. Did you find them all?

*How can paper folding help you find lines of symmetry?*

# SHAPE Safari

**What You'll Need**

- *gameboard*
- *6 counters per player (a different color for each player)*
- *number cube*

## ACTIVITY 4 Shape Hunt

**With Your Group** How much have you learned about shapes? Play this game to find out.

1. **Moving Ahead** **Place one of your counters at *Start*. Roll the number cube. Move forward that number of spaces. More than one player can occupy the same space.**

2. **Landing on Shape Spaces** **Shape spaces name or describe a shape. If you land on a shape space, find that shape on the board. Place a counter on the shape to claim it.**

*Draw each shape on the board on a separate piece of paper. Then sort the shapes in as many ways as you can think of.*

**3 Landing on Direction Spaces**
**Direction spaces let you gain shapes, lose shapes, or move again. If you land on a direction space, follow the directions.**

**4 Declaring a Winner** **The first player to claim five shapes wins.**

## Try It!

Draw each shape. Then sketch any lines of symmetry.

1. triangle
2. parallelogram
3. rectangle
4. square
5. hexagon
6. quadrilateral

Write an odd number that is between the two numbers.

7. 7 and 12
8. 92 and 96
9. 560 and 573
10. 999 and 1,002
11. 7 tens and 8 tens

### Think About It

12. Do all triangles have the same number of lines of symmetry? Use writing and drawings to explain.

# Same Size and Shape

*Use your Tracing Tool to help you find congruent shapes.*

## ACTIVITY 1 Slide It, Flip It, Turn It

### With Your Partner

**1** Which shapes on this stained-glass dome are **congruent,** or the same size and shape? How could tracing shapes help you find out?

**2** Congruent figures match exactly, even when you **slide, flip,** or **turn** them.

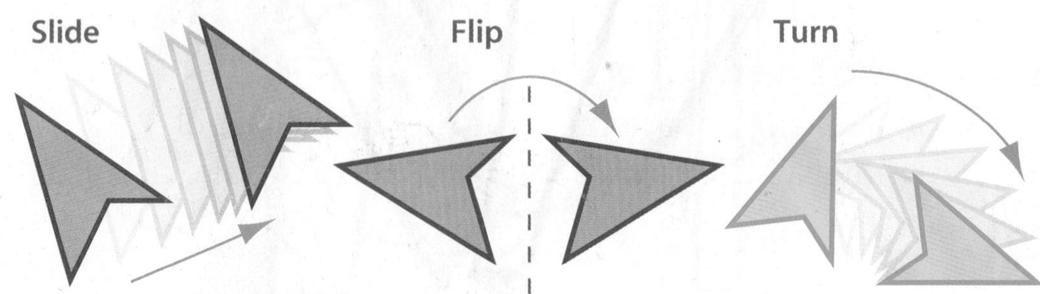

Which pairs of figures show a flip? a slide? a turn?

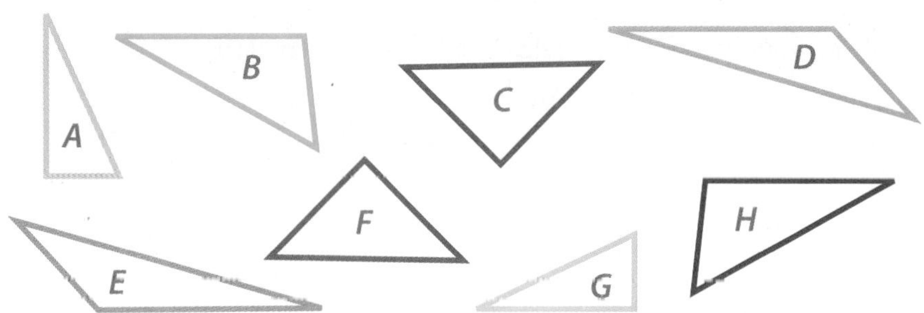


**Self-Check** *Can you draw a figure that will look exactly the same after you flip it?*

## ACTIVITY 2 Pattern Pieces

### On Your Own

1. Cut out a shape from heavy paper or cardboard. Trace around the piece. Then slide, flip, or turn the piece and trace around it again. Compare the sizes and shapes of your drawings. Are the shapes congruent?

2. See what patterns you can create when you slide, flip, and turn several shapes. Share your patterns with the class.

**What You'll Need**

- *heavy paper or cardboard*
- *colored pencils*
- *scissors*

What You'll Need

- *2–3 sheets of construction paper*
- *scissors*
- *glue*

# ACTIVITY 3 Making Masks

**On Your Own** Many cultures use masks to tell about history. This mask from Zaire is the mask of a royal ancestor. It is worn in ceremonial dances. The shells stand for wealth and power. The congruent triangles on the forehead form a pattern. Use congruent shapes to make a mask that tells about your culture or history.

1. **Fold a piece of construction paper in half. Draw a shape for the whole mask. Draw shapes for the eyes and mouth. Cut out the mask and the holes.**

2. **Think about how to decorate your mask. What shapes will you use for the nose and mouth? What patterns could you make around the eyes, mouth, or other parts? Sketch your ideas.**

In 1791 President George Washington chose a team of surveyors to measure land for the capital city of the United States. The city covered ten square miles.

One member of the team was Benjamin Banneker. He brought his knowledge of astronomy to the task. Banneker used a special telescope to sight on the stars. That way, the team was able to use straight lines.

*Benjamin Banneker, an astronomer, helped plan the new capital.*

## ACTIVITY 1 Street Smarts

**With Your Partner** Write your answer to three of the following questions. Use only the streets that have names.

1. Find Constitution Avenue. What streets intersect it?
2. Name a street perpendicular to 12th Street. What type of angle is formed by these two streets?
3. Suppose you walk from the Capitol to the White House.

   What street are you on? What streets do you cross?
4. Which streets shown are parallel to E Street?

*Can you explain your answers to your partner?*

*Draw your answers for this activity in your journal.*

# ACTIVITY 2 Getting from *A* to *B*

**With Your Class** Take a look at this simplified map of Washington, D.C. It uses only letters to label the intersection of streets. Read and respond to the items below to name the streets in a different way.

**1 Point *J*** A specific place is called a **point.** A point is named with one letter. Name five other points.

**2 Line *FM*** A **line** goes on and on in both directions, as shown by the arrows. A line is named with two letters. Name line *FM* in other ways.

**3 Ray *EB*** A **ray** is a part of a line with one endpoint. It goes on and on in one direction, as shown by only one arrow. A ray is named with two letters starting at the **endpoint.** Name three other rays.

**4 Line segment *PT*** A **line segment** is a part of a line. A line segment is named with the letters of its two endpoints. How else can you name line segment *PT*? Name three other line segments.

In 1791 President George Washington chose a team of surveyors to measure land for the capital city of the United States. The city covered ten square miles.

One member of the team was Benjamin Banneker. He brought his knowledge of astronomy to the task. Banneker used a special telescope to sight on the stars. That way, the team was able to use straight lines.

*Benjamin Banneker, an astronomer, helped plan the new capital.*

## Activity 1 Street Smarts

**With Your Partner** Write your answer to three of the following questions. Use only the streets that have names.

1. Find Constitution Avenue. What streets intersect it?

2. Name a street perpendicular to 12th Street. What type of angle is formed by these two streets?

3. Suppose you walk from the Capitol to the White House.

   What street are you on? What streets do you cross?

4. Which streets shown are parallel to E Street?

*Can you explain your answers to your partner?*

*Draw your answers for this activity in your journal.*

# ACTIVITY 2 Getting from *A* to *B*

**With Your Class** Take a look at this simplified map of Washington, D.C. It uses only letters to label the intersection of streets. Read and respond to the items below to name the streets in a different way.

**1 Point *J*** **A specific place is called a point. A point is named with one letter. Name five other points.**

**2 Line *FM*** **A line goes on and on in both directions, as shown by the arrows. A line is named with two letters. Name line *FM* in other ways.**

**3 Ray *EB*** **A ray is a part of a line with one endpoint. It goes on and on in one direction, as shown by only one arrow. A ray is named with two letters starting at the endpoint. Name three other rays.**

**4 Line segment *PT*** **A line segment is a part of a line. A line segment is named with the letters of its two endpoints. How else can you name line segment *PT*? Name three other line segments.**

**3** Change the loop from a rectangle to a parallelogram with no right angles. Sketch the parallelogram and write a letter at each corner. How is it different from a rectangle?

Susan

**On Your Own** Use pentagon *HOUSE* to answer these questions.

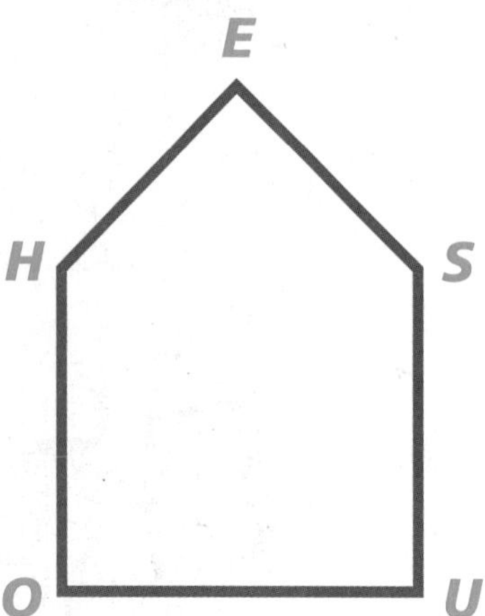


**4** Name all the vertexes, or corner points.

**5** Name a side that is perpendicular to side *OU*.

**6** Name all five line segments, or sides.

**7** In what other ways can you describe *HOUSE*?

## ACTIVITY 2 Points in the Past

**On Your Own** The ancient Egyptians used a loop of rope with 12 equally spaced knots to form a right angle. The rope was stretched with 3 units on one side and 4 on another. The loop always formed a triangle with a right angle, like this one.

You can use something with a right angle, like the corner of a piece of paper, to compare sizes of angles.

1. An **angle** in a polygon is a corner where two line segments meet. Look at triangle *ABC* on the notebook. Notice that angle *A* is greater than a right angle. Which of the angles below is greater than a right angle?

a.

b.

c.

*Remember to line up one side of the paper with one side of the angle.*

**2** Sometimes you need three letters to name an angle. The middle letter is the vertex. Name three angles that have *S* as a vertex.

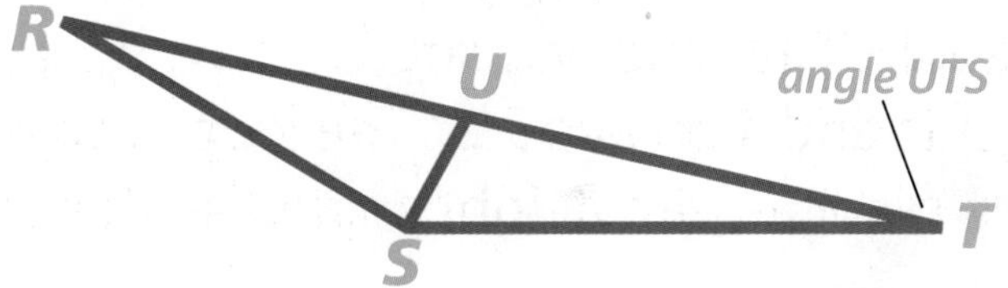


**3** Draw a triangle. Write a letter at each vertex. Name the angles at least two ways. Then tell if each angle is greater than, less than, or the same size as a right angle.

> ✓ **Self-Check** *How can you tell if an angle is greater than or less than a right angle?*

Use shape *MATH* for Exercises 1–5.

1. Name the vertexes.
2. Name the line segments.
3. Name each angle in two ways.
4. Which angles are greater than a right angle?
5. Name two parallel sides.

Draw each figure.

6. a pentagon
7. a triangle with a right angle
8. a quadrilateral with two right angles
9. ray *BC*
10. a line containing points *J, K,* and *L*

**Think About It**

11. Trace figure *MATH* and draw a line of symmetry. Explain how symmetry relates to the size of angles.

Investigation

# Tricky Triangles

These three triangles might look different, but are they? How can you check to make sure that none of them is congruent? In this investigation, you will produce different triangles and explore what you know about congruent shapes.

## 1 Make Your Triangles

**Connect dots on four-by-four dot arrays to make triangles. Make as many different shapes and sizes of triangles as you can. Design a plan to help you find as many different triangles as possible.**

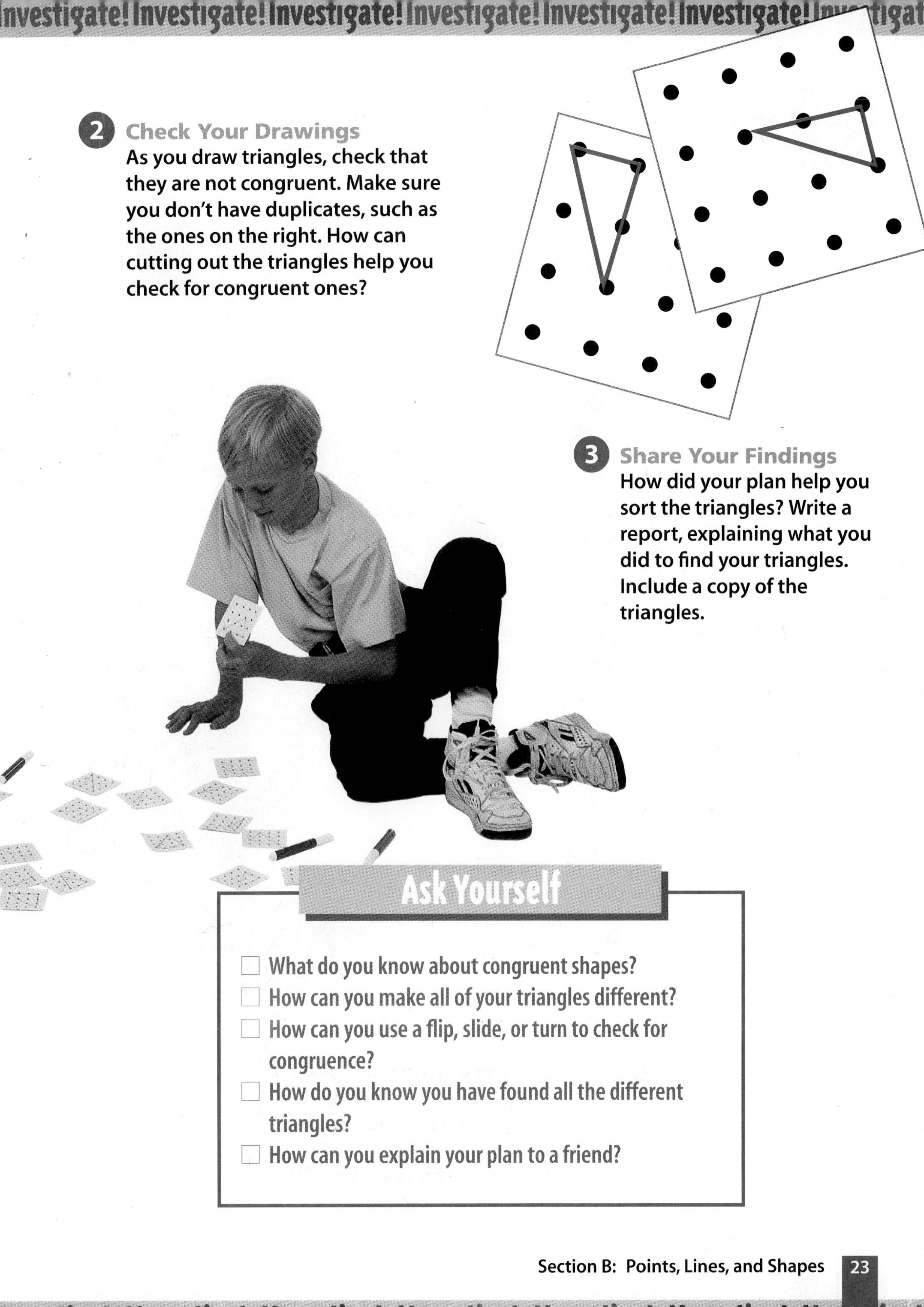

**2 Check Your Drawings**

As you draw triangles, check that they are not congruent. Make sure you don't have duplicates, such as the ones on the right. How can cutting out the triangles help you check for congruent ones?

**3 Share Your Findings**

How did your plan help you sort the triangles? Write a report, explaining what you did to find your triangles. Include a copy of the triangles.

## Ask Yourself

- ☐ What do you know about congruent shapes?
- ☐ How can you make all of your triangles different?
- ☐ How can you use a flip, slide, or turn to check for congruence?
- ☐ How do you know you have found all the different triangles?
- ☐ How can you explain your plan to a friend?

# Giants of the Sky

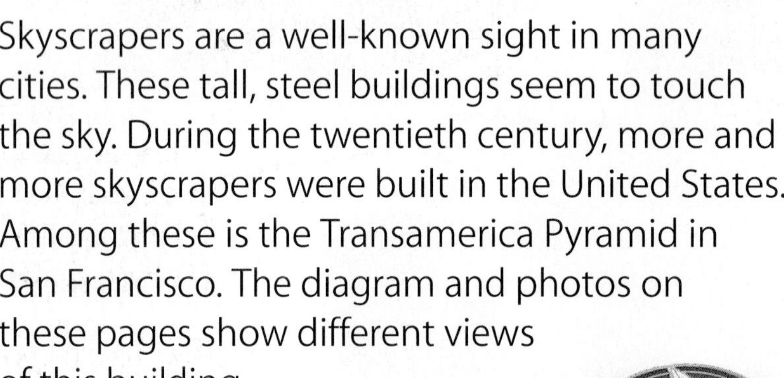

Skyscrapers are a well-known sight in many cities. These tall, steel buildings seem to touch the sky. During the twentieth century, more and more skyscrapers were built in the United States. Among these is the Transamerica Pyramid in San Francisco. The diagram and photos on these pages show different views of this building.

Use the diagram on the opposite page to answer the following questions.

1. **Suppose you are on floor 16. How many floors above you is the observation deck?**
2. **Suppose you are on the top floor, 48. How many floors down is the observation deck?**
3. **The Transamerica Pyramid has 18 elevators, but only 2 reach the top floor. How many don't go all the way up?**
4. **What is the total height of the Transamerica Pyramid?**

**5** How many triangles do you see in the diagram below?

**6** Does the side of the building show symmetry? Sketch it.

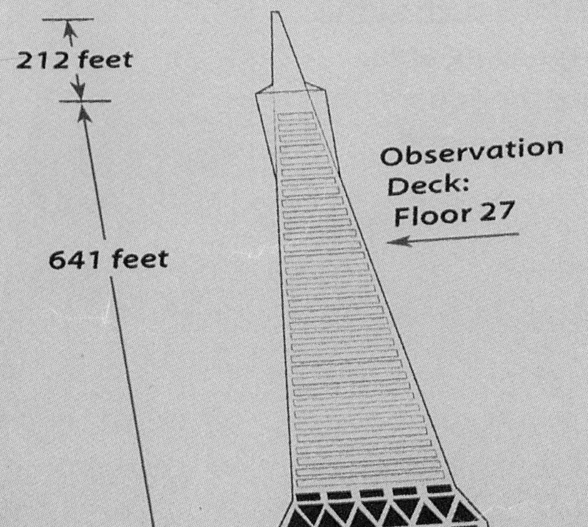


**7** There are 280 parking spaces in the basement parking lot. If 180 spaces are taken, how many parking spaces are empty?

**8** The Transamerica Pyramid was completed in 1972. How many years ago was that?

**9** Suppose you arrived at the observation center at 3 o'clock and stayed for 2 hours. What time did you leave?

## Check Your Math Power

**10** Look for parallelograms in the diagram above. Make sketches to show how connected triangles can form parallelograms.

# LESSON 5 Square Spaces

## ACTIVITY 1 Over and Around

### With Your Class

1. **Area** is the space a shape covers. You can use **square units** such as this one to measure area. Estimate the square units in this photograph.



2. This is a unit of length. Use this unit to estimate the **perimeter,** or distance around the edges, of the photo.

3. When might you need to find area? When might you need to figure out perimeter?

## ACTIVITY 2 Area Explorations

**With Your Partner** How many different shapes can cover the same area? Use grid paper to find out.

**What You'll Need**

- *grid paper*

1. Let one square on the grid paper stand for one square mile. Draw different shapes for a city of ten square miles. What shapes did you come up with?

2. Choose one shape. Label the number of units on each side of it. What is the perimeter?

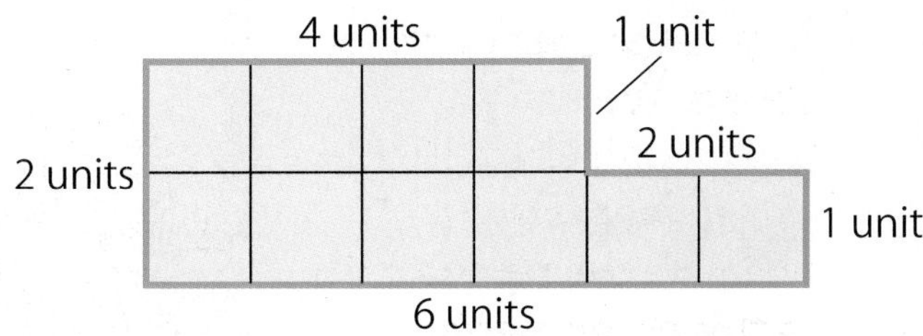


**The area of this shape is 10 square units.**
**The perimeter of this shape is 16 units.**

3. Find the perimeter of your other shapes. Which one has the largest perimeter? the smallest?

*Square tiles can help you find area and perimeter.*

**4** Draw one rectangle and three other shapes that have an area of 16 square units. Then find the perimeter of each shape.

**5** Do all shapes with the same area always have the same perimeter? Explain your answer.

Do You Remember?

## Try It!

Find the area of each figure in square units. Then find the perimeter.

**1.** 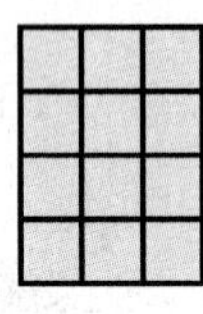

**2.** 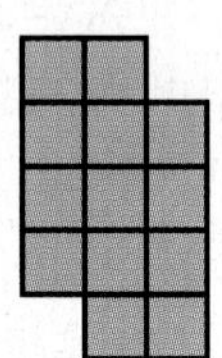

**3.** 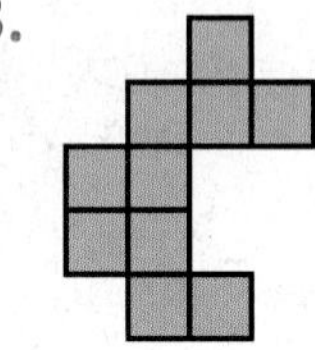

**4.** 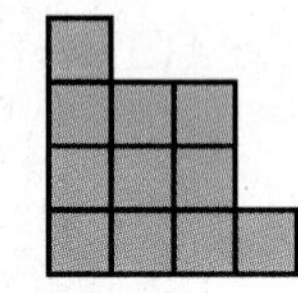

Use the three numbers to write a number sentence.

**5.** 3, 8, 11
**6.** 7, 15, 8
**7.** 100, 40, 60
**8.** 3, 12, 4
**9.** 20, 2, 18
**10.** 14, 2, 7

### Think About It

**11.** Why didn't any figure in Exercises 1–4 have an odd number for its perimeter?

# Seeing SHAPES

You know a lot about flat shapes. But most things you see are solid, not flat. You can learn about solids by comparing their sides to flat shapes.

## ACTIVITY 1 All Sorts of Solids

**With Your Class** All of these real objects are also solids. Find out the names of the solids, and discuss these questions.

**sphere**

Do you see any flat sides?

**cylinder**

What shape are the flat sides?

**cube**

What shape are the sides?

**rectangular prism**

How many sides does it have?

**pyramid**

If the bottom is a square, how many sides are triangles?

**cone**

What other things have this shape?

**With Your Group** Gather some objects of various shapes.

1. How are the objects alike? How are they different? Sort them as many ways as you can.

2. One way to sort objects is by the number and shapes of their sides. Make a chart like the one shown below. Then look at each object and count its sides. Do all the sides have the same shape, or do they have different shapes? Note on the chart how many sides have a given shape.

3. What do you find out by charting the sides of solids? How do the shapes of sides help you group solids? Discuss and record your findings.

CONNECT AND COMMUNICATE

*Rectangular prisms are easier to stack than cones. Can you explain why?*

4. You may have discovered that some solids have all flat sides. The flat side of a solid is a **face.** Two faces meet along an **edge.** Three faces meet at a vertex. How many faces, edges, and vertexes does this solid have?

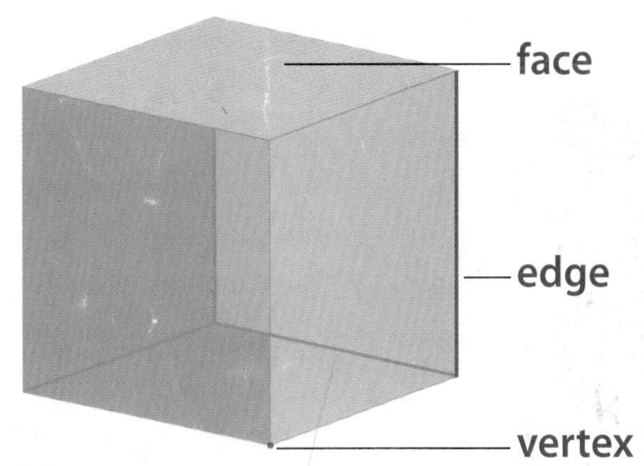


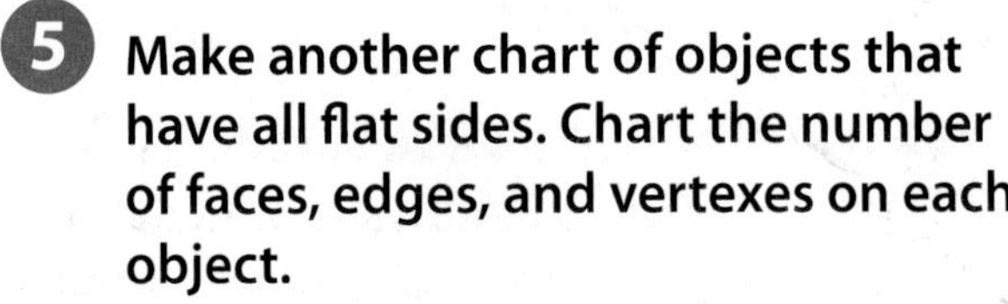

5. Make another chart of objects that have all flat sides. Chart the number of faces, edges, and vertexes on each object.

## Activity 2 Sizes of Faces

### With Your Group

1. On grid paper, trace around one face of a solid. About how many whole squares are inside the shape you traced? Estimate. Then count.

2. Will other faces cover more squares or fewer squares than the face you traced? Estimate. Then check by tracing and counting.

**What You'll Need**

- *grid paper*
- *box*

*Did you use any short cuts for counting the squares? Explain.*

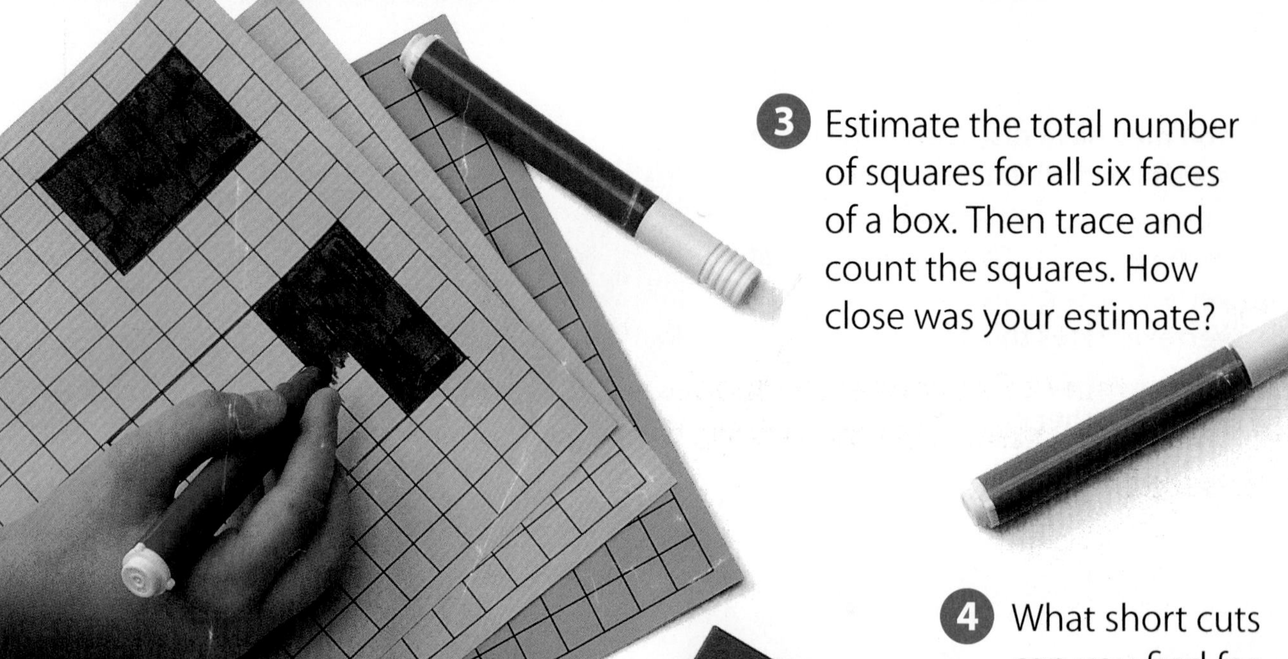

3 Estimate the total number of squares for all six faces of a box. Then trace and count the squares. How close was your estimate?

4 What short cuts can you find for Exercise 3? Explain.

Do You Remember?

## Try It!

Answer these questions about this figure.

1. What is the name of this solid?
2. How many faces does it have?
3. How many edges does it have?
4. What flat shapes are its faces?
5. Name a different solid with the same number of faces.
6. How many vertexes does it have?

Write at least two more numbers in each pattern.

7. 4, 8, 12, ■, ■
8. 8, 14, 20, ■, ■
9. 35, 30, 25, ■, ■
10. 98, 95, 92, ■, ■

### Think About It

11. Which faces of the box are congruent to each other? Explain, using the words *top, front, left side, right side, bottom,* and *back.*

# Net Work

**A** pattern of flat, connected shapes is called a **net.** Try working with nets made from the faces of solid shapes.

## ACTIVITY 1 Sketch a Net

### With Your Partner

1 **Choose a box. Label each side—*front, back, top, bottom, left,* or *right.***

2 **Flatten and unfold the box by cutting it along some edges. Remove extra flaps. Draw the net.**

3 **Cut off one rectangle. Tape it to the net in a different place.**

4 **Fold the net back into a box. Does the net still make a box? Draw the new net.**

**What You'll Need**

- *box*
- *scissors*
- *tape*

*Draw other nets that would make the same box. Use your box to see if the nets will work.*

What You'll Need

- *grid paper*
- *2–3 sheets of construction paper*
- *scissors*
- *tape*

ACTIVITY 2

# Connect a Net

**With Your Partner** If you know how to make a net, you can make a building.

1. Use grid paper to make rectangles of each of these sizes: three by six squares, six by eight squares, and three by eight squares.
2. Cut out two of each rectangle from construction paper or heavy paper. Make sure they are the right size.
3. Decide which pieces to use for all sides of your building. Decorate each piece to look like parts of the building.

✔ **Self-Check** *Be sure you have correctly labeled all pieces of your net.*

4. Tape the pieces together to make a net. Keep all the pieces flat as you connect them. Then fold the pieces to make a solid shape.
5. Compare your building with ones other students made. How are they alike? How are they different?

## Try It!

Which of these nets can be folded to make a cube?

1. 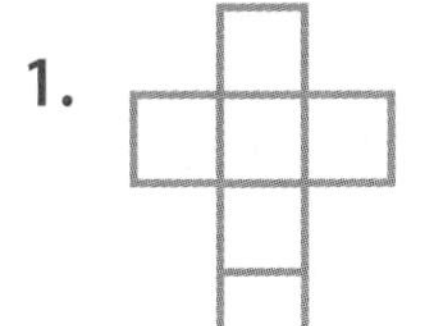
2. 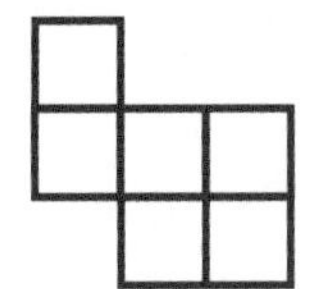
3. 
4. 

Decide if any of the line segments is an edge of the cube shown. If it is, name any edge parallel to it.

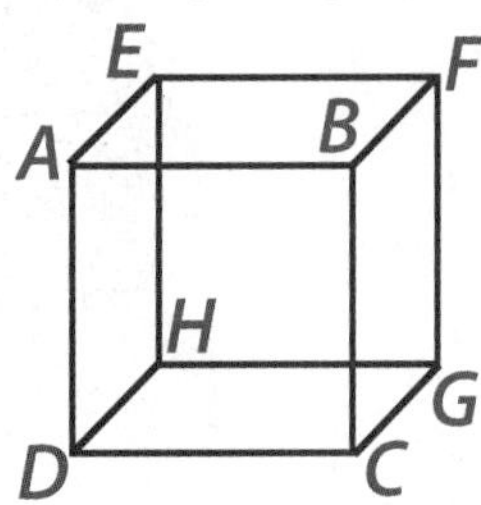


5. *AE* 6. *BG* 7. *CD*
8. *FG* 9. *AC* 10. *DF*

### Think About It

11. All the nets have six squares. Why don't they all form cubes?

## Section D: Exploring Volume

# Lesson 8: Fill It Up!

**LITERATURE**

*Frank is a big, helpful dog. He can be counted on to help his owner solve mathematical problems.*

Going shopping with Mom is a big event. She is lucky to have such an intelligent helper.

It takes forty-seven cans of dog food to fill one shopping bag, but only one Frank to knock over one hundred and ten!

Because of Frank, my knuckles will scrape along the ground by the time I'm twenty-five!

From *Counting on Frank*
by Rod Clement

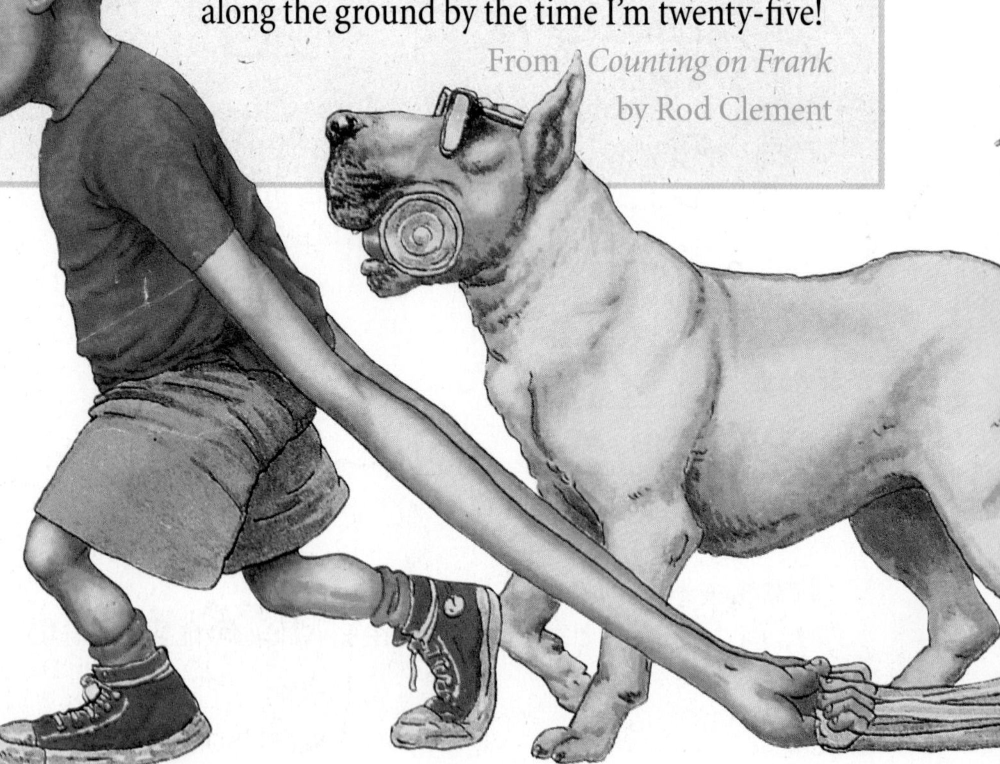

# Activity 1 Shop with Frank

**With Your Class** Discuss these questions.

1. Do you think a grocery bag can hold 47 cans of dog food? Estimate how many will fit. Explain your reasoning.
2. Choose a container in your classroom, such as a wastebasket. Estimate how many cans would fill it. How many grapefruits? How many eggs?

**With Your Group** Estimate with some real bags. Collect bags in three different sizes and 40 small milk cartons.

3. Estimate how many cartons each bag will hold.
4. Fill each bag. Count and record the number of cartons each bag holds. How close are your predictions?
5. One of Frank's cans is twice as big as a small milk carton. How many cans would fit in each of your bags?

**What You'll Need**

- *bags in 3 sizes*
- *40 small milk cartons per group*

*Estimate how many milk cartons your class uses each week. Use your calculator. How many of your largest bags would these cartons fill?*

What You'll Need

- *popped popcorn*
- *boxes in 3 sizes*

*How can you use a calculator to help you estimate?*

## ACTIVITY 2 Pops to the Top

**With Your Group** If you have two boxes, how can you tell which one is bigger? In this activity you will compare boxes, using popped popcorn.

1. Estimate which box will hold the least amount of popped popcorn and which will hold the most. Label the boxes 1, 2, and 3 from least to greatest.
2. Fill box 1 with popcorn and pour it into box 2. Which holds more?
3. Fill box 2 and pour the popcorn into box 3. Which holds more?
4. Compare your estimate with the results.
5. Estimate how many handfuls of popcorn will fill each box. Then fill the boxes. How many handfuls were needed to fill each box? Compare your estimates with your results.

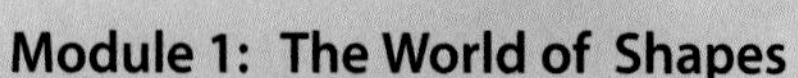

## Activity 3 Space Fillers

### With Your Group

Use a small milk carton and a new filling material, such as marshmallows, pasta, or packing peanuts. Estimate how many handfuls of the material would fill the carton. Compare estimates within your group. Then count the number of handfuls.

**What You'll Need**

- *small milk cartons*
- *uncooked pasta, marshmallows, or packing peanuts*

*Does the volume of the box change when a different filler is used? Explain.*

## Try It!

Write the letters of one or more boxes that match the clue.

1. It holds the most.
2. It holds the least.
3. It holds about two times as much as *c*.
4. A book could fit in it.
5. It holds less than *b*.

a. b. c. d.

Name these parts of figure *BLUE*.

6. vertexes
7. line segments
8. two perpendicular sides
9. two parallel sides
10. a right angle

### Think About It

11. Does a tall box always hold more than a shorter box? Explain.

# Counting Cubes

1 cubic unit

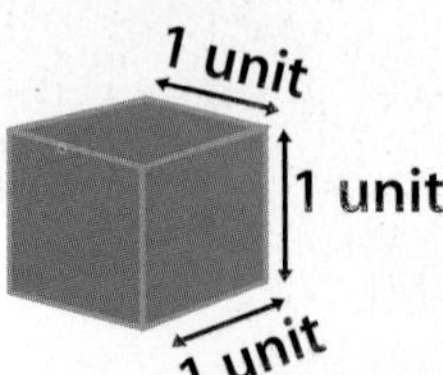


The amount of space taken by a solid shape is **volume.** You can measure volume with **cubic units.**

The solid figures on the left are models of buildings. Both buildings contain ten cubes. The diagrams below are an easy way to show the solid figures on paper. Which diagrams match which buildings? How do you know?

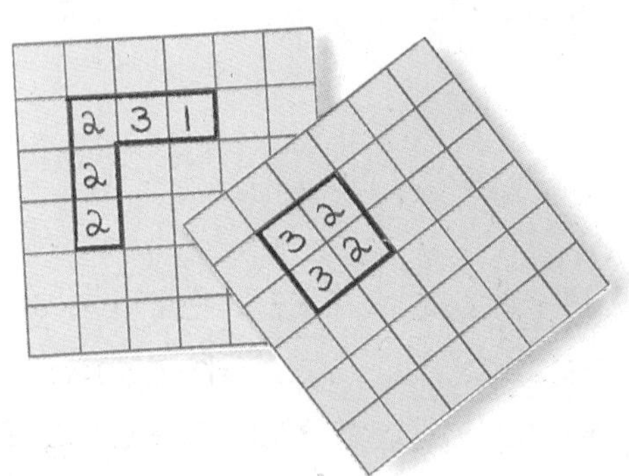


## ACTIVITY 1 Building Plans

### With Your Partner

1. Use 10 to 20 cubes to make a building. Trade buildings with your partner. Then use grid paper to make a diagram of your partner's building, like the ones above.
2. Trade diagrams with another group. Follow their diagram to make a building. How does your building compare with their original building?

**What You'll Need**

- *grid paper*
- *cubes*

*Draw a diagram of your building before trading buildings with your partner.*

**With Your Partner** Choose one of the diagrams on the right.

3. Follow the diagram to make a rectangular prism. Compare your figure with your partner's. What do you notice?
4. What is the volume of your figure in cubic units? Compare your figure's volume with the volume of your partner's figure.
5. Build a different rectangular prism. Draw a diagram. Have your partner try to draw a different diagram for the same shape. What is the volume?

## ACTIVITY 2 Figure Flips

**With Your Partner** Use these diagrams to make buildings from cubes. Which diagrams match when you flip or turn the buildings? Which match the building in the photograph?

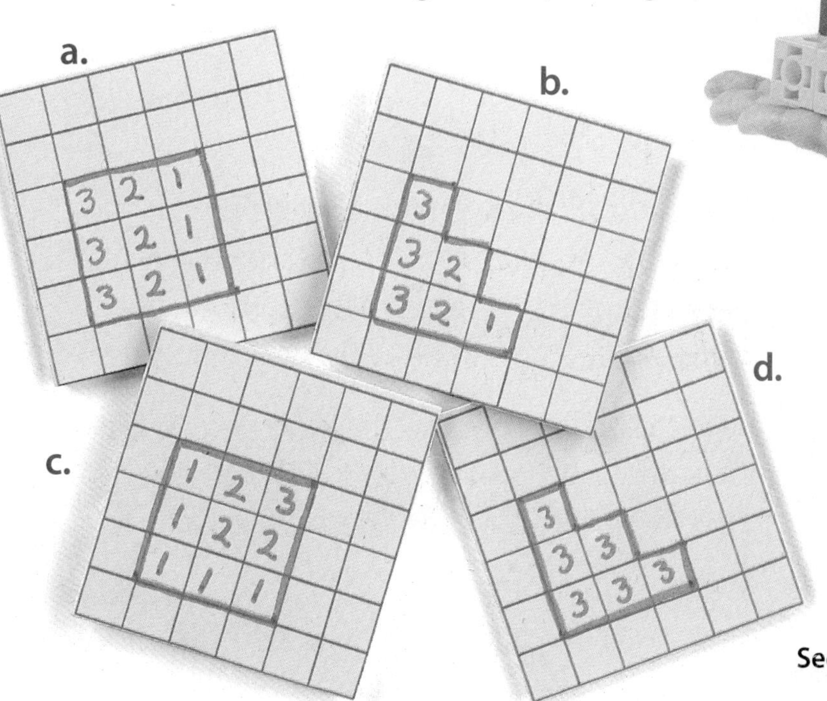


✔ **Self-Check** *Be sure your cube buildings match the diagrams.*

# Cool Cubes

Answer questions 1–4 and two other questions of your choice.

## Missing Cubes

**1** Some small cubes were taken away from the large cube on the right. How many were taken away?

## Cube Copies

**2** All the sides of an actual cube are squares. Trace one face of the cube drawing. Why isn't the tracing square? What shape is it?

## Cubes Times Two

**3** How many small cubes does this large cube contain?

**4** How many cubes would you have if you doubled the length, the width, and the height?

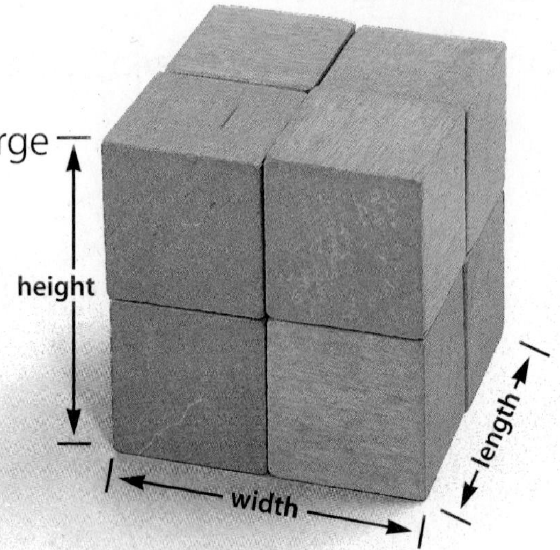

## The Other Side

Use the three views of this cube to answer these questions.

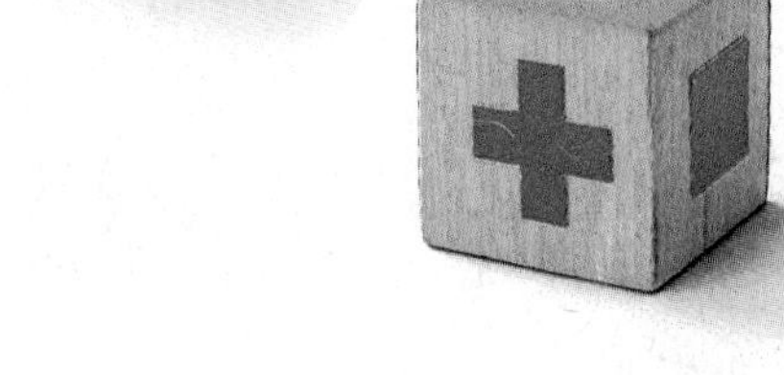

5 What symbol is opposite the star? the cross? the circle?

6 Draw the net that would make this cube. Show all the symbols on their correct faces.

## Painted Cubes

7 How many small cubes are in this large cube?

8 This large cube has been painted on all six sides. Eight of the small cubes are painted on exactly three sides. How many are painted on exactly one side? on two sides? on zero sides?

## Cubic Counts

What is the volume of each figure?

9 ■ cubic units

10 ■ cubic units

Do You Remember? **Cumulative Review**

# Looking Back

Choose the best answer. Write *a, b, c,* or *d* for each question.

**Use these pictures to answer questions 1–5.**

a. 

b. 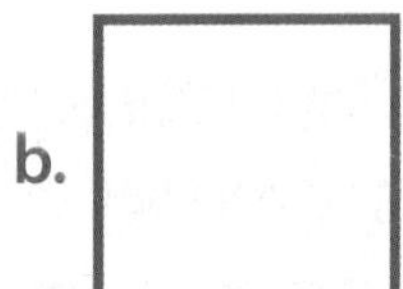

c. 

d. 

1. Which shape is not a polygon?
2. Which shape has only one line of symmetry?
3. Which shape has sides that form right angles?
4. Which shape is a face of a cone?
5. Which shape is a face of a cube?

6. Which of these polygons is not a quadrilateral?

   a. parallelogram b. square
   c. triangle d. rectangle

7. Two different shapes have the same perimeter. Which statement must be true for the shapes?

   a. They are congruent.
   b. They have the same area.
   c. They have the same number of sides.
   d. None of these is true.

**Use these pictures to answer questions 8–9.**

a. 

b. 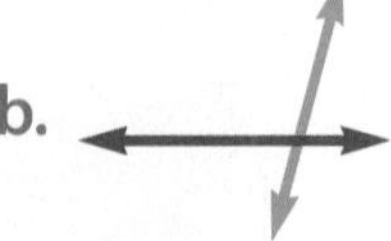

c. 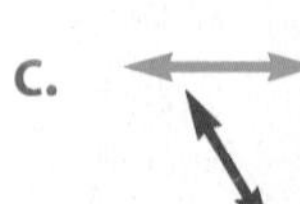

d. 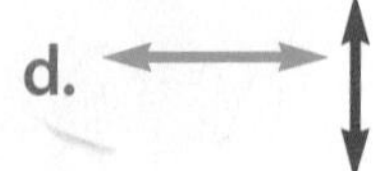

8. Which picture shows perpendicular lines?

9. Which picture shows parallel lines?

**Use this figure to answer questions 10–11.**

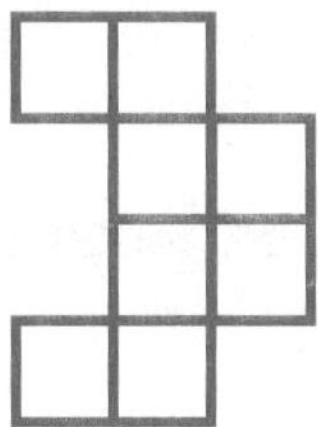

10. The area is:

    a. 6 square units
    b. 8 square units
    c. 10 square units
    d. 16 square units

11. The perimeter is:

    a. 8 units  b. 32 units
    c. 16 units  d. 24 units

**Use these figures to answer questions 12–14.**

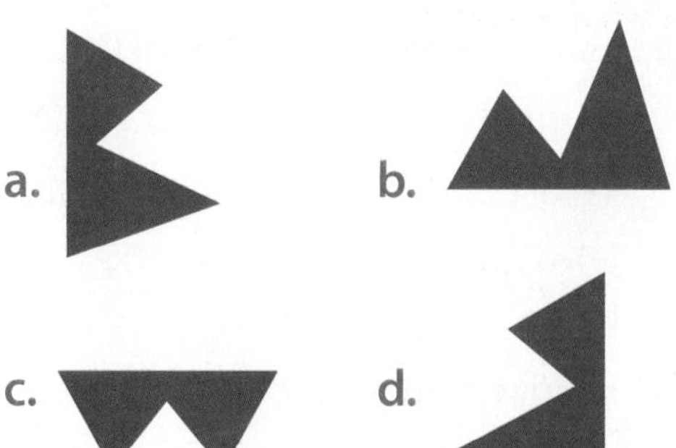


12. Which figure is not congruent to the others?

13. Which figure is a flip of figure *a*?

14. Which figure is a turn of figure *a*?

15. Which of these solids does not have any flat faces?

    a. cube  b. sphere
    c. pyramid  d. rectangular prism

## Check Your Math Power

16. Copy this figure. Draw two line segments by connecting vertexes. Describe the angles and the shapes in your figure. Which angles are larger than a right angle?

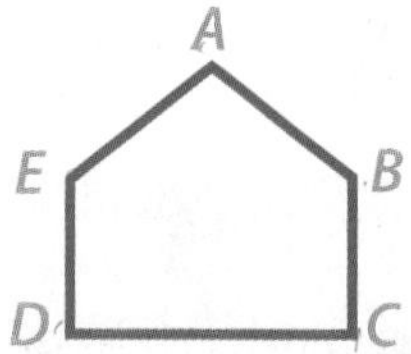


17. Explain how you might find out which box has a greater volume.

# Your Own Building

If you could make your own building, what would it be? You might build a house or an office, a sports stadium or a greenhouse. How would it look? An office building might be tall and rectangular. A greenhouse might have a high, pointed roof. There are many shapes you could use.

## Investigation A: Designing a Plan

Use what you know about shapes to draw a plan for your own building.

1. **Think** about the kind of building you want to make. Then look at several buildings of that kind. What shapes do they have? Sketch the parts of two or three buildings you see.

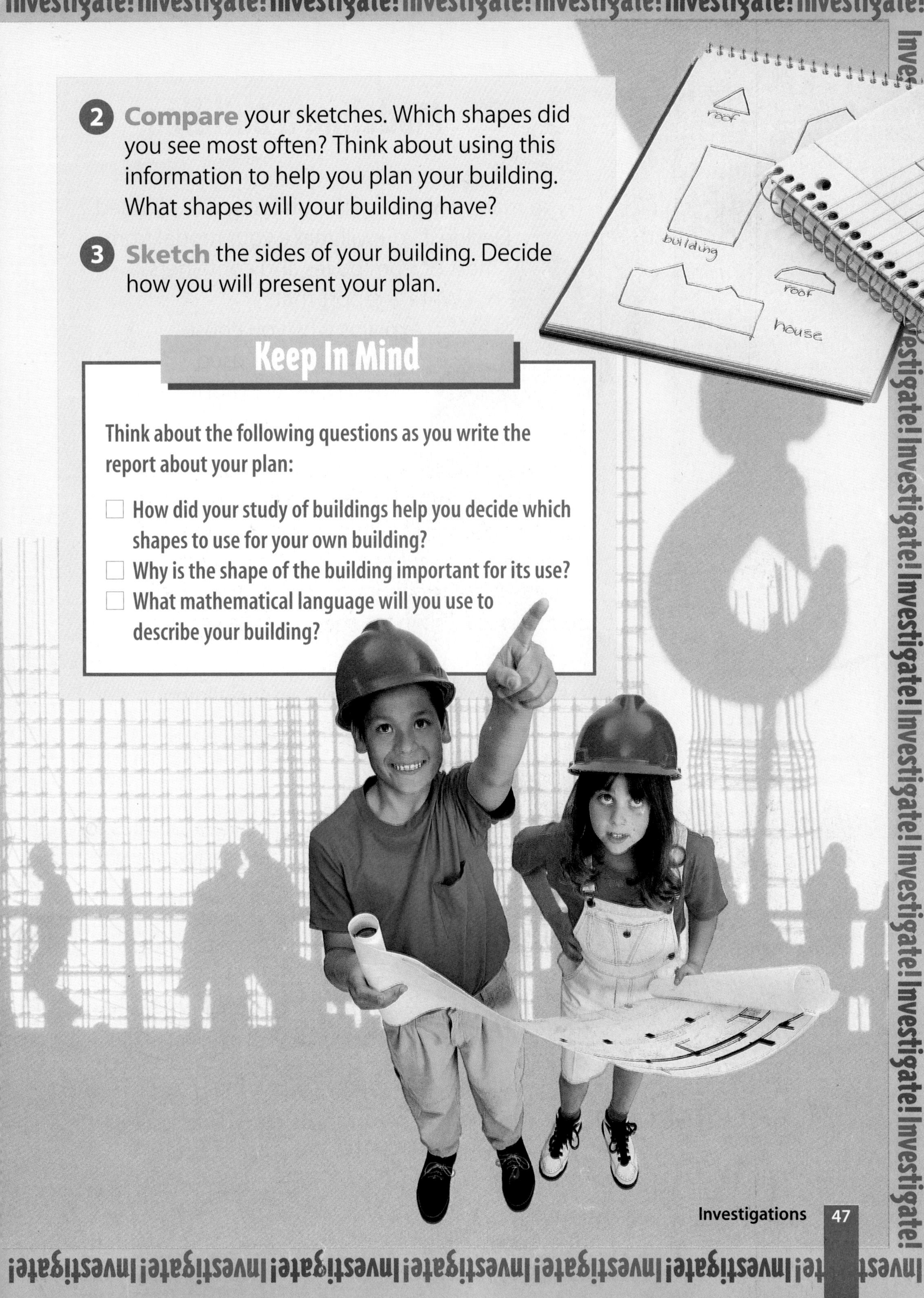


2 **Compare** your sketches. Which shapes did you see most often? Think about using this information to help you plan your building. What shapes will your building have?

3 **Sketch** the sides of your building. Decide how you will present your plan.

## Keep In Mind

Think about the following questions as you write the report about your plan:

- ☐ How did your study of buildings help you decide which shapes to use for your own building?
- ☐ Why is the shape of the building important for its use?
- ☐ What mathematical language will you use to describe your building?

Investigation B

## Modeling a Building

Try to make a model of the building you planned. Decide if you will make your model from nets or from boxes and containers. Write a report that

- explains why you chose the shapes you used;
- describes any problems you had putting the model together.

**Computer Option** If you make your building from nets, you can use a computer drawing program to sketch them. Then you can print the drawings and use them to construct your building.

Investigation C

## Building with Cubes

Plan and put together a small building made from cubes. Then write a report to describe your building and explain what you discovered. Were you able to make any shape of building you wanted? Was it easier or more difficult to make a building with cubes than with other materials?

# Ship It!

In one city, bicycle messengers deliver millions of packages a year. In another city, millions of letters are delivered—all to the same address. Come explore big numbers! You can start right now. Just imagine riding on a fast pony. You're a Pony Express rider carrying a pouch filled with mail bound for California. . . .

Ship It!

# Galloping Mail!

The Pony Express was the first rapid-mail system in the western United States. Pony Express riders were famous for their speedy rides across the country.

*The Pony Express operated from April 1860 until October 1861.*

Carson City

Salt Lake City

Sacramento

*The length of the trail was 1,966 miles between St. Joseph, Missouri, and Sacramento, California.*

## Word Bank

- front-end estimation
- perimeter
- period
- place value
- standard form
- time log

## 1 Getting Ready

The Pony Express was run like a relay race. Each rider rode about 75 miles, changing horses every 10 to 20 miles. Then another rider took over. What place do you know that is 75 miles away?

## 2 By the Numbers

The Pony Express ran for 19 months. Is that more or less than 2 years? How do you know?

Pony Express riders traveled more than 650 thousand miles. Is that more or less than a million miles?

*More than 400 workers staffed 190 stations along the way.*

*Pony Express riders made about 300 trips each way carrying almost 10,000 pounds of letters.*

*Eighty riders and 400 horses moved the mail along.*

Fort Laramie

Fort Kearny

St. Joseph

### Investigations Preview

Learn about perimeter and about adding and subtracting distances. These new tools will help you plan a route and measure items around your classroom and home.

*Ship Shape* (pages 78–79)
Use a 130-inch string to decide if a box is too big to ship. What you know about perimeter is the key.

*Delivery 2000* (pages 94–96)
Plan a route to three cities around the country. You will pick the cities.

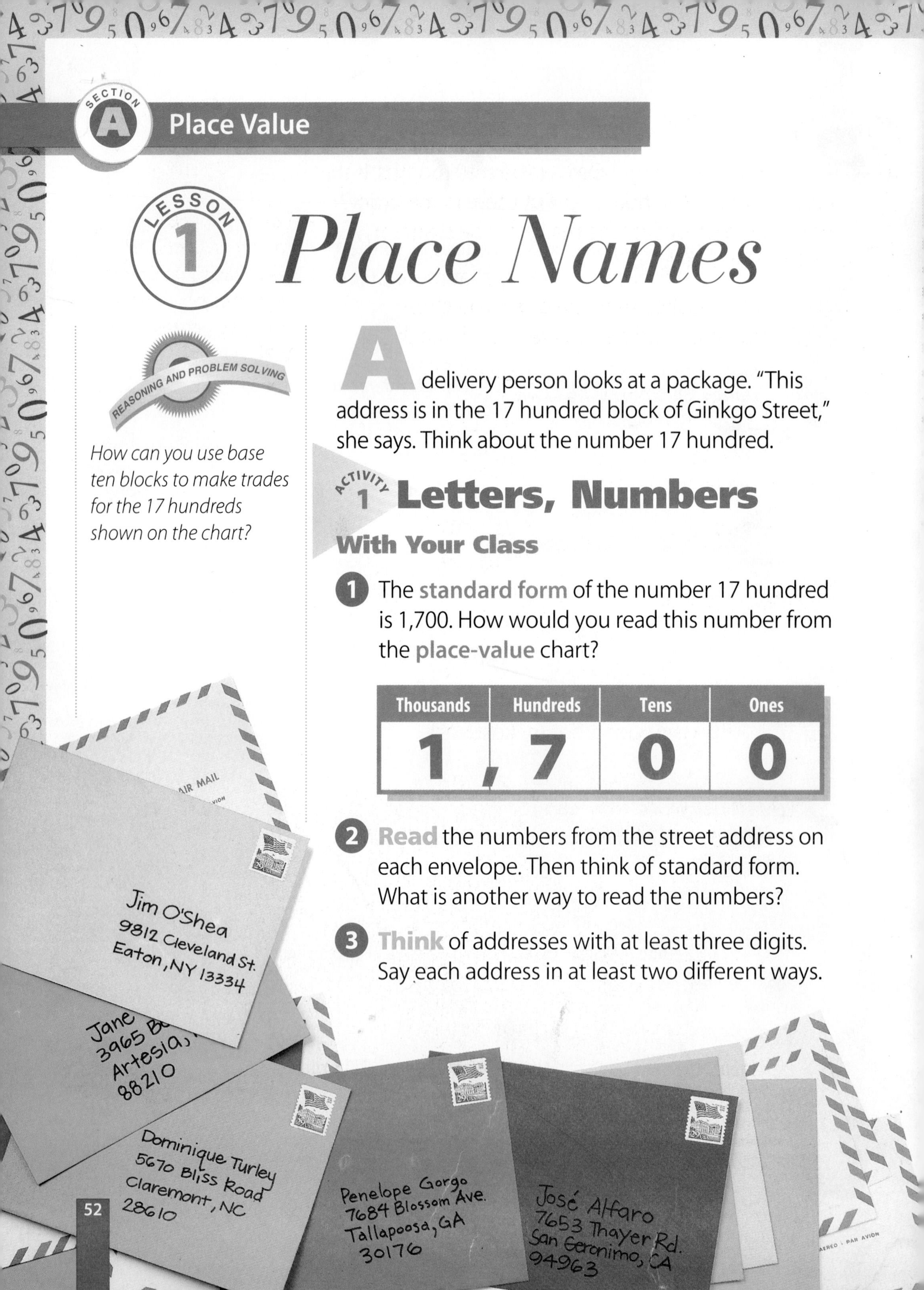




# LESSON 1 Place Names

REASONING AND PROBLEM SOLVING

*How can you use base ten blocks to make trades for the 17 hundreds shown on the chart?*

A delivery person looks at a package. "This address is in the 17 hundred block of Ginkgo Street," she says. Think about the number 17 hundred.

## ACTIVITY 1 Letters, Numbers

### With Your Class

1. The **standard form** of the number 17 hundred is 1,700. How would you read this number from the **place-value** chart?

| Thousands | Hundreds | Tens | Ones |
|---|---|---|---|
| 1, | 7 | 0 | 0 |

2. **Read** the numbers from the street address on each envelope. Then think of standard form. What is another way to read the numbers?

3. **Think** of addresses with at least three digits. Say each address in at least two different ways.

## ACTIVITY 2 Order Your Route

**With Your Group** Deliver the mail! Copy the addresses from the note pad. Put them in the order that you would deliver the mail. Use the diagram at the bottom to help you.

*What is your plan for solving this problem? Can drawing a diagram or map help you? How will you order even and odd numbers?*

1. **List** the addresses in the order you chose. Decide which addresses are in each block.

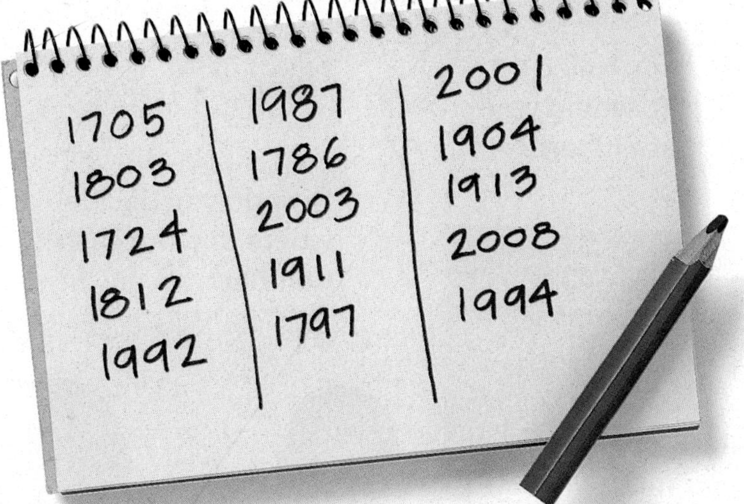


2. **Explain** why your order makes sense.

3. **Explore** a new route. Does your route work if you can carry only half of the mail at one time?

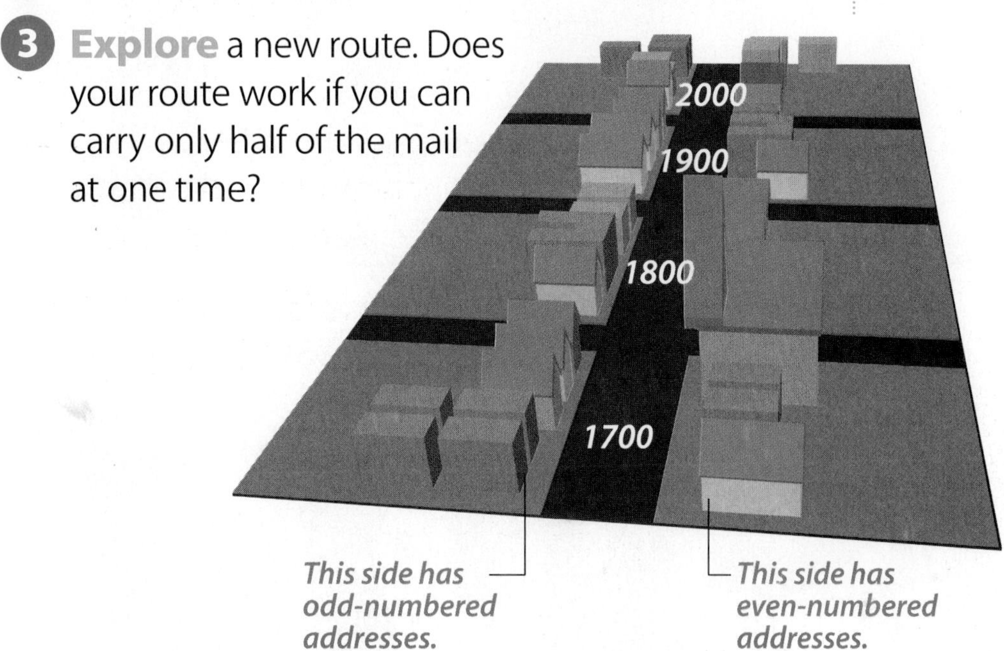

## What You'll Need

- *place-value chart*
- *cube numbered 1–6*

REASONING AND PROBLEM SOLVING

*Do you have a strategy for building the greatest number? How can you make a plan?*

# ACTIVITY 3 Build Big Numbers

**With Your Partner** Your goal is to build the greatest number with four digits. Try it out!

**1** **Roll** a number cube. Choose where to write the number on your place-value chart. You can't move the number once it is written down. Roll the cube three more times and write down the numbers rolled.

**If you rolled a 1 first, would you place it here?**

**How do you decide where to write each number?**

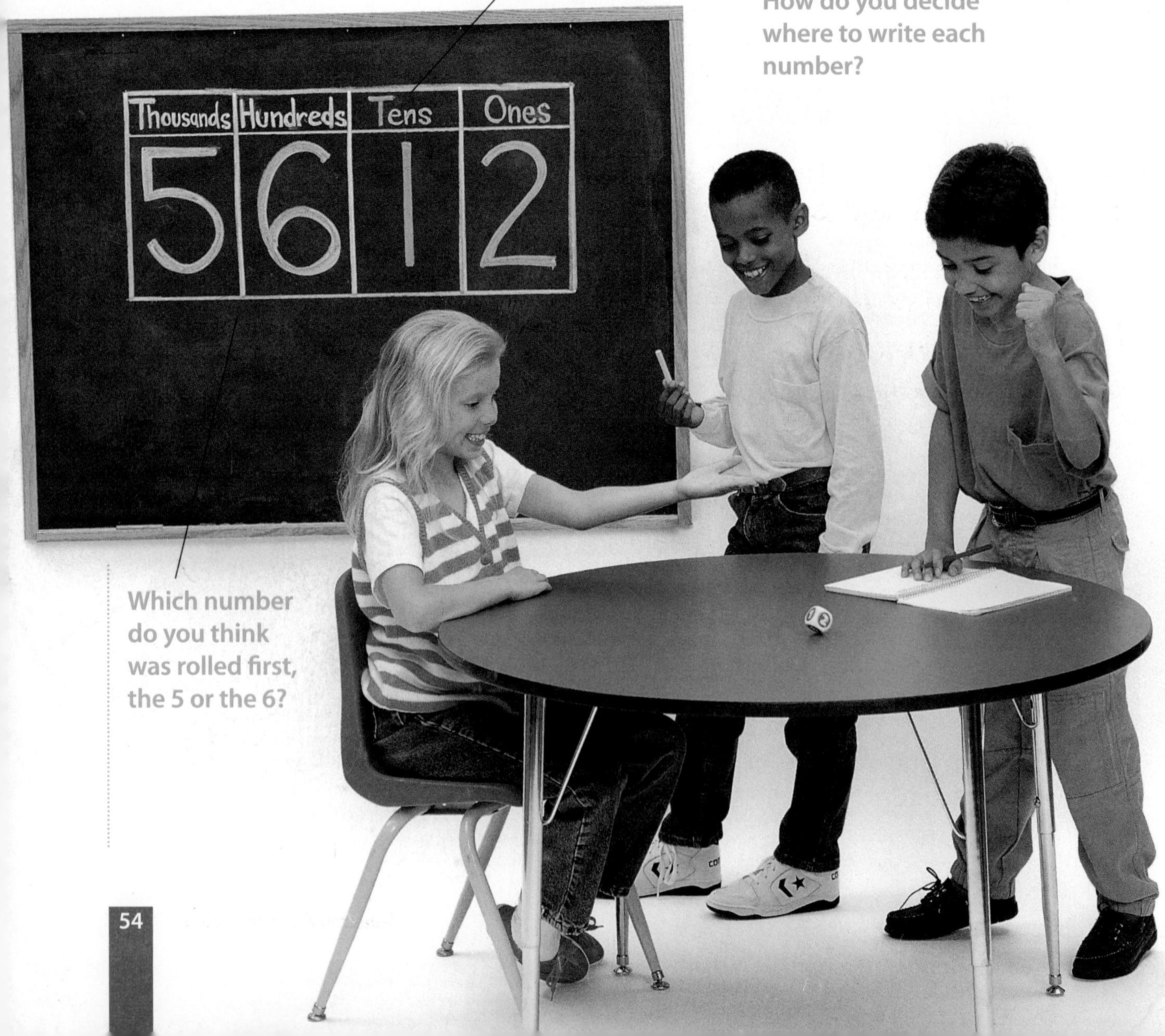
Thousands
Hundreds
Tens
Ones
5
6
1
2

**Which number do you think was rolled first, the 5 or the 6?**

2 **Read** your number out loud. How do you know whether you built the greatest number?

3 **Play** until you each have built six numbers.

4 **Compare** numbers. Which place do you look at first? Use the <, >, and = signs to compare pairs of numbers. Which number is greater?

**2,641 >** (is greater than) **1,246**
**1,246 <** (is less than) **2,641**

5 **Write** a rule for building the greatest number.

**Self-Check** *How do you remember which symbol means "greater than" and which symbol means "less than"? Share your answer with a classmate.*

## ACTIVITY 4 Number Change

**With Your Partner** Your goal is to write a number in standard form.

**What You'll Need**

- *spinner*
- *base ten blocks*

1 Spin the spinner. Write the number in the ones' column. Spin again and fill in the tens' column. Spin a third time for hundreds.

| Thousands | Hundreds | Tens | Ones |
|---|---|---|---|
| | 13 | 8 | 12 |



2 Use base ten blocks to show the amount you spun.

**CONNECT AND COMMUNICATE**

*How is trading with money different from trading with numbers?*

**3** Make as many trades with your base ten blocks as you can. Write the number in standard form.

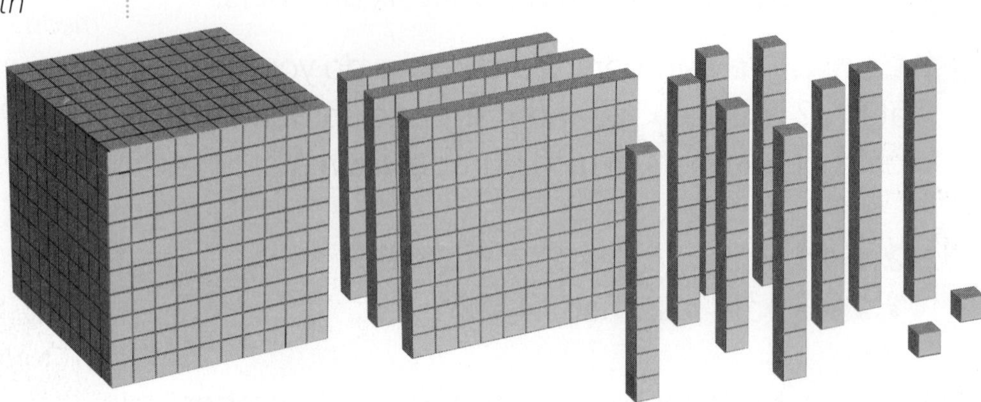

**With Your Group** Discuss how you made your trades.

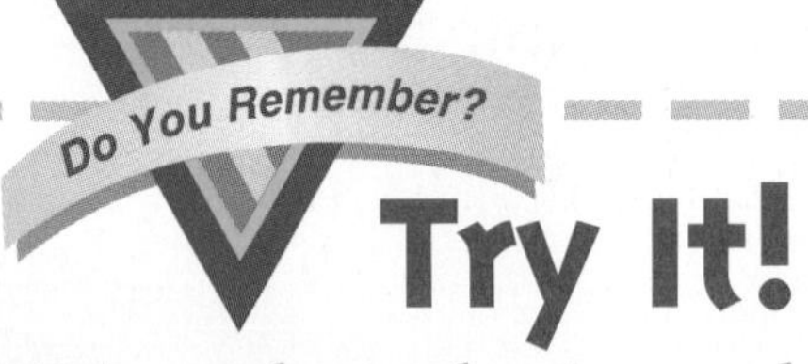


Write each number in standard form.

1. 24 hundreds
2. 73 tens
3. 7 hundreds, 8 tens
4. 2 thousands, 4 hundreds
5. 6 thousands, 5 tens
6. 9 thousands, 10 ones

Use $<$, $>$, and $=$ to compare the numbers.

7. 8,000 ● eight thousands
8. 1,347 ● 12 hundreds
9. 17 hundreds ● 1,900
10. 6 hundreds ● 500

**Think About It**

11. Describe how place value helps you compare numbers.

# A Million Letters

The President of the United States sometimes gets 40,000 letters a week. Is this amount close to a million? How long does it take for the President to get a million letters? One million is 1,000,000.

## ACTIVITY 1 Million Building

### With Your Group

1. **Use** a calculator. In how many weeks will the President get about a million letters?
2. **Explain** your process to another group. Did both groups use the same method? Did both groups get the same result?
3. **Measure** the depth of the 100 letters shown in the picture. How tall would a stack of a million letters be? Tell another group how you solved this problem.

**What You'll Need**
- *ruler*

*You read the number as* four hundred fifty-four million, three hundred eighty-six thousand.

## Activity 2 Mail Millions

**With Your Partner** The chart shows about how many letters are mailed in the United States each day.

*Each group of three digits is called a **period.** To read a number, read each group of three digits and say the name of the period.*

| Millions | | | Thousands | | | Ones | | |
|---|---|---|---|---|---|---|---|---|
| Hundreds | Tens | Ones | Hundreds | Tens | Ones | Hundreds | Tens | Ones |
| 4 | 5 | 4, | 3 | 8 | 6, | 0 | 0 | 0 |

1. Large numbers of letters are sent and received, as shown below. Write the number for each group of letters in standard form. Use a place-value chart.

*In the United States 454 million, 386 thousand letters are mailed each day.*

*The White House got 597 thousand letters in June 1993.*

*Hank Aaron got 900 thousand letters after breaking Babe Ruth's home-run record in 1974.*

*Craig Shergold, a boy in England, got 33 million get-well cards.*

2. Now write your own numbers on a place-value chart. Use up to seven digits. Write at least three numbers. Don't show your partner!

3. Stump your partner. Give clues about one of your numbers. You might tell the digit in the thousands' place or tens' place. You can use other clues about comparing too.

4. Give clues until your partner guesses the number. How many clues did it take?

**My number has a 6 in the thousands' place.**

*Find your own big numbers to play the game with. You might find numbers in the newspaper or in an almanac.*

## Try It!

Use <, >, or = to compare the numbers.

1. 52 million ● 650,569
2. 600,000 ● 8 million
3. 62 million ● 6,000,000
4. 200,000 ● 1 million
5. 5 million, 82 thousand ● 5,800,000

Write each sum in standard form.

6. 20 tens + 80 ones
7. 8 hundred + 25 hundred
8. 27 tens + 13 tens
9. 51 million + 48 million
10. 12 million + 32 thousand

**Think About It**

11. Tell in writing how you found the answer to Exercise 5.

LESSON 3

# Number Smarts!

Use your number sense! Decide which numbers make sense in the story.

## ACTIVITY 1 Fill In the Blanks

**With Your Group** Pick the most sensible number for each blank. The story and picture will help you.

REASONING AND PROBLEM SOLVING

*Each number is used only once. How can this help you choose a strategy for completing the story?*

**1** **Marina is one of about ___?___ bicycle messengers in Chicago, Illinois. Marina rides about ___?___ miles a day, crisscrossing the crowded downtown. That is about ___?___ miles a year!**
**Answers:**
**a. 1,000  b. 50  c. 12,000**

**2** Marina makes about **?** deliveries in one day. Today she made three extra deliveries, or **?**. Marina makes about **?** deliveries a month.

Answers:

a. 16 b. 320 c. 19

**3** About **?** people come into the city each day. The number of cars is much less, about **?**. The number of bikes is even smaller, about **?**.

Answers:

a. 1,000 b. 900,000 c. 85,000

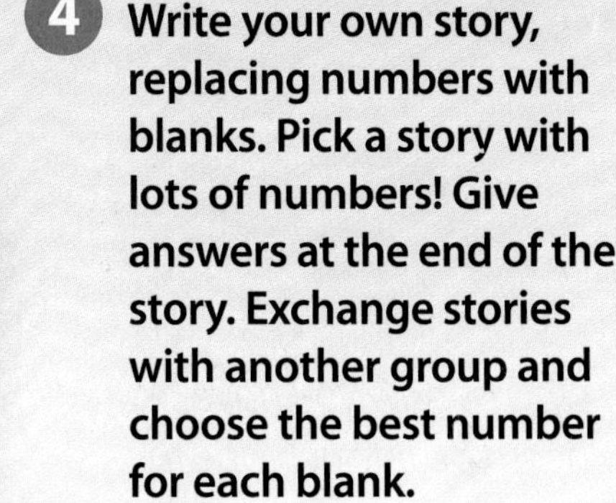

**4** Write your own story, replacing numbers with blanks. Pick a story with lots of numbers! Give answers at the end of the story. Exchange stories with another group and choose the best number for each blank.

## Try It!

Write a reasonable estimate of the following.

1. students in your school
2. people on a bus
3. wheels on a truck
4. floors in a tall building
5. windows in an office building

Add mentally. Use sums of 10 or 100 to help you.

6. $7 + 9 + 3$
7. $1 + 6 + 2 + 8$
8. $4 + 5 + 6 + 2$
9. $50 + 2 + 50$
10. $7 + 9 + 91 + 3 + 13$

### Think About It

11. How does finding reasonable numbers help you solve problems?

On Time!

LESSON 4

# Order Time!

## ACTIVITY 1 30 Minutes Later?

*Discuss how you have heard people describe the time. Why do you think people say the time in different ways?*

**On Your Own** Hot pizza in 30 minutes or less! Can you deliver it on time? Letters and packages aren't the only things to deliver.

1. **The clock shows the time a pizza was ordered. Say the time in two different ways.**
2. **Find the time that is 30 minutes after the time shown. Write the time.**
3. **You deliver a pizza at 9:50. What time was 30 minutes earlier?**

4 The 12 hours from midnight to noon are called A.M. The 12 hours from noon to midnight are called P.M. How can you tell the number of hours in a day?

5 The pizza store is open from 10:00 A.M. to 11:00 P.M. Below are the times one person worked. Rewrite the times, using A.M. and P.M. Then find the number of hours worked each day.

**10:00 to 4:45**

**5:15 to 11:00**

**10:08 to 12:23**

**11:22 to 6:17**

6 Each watch shows when a pizza was ordered. The minute hands are missing, but the watches show about the right time. Match each watch with a time shown. Explain your process.

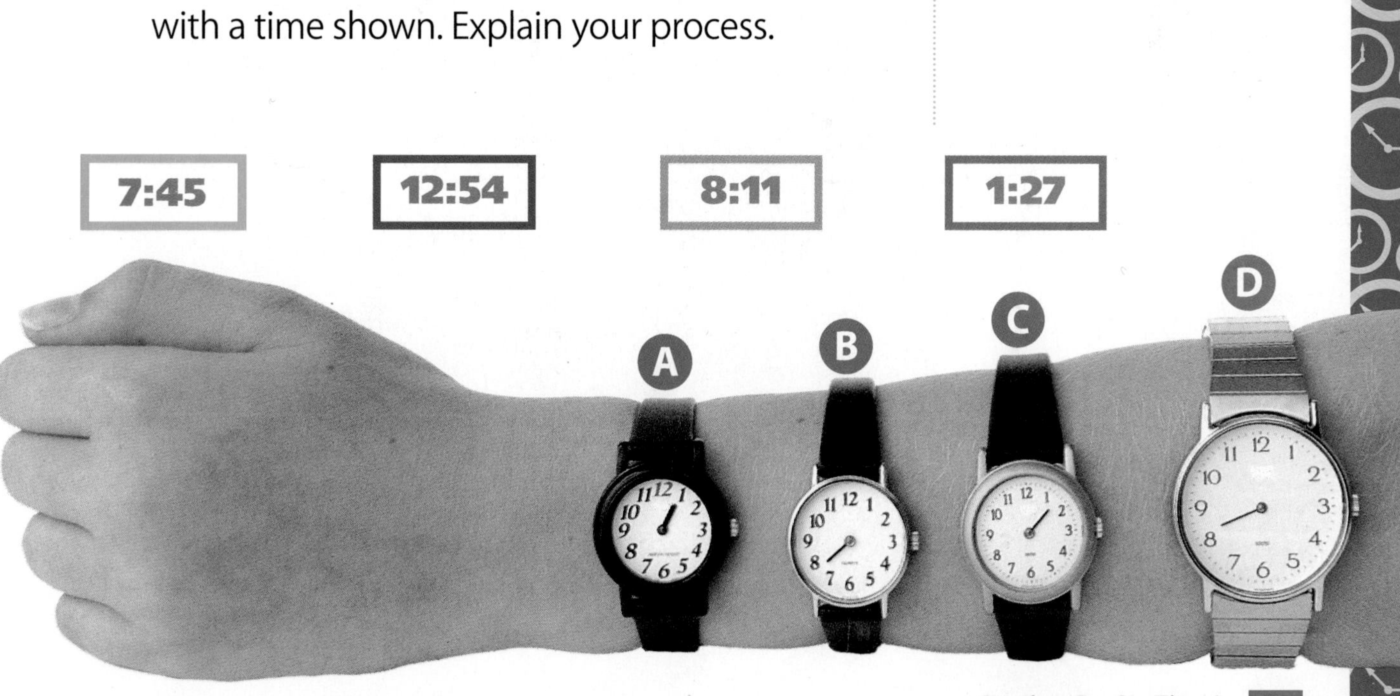

*Explain how you would change 240 minutes to hours. Can you use mental math to solve the problem?*

## ACTIVITY 2 Pizza Time

**On Your Own** Seconds and minutes count! Talking about time is important too.

1. There are 60 seconds in a minute. It takes about 30 seconds for someone to call and order a pizza. About how many minutes does it take for 6 calls in a row? 7 calls?
2. Estimate how many orders you can take in 2 minutes.
3. Use the list below. How long did it take Jan to make four deliveries?
   a. Say the total time in a different way.
   b. Explain how to change time from minutes to hours.

***How many minutes are in an hour? If you are not sure, use the clock to find out.***

Jan's Delivery List
1. 17 minutes
2. 18 minutes
3. 28 minutes
4. 20 minutes

5 minutes

30 MINUTE PIZZA PALACE

## ACTIVITY 3 In 30 Minutes . . .

**With Your Group** Telling time is only one part of having time sense. Here are some ways to use what you already know to explore time.

1. Think of some activities you can do in about 30 minutes. Don't limit your ideas. Brainstorm activities you do at home and activities you do with your friends.
2. Have one group member record your ideas.
3. Make a list of activities that take about a minute or activities that take about an hour. How might your list help you think about time?
4. Share your list with another group. How do the lists compare?

*Brainstorming is just another name for bouncing ideas around. Start with a topic. List all the ideas that come up. Everyone should join in!*

How long does it take to get to school?

How long does it take to play a soccer game?

How long does it take to get ready for school?

How long does it take to eat lunch?

# ACTIVITY 4 All in a Day

**On Your Own** Read this poem to learn about one girl's day during the winter.

LITERATURE

*Alice Yazzie is a Navajo girl. This poem can help you think about the seasons and how you spend your days.*

### *January (Yas Nilt'ees)*

The snow slowed the world,
the Navajo world.
"Go see if the sheep are fine,"
Grandfather Tsosie tells Alice Yazzie.
"The hay is frozen
and so is the ground," says Alice, returning.
"The horses look like they blame me
for causing this cold."

Her nose red, her chin buried in sheepskin,
she carries the smallest lamb
into the hogan.
"Just for the night," says Alice Yazzie
holding the lamb.
"He's all new and starry.
He's too new to be cold."
Grandfather grunts.
He doesn't say no.

From *Alice Yazzie's Year*
by Ramona Maher

*Draw a picture of an activity you do at a certain time. Show it to a classmate. Can another student guess what time it is in the picture?*

1. Make a **time log**—a record of the time spent on an activity. Keep track of six activities you do during the day.

2. Write down the time you begin each activity. Write the time you stop. Find the amount of time spent.

3. How did you spend your time during the day? Which activities took a long time? Which activities took less time?

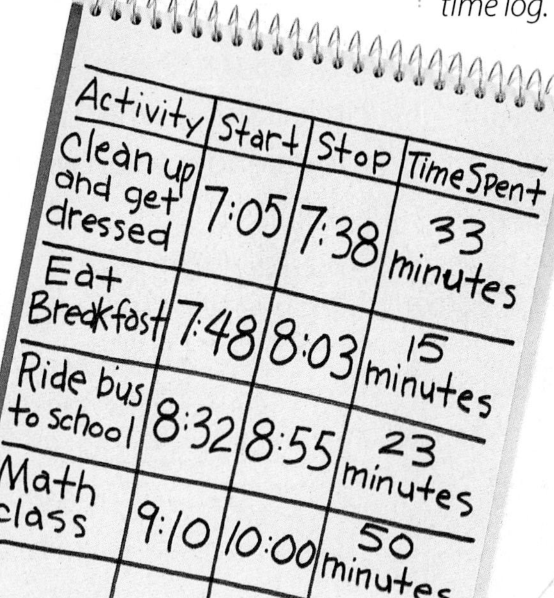


TOOLS AND TECHNIQUES

*You may wish to use a computer spreadsheet program to make your time log.*

Do You Remember?

## Try It!

Write each time in a different way.

1. 2 minutes
2. 130 seconds
3. 5 minutes
4. 220 seconds
5. Order the times above from least to greatest.

Tell the hours and minutes between each pair of times.

6. 10:45 A.M. to 3:16 P.M.
7. 5:54 A.M. to 11:35 P.M.
8. 1:07 A.M. to noon
9. midnight to 7:34 P.M.
10. 11:15 A.M. to 2:12 A.M.
11. 9:00 P.M. to midnight

**Think About It**

12. Tell in writing how you found your answer for Exercise 5.

# LESSON 5 Calendar Clues

*How would you count weeks on the calendar? How would you find three days before or after June 1?*

## ACTIVITY 1 Delivery Dates

**On Your Own** Look at the calendar. The days circled show when packages were shipped. Use the calendar to answer questions about deliveries.

| Sunday | Monday | Tuesday | Wednesday | Thurs |
|---|---|---|---|---|
| 30 | MAY 1 | 2 | 3 | |
| 7 | 8 | 9 | 10 | |
| 14 | (15) | 16 | 17 | |
| 21 | 22 | 23 | 24 | |
| 28 | 29 | 30 | (31) | |
| 4 | World Environment Day 5 | 6 | 7 | |
| 11 | 12 | (13) | 14 | |
| 18 | 19 | 20 | Summer Solstice 21 | |

**1 A package was ordered May 29. It was delivered on this date. How long did it take to get the package?**

**2** Write each circled date in two ways. An example is shown below.

*June is the sixth month.*

**June 5, 1995** ⟷ **6/5/95**

**3** Each package is delivered in three days. Don't count Saturday or Sunday. Write the day and date each package will arrive.

✓ **Self-Check** *How many days are in this month? Remember this simple rhyme: Thirty days have September, April, June, and November.*

| ay | Friday | Saturday |
|---|---|---|
| 4 | Cinco de Mayo 5 | 6 |
| 11 | 12 | 13 |
| 18 | 19 | 20 |
| 25 | 26 | International Frog Jumping Jubilee 27 |
| JUNE 1 | 2 | 3 |
| 8 | 9 | 10 |
| 15 | 16 | 17 |
| 22 | 23 | 24 |
| | | JULY |

**4 You want delivery by Cinco de Mayo. By what day should you order a package that takes 2 weeks for delivery?**

**5 You order a shirt on 5/27/95. Suppose delivery takes 4 weeks. Will you have it by 6/21/95? Explain.**

**6 Share your answers with your class. Did everyone count the days the same way? Describe two ways to count 15 days on the calendar.**

**7 Write a problem about the calendar.**

# Coast to Coast

Traveling coast to coast is faster now than it was in 1895. Messages move faster too! Look at the differences between Dottie's trip and Carolyn's trip.

1. **Dottie was planning a train trip. On June 11, 1895, she sent a letter from San Francisco to New York. She got a letter back 12 days later. What date did she get the letter?**

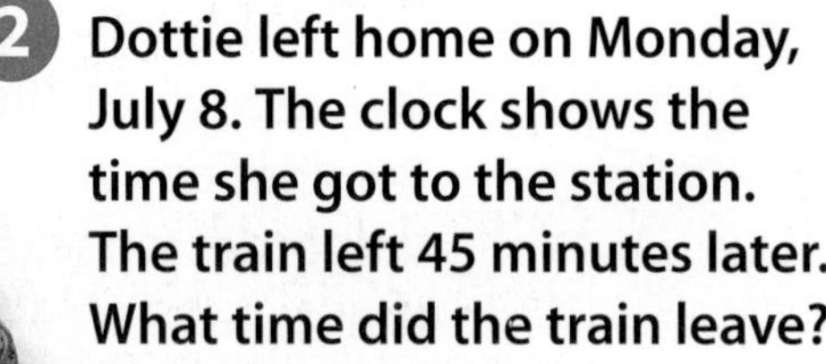

2. **Dottie left home on Monday, July 8. The clock shows the time she got to the station. The train left 45 minutes later. What time did the train leave?**

3. **Dottie changed trains in Kansas City, Missouri, on July 11. How many days did it take her to travel from San Francisco to Kansas City?**

4. **Dottie arrived in New York five days after leaving San Francisco. What day and date did she arrive?**

1895 | 1915 | 1935

5 Carolyn lives in San Francisco 100 years later. She also planned a trip to New York. She sent a letter by electronic mail at 3:55 P.M. and got a letter back at 4:02 P.M. How long did Carolyn wait for an answer?

6 Carolyn left on the second Monday in June. Look at the calendar to find the date.

7 Carolyn got to the airport at 10:45 A.M. This was 35 minutes before the plane took off. What time did the plane take off?

8 Carolyn's flight arrived in New York at 3:50 P.M. San Francisco time. How long did the flight take?

9 Carolyn stayed in New York until the date circled on the calendar. How long did she stay?

10 Write your own problem about traveling by train or plane. Share your problem with your class.

1955 1975 1995

## Cumulative Review

# *Mayan Calendar*

More than 1,000 years ago the Mayan people created a civilization in what is now Mexico and Central America. The Mayan calendar had 365 days, like the calendar you probably use. However, the months and days were named and numbered differently.

### Mayan Months

**1** **The picture symbols below, called hieroglyphics, show the months of the Mayan year. Write a multiplication sentence for the array. How many months does the year have?**

**Months**

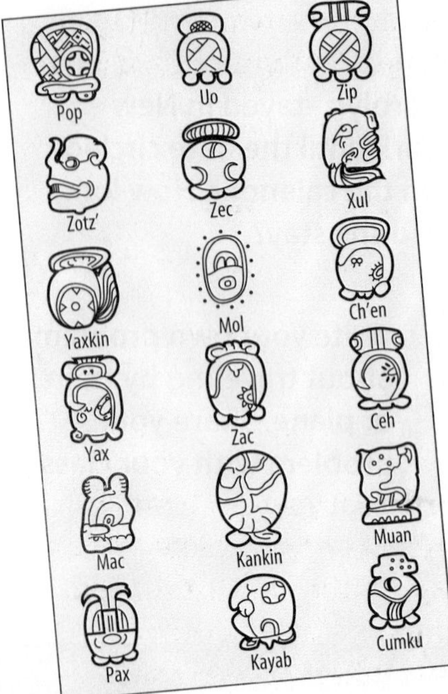


**2** **Each month had 20 days. How many days were in 2 months? 3 months? 4 months?**

**3** **How can you find the number of days in 18 months?**

**4** **After 18 months, there were extra days to make a total of 365 days. The Maya called these unlucky days *Uayeb*. How many days were in *Uayeb*?**

Uayeb

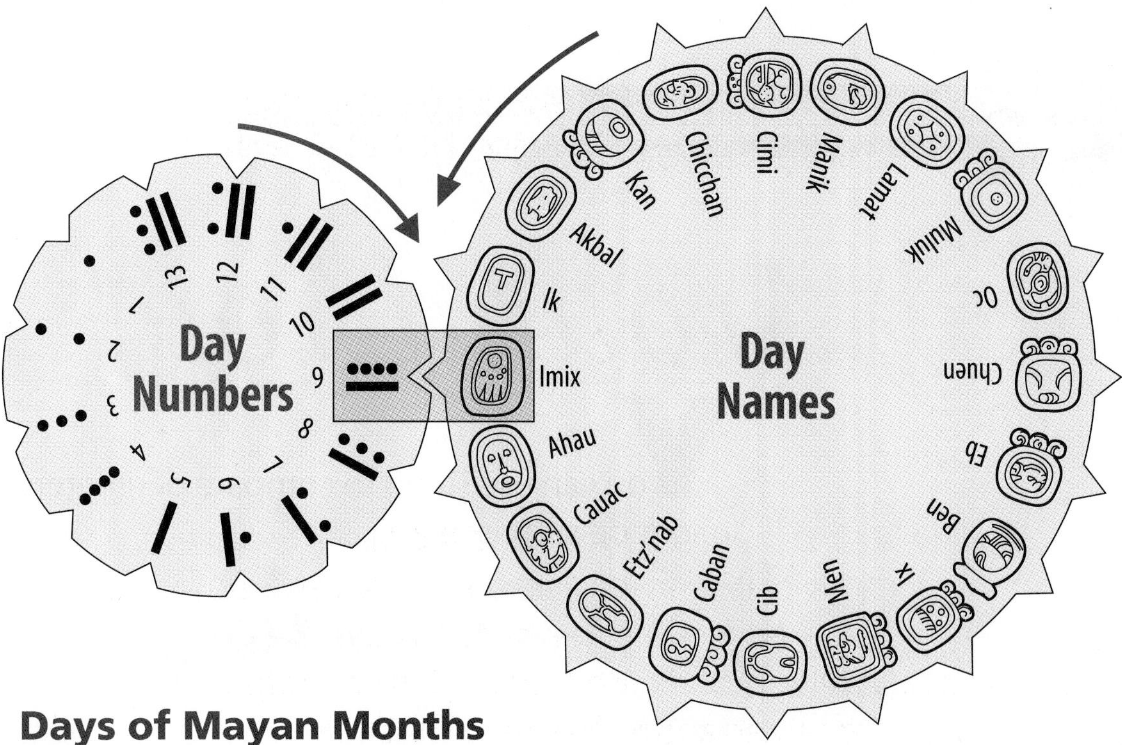


## Days of Mayan Months

**5** Each day of a month had a number and a name. The day shown on the wheels is 9 *Imix*. If you turned the wheels one space, the next day would be 10 *Ik*. Write the names for the next five days.

**6** Count 20 days after 9 *Imix*. What is the number and name of the day?

**7** Count 13 days after 9 *Imix*. What is the number and name of the day?

## Mayan Numbers

**8** The Maya used a dot for 1 and a bar for 5. Show how the Maya wrote 14 and 17.

**9** Find the sum or difference of these Mayan numbers. Write your answer in Mayan numerals or in standard form.

**a.** •••• + ———

**b.** $\overset{\bullet}{\text{—}}$ + $\overset{\bullet\bullet}{\text{—}}$

**c.** $\overset{\bullet}{\underset{\text{—}}{\text{—}}}$ − •••

*This stone carving shows an example of Mayan writing. The symbols form an array. How many symbols are shown in all?*

# Check Your Math Power

**10** The first month of a particular year starts with day 9. Turn the right wheel one complete turn, or 20 spaces. What day number starts the next month? What day numbers start the other months that year? What pattern do you see?

SECTION C Made to Measure

# LESSON 6 Around You!

You can use string to compare perimeters. You might be surprised!

What You'll Need
- *piece of string, 4–5 yd*
- *tape measure*

## ACTIVITY 1 Use Your Head

### With Your Group

1. **Use** a long string. Find which is longer:
   - **a.** your arm or the distance around your waist
   - **b.** your height or the distance around the top of a wastebasket
   - **c.** a desk or the distance around your body

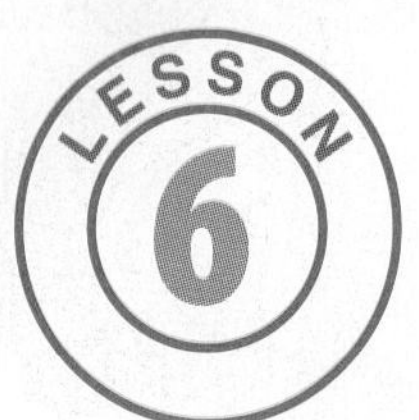

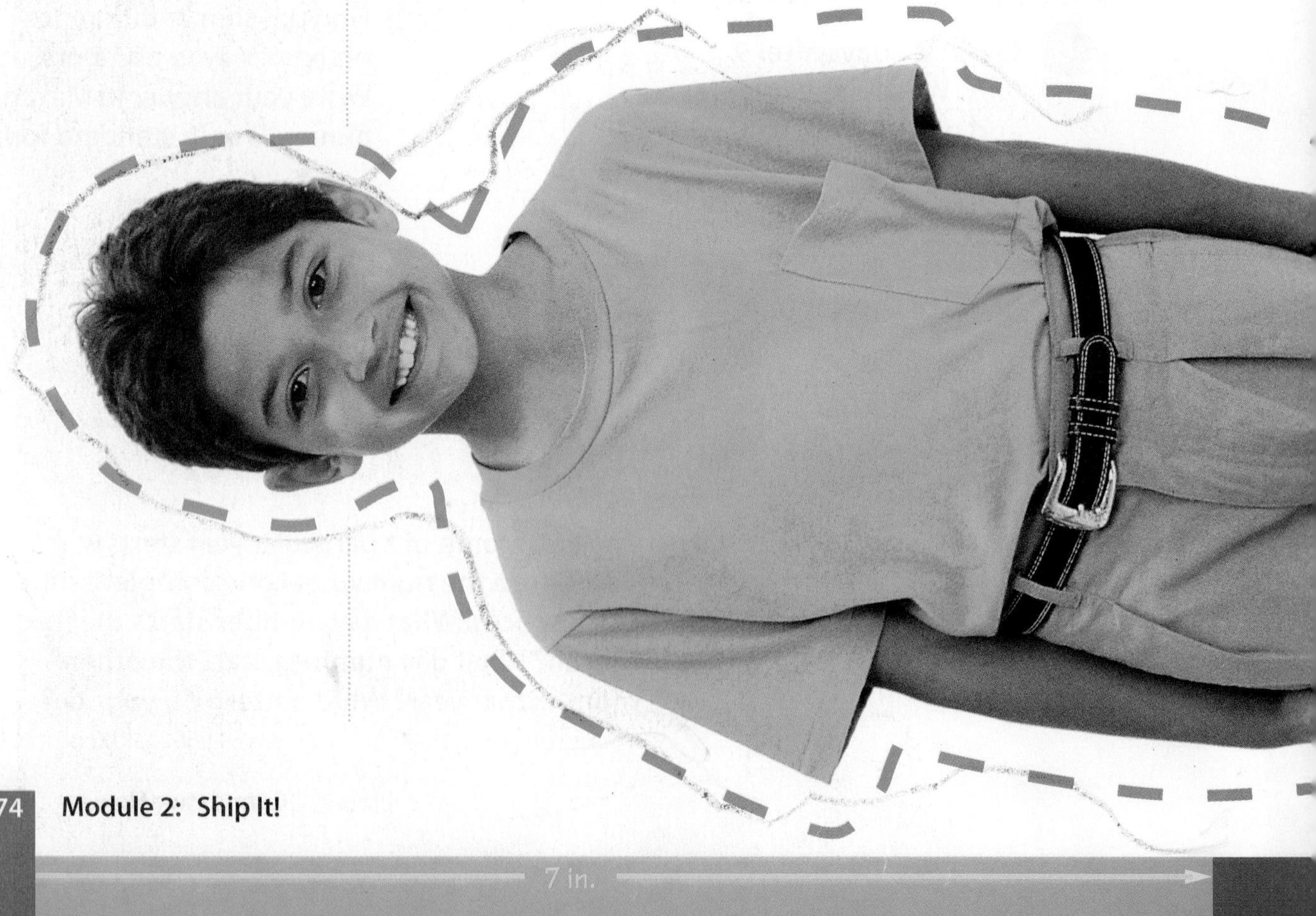

7 in.

2 **Estimate** how many times the string can wrap around your head. Have each person record an estimate. Then count the number of wraps for each person.

3 **Share** your data with the class. Did the length of the string used make a difference? Explain.

✓ **Self-Check** *How close were the estimates and measurements that your class collected?*

## ACTIVITY 2 Check Your Yards

**On Your Own** To compare things, people use standard units like these.

### What You'll Need

- *piece of string, 1 ft*
- *piece of string, 1 yd*
- *tape measure, 12-in. ruler, or yardstick*

**Standard Units**

| | | |
|---|---|---|
| **1** yard (yd) | = | **36** inches (in.) |
| **1** foot (ft) | = | **12 in.** |
| **1 yd** | = | **3 ft** |

1 **List** three things you think have a perimeter of about 1 yd. List three other things with perimeters of about 1 ft.

2 **Check** your guesses by using a string 1 ft or 1 yd long. Measure the perimeter of each object. How well did you estimate?

7 in.

**What You'll Need**

- *12-in. ruler*
- *grid paper*

*Drawing shapes can help you understand how to find perimeter. Label your drawings with measurements like length and width.*

# Activity 3 Shape Up the School

**With Your Group** Now get closer measurements of perimeters by using a ruler.

1. **Look** for things in the classroom that are shaped like a rectangle. Measure the length and width of each to the nearest inch or foot.
2. **Use** grid paper to make a drawing of each rectangle. Use one grid square to show either 1 ft or 1 in. Label each drawing.

*This is the perimeter of a sketch of a book cover.*

| Object | Length | Width | Perimeter |
|---|---|---|---|
| Desktop | 28 inches | 20 inches | 96 inches |
| Notebook | 7 inches | 5 inches | 24 inches |

8 inches

5 inches

**3** **Make** a chart that lists the rectangles you found. Record the length and width of each.

**4** **Use** your chart and drawings to calculate the perimeter of each rectangle. Record the perimeters on the chart you made.
a. Which object has the largest perimeter?
b. Which object has the smallest perimeter?
c. Write a rule for calculating the perimeter of rectangles.

*How can you use your drawings to make a general rule about how to calculate perimeter?*

Do You Remember?

## Try It!

Write each measurement in feet and inches.

1. 22 in.
2. 37 in.
3. 3 yd
4. 1 yd, 13 in.
5. 4 yd, 6 ft

Sketch these rectangles on a grid.

6. 13 in. by 2 in.
7. 3 ft by 2 ft
8. 4 yd by 5 yd
9. 20 in. by 7 in.
10. Find the perimeter of each rectangle in Exercises 6 through 9.
11. Find the area in square units of each rectangle.

### Think About It

12. When is it useful to change feet to inches? When is it useful to change inches to feet?

Investigation

# *Ship Shape*

Today you are working for a shipping company. The company will not send boxes larger than a particular size. Your job is to decide which boxes are too big. You look around for your boss and a ruler. You find only a string and this note.

This string is 130 inches long. Use it to measure the sum of the shortest perimeter and the longest length. We will only ship boxes with sums less than 130 inches.

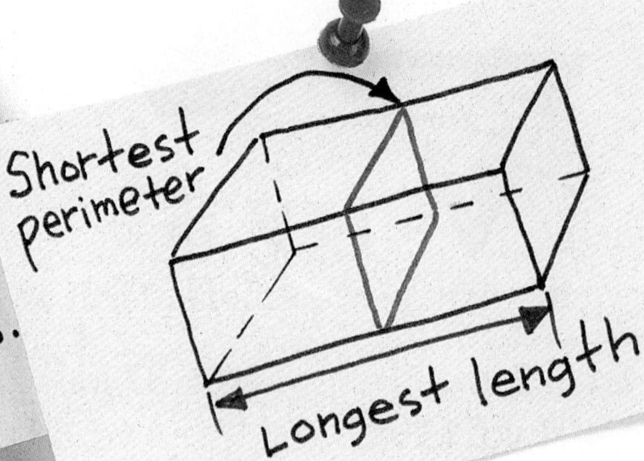


## Ask Yourself

- ☐ What is my task?
- ☐ Do I have everything I need?
- ☐ How will I use what I know about perimeter to help me?
- ☐ Can I think of another way to do this task?
- ☐ How might I describe my method to my boss?

1. Draw pictures and write step-by-step instructions to show how you do your job. Work on one box at a time.

2. When you check a box, how do you know which perimeter is shortest?

3. How do you add perimeter and length on a string? How do you know if a box is too big?

4. Use a 130-in. string to make a list of things that you can ship and things that are too big to ship. How can you use estimation to help you with your list?

*Explore how to use a string to do your job. You can practice on things in your classroom like bookshelves and lunch boxes.*

# Lesson 7 Mail Train

## Activity 1 Get the Mail

**On Your Own** The mail train leaves letters every 10 miles. People get letters from the letterbox closest to them.

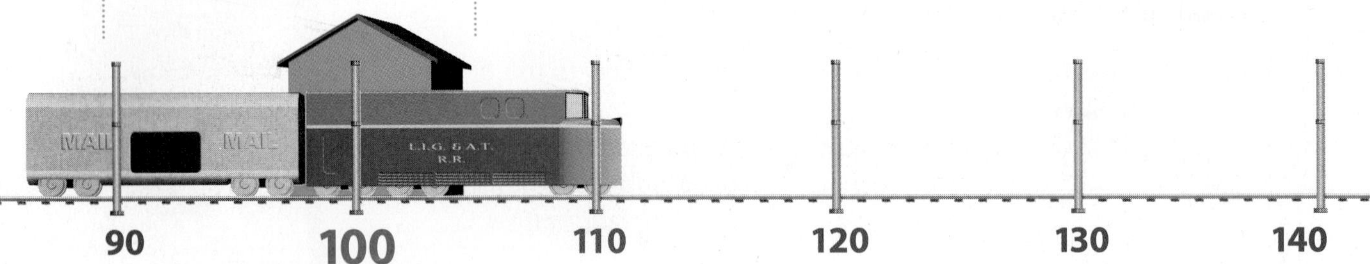


1. Ramon lives at milepost 123. Where does he go to pick up a letter?

2. Shantay lives at milepost 96. Where does she go to pick up a letter?

3. People live at each of these mileposts. Where do they go to get their letters?

   a. 147 b. 192 c. 189 d. 114

4. Deciding where people go to get letters is just like rounding. Describe your way of rounding.

*What if people lived at 115, halfway between two letterboxes? They would go to the greater ten.*

**5** Every 100 miles, the train leaves packages at a station. People get packages from the station closest to them. Teresa lives at milepost 178. Which station is closer to her, 100 or 200?

**6** Which package station would people use if they lived at these mileposts?

a. **84** b. **130** c. **151** d. **247**

*How would you explain rounding to a friend? What rules would you make for rounding?*

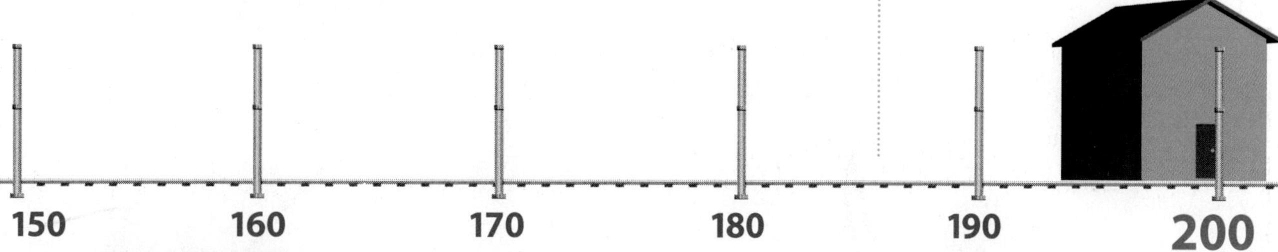


Do You Remember?

## Try It!

Round to the nearest hundred. Then round to the nearest ten.

1. 72 2. 202 3. 555 4. 787 5. 1,417

What numbers could have been rounded to the nearest ten to give the numbers below?

6. 40 7. 130 8. 110 9. 200 10. 2,480

Complete the addition and subtraction sentences.

11. ■ + 29 = 80 12. 63 − 12 = ■ 13. 73 − ■ = 38

**Think About It**

14. Explain how rounding helps you work with numbers.

# LESSON 8 Estimation Pass

What You'll Need
- *gameboard*
- *spinner*
- *game pieces*

## ACTIVITY 1 Delivery Run

### With Your Group

How many moves will you need to reach the finish line? Play Estimation Pass. The first player to reach Sum's Outpost wins.

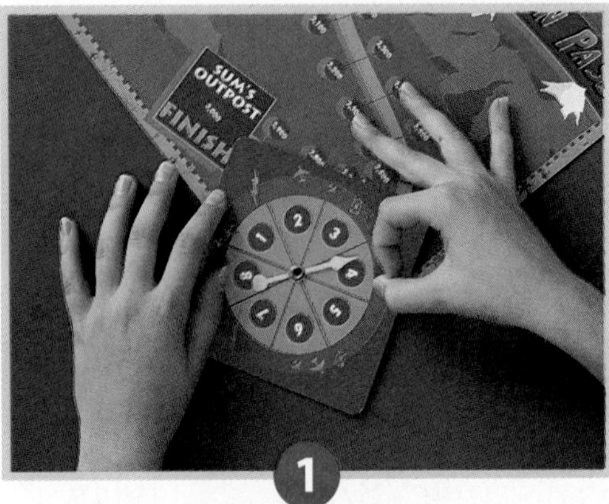


1 **Spin the spinner three times. Use your three digits to make any three-digit number. Round that number to the nearest hundred.**

2 **List both numbers in a chart like the one above. Move your game piece forward by the amount of your rounded number.**

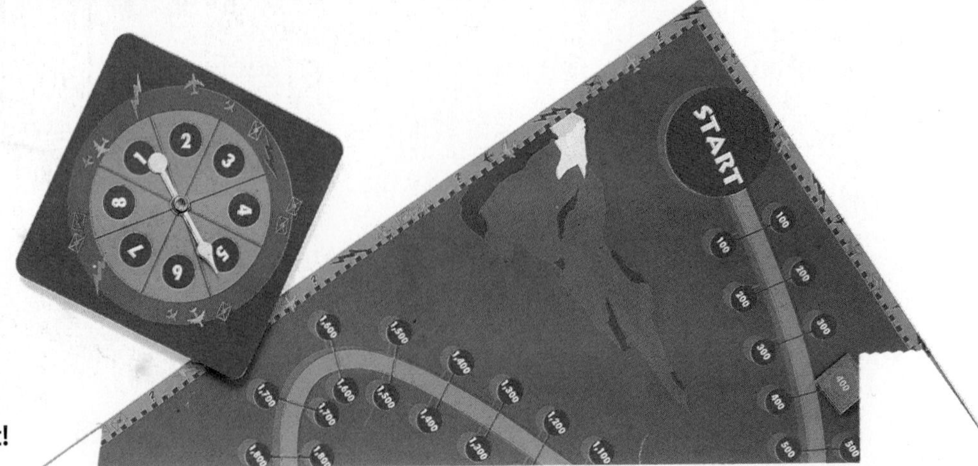

3. Take turns until one player reaches the end. Then add the numbers on each of your lists. Find the difference between the two sums. Compare your difference with that of the other players. Who has the smallest difference? the largest?

Self-Check *Does rounding always give a higher estimate than the front-end method? Try both methods. Write about what you find out.*

# Activity 2 Air Delivery

**With Your Group** Where there are few roads, airplanes deliver almost everything. Bush pilots fly small planes into remote areas all over Alaska. Use the map on the right to answer the following questions.

1. **Estimate** the distance from Takotna to Skwentna, then to Kokrines, and back to Takotna. Use either **front-end estimation** or rounding.

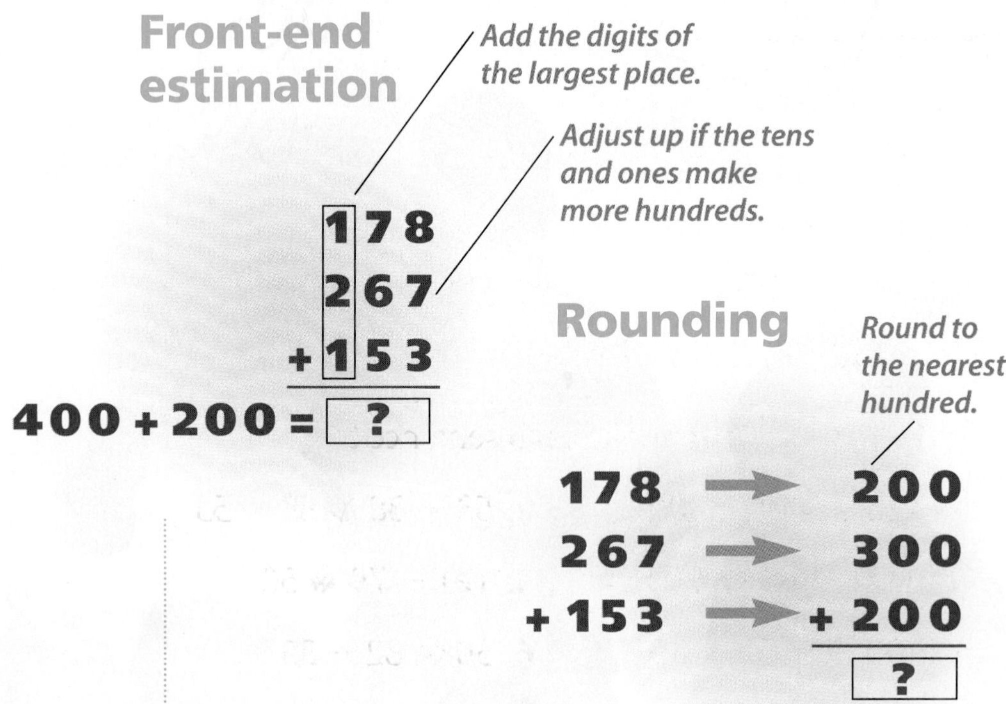


2. **Plan** other routes shorter than 850 miles.
3. **Tell** about how much farther from Fairbanks Kokrines is than Venetie. Did you round to the nearest hundred or the nearest ten?
4. **Explain** your method of estimating.

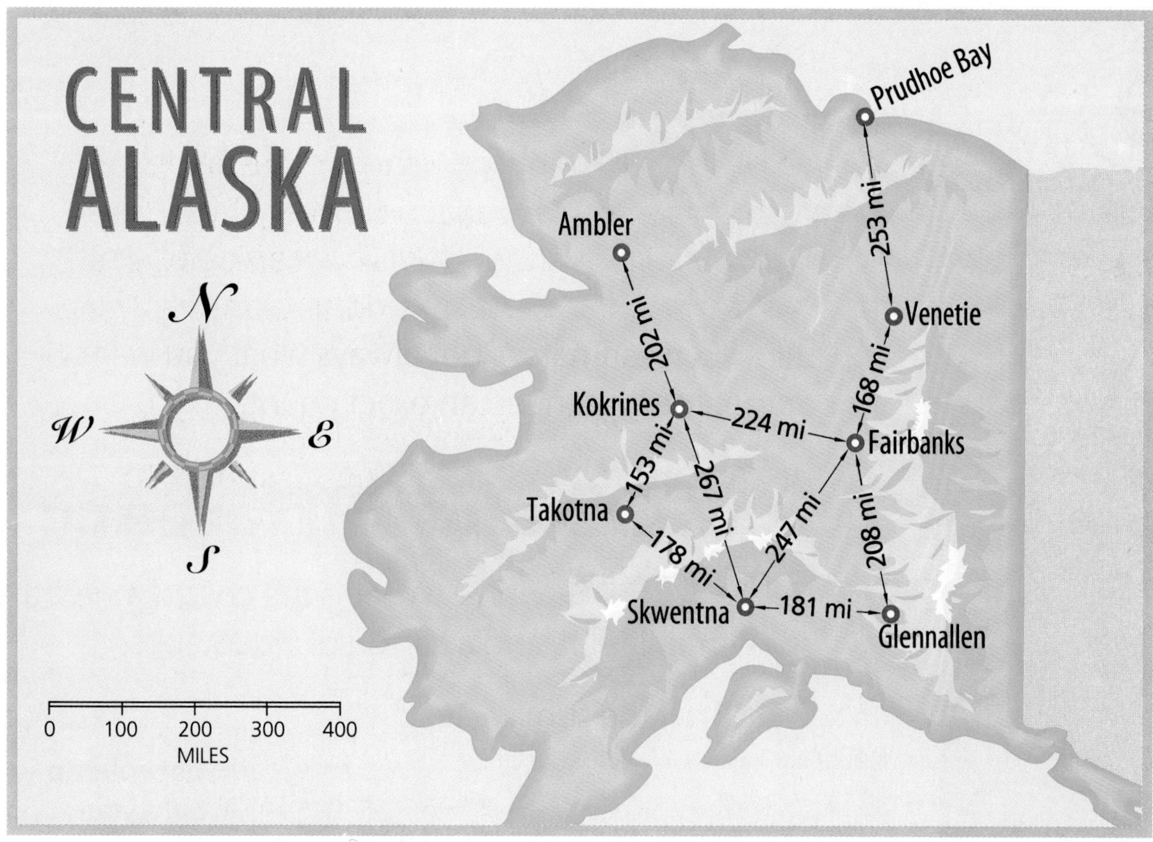

## Try It!

Write <, >, or = to make each sentence true.

1. 426 + 449 ● 500
2. 53 + 88 ● 88 + 53
3. 242 + 183 ● 500
4. 121 − 79 ● 50
5. 700 ● 958 − 349
6. 50 ● 82 − 35

Estimate. Find the exact answer for estimates less than 500.

7. 792 + 676
8. 764 − 339
9. 462 − 279
10. 847 + 778

### Think About It

11. When is an estimate better than an exact answer?

# Air Wilderness

**A**n estimate is not always what you want. Sometimes you need an exact count.

## ACTIVITY 1 Sum and Difference

**With Your Group** What is the cost of a sled, a snowmobile suit, and a carton of videotapes?

**1** **Find** the sum.

What column would you add first?

How would you add the tens? the hundreds?

$$\begin{array}{r} \$138 \\ 278 \\ +\ 126 \\ \hline ? \end{array}$$

**2** **Explain** how you add.

*How does knowing* 7 + 6 = 13 *help you find these sums?*

17 + 6
27 + 6
77 + 6

*videotapes*

**3** **Invent** your own shipment of two or more items to deliver. Then find the cost. For example, the cost of a shipment of a computer, a sled, and video tapes would be

**$3,095 + $138 + $126**

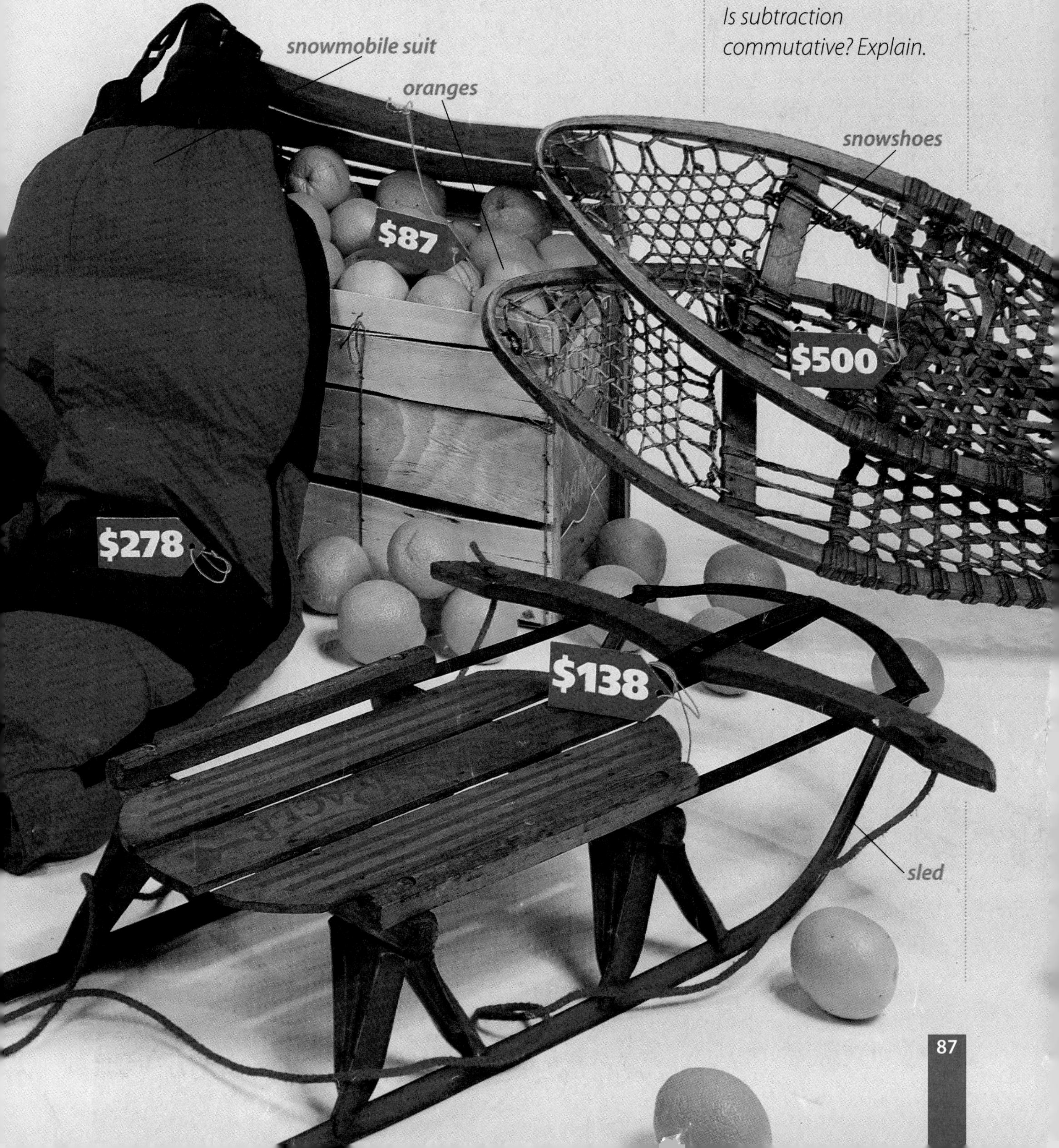

*The Commutative Property says that* 24 + 56 = 56 + 24. *Is subtraction commutative? Explain.*

**4** **Find** the difference between the costs of snowshoes ($500) and oranges ($87). Here are two methods to show renaming.

How could you use rounding to estimate the difference?

Explain these two ways to rename 500.

Explain how to find the difference. How can you use addition to check your work?

49 10
$500
− 87
□□□

4 9 10 10
$500
− 87
□□□

**5** **Create** five other subtraction exercises using numbers of your own. Exchange with another group and solve.

## Try It!

**365 265 98 102 429 115**

Choose two of the green numbers that have the given sum.

1. 380   2. 694   3. 363   4. 213

Choose two green numbers that have the given difference.

5. 163   6. 17   7. 64   8. 250

Complete the number sentence.

9. 190 + ■ = 285   10. 423 = 337 + ■   11. ■ − 45 = 710

**Think About It**

12. How are addition and subtraction related?

# *Exact Enough?*

Mental Math?

**B**efore you calculate, think about your purpose.

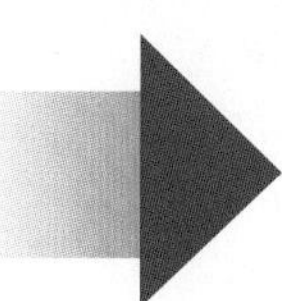

Exact or Estimate?

## ACTIVITY 1 Stop and Think

**With Your Class** Think through a problem before you start to compute.

1. Which of these needs an exact number? Will an estimate do for each of these?
   - the street address on a letter
   - the size of a new pair of shoes
   - the number of baseball players on a field
   - the amount of fuel for an airplane flight
2. Did your class agree about when to use exact numbers? How do you choose between an exact number and an estimate?

**On Your Own** Write a word problem that needs an estimated answer. Revise the problem so it needs an exact answer. Exchange problems with a classmate.

*Describe your way of deciding when to estimate.*

**Exercises and Problems**

# *Truckloads of Baseballs*

The baseballs on the map show cities that have major-league baseball teams. Each team buys about 18,000 baseballs a year. Use the map to help solve the problems. Think about these questions:

- Do you want an exact number or an estimate?
- Will you use mental math, paper and pencil, or a calculator?

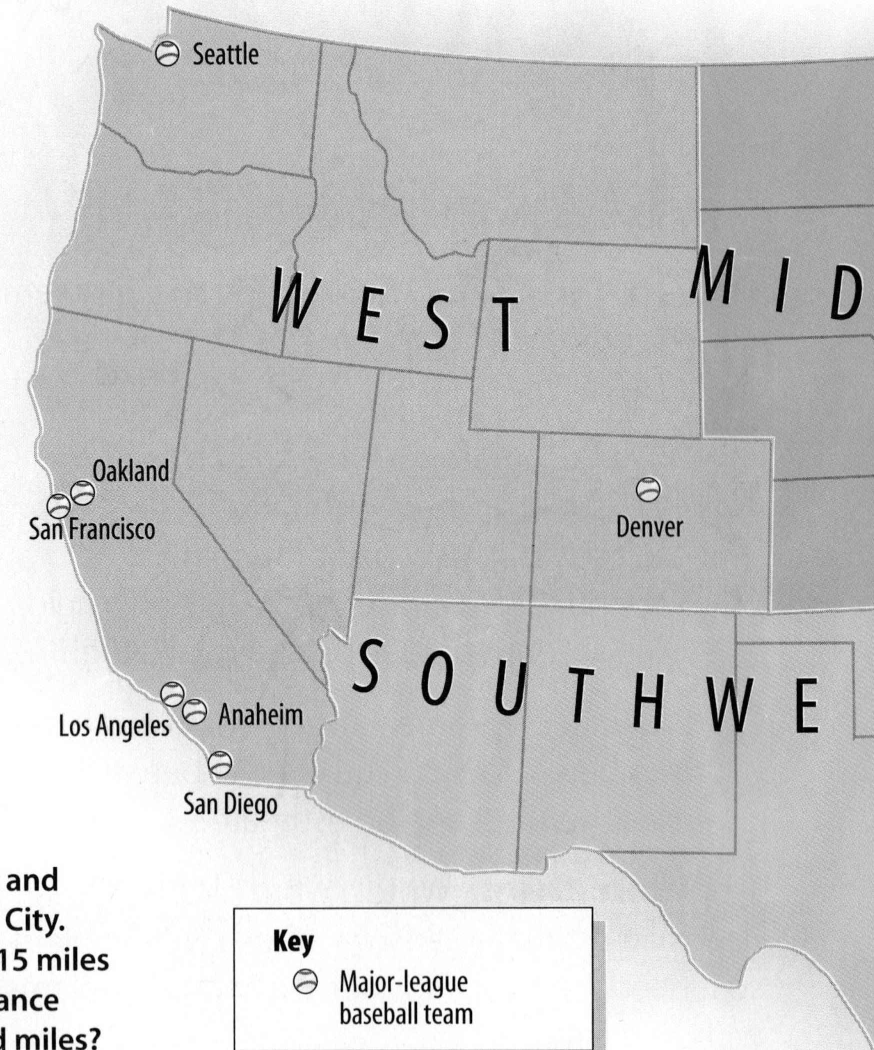


**1** **How many teams are in the Southeast? How many baseballs would go to them?**

**2** **Two trucks delivered 18,000 baseballs to a team. The first truck had 7,200. How many baseballs were in the second truck?**

**3** **How many more teams are in the Midwest than in the Northeast?**

**4** **A delivery truck left St. Louis and traveled 256 miles to Kansas City. After a delivery, it traveled 615 miles to Denver. Was the total distance more or less than a thousand miles?**

**5** A delivery truck went from St. Louis to Houston, then back to St. Louis. The distance each way is 800 miles. How many miles did the truck travel for the round trip?

**6** Before and after a game, players signed 216 balls. They signed 46 before the game. How many did they sign after the game?

| Baseball Fans in Anaheim Stadium, July 8 through July 10, 1993 | |
|---|---|
| **29,147** | Thursday, 7/8/93 |
| **23,276** | Friday, 7/9/93 |
| **33,225** | Saturday, 7/10/93 |

**7** The chart shows how many people went to three games. Was the total more than eighty thousand? Explain.

**8** How many more people came to Saturday's game than to Thursday's game?

**9** One stadium has 64,593 seats. During a game about 1,500 seats were empty. About how many seats were filled?

**10** What way of adding works best for you? What kinds of problems can you do mentally? When do you prefer to use a calculator?

## Cumulative Review

# Looking Back

**Choose the best answer. Write *a, b, c,* or *d* for each exercise.**

1. Which sentence is true?
   a. 2,007,000 = 2,000,700
   b. 7,000,000 = 7 million
   c. 135,800 > 1 million
   d. 3,000,000 < 560,984

**Use the clock to answer Exercises 2 and 3.**

2. What is the time 1 hour and 10 minutes after the time shown?
   a. 2:43  b. 1:43
   c. 3:16  d. 4:20

3. When it's 7:47, how much time has passed?
   a. 3 hours 15 minutes
   b. 7 hours
   c. 4 hours 32 minutes
   d. 6 hours 14 minutes

**Use the calendar to answer Exercises 4 and 5.**

| APRIL | | | | | | |
|---|---|---|---|---|---|---|
| S | M | T | W | T | F | S |
| | | | | (1) | 2 | 3 |
| 4 | 5 | 6 | 7 | 8 | 9 | 10 |
| 11 | 12 | (13) | 14 | 15 | 16 | 17 |
| 18 | 19 | 20 | 21 | (22) | 23 | 24 |
| 25 | 26 | 27 | 28 | 29 | 30 | |

4. A package is sent on each circled date. Each package takes one week to deliver. Which date is not an arrival date?
   a. April 29  b. April 20
   c. April 14  d. April 8

5. What day of the week is three days later than April 23?
   a. Tuesday  b. Thursday
   c. Sunday  d. Monday

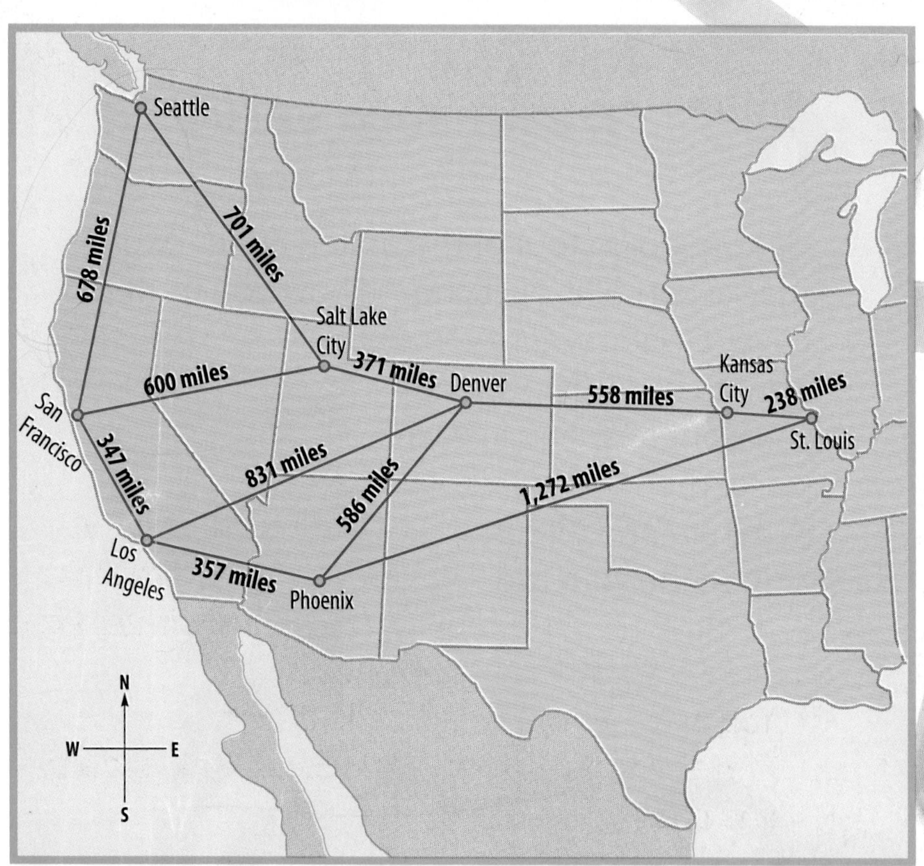


*a dancer's ballet shoes*

To: Denver

**3** Use words, numbers, and pictures to describe your trip. You may write a letter to a friend, keep a journal, or keep a travel log. Do these things.

- List each city you visited.
- List the items you delivered.
- Explain why your route is the shortest.

*the baseball glove of an all-star*

To: St. Louis

## Keep in Mind

**Your report will be judged by how well you do the following things.**

- ☐ Use addition and subtraction to show distances.
- ☐ Explain why your route is the shortest possible one for the items you chose.
- ☐ Describe the highlights of your trip.

## Investigation B: Travel Your Way

*You might plan a walking tour or a tour by in-line skates. You might hike or ride a horse. How far could you go in a day? Here are some estimates of distances you could travel in one day:*

- *walking, 10 miles*
- *in-line skating, 15 miles*
- *biking, 25 miles*
- *horseback riding, 30 miles*

Plan your own tour of the United States or one special part of it. First choose how you want to travel. Decide where you want to go and how long you want to spend in each place. Then use words, numbers, and pictures to describe your trip.

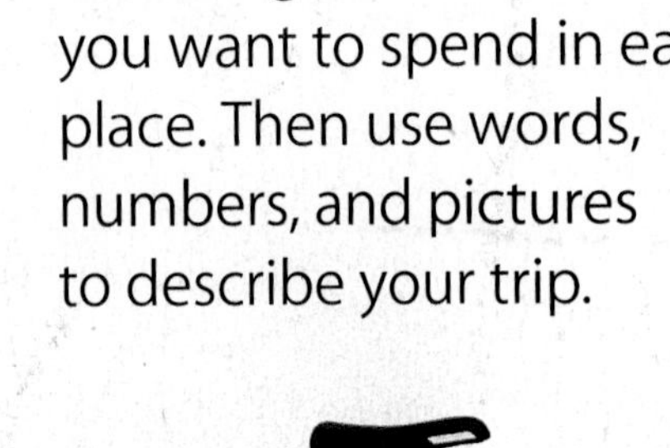

## Ongoing Investigation: "How Much Is a Million?" Revisited

How quickly are you collecting one million? Find out about how many items you have collected so far. Also take a look at your log to see how many items you've collected each week. Is there a pattern? Write a summary of your data and your observations about it. Be sure to include

- your prediction of how long it will take to collect one million
- any suggestions you have for collecting more items faster

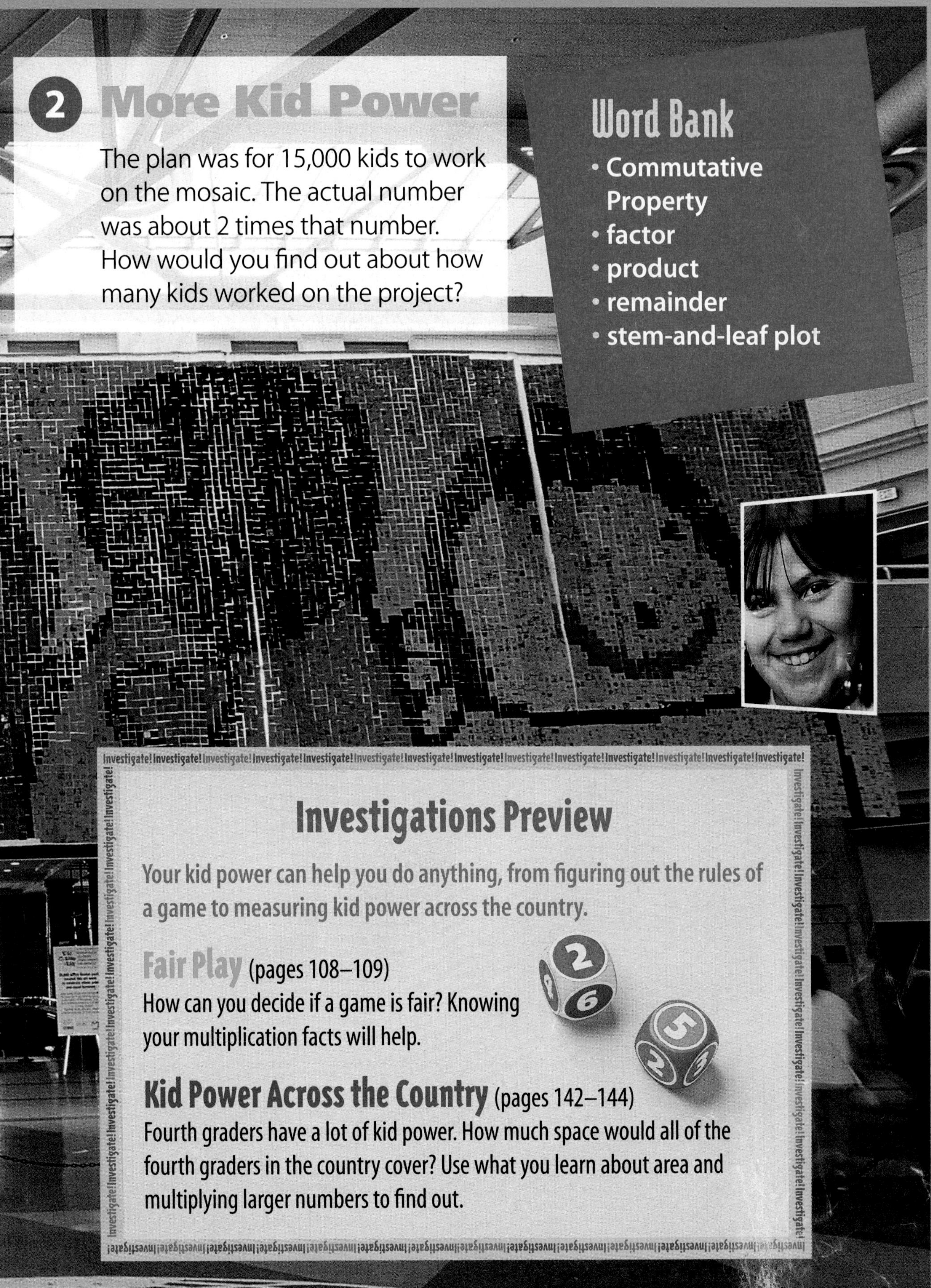

# 2 More Kid Power

The plan was for 15,000 kids to work on the mosaic. The actual number was about 2 times that number. How would you find out about how many kids worked on the project?

## Word Bank

- Commutative Property
- factor
- product
- remainder
- stem-and-leaf plot

## Investigations Preview

Your kid power can help you do anything, from figuring out the rules of a game to measuring kid power across the country.

**Fair Play** (pages 108–109)
How can you decide if a game is fair? Knowing your multiplication facts will help.

**Kid Power Across the Country** (pages 142–144)
Fourth graders have a lot of kid power. How much space would all of the fourth graders in the country cover? Use what you learn about area and multiplying larger numbers to find out.

## Section A: The Basic Facts

# Lesson 1: Just the Facts

Powerful fifth graders attend Adamsville School in Bridgewater, New Jersey. They raised more than $1,000 for the Yanomami people in the Brazilian rain forest. Students asked every governor in the United States for a favorite recipe. They put the recipes together in a cookbook and sold copies.

## Activity 1: Powerful Kids

**With Your Class** What if your class sold a cookbook? Use what you know about multiplication to answer these questions.

1. There are 50 recipes in the cookbook. Each recipe is 2 pages long. How many pages are used for recipes?
2. If each person in your class sells 30 books, how many books are sold in all?
3. If the price of the book is $9, about how much money could your class raise?

## ACTIVITY 2 Table It!

**With Your Class** How did you use multiplication facts to answer the cookbook questions? How many other multiplication facts do you know?

*Be sure to write products in the correct boxes.*

1. Take turns calling out pairs of numbers to multiply together, or **factors.** As each factor pair is called, write the answer, or **product,** in the correct box on your multiplication table. If you don't know a product, outline its box and leave it blank.

2. After all the factor pairs are called out, look at the boxes you left blank. Make a list of the factor pairs with which you had trouble.

3. Compare your table with your classmates'. Work together to fill in all blank boxes on your table.

**Self-Check** *What patterns do you see on the table?*

**c. Count the boxes you haven't crossed out. How many of the leftover facts do you need to work on?**

Do You Remember?

## Try It!

Find the products. Arrange them in a list from least to greatest.

1. $6 \times 9 =$ ?
2. $7 \times 7 =$ ?
3. $3 \times 6 =$ ?
4. $5 \times 8 =$ ?
5. $4 \times 9 =$ ?
6. $8 \times 6 =$ ?

Estimate the sum or difference.

7. $23 + 38$
8. $89 - 51$
9. $32 + 46$
10. $104 - 41$
11. $19 + 59$
12. $203 - 146$

### Think About It

13. How is doubling a number the same as adding it to itself?

# LESSON 2 Fact Power

LITERATURE

*Ernie teaches everyone in his fourth grade class how to knit. How does Ernie's class use their kid power?*

Now that they could all knit, they could have a Christmas fair or something to raise money to buy games and books for children in the town hospital. All the things sold at the fair were knitted by the fourth grade. Frankie was good at mittens and so was Edward. Frankie knitted all the right-hand ones and Edward all the left-hand ones. Between them they made five pairs of mittens for the fair.

From *Ernie and the Mile-Long Muffler*
by Marjorie Lewis

## ACTIVITY 1 Multiplying Mittens

**With Your Class** Discuss these questions.

1. If each mitten had 4 yellow triangles, how could you figure out how many yellow triangles were knitted on all the mittens? Is there more than one way to find out?
2. Frankie and Edward used a plan, or strategy, to solve a problem. What strategies do you use to figure out multiplication facts?

*Can you think of a fast way to find the number of triangles on 10 pairs of mittens? Explain.*

# ACTIVITY 2 Choose Your Strategy

**With Your Class** What if there is a multiplication fact you don't know? Facts you already know can help you learn facts you don't know. Discuss which strategy you would use first.

*In your strategies use facts that are easy to remember. You might already know the fives facts, such as 2 × 5 and 3 × 5.*

**Add** **If you don't remember 8 × 7, do you know 7 × 7? How will that help you?**

**Subtract** **Maybe you know 8 × 8. How can this fact help you find 8 × 7?**

**Double** **Perhaps you know 4 × 7. How can you use this fact to find 8 × 7?**

**With Your Group** Use the multiplication facts you know to play this strategy game.

1. The group needs one sheet of paper. Make two columns on it. Label the first column *Question* and the second one *Strategy*. Divide the group into two teams.

*Try to play the game staying with only one fact. How many strategies did you come up with?*

2. The first team thinks of a fact. A team member writes it in the *Question* column.

3. The other team comes up with a strategy for the fact. They have 20 seconds to write it in the *Strategy* column. The first team checks the strategy. If the strategy works, the second team gets a point.

4. Change roles and continue with a different fact. Keep taking turns. The team that gets ten points first wins.

**What You'll Need**

- *note pad*

## ACTIVITY 3 Kid Power Pad

**On Your Own** Start a kid power pad of multiplication facts to concentrate on. Use it whenever you need help with a difficult fact.

1. List facts that are difficult for you.
2. Write each fact on a separate page of your power pad. (Use your journal if you don't have a note pad.)

3. Think of a helpful strategy for each fact. Write it in a sentence under the fact.

**With Your Class** Work together to come up with more strategies.

4. Collect everyone's list of difficult facts. Write them all on the board.
5. Discuss strategies found in the game for each fact listed. Do your classmates know any useful strategies for your difficult facts? Add them to your power pad.

Do You Remember?

## Try It!

Find the products and list a strategy for each fact.

1. $4 \times 5 =$ ?
2. $3 \times 8 =$ ?
3. $9 \times 6 =$ ?
4. $7 \times 8 =$ ?
5. $6 \times 4 =$ ?
6. $5 \times 9 =$ ?

Write the greater number in words. Round the smaller number to the nearest hundred.

7. 8,345; 8,453
8. 752; 725
9. 1,100; 1,101
10. 300,590; 305,900
11. 17,090; 17,901

**Think About It**

12. Could there be more than one strategy for each fact? Explain.

Investigation

# Fair Play

A toy company has created a new math game. Before selling the game, the company needs to make sure the rules are fair. They want students to test the rules and give feedback. If the rules aren't fair, how can they be changed?

1. **Game Rules** **The game includes two cubes, each numbered 1 through 6. Players roll the number cubes and multiply the numbers. The first player scores a point when the product is even. The other player scores a point when the product is odd.**

**2 What's Fair?** A game is fair if all players have the same chance of winning.

- What do you know about this game?
- Does it seem fair?
- How could it possibly not be fair?

**3 Test the Rules** Conduct a fairness test by rolling two number cubes and finding their products. Record the results of your rolls. How many times should you roll the cubes to test the rules? How should you record your results?

**4 Draw Conclusions** What did you find out? Are the rules fair to all players? If the rules are fair, explain how you know. If the rules are unfair, explain why and suggest how to change the rules to make them fair.

## Ask Yourself

- ☐ Why should a game be fair?
- ☐ What are some fair games you can think of?
- ☐ How do you decide how many times you should test the rules?
- ☐ How do you know if the rules are fair or unfair?
- ☐ How would you explain the rules to your classmates?

Section B: Dividing by Multiplying

Lesson 3

# Factor Factory

Some machines need electricity to make them work. The machines on these pages are different. How can you use your kid power to figure out what makes these machines work?

## Activity 1 Function Machines

**With Your Class** Discuss how the numbers on the function tables provide clues about what each machine does. How can you use what you know when you don't have all the facts?

1. Copy the table below. What does the machine do to make the bottom numbers come out?

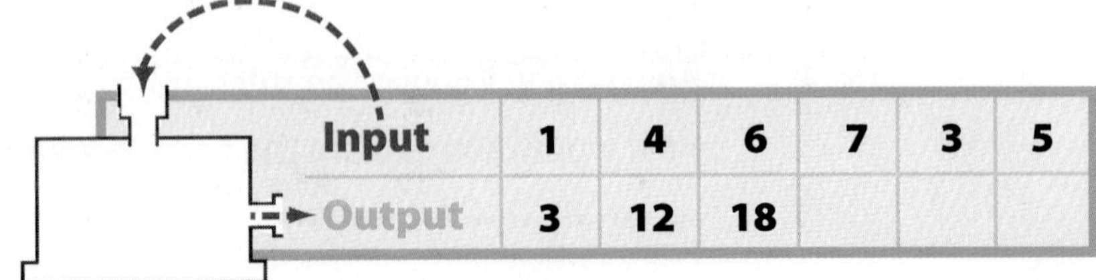

| Input | 1 | 4 | 6 | 7 | 3 | 5 |
|---|---|---|---|---|---|---|
| Output | 3 | 12 | 18 | | | |

*What pattern do you see in this function machine?*

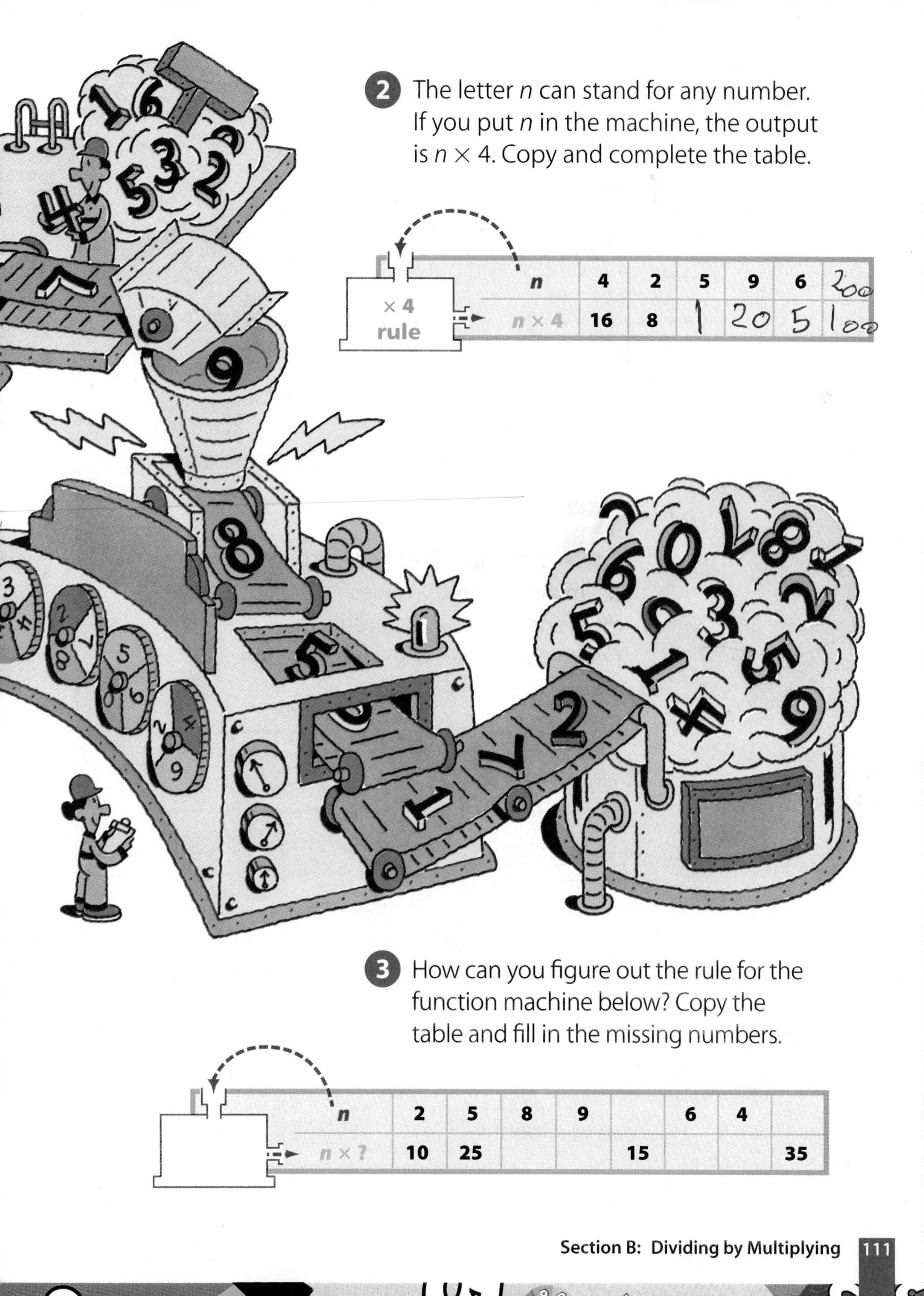

**2** The letter $n$ can stand for any number. If you put $n$ in the machine, the output is $n \times 4$. Copy and complete the table.

× 4 rule

| $n$ | 4 | 2 | 5 | 9 | 6 | |
|---|---|---|---|---|---|---|
| $n \times 4$ | 16 | 8 | | | | |

**3** How can you figure out the rule for the function machine below? Copy the table and fill in the missing numbers.

| $n$ | 2 | 5 | 8 | 9 | | 6 | 4 | |
|---|---|---|---|---|---|---|---|---|
| $n \times ?$ | 10 | 25 | | | 15 | | | 35 |

*In Your Journal* Explain how you figured out another player's rule.

# ACTIVITY 2 Function Fun

**With Your Group** Try this function game.

1. Each student thinks of a rule.
2. Player 1 draws a function table and fills in one input and output for the rule.

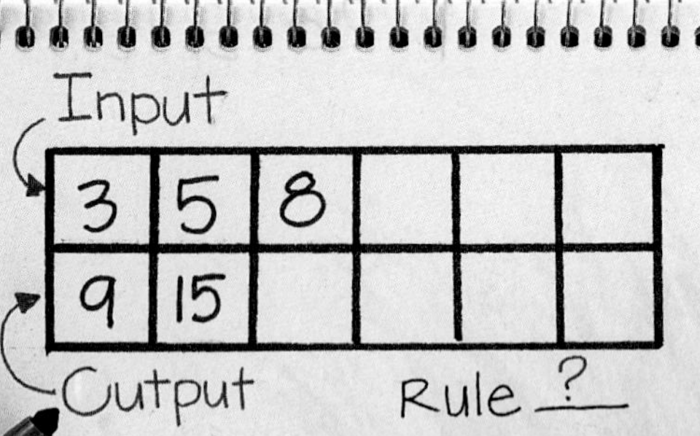


3. The other players give input numbers, and player 1 fills in output numbers.
4. When the other players figure out the rule, a new player begins.

Do You Remember?

## Try It!

Fill in the missing factors or products.

1.

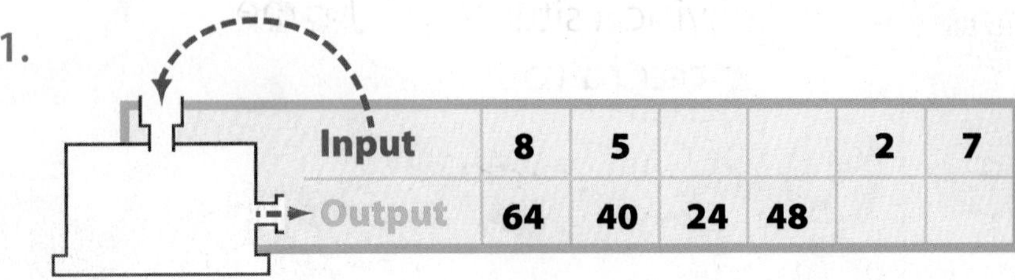

| Input | 8 | 5 | | | 2 | 7 |
|---|---|---|---|---|---|---|
| Output | 64 | 40 | 24 | 48 | | |

2. What's the rule for Exercise 1?

3. ■ × 4 = 28 4. 6 × ■ = 24 5. 5 × ■ = 30

Use <, >, or = to complete these statements.

6. 9 × 6 ● 8 × 7 7. 4 × 3 ● 6 × 2 8. 8 × 9 ● 9 × 7

9. 8 × 3 ● 6 × 4 10. 5 × 7 ● 6 × 6 11. 4 × 7 ● 3 × 9

**Think About It**

12. How can you identify $n$ in $4 \times n = 36$?

# Division Power

You can use kid power in many ways. At a summer program students like Wesley Morrissette, shown here, became inventors. They used their kid power to invent machines to solve everyday problems.

## ACTIVITY 1 Dividing Up

**With Your Group** Use counters to act out each of the following division situations. Use the division symbol $\overline{)\quad}$ to record your work.

1. **There are 30 students in the program and 6 students in each group. How many groups are there?**

2. **Suppose 3 students made 18 machines. If each student made the same number of machines, how many did each make?**

3. **One student made an automatic table setter. If the machine sets 20 plates into 5 groups, how many plates are there in each group?**

**What You'll Need**

- *counters*

*You can arrange counters in arrays to help you act out the situations.*

**On Your Own** Student inventors use many materials. Decide how to divide these materials. If you can't divide equally, how will you show the **remainder,** or leftover part? Record your work. One student showed her work like this.

*Khushali Tripathi, age 10, made an automatic table setter.*

Answer any three of these questions. Exchange answers with a partner. Discuss how you answered the questions.

4. **How would 5 students share 25 blocks of clay?**
5. **If there are 17 pieces of metal for 8 students, how many pieces would each student get?**
6. **How would 9 students divide 72 in. of string?**
7. **How would 9 students divide 75 in. of string?**

## ACTIVITY 2 Multiplication Undone

### With Your Class

1. Copy the function table below. How is this machine different from a multiplication machine?

? rule

| Input | 49 | 14 | 21 | 63 | 35 | 28 |
|---|---|---|---|---|---|---|
| Output | 7 | 2 | | | | |

2. Fill in the missing numbers. What's the rule? How do you know?

3. What is different about these sentences? What is alike?

$$14 \div 7 = n$$

$$n \times 7 = 14$$

### With Your Group

4. Make a function machine for another set of division facts. Include the rule for your machine. How can you check your work?

✔ **Self-Check** *How are multiplication and division related?*

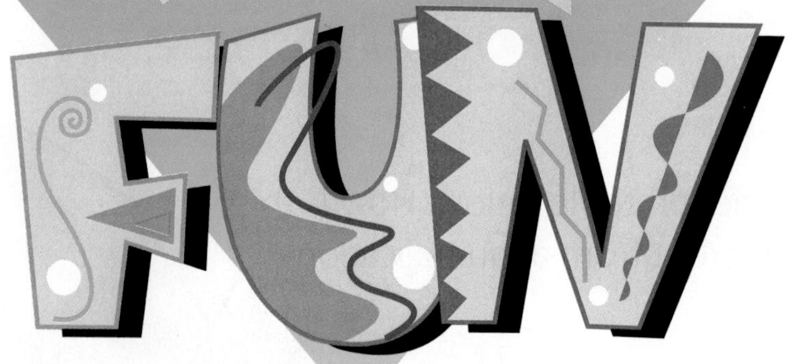


## Activity 3 Spin to Win

**What You'll Need**
- *gameboard*
- *spinner*
- *washable markers*

### With Your Group

You've learned much about multiplying and dividing. Use what you know to play this game. Two to four people can play.

**1 Spin a Factor**
**Spin the spinner. Then choose a product on the board that has your spinner number as one of its factors.**

**2 Match the Factor**
**State the other factor that makes the product. Divide the product by the spinner number to check your choice. If your answer is the number you stated, you win the circle.**

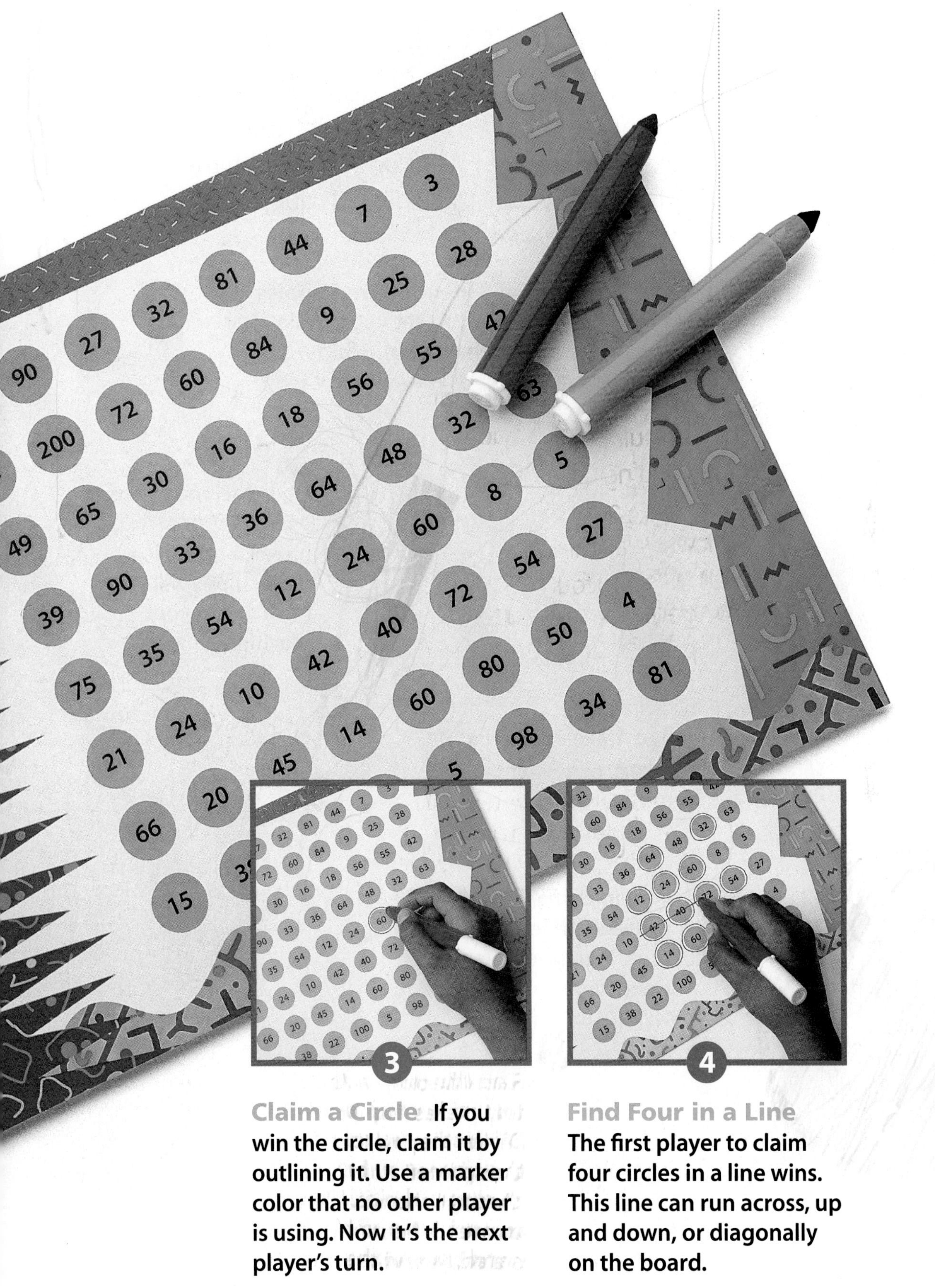

**Claim a Circle** If you win the circle, claim it by outlining it. Use a marker color that no other player is using. Now it's the next player's turn.

**Find Four in a Line** The first player to claim four circles in a line wins. This line can run across, up and down, or diagonally on the board.

*Explain how each situation helps you decide what to do with the remainder.*

## ACTIVITY 4 Leftovers

**With Your Partner** You're using some inventions to set up a class picnic. How will you divide everything? What do you do with the leftovers? Choose three division questions. Record your work.

1. **You and 3 friends have 6 apples to share. If you set your apple cutter to divide them fairly, how many apples would each of you get?**
2. **One machine opens 6 cans at once. You have 23 cans. How many times will you have to run your machine?**
3. **A sandwich machine uses 2 slices of bread to make a sandwich. How many sandwiches can it make from 13 slices?**
4. **Your juice machine can squeeze three lemons at a time. You have 22 lemons. How many groups of lemons will the machine squeeze?**

## On Your Own

**5** **There are three ways to deal with remainders. Write what you did with the remainders in Exercises 1–4.**

**a. Ignore the remainder. The leftover part is not needed.**
**b. Round the answer to the next number.**
**c. Write the answer as a fraction.**

*Write some remainder problems of your own. Trade problems with a classmate.*

**6** **Compare your answers with your partner's.**

# Try It!

Write how many each kid gets. What happens to each remainder?

1. 27 cookies ÷ 6 kids
2. 17 marbles ÷ 8 kids
3. 35 apples ÷ 4 kids
4. 45 bananas ÷ 7 kids
5. 7 hot dogs ÷ 3 kids
6. 57 pencils ÷ 9 kids

Write a multiplication fact to match each division.

7. 27 ÷ 3
8. 24 ÷ 8
9. 30 ÷ 6
10. 49 ÷ 7
11. 56 ÷ 8
12. 72 ÷ 9

### Think About It

13. Can you divide your class into 3 groups of equal size? Explain what to do if there is a remainder.

Do You Remember?

## Cumulative Review

# Record Breakers

Kids can show their power by breaking records. Find out more about these kids from around the world.

### United States

1. In April 1990, Richard Daff, Jr., became the youngest bowler to score a perfect 300. He did this 4 months before his 12th birthday. What year was he born?
2. If his score was 2 times what he scored when he was 8, what was his score at age 8?

### Jamaica

3. Joy Foster of Jamaica was the youngest table tennis player ever to compete internationally. Joy was 8 years old at the 1958 championship. How old would she be now?
4. A table tennis table is 9 ft by 5 ft. Give its perimeter.

## Great Britain

5. About 160,000 kids attended the world's largest children's party. If 16 kids sat at 1 table, about how many tables were needed?

6. The party took place in 1979. About how many decades ago did it happen?

## China

7. In 1991, at age 12, Fu Mingxia of China won the women's world title for platform diving. What year was she born?

8. If the diving platform was 6 yd high, how many feet high was it?

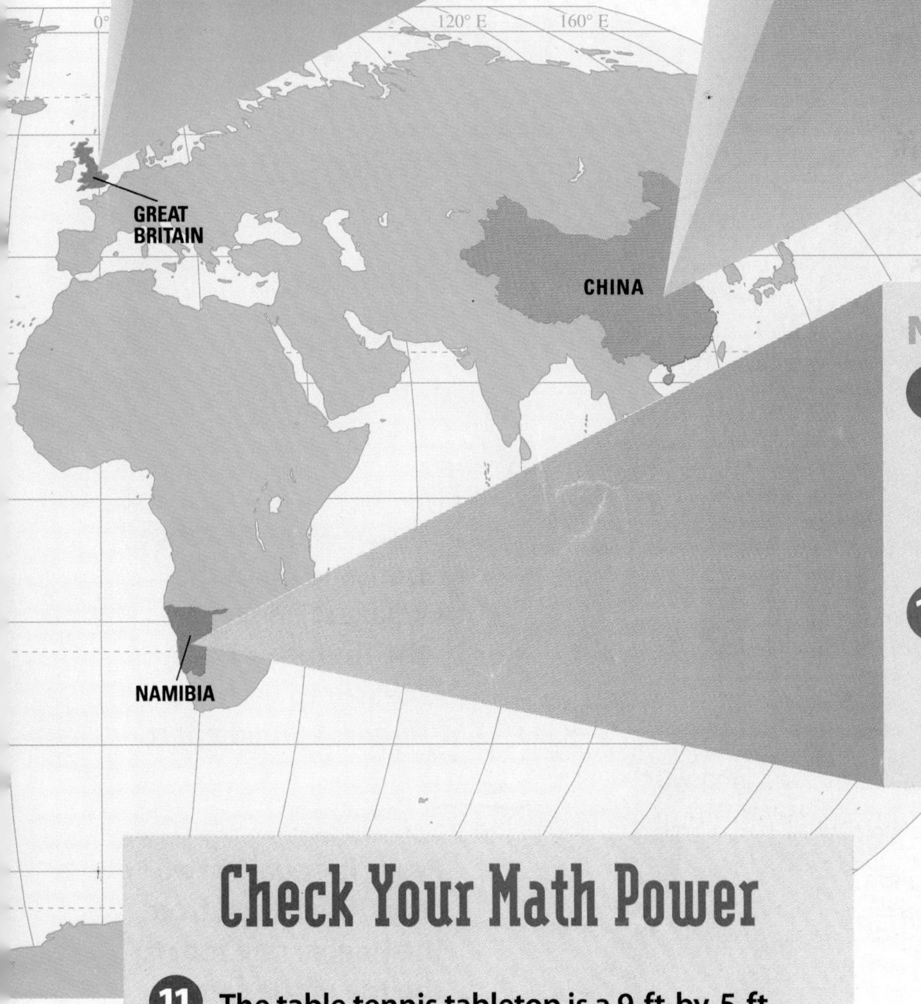

0°
120° E
160° E
GREAT BRITAIN
CHINA
NAMIBIA

## Namibia

9. A girls' school set a record for the longest kebab in July 1993. It measured 3,310 ft. About how many yards was it?

10. The previous record was set in September 1991. How many months later was it broken?

# Check Your Math Power

11. The table tennis tabletop is a 9-ft-by-5-ft shape divided in width by a net. Use geometric terms and drawings to describe it.

# Kid Sizes

**H**ow can you measure without using a ruler? The ancient Egyptians used parts of the body as measuring tools. You can too.

## Activity 1 Ancient Units

What You'll Need
- *inch ruler*

**With Your Group** Use a ruler to find the following personal measures in inches. Record your work.

**Cubit** is the distance from the tip of the middle finger to the elbow. It was used to measure height and width.

**Span** is the distance from the tip of the smallest finger to the thumb. It is measured with the fingers spread apart.

**Foot** is the length of an adult foot and was used by the Egyptians to measure short distances.

**Pace** is equal to two steps, measured from the heel of one foot to the toe of the same foot on touching the ground again.

## ACTIVITY 2 Use Your Units

**With Your Group** Take turns using your personal units to measure each item listed on the chart. Record your results. Then estimate each measurement in inches.

*Trace around your hand or foot and use your drawing as a "ruler."*

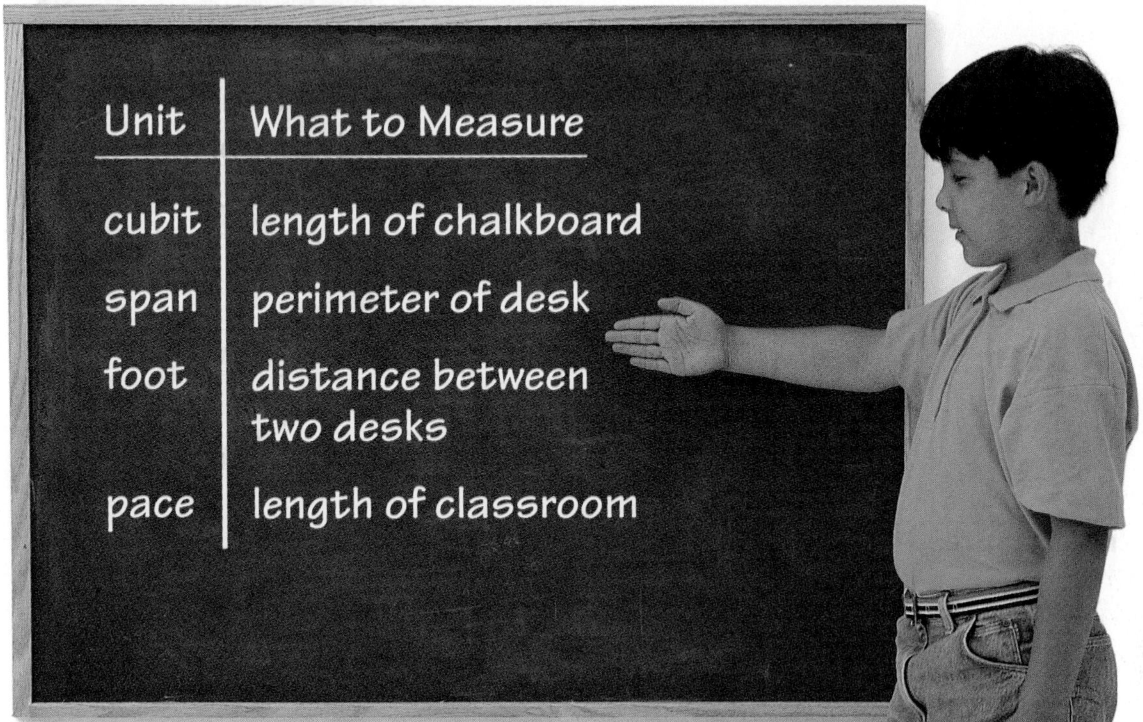

| Unit | What to Measure |
|---|---|
| cubit | length of chalkboard |
| span | perimeter of desk |
| foot | distance between two desks |
| pace | length of classroom |

## ACTIVITY 3 Use What You Know

**With Your Group** Now find the measurement of each object in inches.

1. How can you use the data in Activity 1 and Activity 2 to calculate the total inches? What method would you use to find your totals?

2. Compare your estimates with your results. How did knowing your personal measures help you make estimates?

## ACTIVITY 4 Find the Length

**With Your Class** Suppose your step measures 21 in. How can multiplication help you find the length of 4 steps?

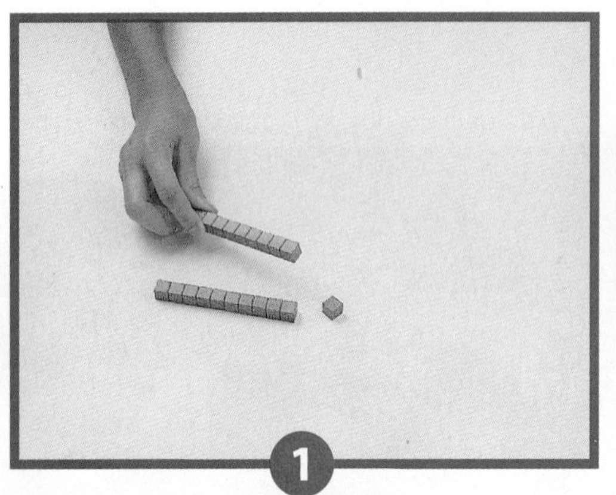

**1** **First find 1 group of 21.**

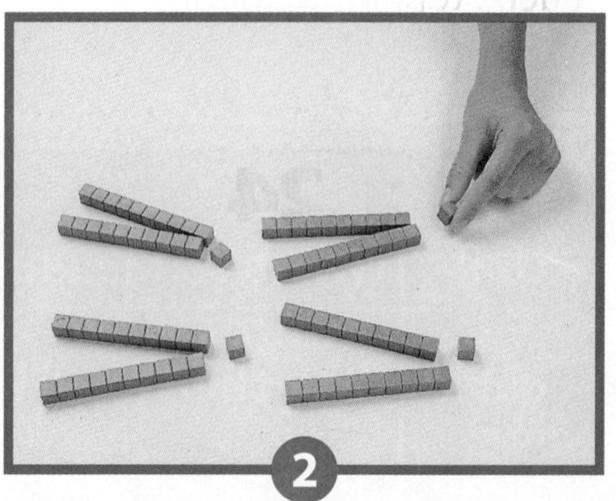

**2** **Then find 4 groups of 21. How many tens are in each group? How many ones?**

**You might think about the groupings this way:**

$$\begin{array}{r} 2 \text{ (tens)} \\ \times 4 \\ \hline 8 \text{ (tens)} \end{array} \qquad \begin{array}{r} 1 \text{ (ones)} \\ \times 4 \\ \hline 4 \text{ (ones)} \end{array}$$

**3** **How many inches are there altogether?**

$$80 + 4 = ?$$

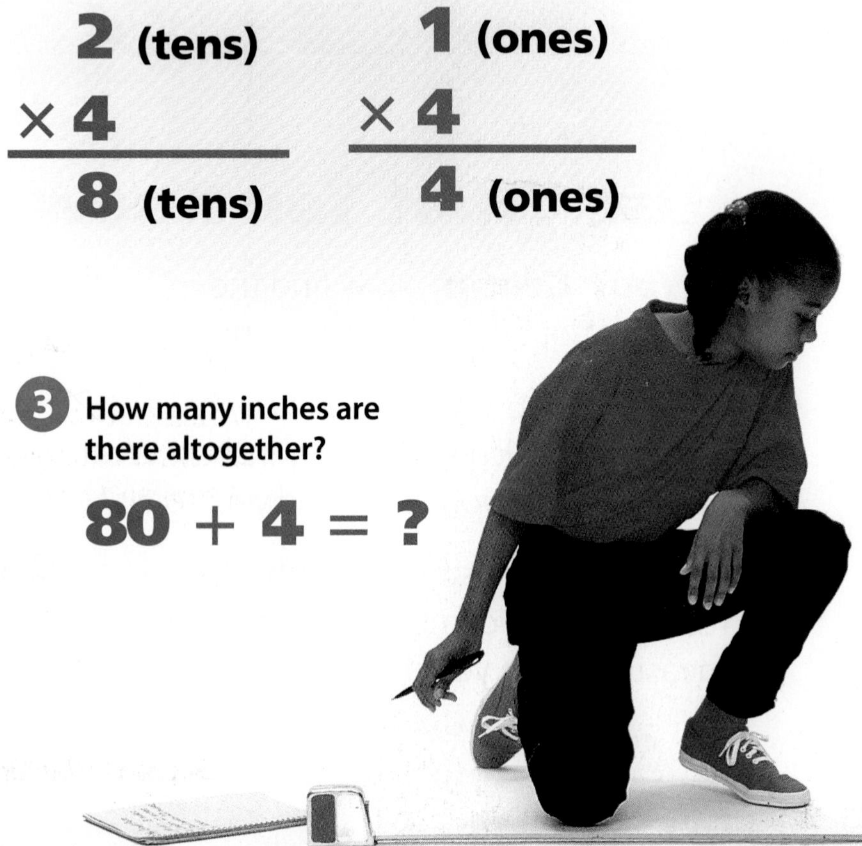

✔ **Self-Check** *When you worked through the multiplication, did you get the same answer as your classmates or a different one? Explain how you found the product.*

## ACTIVITY 5 Tricks of a Trade

**With Your Class** Suppose your pace measures 24 in. How can multiplication help you find the length of 3 paces? Record your work after each step.

$$3 \times 24 = ?$$

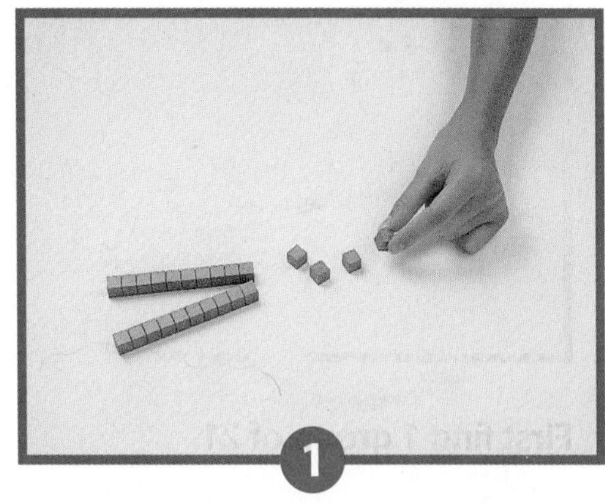

1

**How many tens and ones are there in 1 group of 24? How many are there in 3 groups of 24?**

2

**Where can you make a trade? How does this change the total number of tens and ones?**

![CONNECT AND COMMUNICATE]

*In Your Journal* *If you use mental math, how does your method compare with what's on these notebooks?*

**3** **These notebooks show different ways to find the answer. How do these compare with your method of recording multiplication?**

**On Your Own** Suppose your span measures 6 in. The length of a table is 12 spans, and the width is 5 spans. What is the perimeter of the table in inches? Record your work and compare your method of finding the answer with the method used by your classmates.

*Explain your strategy for finding the answer.*

## Try It!

Use a pencil and paper, mental math, or a calculator. Give the reason for your choice.

**1.** $3 \times 26 = \blacksquare$ **2.** $4 \times 15 = \blacksquare$ **3.** $5 \times 23 = \blacksquare$

**4.** $\begin{array}{r} 37 \\ \times\ 5 \\ \hline \end{array}$ **5.** $\begin{array}{r} 40 \\ \times\ 8 \\ \hline \end{array}$ **6.** $\begin{array}{r} 24 \\ \times\ 6 \\ \hline \end{array}$ **7.** $\begin{array}{r} 50 \\ \times\ 4 \\ \hline \end{array}$

Estimate your answer. Then find the product.

**8.** $7 \times 19 = \blacksquare$ **9.** $6 \times 29 = \blacksquare$ **10.** $4 \times 28 = \blacksquare$

Find two other factors that give the same product.

**11.** $8 \times 3 = \blacksquare \times \blacktriangle$ **12.** $9 \times 2 = \blacksquare \times \blacktriangle$ **13.** $10 \times 4 = \blacksquare \times \blacktriangle$

### Think About It

**14.** Why is one method better for finding some answers?

# LESSON 6 The Next Step

*These children participated in the March of Dimes Walk America walkathon.*

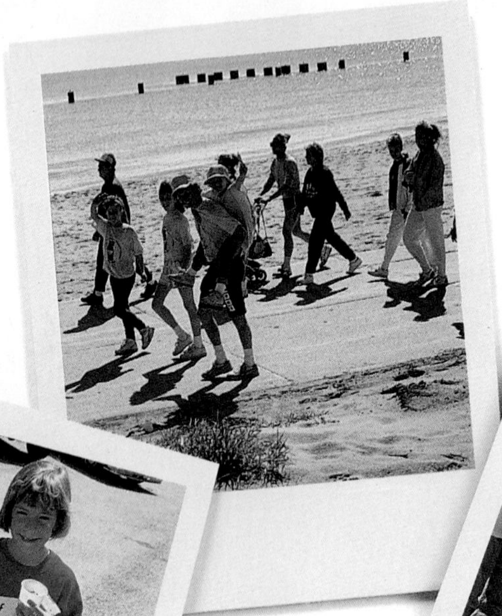

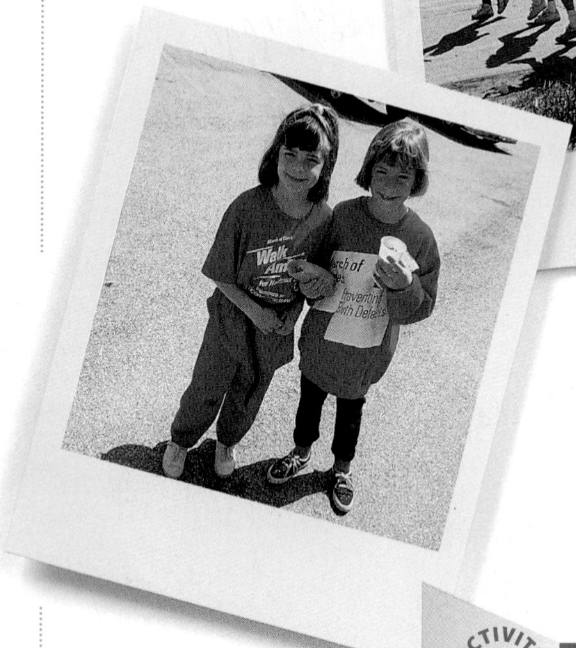

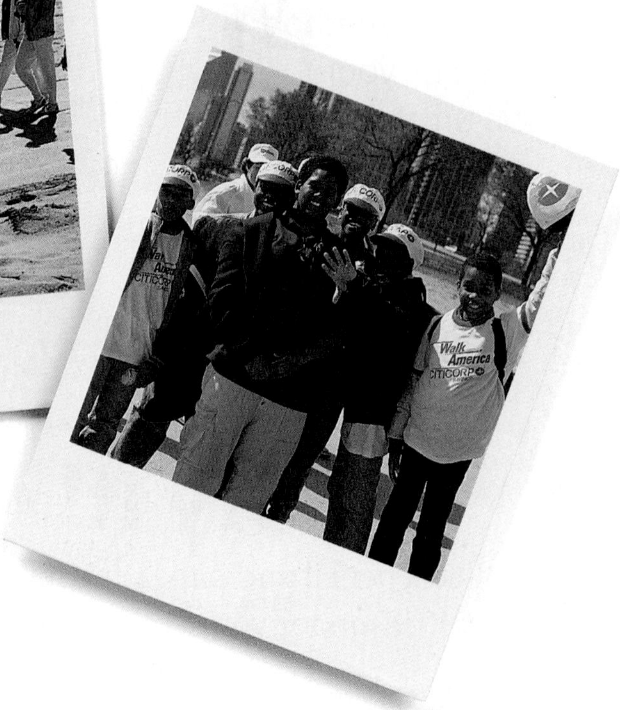

## ACTIVITY 1 Miles to Multiply

**With Your Partner** Many children go on walkathons to raise money for charity. The more miles walked the more money raised. Suppose 126 children each walked 4 mi. What is the total number of miles walked? How would you multiply with a large number like 126?

*The Commutative Property allows you to multiply in more than one way.*

1. Think about how you'll set up the multiplication. Is it easier to work with 4 groups of 126 or 126 groups of 4?

2. In what order will you record your work? Will you need to make a trade?

3. There is more than one way to find the answer. Which is most like your own?

*Use mental math to figure out 4 3 120. Then work through the problem on paper to check your answer.*

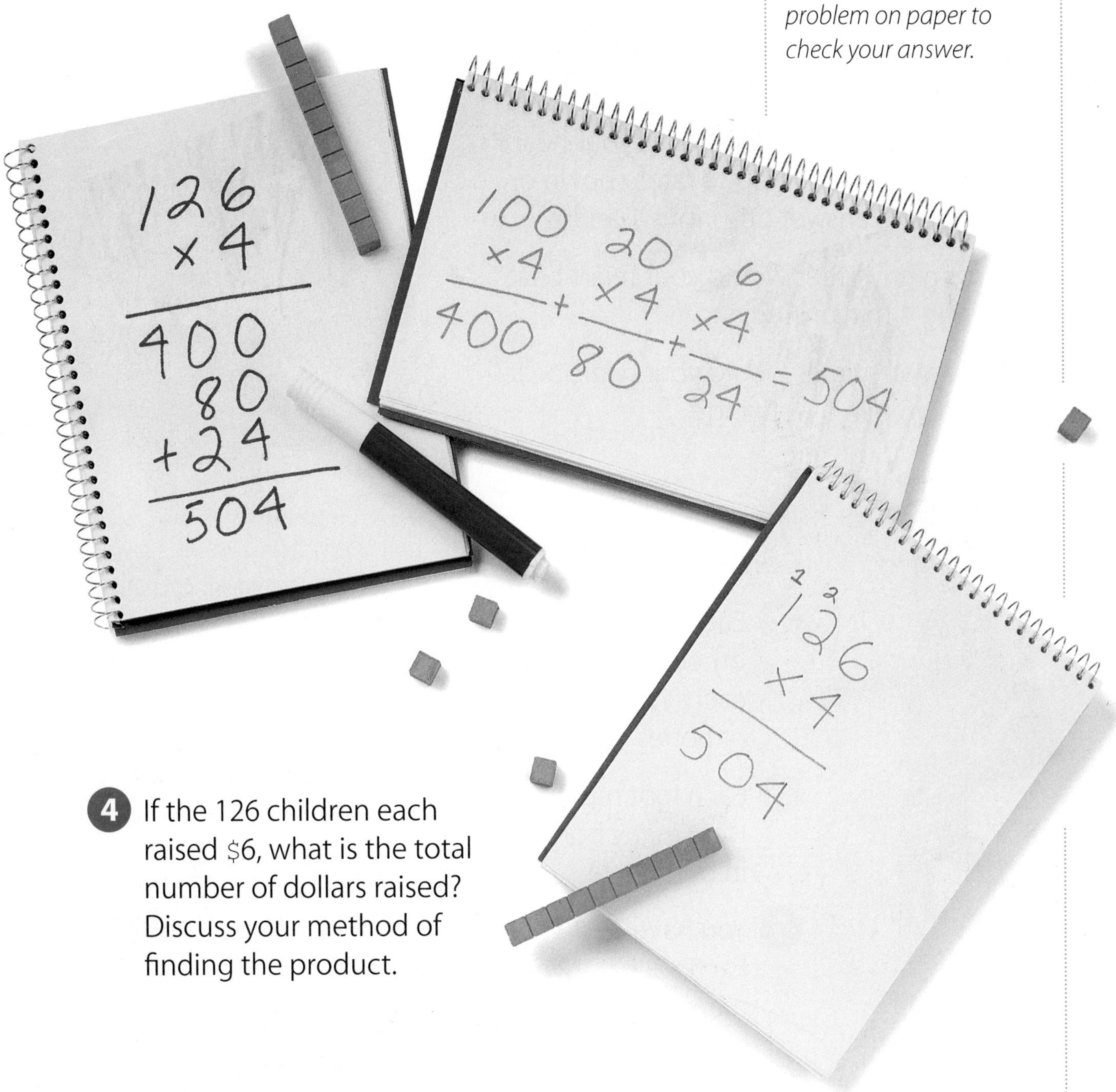

4. If the 126 children each raised $6, what is the total number of dollars raised? Discuss your method of finding the product.

**Exercises and Problems**

# Facts About You

Your body is an amazing machine. How much do you know about it? Use multiplication to discover facts about your body.

## Heart Beats

Your pulse is the number of times your heart beats in 1 min. Use the pulse rates shown on these pages to answer questions 1 and 2.

1. How many times would your heart beat during 4 min of studying?
2. How many times would your heart beat during 8 min of walking?

## Bones

3. Each thumb has 2 bones. All other fingers have 3 bones each. What is the total number of bones in 10 fingers?
4. Each foot has 26 bones. How many bones are there in both feet?
5. You have 2 sets of ribs. Each set has 12 ribs. How many ribs do you have altogether?

**calories burned: 2 per minute**
**pulse rate: 70 per minute**

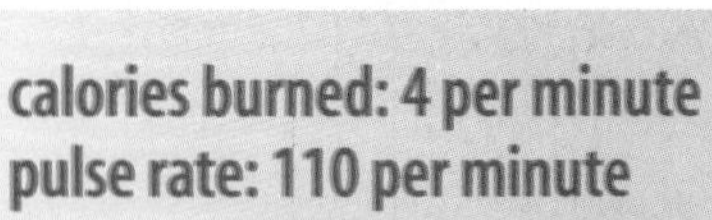

**calories burned: 4 per minute**
**pulse rate: 110 per minute**

## Calorie Count

The amount of energy in food is measured in calories. Use the calories shown for the activities on these pages to answer questions 6–10.

6 If you studied for 15 min, how many calories would you burn?

7 If you walked for 60 min, how many calories would you burn?

**calories burned: 9 per minute**
**pulse rate: 140 per minute**

8 How many calories are burned during 18 min of skating?

9 If you ran for 14 min, how many calories would you burn?

10 How many calories would you burn during 12 min of walking?

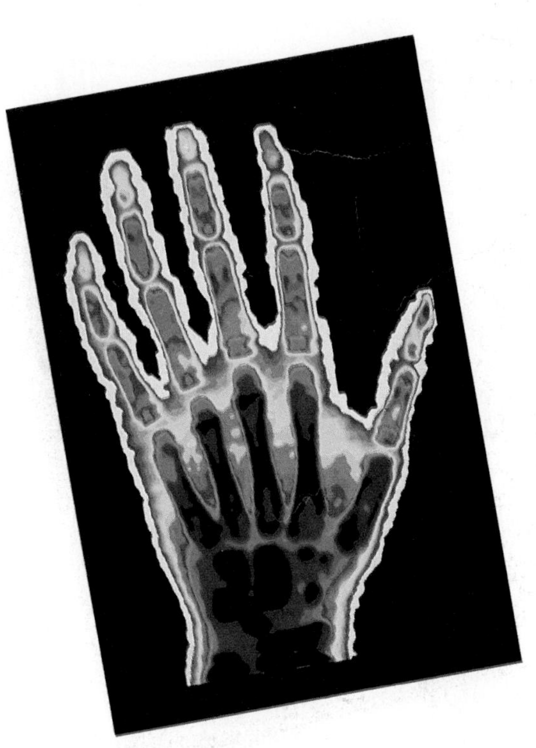

**calories burned: 8 per minute**
**pulse rate: 120 per minute**

11 How can you use multiplication to find out how many days old you will be on your next birthday?

# Birthday Mystery

## ACTIVITY 1 Gather the Data

**With Your Class** Do you share the same birthday with another classmate? Try plotting class birthdays.

1. Write your birthday on a piece of paper. Use numbers to represent the month and day.
2. Collect the papers. Organize the months and days by making a **stem-and-leaf plot.** The stem-and-leaf plot below shows two sets of data—the months of the year and the days of the month.

**Make the stem. The numbers for the months form the stem.**

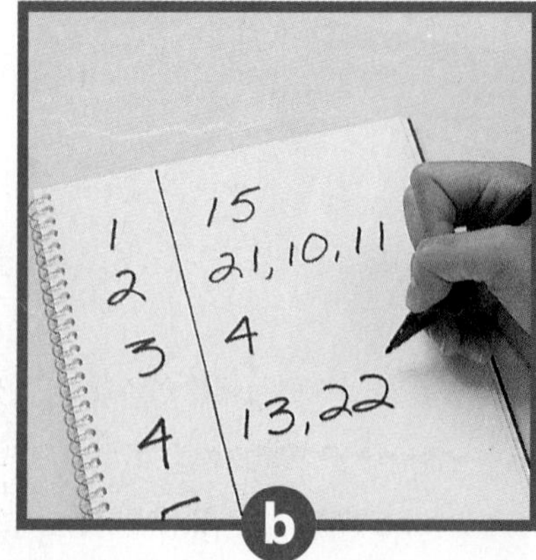


**Add the leaves. The numbers for the days are the leaves.**

**3** This stem-and-leaf plot shows the birthday data for one class. Discuss the questions with your class.

*The stem-and-leaf plot is a special way to plot data. What other ways do you know?*

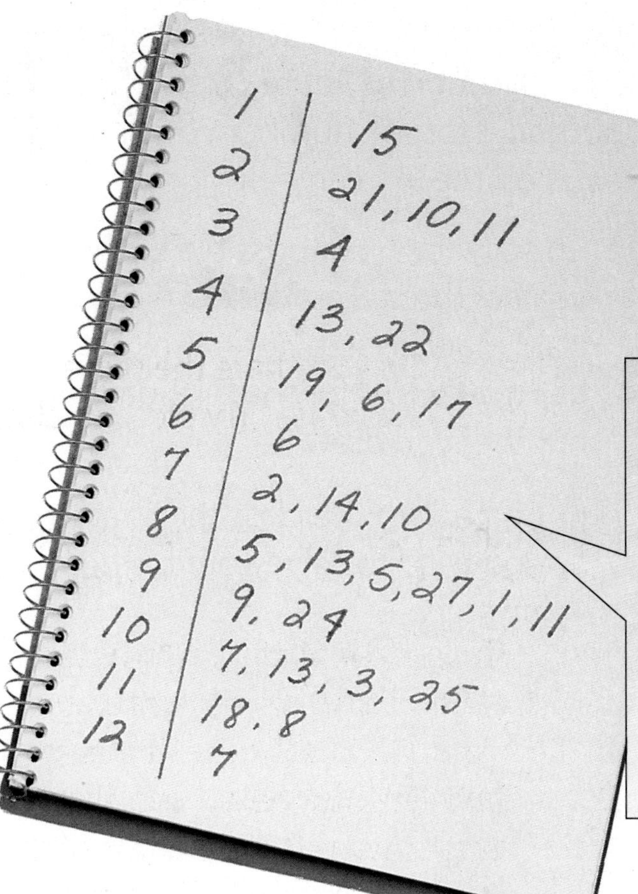


- **Are there birthdays in every month?**
- **Which months have the most birthdays?**
- **Which months have the fewest birthdays?**
- **How many birthdays are in summer? in winter?**
- **Do any students have the same birthday?**

## ACTIVITY 2 Solve the Mystery

**With Your Class** Find out how you can use multiplication to figure out the birthday mystery!

**1** Multiply the month (*m*) of your birthday by the day (*d*) to find your birthday number. Use a calculator if you need to. Write your number on a piece of paper.

$m \times d =$ **Birthday number**

2. Collect the papers for the whole class. Then have each person draw a birthday number from the pile.

3. Now use what you have learned about multiplication to figure out the possible birthdays for the number you drew. The clues on the left can help you.

4. Check your list of possible birthdays against the stem-and-leaf plot your class made in Activity 1. Which date has the factors for the birthday number you drew?

5. Share with the class the strategy you used to solve your birthday mystery.

## Clues

- One factor is always the month number. For example, 5 is a factor of all the birthday numbers for May. That means that all May birthday numbers have 5 as a common factor.
- You can also say that all the May birthday numbers are multiples of 5 (such as 5, 10, 15, and so on). Do you recognize your birthday number as a multiple of some number between 1 and 12?
- If your number is odd, you can eliminate half the months. Which months are those? Why?

**With Your Group** Choose one of these questions to investigate. Be prepared to share what your group discovers.

**6** Six different days of the year have the birthday number 36. What are they? Can you find a birthday number that works with more than six dates?

**7** June has many birthday numbers in common with other months. Which month has the most birthday numbers in common with June?

**8** How many different birthday numbers are there altogether?

✔ **Self-Check** *Why is the stem-and-leaf plot helpful for figuring out the birthday numbers?*

## Try It!

Find each missing day for birthday number 24.

1. June ■
2. December ■
3. August ■
4. March ■
5. April ■
6. February ■

Rewrite each multiplication as a division statement.

7. $8 \times 7 = 56$
8. $9 \times 4 = 36$
9. $9 \times 7 = 63$
10. $5 \times 7 = 35$
11. $5 \times 9 = 45$
12. ▲ × ■ = ●

**Think About It**

13. If you know a birthday number and day, how could you find the month?

# Area for Kids

Your class wants to show that kid power can help make the world a better place. The class will create a kid power mural made up of 12 panels, or parts. The mural will be displayed in a hallway.

## Activity 1 How Much Space?

**What You'll Need**

- *grid paper*
- *ruler*

**With Your Partner** How much wall space, or area, do you need for the mural?

1. **Each panel measures 2 ft long and 2 ft wide. Let each square on your grid paper stand for 1 square foot. Draw a shape on your paper to stand for 1 panel. What is the area of 1 panel? How did you find it?**

2. **Draw a rectangle that's made up of the 12 panels connected together. What is the area of the whole mural? How does your rectangle compare with your classmates' panels?**

*Explain how using an array is like finding the area of a rectangle.*

*Could you display your mural on a wall 3 ft wide and 16 ft long? Explain.*

**3** **How many feet long does your wall space have to be? How many feet wide? What is the area of the needed wall space?**

**4** **Describe what area is and how you find it.**

## ACTIVITY 2 Different Shapes

**With Your Partner** What if the wall space for the mural isn't shaped like a rectangle? How can you find out if your mural will fit? Will exploring the area of shapes other than rectangles and squares help?

**What You'll Need**
- *grid paper*
- *scissors*

**1** Draw a square 4 units long and 4 units wide. Draw a separate rectangle 8 units long and 4 units wide. What is the area of each shape?

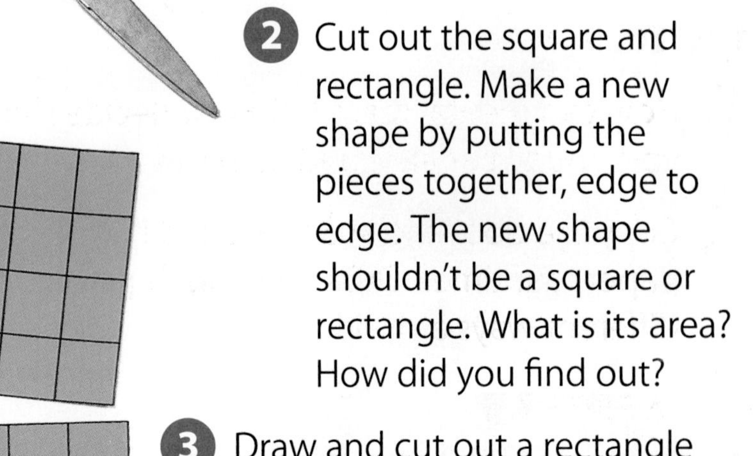

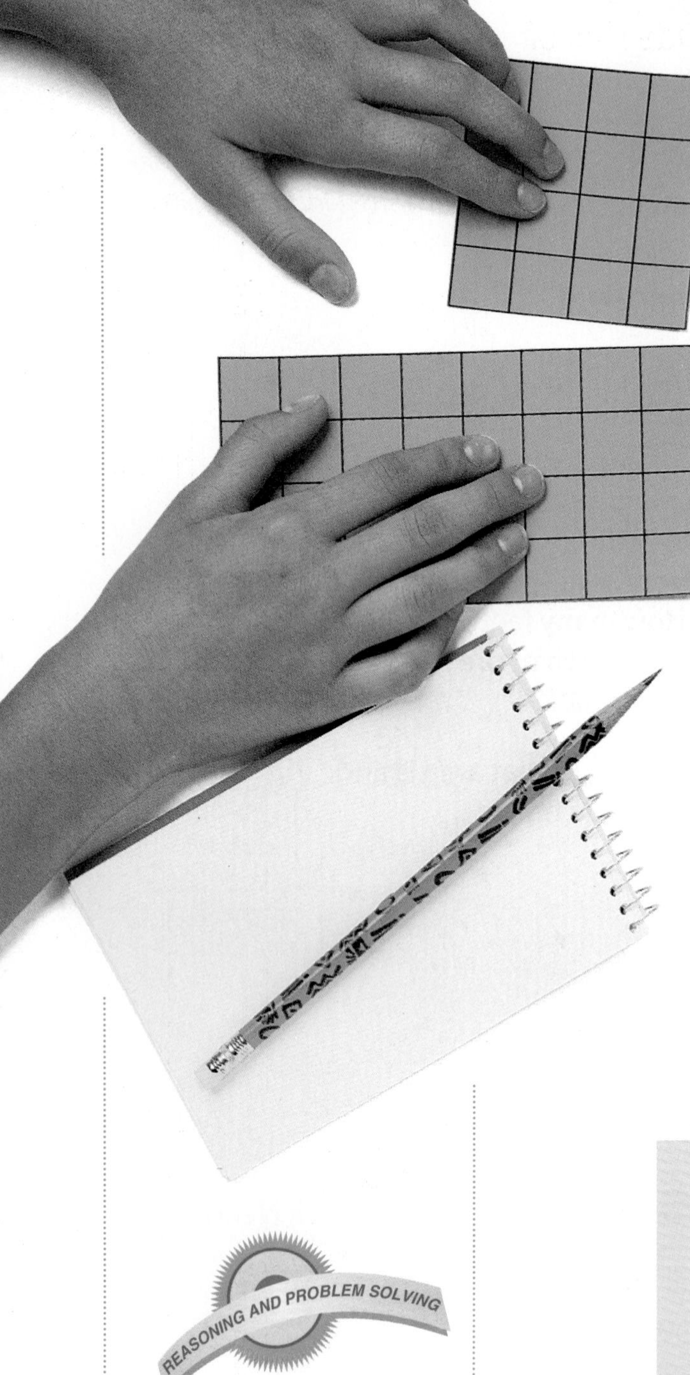

2 Cut out the square and rectangle. Make a new shape by putting the pieces together, edge to edge. The new shape shouldn't be a square or rectangle. What is its area? How did you find out?

3 Draw and cut out a rectangle 10 units long and 6 units wide. What is its area? Cut and throw out four connected squares from one corner. How is the new shape different from the rectangle you started with? Find the area of the new shape. How did you find out?

4 Suppose the wall space for the kid power mural is around a doorway. The measurements for the space are shown below. What is the area of this wall space? How did you find out?

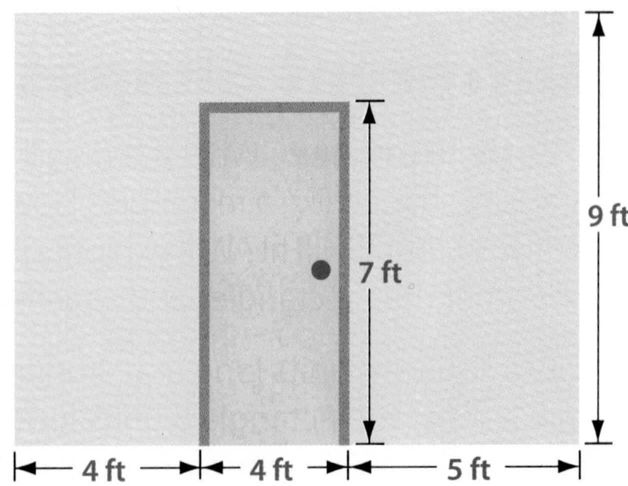


REASONING AND PROBLEM SOLVING

*In Step 2, what would happen to the area if you put the square and rectangle together in another shape?*

## On Your Own

5 How can mental math help you decide if all of your mural panels could fit in this space?

6 Copy the door and space around it on grid paper four times. Draw the panels placed four different ways around the door.

*Could there be more than four ways to place the panels? Draw to find out.*

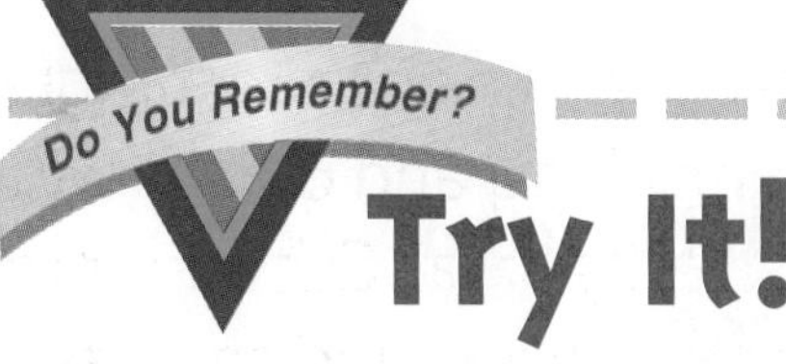


## Try It!

Find the areas of the shapes. The numbers around the shapes stand for units.

1. 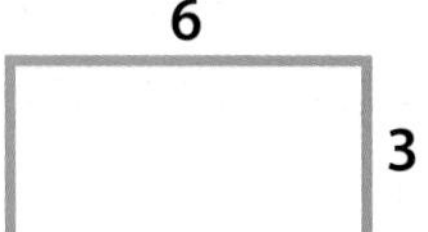


2. 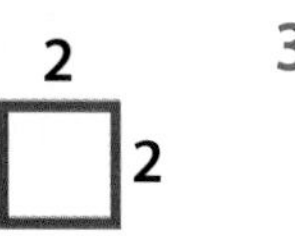


3. 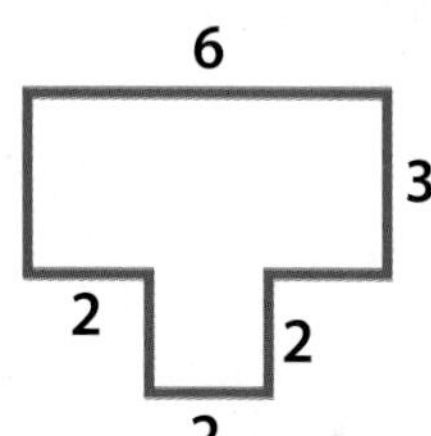


4. 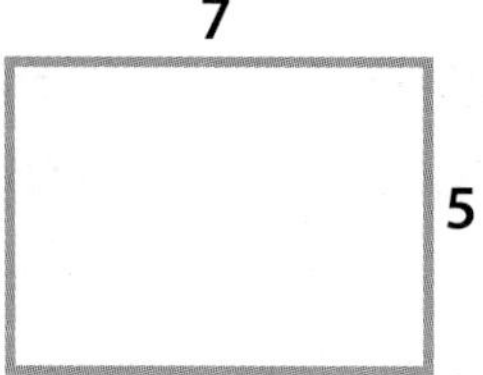


5. 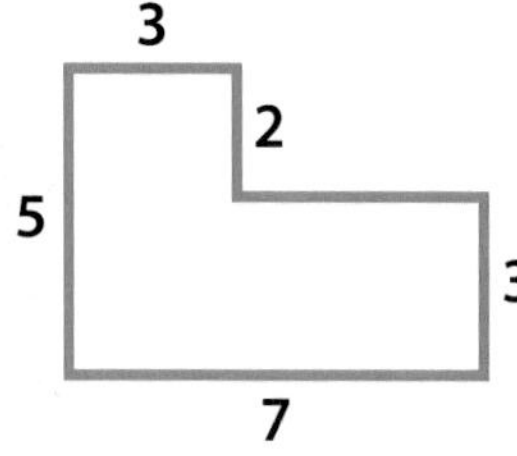


Write the rule to find ■.

6. 4, 12, 20, ■
7. 10, 19, 28, ■
8. 30, 20, 10, ■
9. 0, 1, 2, 3, ■
10. 1; 100; 10,000; ■

### Think About It

11. How does rearranging the shape of a rectangle affect its area? Explain.

Do You Remember?

## Cumulative Review

# Looking Back

**Choose the best answer. Write *a, b, c,* or *d* for each question.**

1. Which is the product of $8 \times 9$?

   a. $50 + 14$  b. $81 - 0$
   c. $50 + 22$  d. $50 + 6$

2. Which is the product of $6 \times 7$?

   a. $21 + 21$  b. $20 + 23$
   c. $55 - 20$  d. $50 - 1$

3. Which is the product of $62 \times 7$?

   a. $21 \times 21$  b. $89 \times 6$
   c. $81 \times 5$  d. $217 \times 2$

4. Which group is made up of nothing but factors of 150?

   a. 3, 50, 10, 30, 8, 75, 2, 1
   b. 150, 5, 3, 50, 30, 10, 75, 2
   c. 150, 3, 50, 30, 75, 5, 80
   d. 10, 30, 50, 75, 2, 3, 25, 42

5. $24 \times \blacksquare = 16 \times 6$

   a. 8  b. 24
   c. 4  d. 3

**Use this table to answer questions 6–8.**

| Input | 2 | | 10 | 24 | | 5 |
|---|---|---|---|---|---|---|
| Output | 18 | 54 | | | 180 | 45 |

6. What's the rule for the table?

   a. $n + 12$  b. $n \times 9$
   c. $n \times 6$  d. $n \div 9$

7. If the output is 180, the input is

   a. $90 - 80$  b. $18 + 2$
   c. $45 - 20$  d. $11 + 11$

8. If the input is 10, the output is

   a. 70  b. 80
   c. 90  d. 100

9. What is the area of this banner?

   a. $3 \times 8$  b. $8 - 3$
   c. $3 + 3 + 8 + 8$  d. $8 \div 3$

8 units

3 units

10. What is the area of this bulletin board?

a. $6 \times 4$ b. $6 + 4$
c. $4 \div 6$ d. $10 + 10$

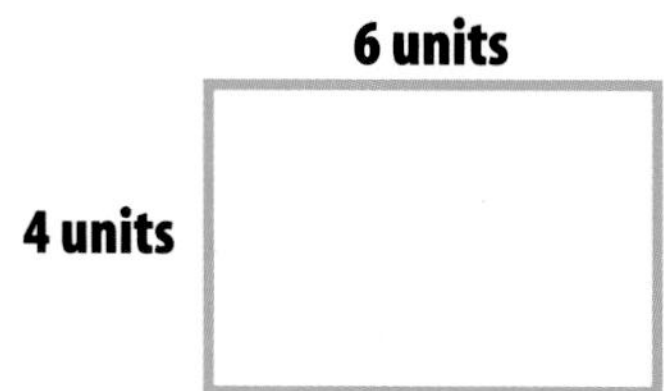


11. Will the banner fit on the bulletin board? Why or why not?

Fifty students went on a walkathon. Some walked the entire 13 mi. Others walked fewer miles. Use the bar graph to answer Exercises 12–17.

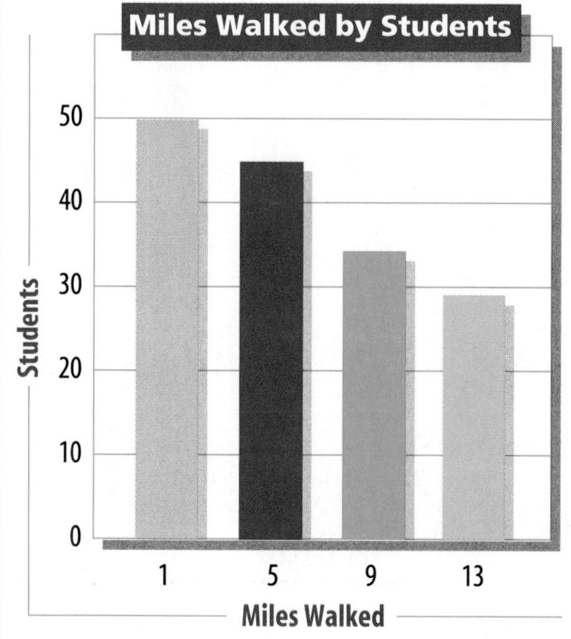


12. About how many students walked the first mile?

a. 42 b. 50
c. 46 d. 35

13. About how many students were still walking through the ninth mile?

a. 45 b. 40
c. 34 d. 30

14. About how many students finished every mile of the walkathon?

a. 29 b. 35
c. 45 d. 50

## Check Your Math Power

15. Write a few sentences that describe how well this group of students did on the walkathon.

16. Suppose riding each mile of a 15 mi bike ride earns $2 for a charity. How can 4 friends together earn $100 for the charity? Explain two ways.

MODULE 3 Investigations

# Kid Power Across the Country

You have already discovered ways that you can use your kid power. Now imagine the kid power of 3,670,000 students. That's about the number of fourth graders in the United States. Suppose all these fourth graders joined together in one place. How much space would they take up?

## Investigation A Kid Space

1. **Use** what you know about multiplication and area to gather data and find the area.

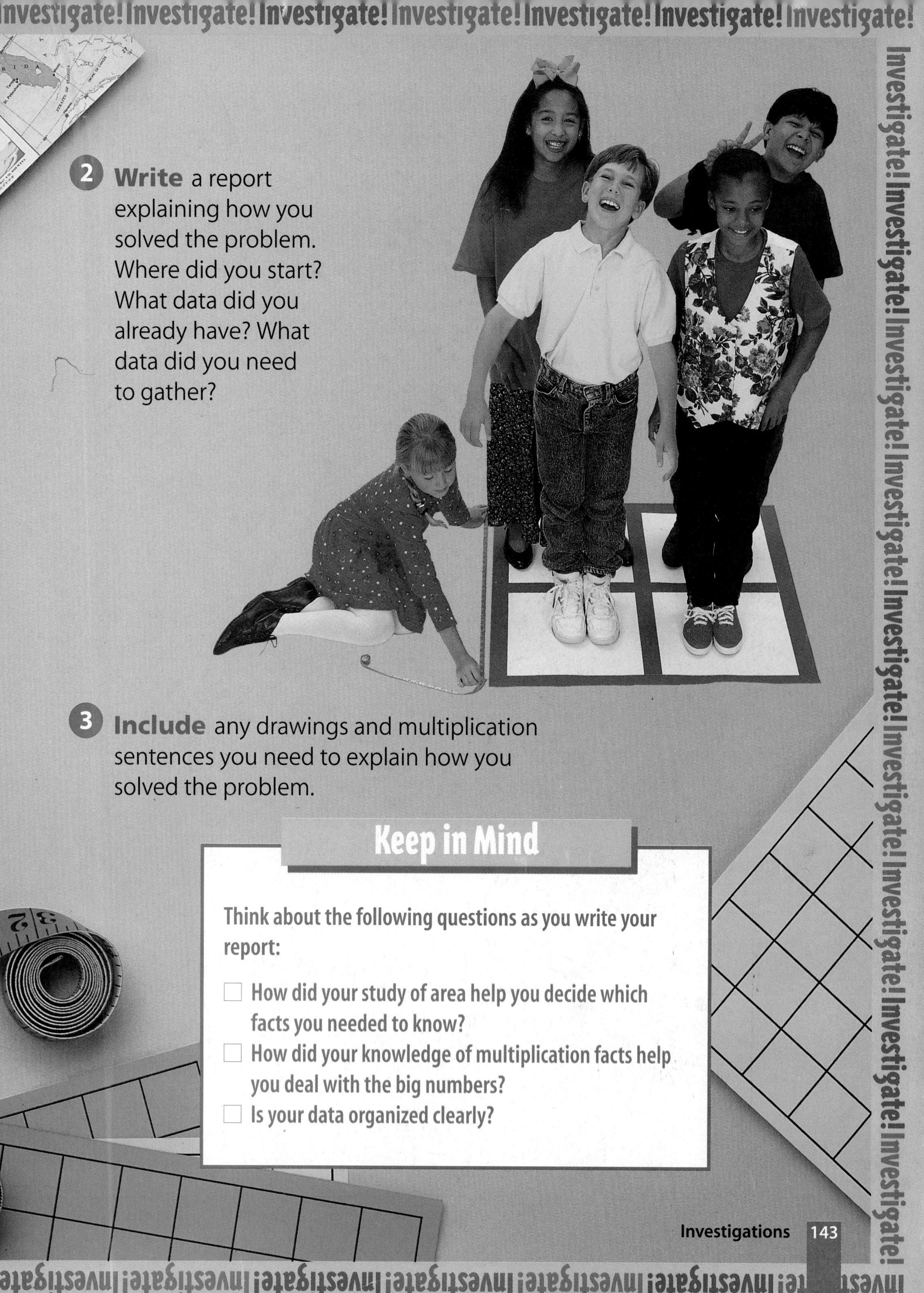

2 **Write** a report explaining how you solved the problem. Where did you start? What data did you already have? What data did you need to gather?

3 **Include** any drawings and multiplication sentences you need to explain how you solved the problem.

## Keep in Mind

Think about the following questions as you write your report:

- ☐ How did your study of area help you decide which facts you needed to know?
- ☐ How did your knowledge of multiplication facts help you deal with the big numbers?
- ☐ Is your data organized clearly?

Investigate! Investigate! Investigate! Investigate! Investigate! Investigate! Investigate!

Investigation B

## A Wave of Kids

You might have seen "the wave" at a sporting event. How much time would it take all the fourth graders in the United States to complete one wave? Suppose they are sitting on stadium seats that are 100 yd deep. Would you time the wave using minutes, hours, days, or something longer? Your report should include these:

- A reason for timing the wave the way you did;
- An explanation of how you solved the problem and what data you used.

Investigation C

## A Kid Mural

What if you create and place a 12-paneled mural on one of your classroom walls? All of the panels will have the same area. They'll be as large as possible but also fit the space.

- Choose a large space and find its area.
- Decide how large the mural panels can be. Explain how you did it.
- Draw three ways to arrange the panels.

**Computer Option** If you have a computer, you can use a drawing program to explore different ways to arrange your mural.

# Fraction Action

You don't have to look far to find **fractions.** A fraction is a number that shows part of a whole. You use fractions when you share something equally with a friend. How else do you use fractions?

**Exploring Fractions of a Whole**

**Measuring with Fractions**

**Fractions and Data**

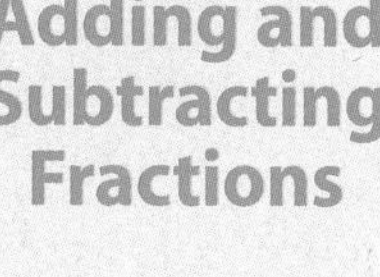

**Adding and Subtracting Fractions**

# Fractions Everywhere!

**Y**ou can find fractions anywhere you see equal parts. For example, you might use fractions to measure cooking ingredients. What other uses of fractions do you know about?

## 1 Looking for Equal Parts

Use the pictures on these pages to help you think of other examples of fractions. Look in places like a craft kit, a cookbook, a grocery store, or a gymnasium. Use your imagination!

Play dough:
2 cups flour
$1\frac{1}{2}$ cups water
$\frac{1}{4}$ cup salt
2 tbsp oil
2 tsp cream of tartar

## 2 Collecting and Recording

Record any uses of fractions you find. Write them in your journal. Draw them. Show the whole or the group that each part came from.

## 3 Sharing

What fractions did you find? Where did you find them? What was the most interesting example you found?

### Word Bank

- denominator
- equivalent fractions
- mixed number
- numerator
- simplest form

### Investigations Preview

Fractions can help you do everything from measuring your height to organizing data.

**Invent a Fraction** (pages 160–161)

What fraction of your height is your hand length? You'll make a body fraction to find out.

**Which Do You Prefer?** (pages 190–192)

Ask your class and another group a survey question. You can use fractions to describe your results.

## Exploring Fractions of a Whole

# Lesson 1 Fractions of Time

LITERATURE

*Ramona thinks a quarter of something is always 25. Is she right? Read and find the answer for yourself.*

Ramona sat down at the kitchen table to wiggle her tooth and watch the clock. The little hand was at eight, and the big hand was at one. . . .

The big hand moved slowly to three. Ramona continued to sit on the chair wiggling her tooth and being a very good girl as she had promised. The big hand crawled along to four.. When it reached five, Ramona knew that it would be quarter after eight and time to go to school. A quarter was twenty-five cents. Therefore, a quarter past eight was twenty-five minutes after eight. She had figured the answer out all by herself.

From *Ramona the Pest*
by Beverly Cleary

# ACTIVITY 1 Dividing Up Time

## With Your Class

1. Discuss the story. Did Ramona leave at the right time? Explain.

**This clock face is divided into four equal parts. The shaded part is $\frac{1}{4}$. The numerator, or top number in the fraction, shows the number of parts shaded. The denominator, or bottom number, shows the total number of equal parts.**

2. What part of the clock face is not shaded? How would you write that as a fraction?

$$\frac{\text{shaded parts}}{\text{total parts}} \quad \frac{1}{4} \quad \frac{\text{numerator}}{\text{denominator}}$$

3. What fraction of each clock face below is shaded?

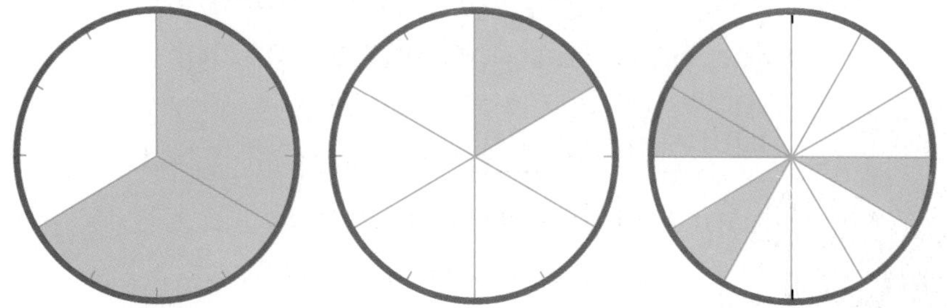

What You'll Need

- *Fraction Tool or circle shape and ruler*

# ACTIVITY 2 Circle Fractions

**With Your Partner** Now try drawing some fractions on a circle.

1. Draw a circle. Divide it into six equal parts.

✓ **Self-Check** *Does the shaded part below show $\frac{1}{3}$? Why or why not?*

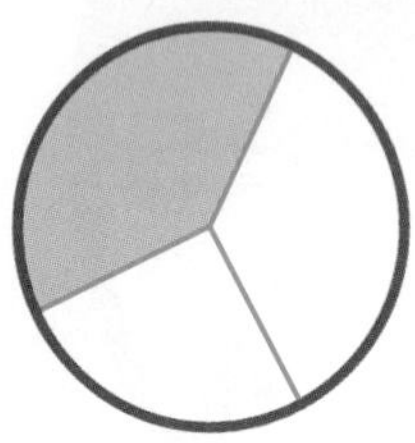

**2** Shade some of the parts. Ask your partner to name the fraction you shaded.

**3** Try the same thing for a circle with 8 equal parts. Then try 12 equal parts.

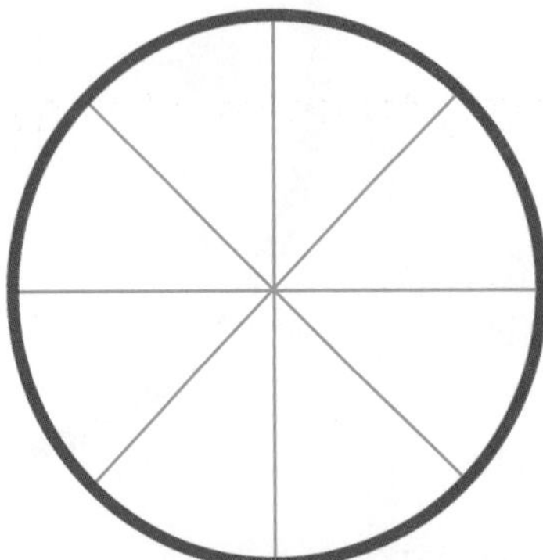

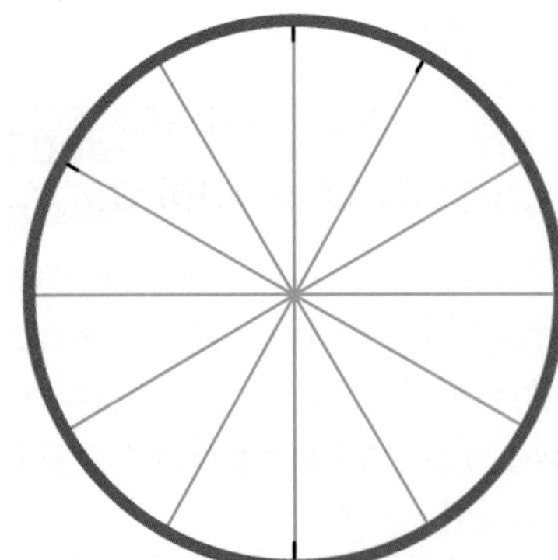

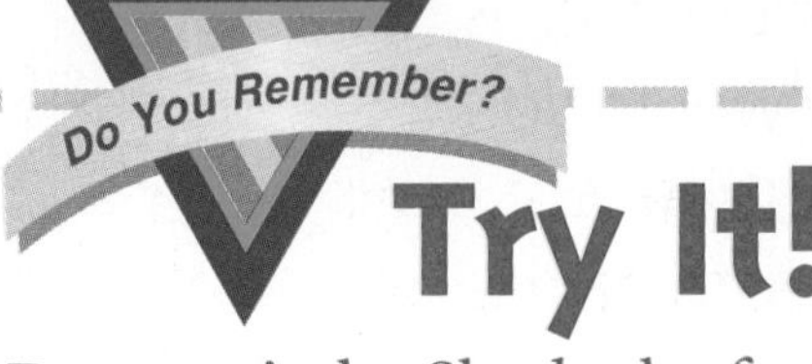


## Try It!

Draw a circle. Shade the fraction.

1. $\frac{1}{2}$
2. $\frac{3}{4}$
3. $\frac{1}{8}$
4. $\frac{1}{3}$

Complete. Some answers may be fractions.

5. 1 hour = ■ minutes
6. $\frac{1}{2}$ hour = ■ minutes
7. $\frac{1}{4}$ hour = ■ minutes
8. 60 seconds = ■ minute
9. 30 seconds = ■ minute
10. 15 seconds = ■ minute

### Think About It

11. Which circle in Exercises 1 through 4 has the greatest fraction not shaded?

# Beyond Circles

You can divide squares and rectangles into any number of equal parts.

## ACTIVITY 1 Draw It Your Way

**What You'll Need**
- *dot paper or grid paper*

### With Your Group

1. Look at the square on the right. How are the parts alike? How are they different?

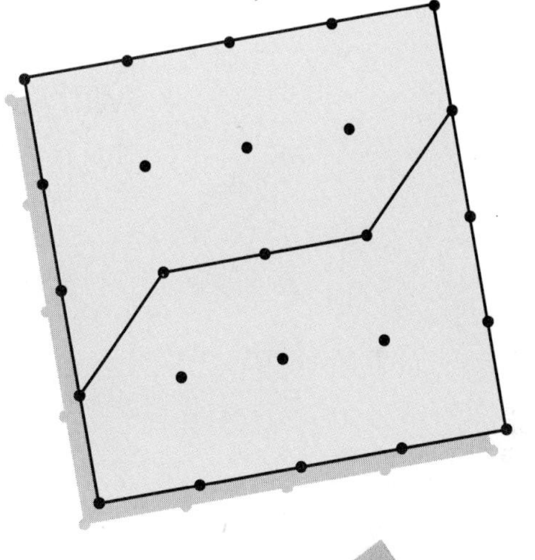

2. Draw at least three different ways to divide a square into halves on dot or grid paper.
3. Divide a square into fourths. Show at least three ways to do it. An example is below.

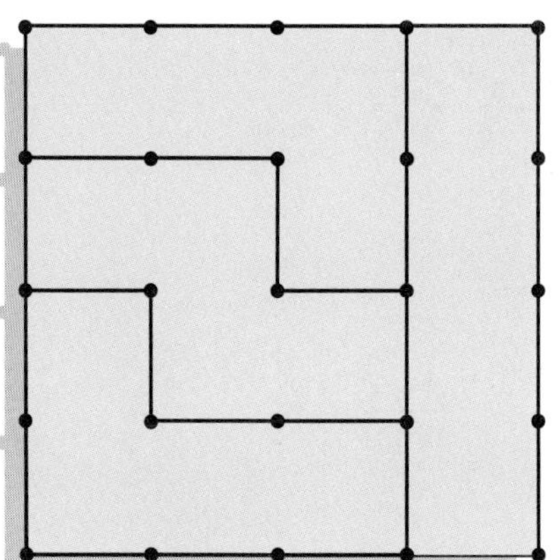

4. Discuss and compare the divided squares. How can you be sure the parts are the same size?

## What You'll Need

- *grid paper*
- *crayons*

*Draw a square with 16 equal parts. Choose four different colors, and color the parts. Describe your sketch with fractions.*

# ACTIVITY 2 Colorful Fractions

**On Your Own** Sometimes it's easier to see fractions if you color the equal parts. You will do that in this activity.

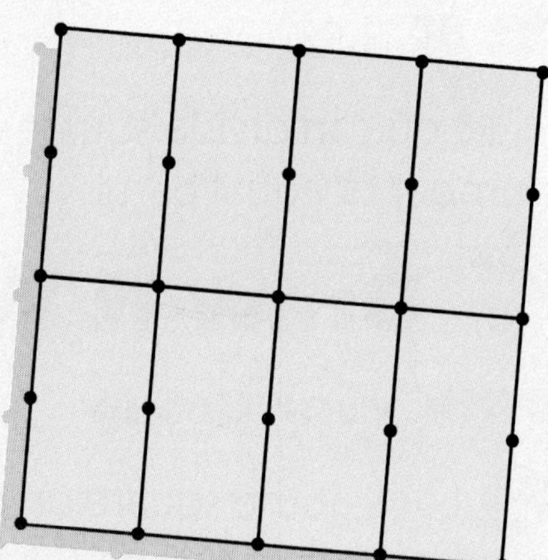

1. Draw at least three different ways of dividing a square into eight equal parts.
2. Select one of your drawings. Color the parts with three or four colors.
3. Use fractions to describe your drawing.

3/8 red

2/8 orange

3/8 purple

# Activity 3 Keep On Dividing

## With Your Group

**What You'll Need**
- *grid paper*

1. Take a look at these drawings. Now find another way to divide a rectangle into thirds, into sixths, and into twelfths.

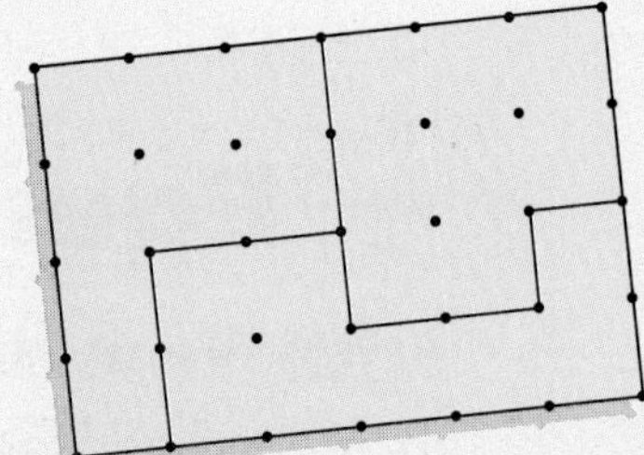

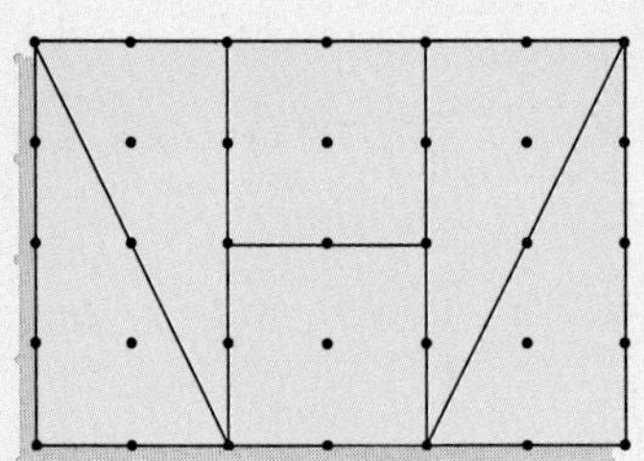

2. Share your drawings with the class. How many different ways did the class find in all?

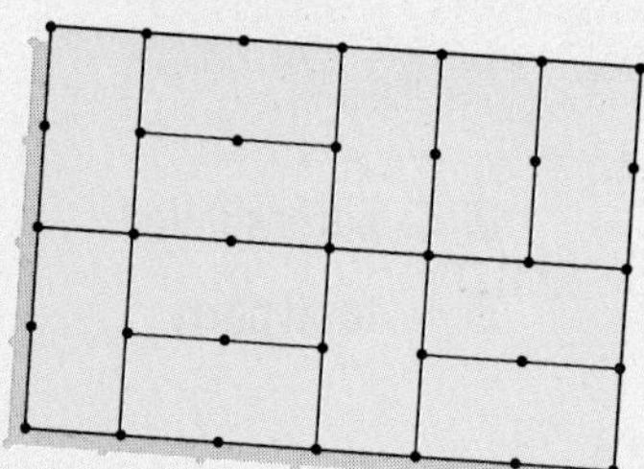

Do You Remember?

## Try It!

Draw a shape and shade the fraction.

1. $\frac{1}{3}$ 2. $\frac{1}{4}$ 3. $\frac{1}{8}$ 4. $\frac{1}{10}$ 5. $\frac{3}{4}$

6. $\frac{5}{8}$ 7. $\frac{7}{8}$ 8. $\frac{1}{16}$ 9. $\frac{7}{10}$ 10. $\frac{5}{6}$

Find each product. What pattern do you see?

11. $4 \times 3$
12. $4 \times 30$
13. $4 \times 300$
14. $4 \times 3{,}000$
15. $4 \times 30{,}000$
16. $4 \times 300{,}000$

### Think About It

17. Which fractions in Exercises 1 through 10 are greater than $\frac{1}{2}$? How do you know?

*Each of the shapes below is a fourth of something. Choose one shape and draw the whole.*

# Are They Equal?

## ACTIVITY 1 Equals by Folding

**With Your Group** Can different fractions show the same amount? This activity will help you decide.

1. **Start with a sheet of paper like the one shown here. Write a fraction for the shaded part.**

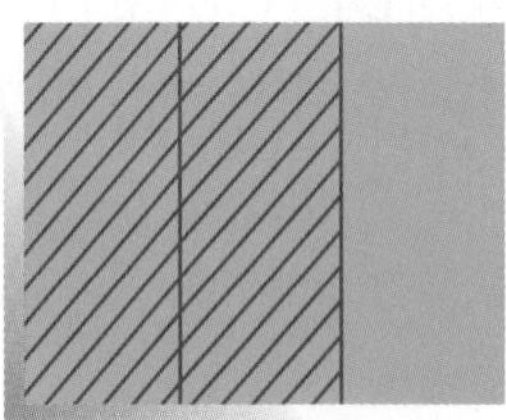

$\frac{2}{3}$ ← parts shaded / ← total parts

2. **Fold the paper in half, as shown here.**

3. **Unfold the paper. Write the fraction.**

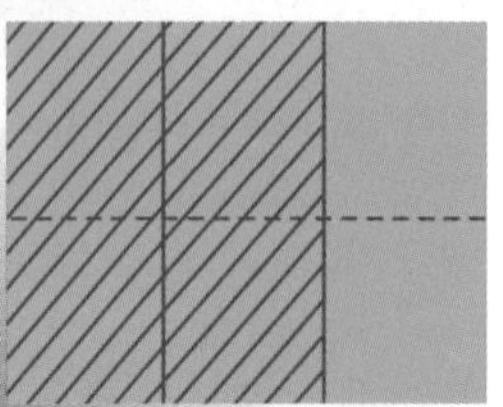

4. **Refold the paper. Then fold it in half again, as shown.**

$\frac{?}{?}$ ← parts shaded / ← total parts

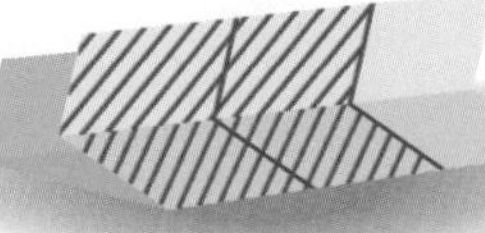

5. **Unfold the paper. Write the fraction.**

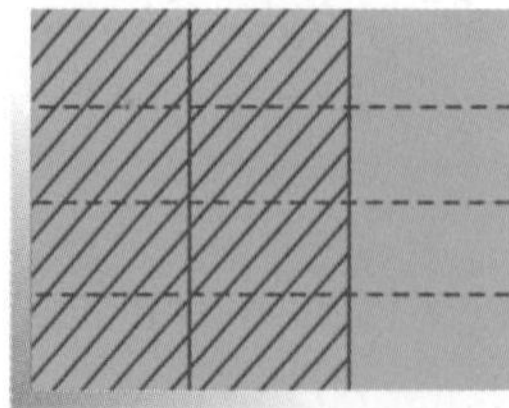

$\frac{?}{?}$ ← parts shaded / ← total parts

6 What happened to the shading when you folded the paper? Did it grow? shrink? stay the same?

7 Write number sentences to compare the fractions you wrote. Use <, >, or =. Fractions that name the same amount are called **equivalent fractions.**

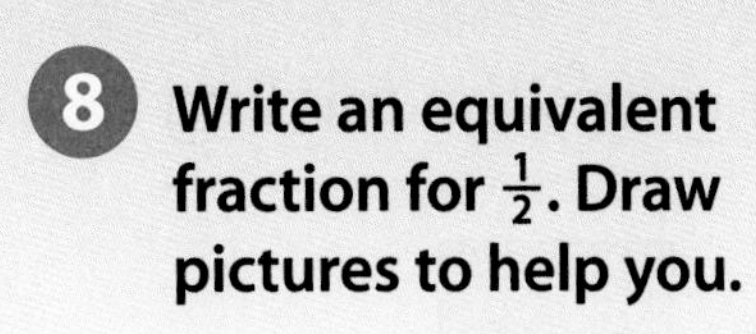

8 **Write an equivalent fraction for $\frac{1}{2}$. Draw pictures to help you.**

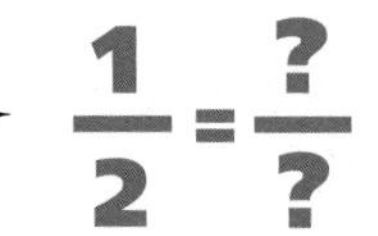

$\frac{1}{2} = \frac{?}{?}$

*Repeat the paper-folding activity, using a sheet of paper that is divided and shaded as shown below.*

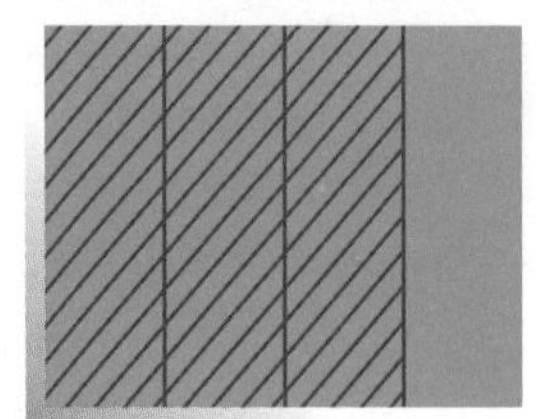

## ACTIVITY 2 Simplifying Things

**With Your Group** Sometimes it makes sense to use one equivalent fraction instead of another. In real life we often use the equivalent fraction that is in **simplest form.** A fraction is in simplest form if its numerator and denominator have no common factors other than 1.

1 Suppose you are told to go to the store and buy $\frac{2}{4}$ gallon of milk. How would you write that amount in simplest form?

2 Suppose a recipe calls for $\frac{4}{6}$ cup of flour. How would you write that amount in simplest form?

3 Write three number sentences using fractions not in simplest form. For example, you might write $\frac{3}{9} = \frac{?}{?}$. Exchange sentences with another group. Write their fractions in simplest form.

*In Your Journal* Write a definition of equivalent fractions in your own words. Use paper folding, multiplication, or division to describe an example.

## Activity 3 Mystery Fractions

**With Your Partner** Each partner should have at least three turns.

1. Write two fractions that name the same amount. Don't show your partner.
2. Cover up one of the numerators or denominators.
3. Have your partner guess the missing number.

$$\frac{2}{3} = \frac{\blacksquare}{12}$$

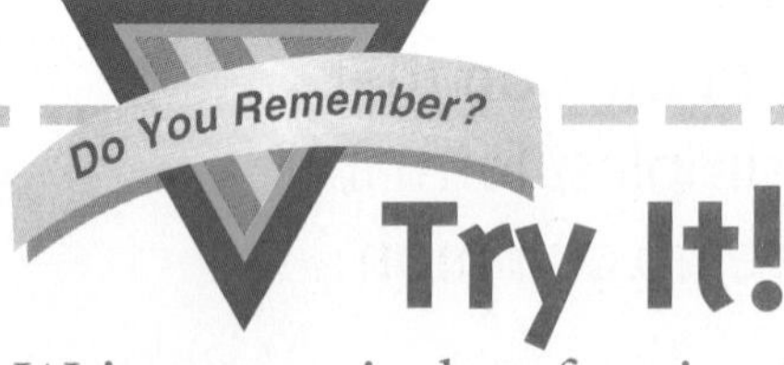


## Try It!

Write an equivalent fraction in simplest form. Use the pictures.

1. $\frac{4}{8} = \frac{1}{\blacksquare}$
2. $\frac{4}{10} = \frac{\blacksquare}{\blacksquare}$
3. $\frac{2}{6} = \frac{\blacksquare}{\blacksquare}$
4. $\frac{2}{4} = \frac{\blacksquare}{\blacksquare}$

Draw the figure and shade $\frac{1}{4}$.

5. rectangle
6. square
7. parallelogram
8. circle
9. octagon
10. hexagon

### Think About It

11. Is $\frac{1}{2}$ of every rectangle the same size? Explain in writing.

# Comparing Fractions

## ACTIVITY 1 Circle Pieces

**With Your Partner** Try cutting up some circles to compare the size of different fractions.

**What You'll Need**

- *Fraction Tool or circle shape and ruler*
- *construction paper*
- *scissors*

1. Draw five circles, each on a different color of construction paper. Use your Fraction Tool to divide each circle into equal parts. Make one circle for each of these fractions: halves, thirds, fourths, sixths, and twelfths. Cut out the fraction pieces.

2. Which fraction piece is larger, $\frac{1}{2}$ or $\frac{1}{4}$? How many fourths are equal to $\frac{1}{2}$?

3. Compare $\frac{1}{3}$ and $\frac{2}{6}$. Are they equal? What other equivalent fractions can you find?

4. Write sentences using >, <, or = to compare pairs of these fractions.

$\frac{3}{4}$ $\frac{2}{3}$ $\frac{4}{6}$ $\frac{7}{12}$

*What happens to the size of the fraction as the numerator increases? Try* $\frac{1}{4}, \frac{2}{4}, \frac{3}{4}$. *What happens as the denominator increases? Try* $\frac{1}{4}, \frac{1}{5}, \frac{1}{6}$.

### What You'll Need

- *fraction circle pieces from Activity 1*
- *Fraction Tool or circle shape and ruler*
- *construction paper*
- *scissors*

*How can you tell from looking at a fraction whether its value is greater than one?*

# Activity 2 Mixed Numbers

**With Your Group** Use your circle pieces from the last activity.

1. Take nine circle pieces for thirds. Nine thirds is a fraction greater than one. What whole number is the same as $\frac{9}{3}$?

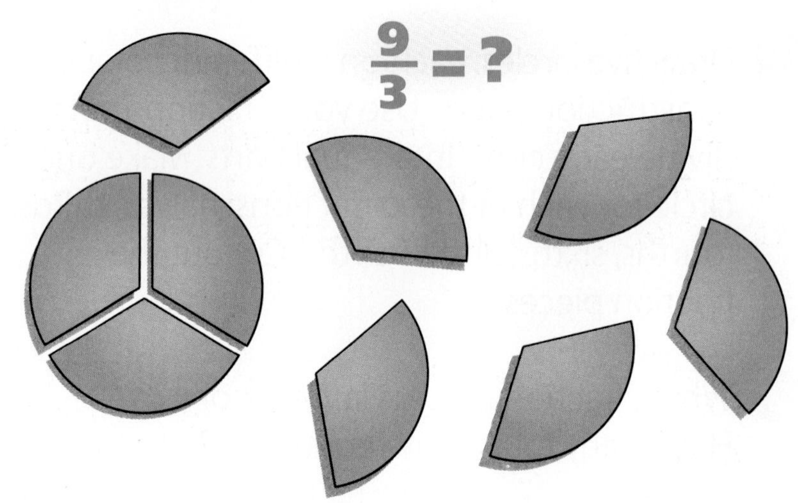


2. Take eight thirds, or $\frac{8}{3}$. How many wholes do you have? How many thirds are left? You can write $\frac{8}{3}$ as a whole number and a fraction, or **mixed number.**

$\frac{8}{3} = 2\frac{2}{3}$

3. Use your circle pieces to continue the patterns up to three.

   **a.** $\frac{1}{3}, \frac{2}{3}, 1, 1\frac{1}{3}$

   **b.** $\frac{1}{4}, \frac{2}{4}, \frac{3}{4}, 1, 1\frac{1}{4}$

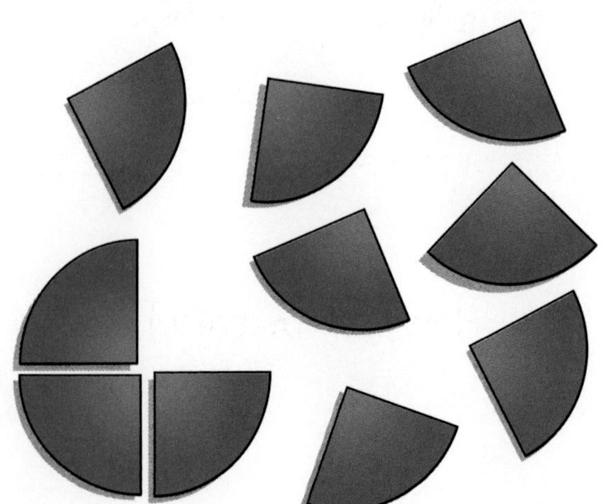

 fractions of a whole

**4** Write $1\frac{7}{8}$ as a fraction greater than one. Then do the same for two of these mixed numbers.

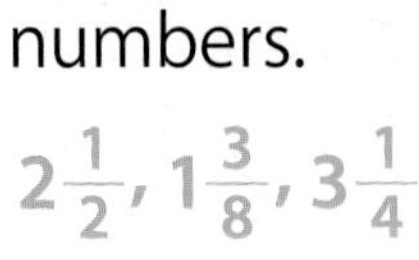

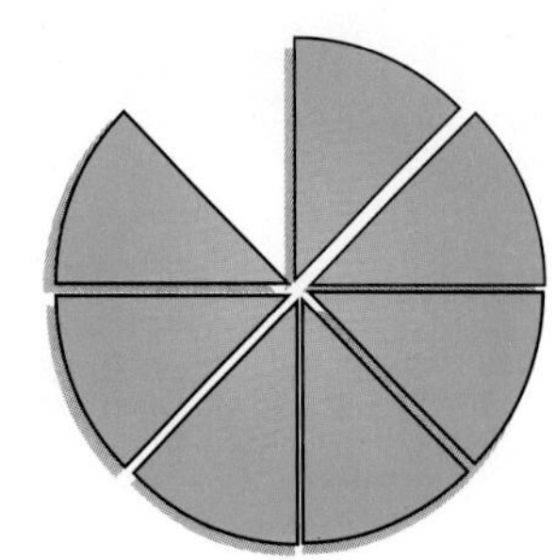

## ACTIVITY 3 Estimating Fractions

**On Your Own** Use the number line to estimate. Is each fraction in green closer to 0, $\frac{1}{2}$, 1, $1\frac{1}{2}$, or 2? Discuss your answers with the class.

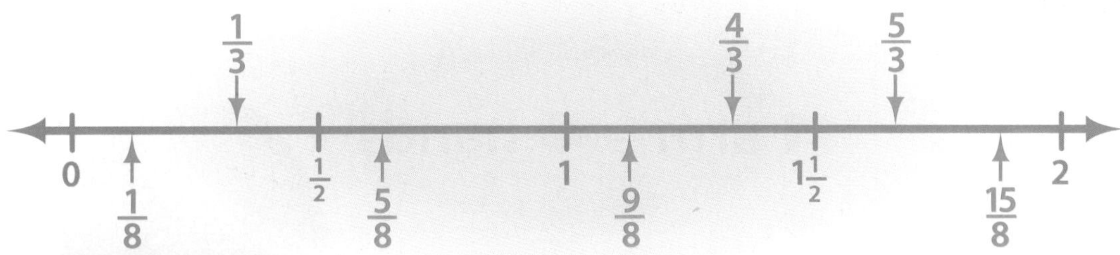


Do You Remember?

## Try It!

Compare. Write >, <, or =. Make drawings to help.

1. $\frac{2}{5}$ ● $\frac{4}{5}$
2. $\frac{4}{12}$ ● $\frac{1}{3}$
3. $\frac{1}{3}$ ● $\frac{1}{6}$
4. $\frac{3}{4}$ ● $\frac{6}{8}$
5. $\frac{7}{8}$ ● $\frac{3}{8}$
6. $\frac{9}{6}$ ● 2
7. $1\frac{2}{3}$ ● $\frac{5}{3}$
8. $\frac{8}{4}$ ● 3

What is the missing number?

9. $4 \times n = 36$
10. $6 \times 28 = n$
11. $7 \times 35 = n$

### Think About It

12. How can you tell whether a fraction is more than 2?

Investigation

# Invent a Fraction

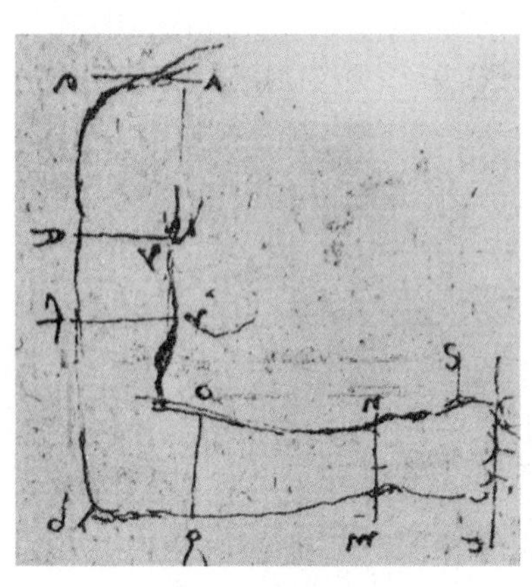

*Leonardo divided body parts like the arm above to help him draw better figures.*

Artists use fractions to help them draw. Leonardo da Vinci, an Italian artist who lived from 1452 to 1519, used fractions to make body measurements. He found that his arm was four hand lengths long. Like Leonardo, you can invent a fraction of your own.

**1 arm = 4 hands**

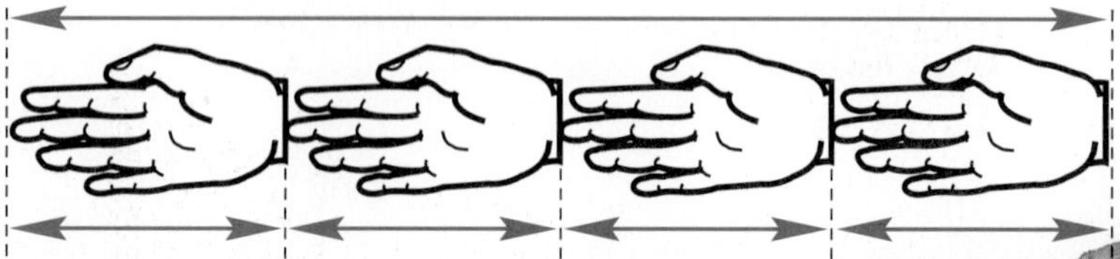

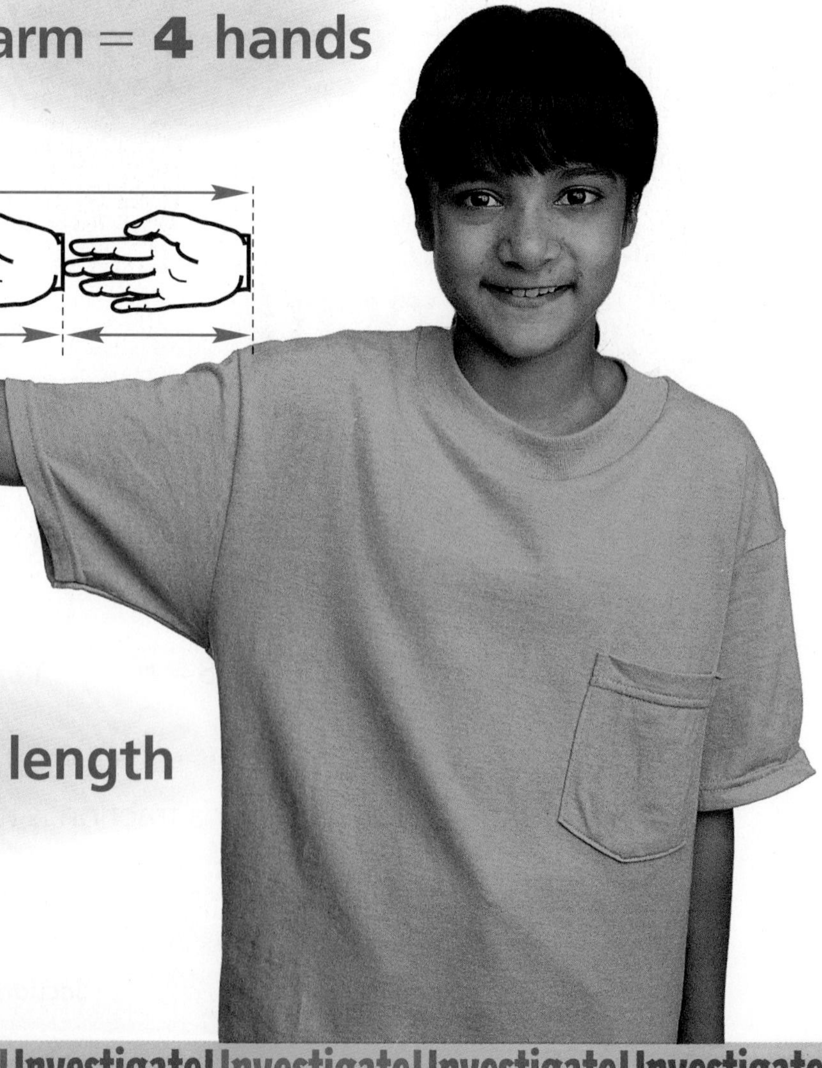

**1 hand = $\frac{1}{4}$ of arm length**

1. Use the length of your hand, face, or foot to invent a fraction. If you use your hand length, estimate how many "hands" tall you are. What fraction of your height is your hand?

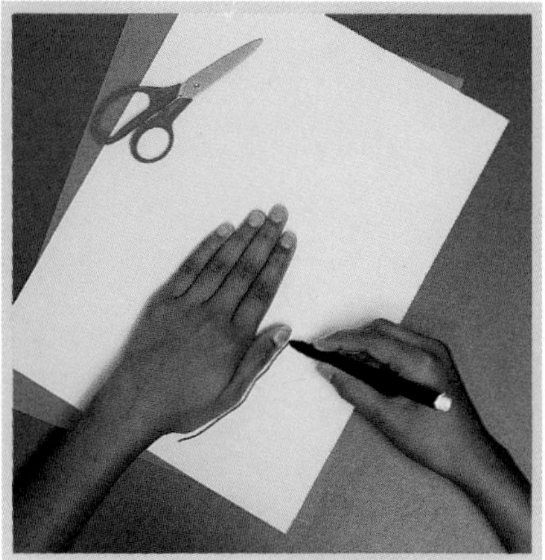

2. Make a paper "ruler" of your hand, face, or foot. Now measure your height.

3. Compare your fraction with others who used the same part of the body to make the ruler. What can you say about how a person's hand, face, or foot compares with that person's height? Explain what you found.

## Ask Yourself

- ☐ What data do I need to collect?
- ☐ How do I collect the information?
- ☐ Can I use rounding to help?
- ☐ Does my data make sense?
- ☐ How can I describe what I found?

Measuring with Fractions

# Fractions on a Ruler

What You'll Need

- *inch ruler*

## Activity 1 Looking at Length

### With Your Group

1. Use the ruler to count by fourths from zero to two inches. Ask yourself: "Should I say $\frac{1}{2}$ or $\frac{2}{4}$?" "Do I say $1\frac{1}{4}$ or $\frac{5}{4}$?"

2. One end of the pencil is next to 0. What mark is closest to the other end? How long is the pencil?

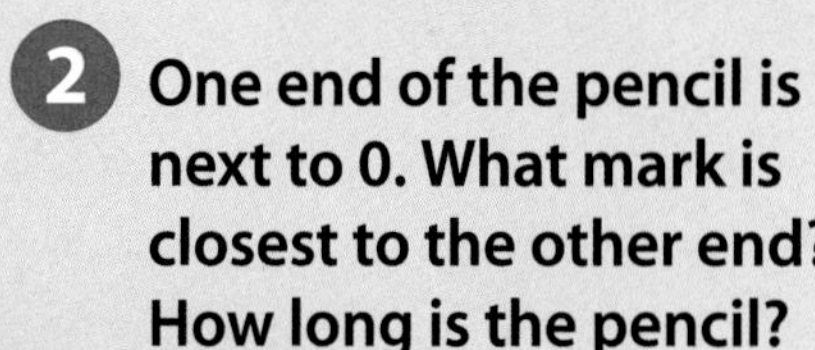

*Would you use fourths in writing the length of every object shown here? Why or why not?*

**3** **Choose one object shown here. Estimate its length to the nearest quarter inch.**

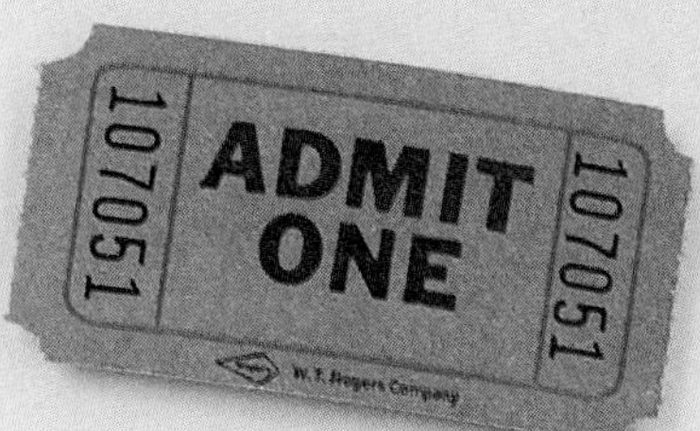

*Hold up an object. Have your friends estimate the length. Then measure to see who was closest.*

**4** **Measure the object with a ruler. Write the measure to the nearest quarter inch.**

**5** **Choose other objects on the page and estimate their length. Then measure them to the nearest quarter inch.**

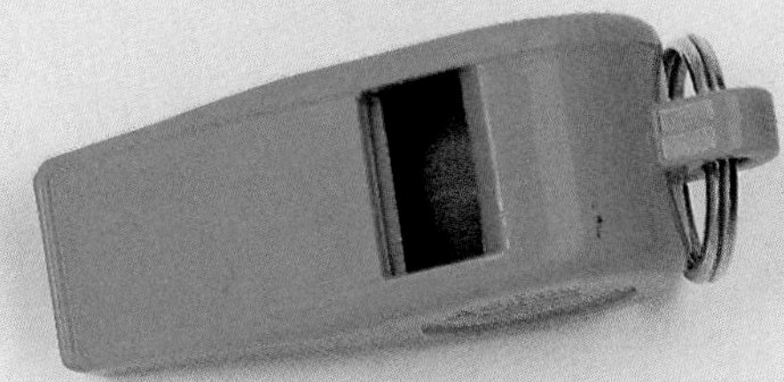

Do You Remember?

## Try It!

Measure these line segments to the nearest quarter inch.

1. ▬ 2. ▬▬▬▬▬▬▬▬▬▬
3. ▬▬▬▬▬▬▬▬▬▬▬▬▬▬▬▬▬▬▬▬
4. ▬▬▬▬▬ 5. ▬▬▬▬▬▬▬▬▬▬▬

Complete. Write <, >, or =.

6. 36 in. ● 1 yd  7. 2 yd ● 100 in.
8. 11 in. ● 1 ft  9. 30 in. ● 2 ft
10. 6 in. ● $\frac{1}{2}$ ft  11. 9 ft ● 2 yd

### Think About It

12. Explain in writing why it is better to use inches, not feet, to measure the line segments in Exercises 1–5.

# Pints, Pounds, and Fractions

*Draw different containers you may find at home or in the classroom. Look for numbers that show capacity. Write these numbers on your container drawings.*

How big is a pint? How much is a cup? Capacity tells how much a container holds.

## ACTIVITY 1 Capacity Connections

**With Your Group** Use the pictures below to help you answer the questions.

1. What do you get when you double a pint?
2. How many cups are in a quart?
3. What unit is half as much as a pint?

**1 cup (c)**

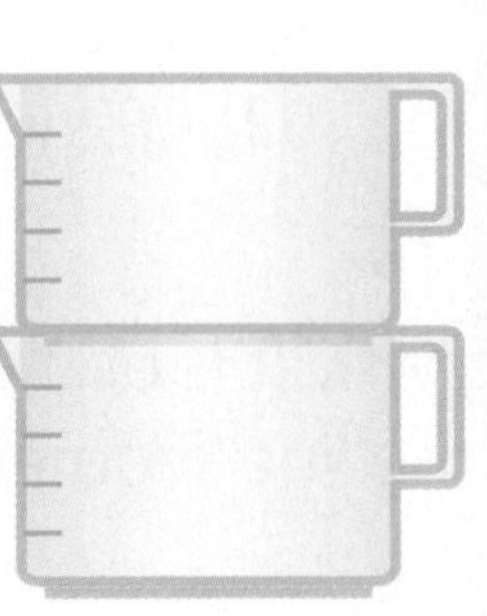

**1 quart (qt)**

**4** How much liquid is in the container below?

**5** Use the picture to help you complete each number sentence.

$1\frac{1}{2}$ pt = ■ c

6 c = ■ pt

$2\frac{1}{2}$ pt = ■ c

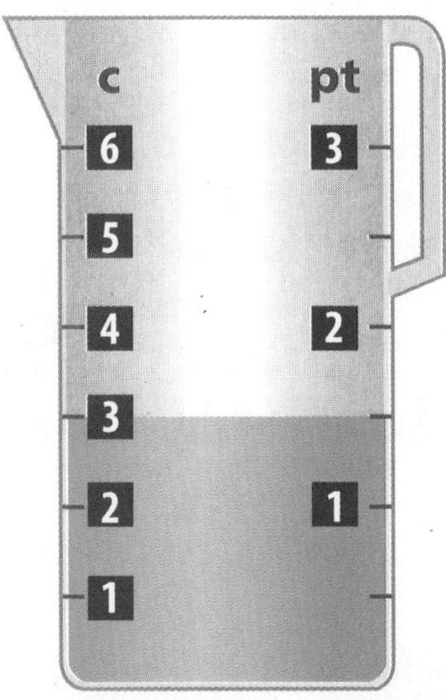


✓ **Self-Check** *How can you use fractions to describe the relationship between cups, pints, and quarts?*

## Activity 2 Charting Fractions

**With Your Partner** Use the orange juice container. Answer the questions below.

**1** **How many quarts are in a gallon?**

**2** **Suppose you have 2 qt of milk. Write the amount in two other ways.**

**2 qt = ■ gal**

**2 qt = ■ pt**

**1 gallon (gal)**

**3** **Copy and complete the chart on the left. What patterns do you notice?**

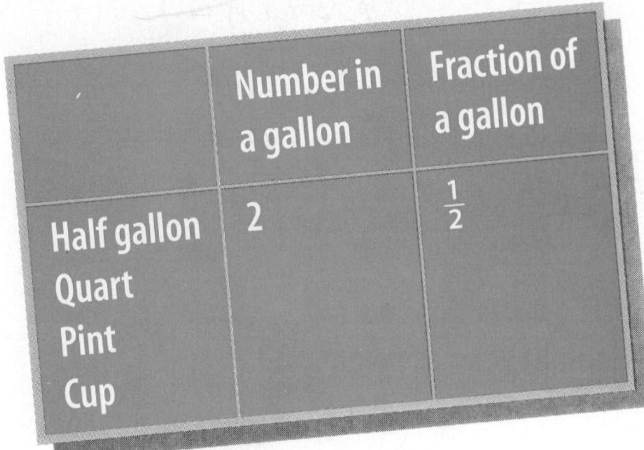

| | Number in a gallon | Fraction of a gallon |
|---|---|---|
| Half gallon | 2 | $\frac{1}{2}$ |
| Quart | | |
| Pint | | |
| Cup | | |

## ACTIVITY 3 What's the Weight?

**On Your Own** To measure weight, we use scales and a different set of units. Use the scale below.

**1** A grapefruit **weighs about one** pound (lb). **How many** ounces (oz) **does it weigh?**

**2** Two strawberries **weigh about 1 oz. About how many strawberries weigh 1 lb?**

**3** Four kiwis **weigh 1 lb. What fraction of a pound does one kiwi weigh?**

*Digital scales use decimals instead of fractions to show weight.*

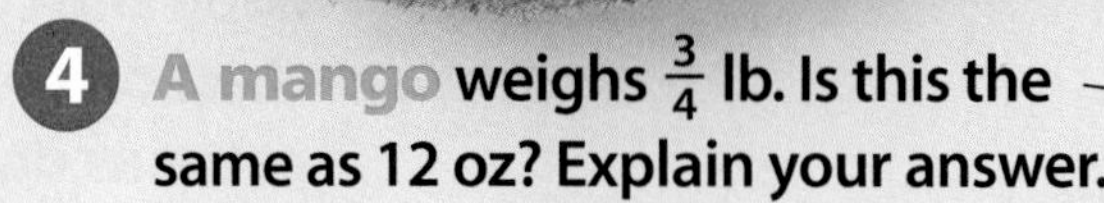

**4** A mango **weighs $\frac{3}{4}$ lb. Is this the same as 12 oz? Explain your answer.**

**5** **A banana** weighs about 5 oz. About how many bananas are in 1 lb?

*In Your Journal* Do you think it is easier to weigh small amounts of fruit in ounces or in fractions of pounds? Why do you think so?

**6** **A kiwano melon** weighs about 1 lb. There are 2,000 lb in one **ton (t)**. If a grocery store buys $\frac{1}{2}$ t of kiwano melons, about how many kiwanos is that?

Do You Remember?

## Try It!

Complete.

1. 1 c = ▢ qt
2. 3 qt = ▢ c
3. 5 gal = ▢ qt
4. 2 lb = ▢ oz
5. 8 oz = ▢ lb
6. $\frac{1}{16}$ lb = ▢ oz

Write the weight in pounds. Remember 1 t = 2,000 lb.

7. 2 t
8. 3 t
9. 5 t
10. 8 t

What is $n$?

11. $8 \times 127 = n$
12. $6 \times n = 72$

**Think About It**

13. Would you measure a bathtub of water in cups? Explain.

Do You Remember?

## Cumulative Review

# Victory Garden

Answer the questions about the picture shown here. Choose a calculator, paper and pencil, or mental math to solve each problem.

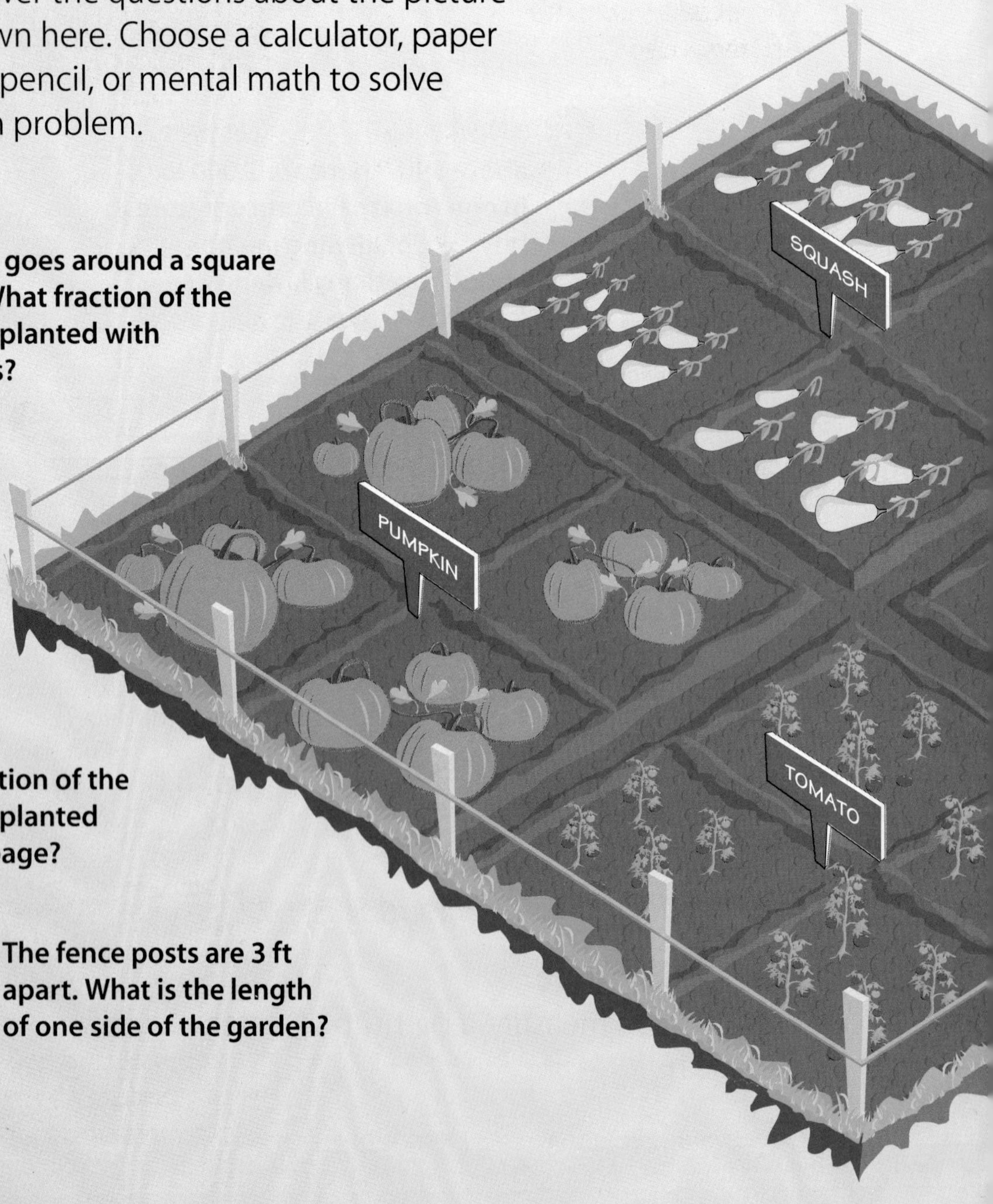

**1** **The fence goes around a square garden. What fraction of the garden is planted with pumpkins?**

**2** **What fraction of the garden is planted with cabbage?**

**3** **The fence posts are 3 ft apart. What is the length of one side of the garden?**

SQUASH

PUMPKIN

TOMATO

*A victory garden is a small vegetable patch. During World War II, people planted gardens like the one shown here. Many people grew vegetables in their own back yard to make sure there would be enough food.*

4 What is the perimeter of the garden?

5 What is the perimeter of the pumpkin patch?

6 What is the area of the pumpkin patch in square feet?

7 What is the area of the entire garden in square feet?

8 One square yard is 3 ft by 3 ft. What is the area of the whole garden in square yards?

**1 yd = 3 ft**

CABBAGE

## Check Your Math Power

9 Sketch a garden that has the same area as this one but a different perimeter.

10 Write the name of the vegetable you would grow in each part of your garden. Label each part as a fraction of the whole.

## Fractions and Data

# Fraction Check-out

*In Your Journal* *Describe how $\frac{1}{3}$ of a book is different from $\frac{1}{3}$ of a group of books.*

*Drawing a picture or using counters can help you find fractions of a group of things.*

The chart below shows the number of materials a library received back in an hour. Librarians can use the data to tell which kind of material people read most.

## ACTIVITY 1 Library Fractions

### With Your Class

1. In all, 16 items were returned. Nine were fiction books. How could you write the number of fiction books as a fraction of the total?

   **Fiction books returned**
   ———
   **Total items returned**

2. What fraction of the returns were magazines? Write your answer in simplest form.

| | Magazine | Fiction | Nonfiction |
|---|---|---|---|
| Materials returned in one hour | // | //// 𝍸 | 𝍸 |

3. Write a fraction that tells how many of the returns were nonfiction books.

## ACTIVITY 2 Stacked Fractions

**On Your Own** To find a fraction of a number, think of equal parts. Use counters to help you.

1. One sixth of the 24 books shown below are about history. How many history books are there?

$\frac{1}{6}$ of 24

2. Which books make up $\frac{1}{4}$ of the total? Explain.

3. What kind of book makes up $\frac{1}{3}$ of all the books?

4. Match each fraction of 30 with a number.

$\frac{1}{6}$ of 30 15 $\frac{1}{5}$ of 30

6 $\frac{1}{2}$ of 30 5

*How can you use division to find fractions of a set?*

**Exercises and Problems**

# At the Library

Use the collection of books shown here to answer some questions.

**Library Books**

| Book Type | Number |
|---|---|
| Fiction | ? |
| Nonfiction | ? |
| Biography | ? |
| Total | ? |

1. **These books can be grouped as fiction, nonfiction, and biography books. Copy and complete the chart.**

2. **What fraction of the books are nonfiction?**

3. **Fiction books make up $\frac{6}{12}$ of the collection. Explain why you can also say that $\frac{1}{2}$ of the books are fiction.**

4. **What fraction of the books is each type of book? Write each fraction in simplest form.**

5. **Together the biographies and the nonfiction books make up what part of the set of books?**

6. **For a special report, you read $\frac{2}{3}$ of the nonfiction books. How many books was that?**

7. **How many books make up $\frac{2}{3}$ of all the books?**

**Nonfiction**

8 *Island of the Blue Dolphins* has about 180 pages. *A River Dream* has about $\frac{1}{6}$ that number of pages. About how many pages long is *A River Dream*?

9 *Paddle-to-the-Sea* has about 54 pages. About $\frac{1}{2}$ of them are pictures. About how many pages are not pictures?

10 Suppose you double the number of each type of book. What happens to the fraction of the group that is nonfiction? fiction? biography?

# "7 out of 10 Kids Prefer..."

*How might including* other *as a choice help you organize your data?*

Fractions are often used in reporting the results of surveys. These activities can help you take your own survey and graph the results.

## Activity 1 What's Your Favorite?

### With Your Class

1. Take a survey to find out what your classmates prefer. Choose any topic. You might choose sports, TV shows, or kinds of music.
2. List three or four answers for your classmates to choose from. You may want to include *other* as a choice.

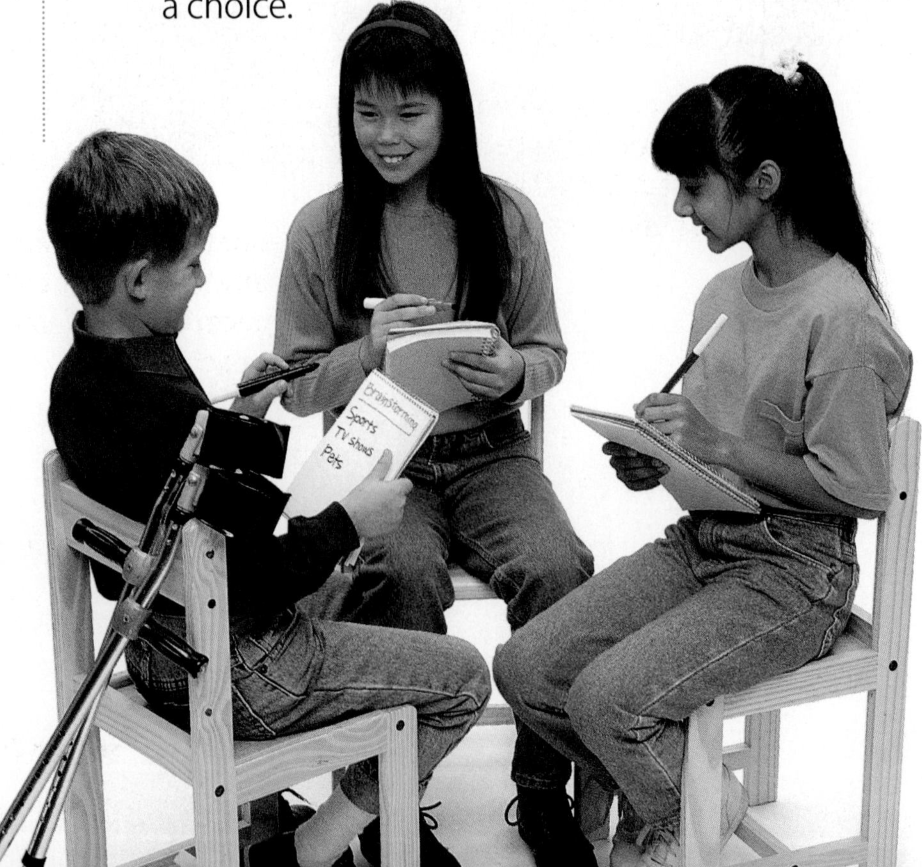

3. Have each student write his or her choice on a piece of paper. Collect the data. Total the votes for each choice.

4. Make a bar graph to show your data. Use the graph to tell what fraction of your classmates voted for each choice.

| Choice | Votes |
|---|---|
| Basketball | ~~////~~ ~~////~~ // |
| Bowling | /// |
| Baseball | ~~////~~ |
| Soccer | ~~////~~ /// |
| Others | //// |

## ACTIVITY 2 Make a Data Pie

**With Your Group** You can use a paper strip to make a **circle graph** of the data you collected.

**What You'll Need**

- *adding machine tape*
- *ruler*
- *crayons or markers*
- *tape*
- *drawing paper*

1. **On your tape, draw an equal-size section for each student you surveyed. Cut off any tape you don't need.**

2. **Color the strip to show how many students voted for each choice. Use a different color for each choice.**

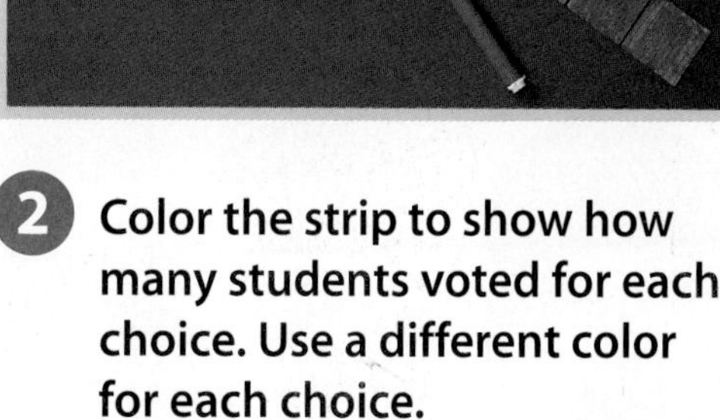

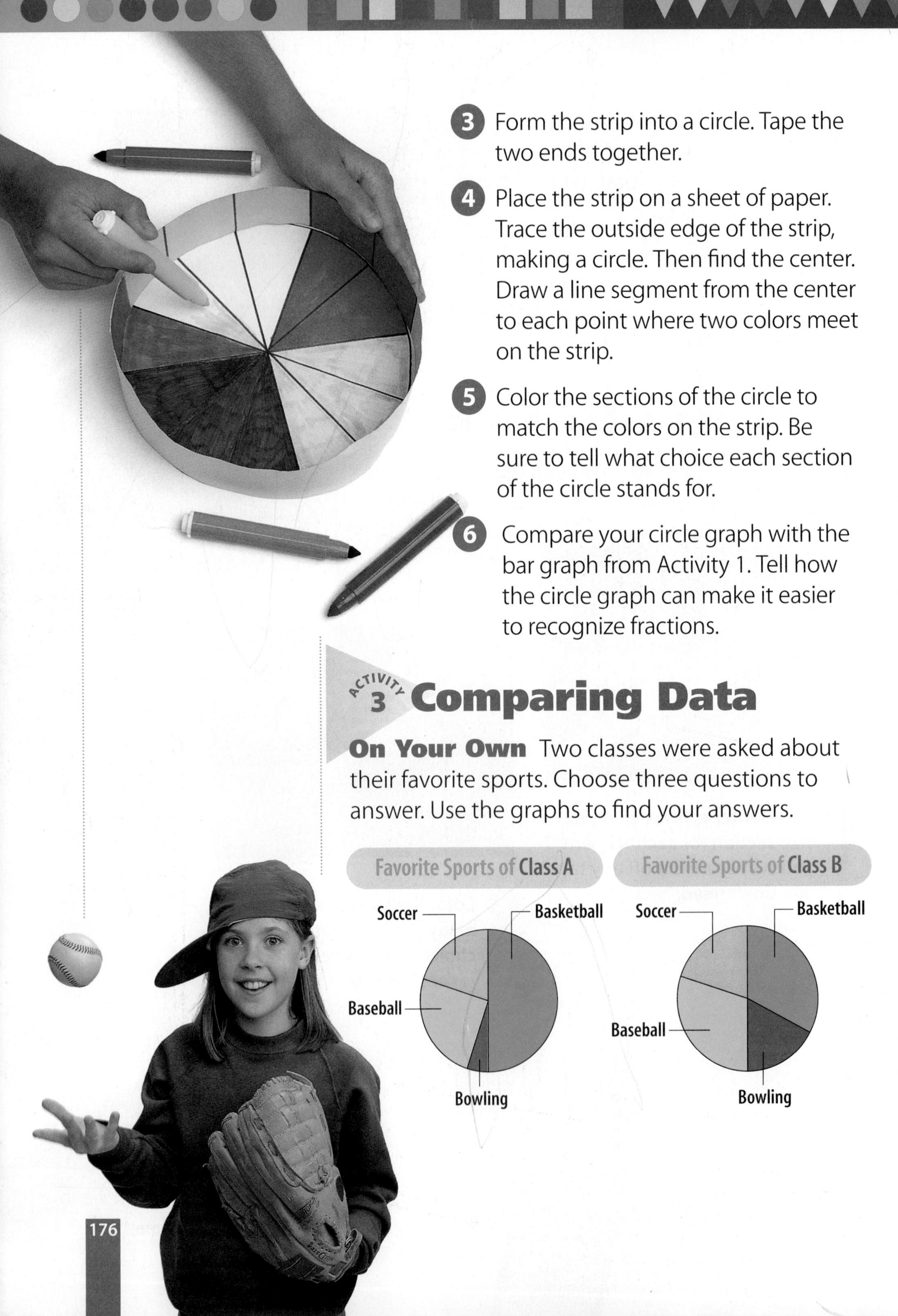


3. Form the strip into a circle. Tape the two ends together.
4. Place the strip on a sheet of paper. Trace the outside edge of the strip, making a circle. Then find the center. Draw a line segment from the center to each point where two colors meet on the strip.
5. Color the sections of the circle to match the colors on the strip. Be sure to tell what choice each section of the circle stands for.
6. Compare your circle graph with the bar graph from Activity 1. Tell how the circle graph can make it easier to recognize fractions.

## Activity 3 Comparing Data

**On Your Own** Two classes were asked about their favorite sports. Choose three questions to answer. Use the graphs to find your answers.

1. Which sport was chosen most in each class? Which sport was chosen least?

2. How does the fraction of students who chose basketball in class A compare with that in class B?

3. About what fraction of students chose soccer in class A? What fraction chose soccer in class B?

4. Which sport was chosen by about $\frac{1}{4}$ of the students in class A?

**✔ Self-Check** *Three out of a group of 18 students say volleyball is their favorite sport. How much of a circle graph would you shade to show this amount? Explain.*

Do You Remember?

## Try It!

The circle graph shows the results of a survey of 50 people. Match each sport with the fraction of people who chose it.

1. $\frac{1}{5}$  2. $\frac{3}{5}$

3. $\frac{2}{25}$  4. $\frac{3}{25}$

**Sport Choices**

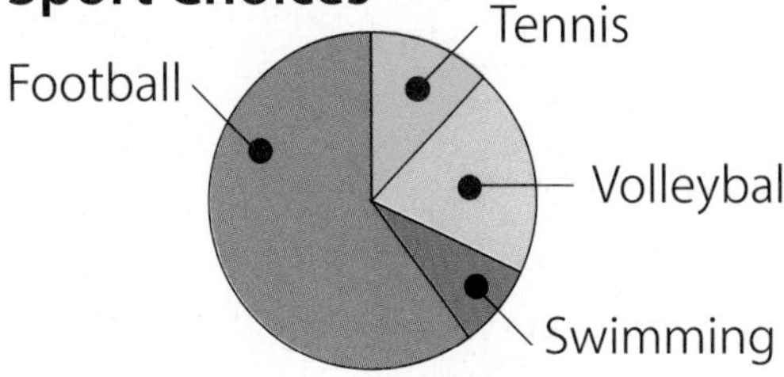


Use the circle graph to compare. Write $>$ or $<$.

5. $\frac{3}{25}$ ● $\frac{2}{25}$  6. $\frac{3}{5}$ ● $\frac{3}{25}$  7. $\frac{3}{5}$ ● $\frac{1}{5}$

8. $\frac{1}{5}$ ● $\frac{1}{2}$  9. $\frac{2}{25}$ ● $\frac{1}{5}$  10. $\frac{1}{2}$ ● $\frac{3}{5}$

### Think About It

11. Write an explanation of how a circle graph can help you compare fractions.

# Lesson 9 Fractions Around You

You can find fractions anywhere that you see equal parts. People use fractions to measure and make things. They also need fractions to organize or share things, like slices of pizza.

## Activity 1 Describing Parts

**With Your Partner** Answer the questions about the pictures below. Record your work.

1. How can fractions help you describe these pictures?
2. Choose a picture to sketch. Label each part with a fraction. What is the total?

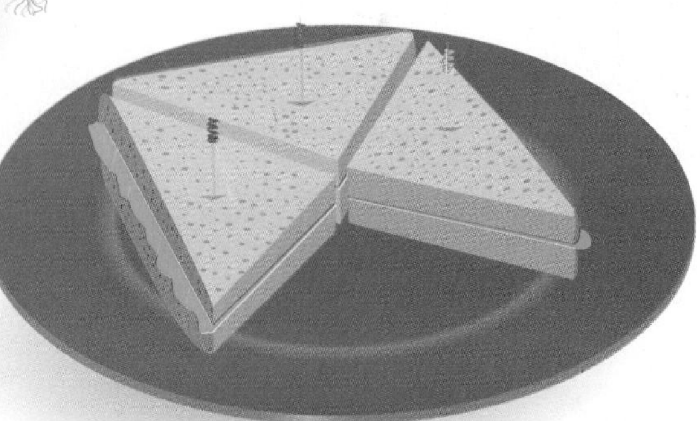

## ACTIVITY 2 Pizza Pieces

**With Your Group** The pizza on the right was cut into eight equal parts. What fraction of the whole pizza is left? Take a fraction circle with eighths, and get ready to solve some more pizza problems.

**What You'll Need**

- *Fraction Tool, or circle shape and ruler*

1. Suppose one friend ate three pizza slices, and you ate two slices. What fraction of the pizza was eaten? What fraction is left?

**3** eighths + **2** eighths = ?

**8** eighths − **5** eighths = ?

2. What other ways can two friends eat $\frac{5}{8}$ of a pizza together? Write the number sentences.

*How can you use what you know about whole number addition and subtraction to help you add and subtract fractions?*

### What You'll Need

- *Fraction Tool, or circle shape and ruler*
- *construction paper*
- *scissors*

# ACTIVITY 3 Pizza Orders

**With Your Group** Suppose four friends give you this order. Each pizza is divided into six equal slices. Use fraction circles to help you answer the questions.

**Pizza Slice Orders**

| | Cheese | Mushroom | Green Pepper |
|---|---|---|---|
| Angelica | 2 | 0 | 1 |
| Brad | 2 | 0 | 2 |
| Ray | 3 | 2 | 1 |
| Maria | 1 | 1 | 1 |

1. For each topping, how many slices do you need?
2. You can order only whole pizzas. How many pizzas of each topping should you order?
3. Suppose you can order "half-and-half." Maybe you want half cheese and half mushrooms. How might this change your order?

*Make a chart like the one above for your own group. Decide what pizzas you would order.*

4. Suppose you ate 2 slices of a pizza cut into twelfths. A friend ate 5 slices. What fraction of the pizza did the two of you eat together?

5. Use subtraction to find out if you and your friend ate more than $\frac{1}{2}$ of a pizza.

6. Show all the different ways that two friends, together, could eat $\frac{9}{12}$ of a pizza. Then do the same for $\frac{6}{12}$ of a pizza. Write the number sentences.

7. How many ways can two friends share $1\frac{1}{2}$ pizzas if the pizzas are cut into fourths? Write the number sentences.

*Draw a pizza. Divide it into equal slices. Choose three toppings and draw a topping on each slice. Write some addition sentences and subtraction sentences about your pizza.*

### What You'll Need
- *gameboard*
- *2 labeled cubes 1–6*
- *game pieces*

*You can use fraction models or circles to help you find the sum or difference.*

## Activity 4 Fractions in Action

**With Your Group** Use your fraction power to play this game. Take turns until each player reaches the end.

1. **Start the Game** On your turn, roll a cube. Move a game piece the number of spaces shown on the cube.

2. **Find the Numerators** Now roll both cubes. The numbers you roll will be your missing numerators.

**3 Add or Subtract** Copy and complete the number sentence.

**4 Score Points** Look at the score chart on the gameboard to see how many points to add to your score.

**5 Finish the Game** The person with the most points is the winner.

*In Your Journal* *Write a short note to a friend, explaining how to add and subtract fractions.*

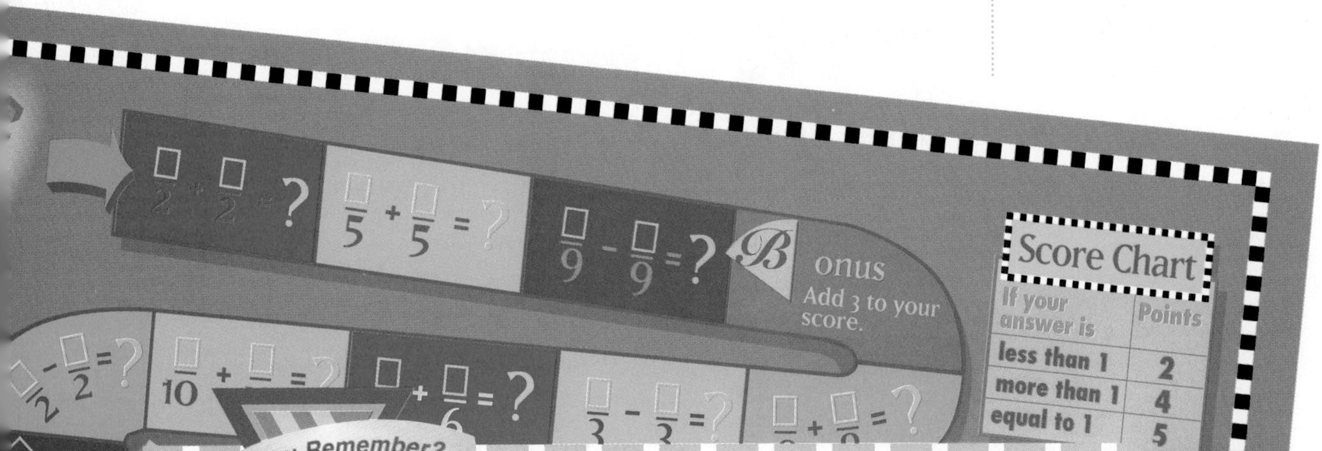

**Score Chart**

| If your answer is | Points |
|---|---|
| less than 1 | 2 |
| more than 1 | 4 |
| equal to 1 | 5 |

Bonus
Add 3 to your score.

Do You Remember?

## Try It!

Find the sum or difference. Decide if the answer is equal to $\frac{1}{2}$.

1. $\frac{3}{4} - \frac{1}{4}$
2. $\frac{8}{6} - \frac{5}{6}$
3. $\frac{1}{4} + \frac{1}{4}$
4. $\frac{7}{10} - \frac{3}{10}$
5. $\frac{7}{8} - \frac{3}{8}$
6. $\frac{5}{8} + \frac{1}{8}$

Add using mental math. Look for sums of 10 or 100.

7. $9 + 3 + 1 + 4 + 7$
8. $17 + 4 + 6 + 1$
9. $20 + 33 + 80 + 11$
10. $40 + 12 + 60 + 5$

### Think About It

11. Explain how you knew in Exercises 1 through 6 whether answers were $\frac{1}{2}$ or not.

LESSON 10

# Mixed Measures

*The kimono is a traditional Japanese gown that men and women wear.*

You can find colorful fabrics all around the world. In this lesson you'll measure fabric in yards and fractions of yards.

## ACTIVITY 1 Fractions of Fabric

**With Your Group** Use what you know about adding and subtracting fractions to answer the following questions.

1. You need 1 yd of fabric to make a kimono sash. You want $\frac{1}{2}$ yd of extra fabric. How much should you buy?
2. You bought $2\frac{3}{4}$ yd of the border material below. You used $1\frac{1}{4}$ yd. How much is left?
3. You bought 3 yd of silk. You have $2\frac{1}{2}$ yd left. How much did you use?

**4** You need $1\frac{1}{2}$ yd of fabric from India for a pillow and $\frac{1}{2}$ yd for a scarf. How much fabric do you need in all?

**5** You have $5\frac{2}{3}$ yd of border fabric. You use $3\frac{1}{3}$ yd. How much is left? Explain how to find the answer without using a yardstick.

**5 wholes 2 thirds**
**− 3 wholes 1 third**

**?**

### On Your Own

**6** Write four different pairs of mixed numbers or fractions that have a sum of $2\frac{3}{4}$.

$\triangle + \square = 2\frac{3}{4}$

**7** Write four different pairs of mixed numbers that have a difference of $\frac{3}{4}$.

*Sari fabric comes from India. Indian women wrap long pieces of the fabric around their bodies.*

**Self-Check** *How can you use addition to check your answer to question 7?*

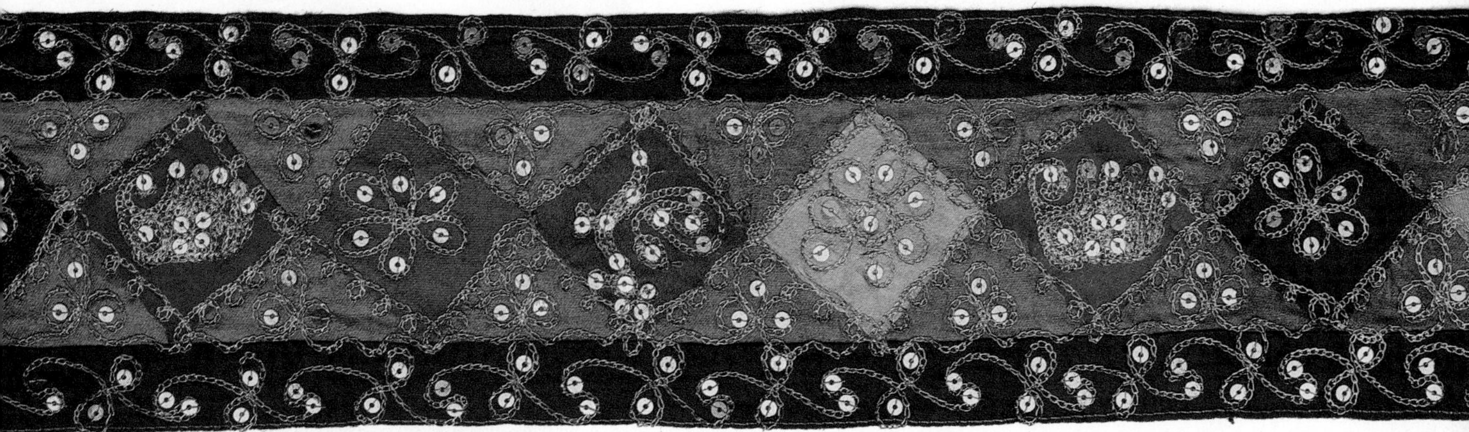

**What You'll Need**

- *ruler*

# ACTIVITY 2 Frame It!

**With Your Partner** Sketching and measuring can help you decide how to make a picture fit in a frame.

1. Will the picture at the left fit in the frame below? Explain.
2. How much wider is the picture than the opening in the frame? How much longer is it?
3. Write or draw how you would trim the picture to make it fit inside the frame.

$$12\frac{1}{4} \text{ in.} - 10 \text{ in.} = ?$$

$$8\frac{1}{2} \text{ in.} - 8 \text{ in.} = ?$$

4. Suppose you buy a larger frame. You decide to add a border that makes the picture 2 in. longer and 2 in. wider. Describe how wide and long the opening in the frame needs to be.

**5** Sketch the picture below at full size. Explain how you would trim it to make it fit the frame.

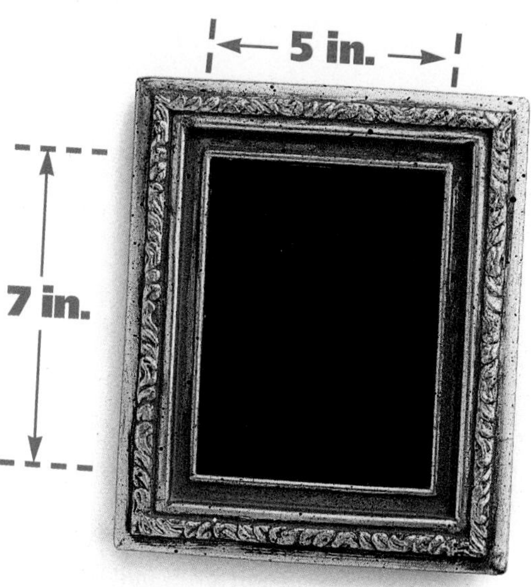


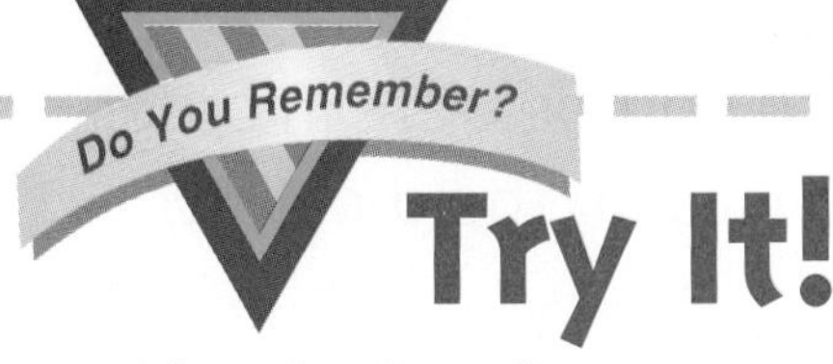


## Try It!

Decide whether the answer will be more or less than 5. Then add or subtract.

1. $5 + \frac{3}{4}$
2. $5\frac{1}{4} - 1$
3. $2\frac{1}{3} + 3\frac{1}{3}$
4. $6 - 1\frac{1}{8}$
5. $4\frac{1}{4} + \frac{2}{4}$
6. $3\frac{1}{5} + 2\frac{3}{5}$

Subtract. What do you notice about the answers?

7. 25,861 − 1
8. 25,861 − 60
9. 25,861 − 800
10. 125,861 − 5,000

**Think About It**

11. How is adding mixed numbers similar to adding fractions? Write your answer.

*Choose one of your own drawings. Measure the length and width. Explain how you could trim your picture or add a border to fit one of the frames shown on these pages.*

Do You Remember? **Cumulative Review**

# Looking Back

**Choose the right answer. Write *a, b, c* or *d* for each question.**

1. A pizza was divided into 8 equal parts. Three pieces were eaten. Which sentence is true?

   a. There is $\frac{3}{8}$ of the pizza left.

   b. Half of the pizza was eaten.

   c. There is $\frac{5}{8}$ of the pizza left.

   d. There are 3 pieces left.

2. What fraction of the square is not shaded?

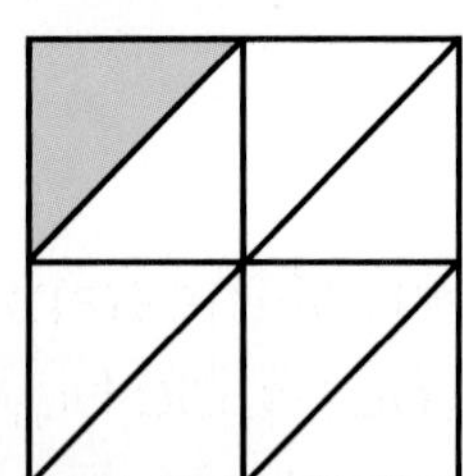

   a. $\frac{1}{8}$ b. $\frac{1}{16}$

   c. $\frac{1}{2}$ d. $\frac{7}{8}$

3. Which fraction is not equivalent to the others?

   a. $\frac{8}{12}$ b. $\frac{9}{15}$

   c. $\frac{3}{5}$ d. six tenths

4. Look at this pattern.

   $\frac{1}{2}, 1, 1\frac{1}{2}, 2$

   Which number comes next?

   a. $2\frac{2}{2}$ b. 3

   c. $2\frac{1}{2}$ d. $3\frac{1}{2}$

5. Which numbers are in order from least to the greatest?

   a. $\frac{1}{2}, \frac{1}{4}, \frac{1}{8}$ b. $\frac{2}{5}, \frac{3}{5}, \frac{4}{5}$

   c. $\frac{1}{2}, \frac{2}{4}, \frac{3}{6}$ d. $\frac{1}{2}, \frac{1}{3}, \frac{1}{4}$

6. Which letter on the number line shows the number $\frac{7}{2}$?

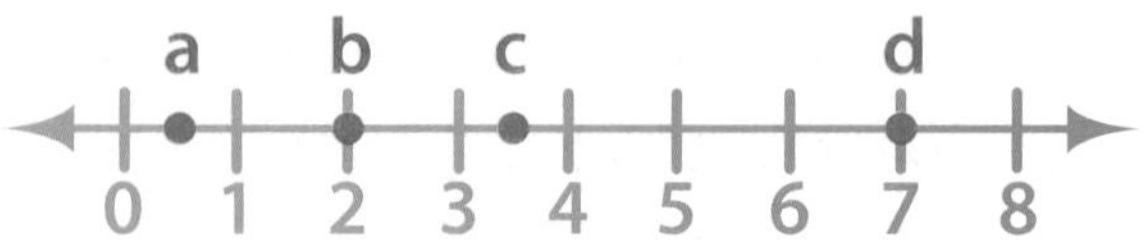


7. Which weight is different from the others?

   a. 4 oz b. $\frac{4}{16}$ lb

   c. 14 oz d. $\frac{1}{4}$ lb

8. Which amount is the same as 6 pints?

   a. 6 c  b. 4 gal
   c. 3 qt  d. 3 pt

9. One-third dozen is how many?

   a. $\frac{1}{3}$  b. 6  c. 4  d. 36

10. Suppose you cut off 2 ft of a 10-ft string. What fraction of the string did you cut off?

   a. $\frac{2}{10}$  b. $\frac{2}{8}$  c. $\frac{8}{10}$  d. 8 ft

11. Which part of the circle graph could represent $\frac{5}{20}$ of a group?

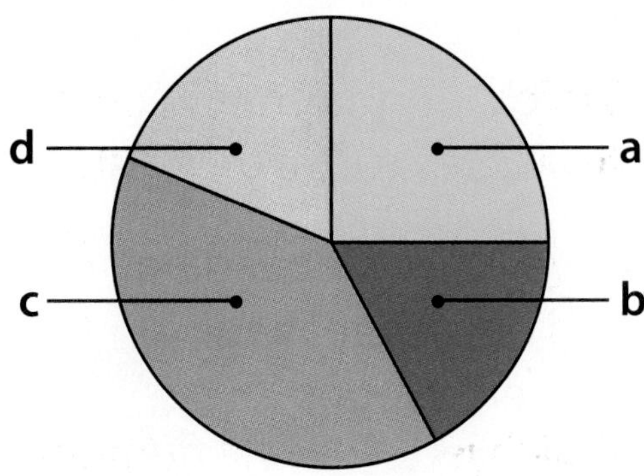


12. Which sum is equal to $\frac{1}{2}$?

   a. $\frac{1}{5} + \frac{1}{5}$  b. $\frac{1}{6} + \frac{1}{6}$
   c. $\frac{1}{8} + \frac{3}{8}$  d. $\frac{3}{4} + \frac{1}{4}$

13. Which difference equals $2\frac{1}{6}$?

   a. $2\frac{5}{6} - \frac{4}{6}$  b. $2 - \frac{3}{6}$
   c. $5 - 3\frac{1}{6}$  d. $2 - \frac{1}{6}$

## Check Your Math Power

14. Copy this design and shade the triangles in two or three different colors. Write the fraction of the design that is each color. Then write at least three addition or subtraction sentences for the design. Explain what each sentence shows.

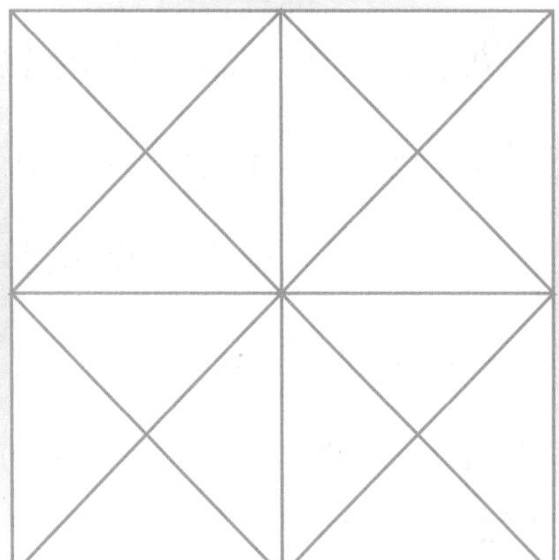

15. Tell which of the frames listed below you would buy to frame a $5\frac{1}{2}$-in.-by-$3\frac{1}{2}$-in. picture. The sizes of the openings are given. Larger frames cost more money. Write your reason for your choice.

   Frame A: 3 in. by 5 in.
   Frame B: 5 in. by 7 in.
   Frame C: 8 in. by 10 in.
   Frame D: 9 in. by 12 in.

MODULE 4 Investigations

# Which Do You Prefer?

You've already learned how to use fractions with data. Fractions can help you understand data. They also can help you report the results of a survey. How can they help you compare survey results from different groups? Find out.

## Investigation A It's Your Choice

How might the results of a survey differ depending on the people you survey? Find out by creating a survey question. Ask two different groups of people the same question. Write a report about what you find.

### Keep in Mind

**Be sure to do the following things in your report.**

- ☐ **Write about the survey results.**
- ☐ **Explain how the way you show data helped.**
- ☐ **Tell how you used fractions to compare the results from the groups.**

Here are some hints.

1. **Form a Question** Work with a partner if you like. What question would interest both groups?

2. **Choose Two Groups** You may choose groups that differ in age, such as adults and fourth graders. You may choose groups that differ in other ways. Ask yourself these questions.
   - How can I describe the groups?
   - Do I expect to get very different answers?

3. **Collect and Organize Data** To collect your data you may work with a partner.
   - Write your own report.
   - Explain how you can use fractions to explain the results.

*Top to bottom: French, Spanish, German, Chinese*

Investigation B

## Kids and Language

You can use surveys to learn about the people around you. Many of your classmates may speak more than one language. Design a survey. Find out how many languages your classmates speak. Find out how another class compares with yours.

1. Share the work of gathering the data.
2. Use your data to make a poster.
3. Compare the two sets of data. Tell how they are alike and different. Use fractions to explain what you found.

Ongoing Investigation

## Fractions of a Million

You're halfway through your math book, but your collection probably isn't halfway to a million yet. What fraction of a million have you collected? Count up the total number of items you have collected. Use that number for your numerator. Use 1,000,000 as your denominator. Can you simplify your fraction? Is it more or less than one-half? How can you tell?

MODULE 5

# Discovering Treasure

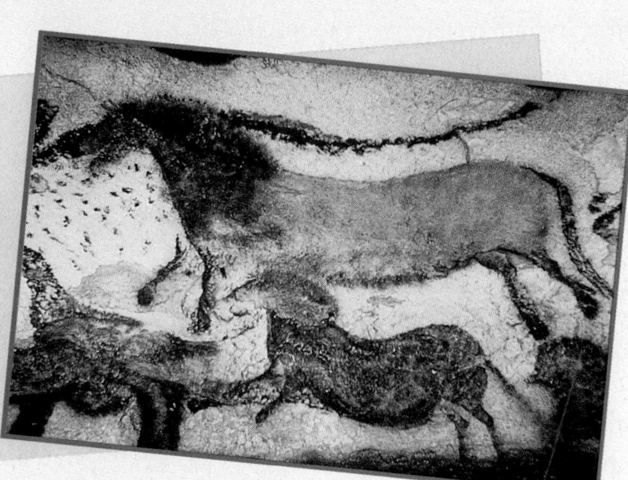

Image of a bull, portion of a prehistoric cave painting, Lascaux, France

It was September of 1940. Four boys were looking for treasure near the Lascaux Manor in France. They found treasure, but not the kind they expected.

Jacques Marsal and three friends saw a small hole on the side of a hill. They started digging, hoping to find gold, silver, and jewels. Instead, they found a cave.

The walls were painted with bulls, horses, and deer. The pictures were nearly 17,000 years old.

You too can be a treasure hunter. You can solve puzzles and learn new skills. Just turn the page. . . .

Shapes and Ordered Pairs

Exploring Money

Equal Shares

Averages and Logic

# Hunting for Treasure

Do you dream of hunting treasure? Maybe you have even found treasure. In this module you'll learn how to hunt, tell about, and share all kinds of treasure. These ideas may help you get started.

## 1 Look Around

**What treasures would you like to find? Think of treasure you have read about. What treasures have you seen at school, at home, or at a museum? Write them down.**

### Word Bank

- average
- compatible numbers
- coordinate grid
- ordered pair
- Roman numerals
- similar figures

## 2 Start Hunting

Suppose you want to hunt for treasure. What information will you need to get started? List several things.

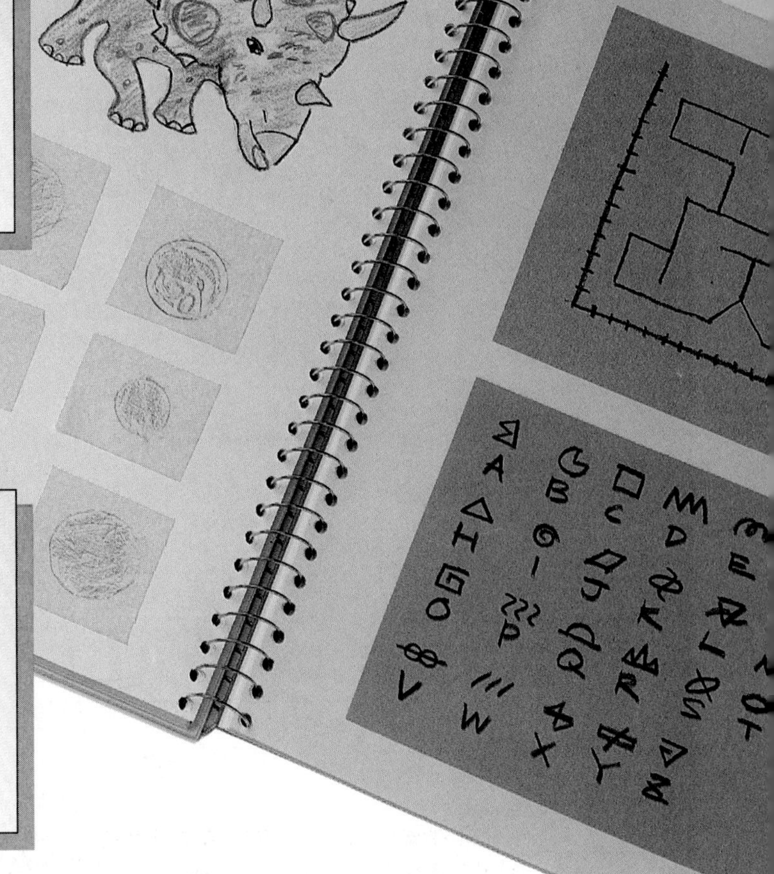

## 3 Show and Tell

Imagine you are hiding a treasure. Draw a map that shows where you found it. Write clues, or hints, telling where it is. Share them with your class.

## Investigations Preview

Thinking logically can make you a better treasure hunter. You can learn to be a logical thinker. You will also try to make and break secret codes.

**Secret Sign** (pages 204–205)

How could you invent a sign for a treasure-hunting club? Knowing how to draw shapes on a grid will help you.

**Treasure Keys** (pages 238–240)

You'll use division and multiplication to design a math code. You also will have a chance to solve a secret message.

Section A: Shapes and Ordered Pairs

# Lesson 1: Unmasking Treasure

A map can lead you to treasure if you know how to read it. The map on the next page shows the tomb of the Egyptian King Tutankhamen.

## Activity 1: Walk This Way

**With Your Partner** The marks on the side of the map show paces, or steps. Count them to find out how far you would walk to reach each treasure. The compass on the map shows directions.

1. Find the leopard mask. What other object is in the same room?
2. Give directions to go from the entrance to the mask.
3. Find the treasure at each site.
   a. From the entrance, walk 12 paces north, 14 paces east, then 10 paces south.
   b. From the entrance, walk 12 paces north, 13 steps east, and 2 paces north.

*Pyramids in Egypt stand above the tombs of ancient kings.*

4. Choose another treasure. Describe how to get to it from the entrance. Compare your directions with ones other students give.

*In Your Journal* Write directions showing how to get from the falcon statue to the leopard mask.

***King Tutankhamen's tomb is in Egypt, south of the great pyramids. It was discovered in 1922.***

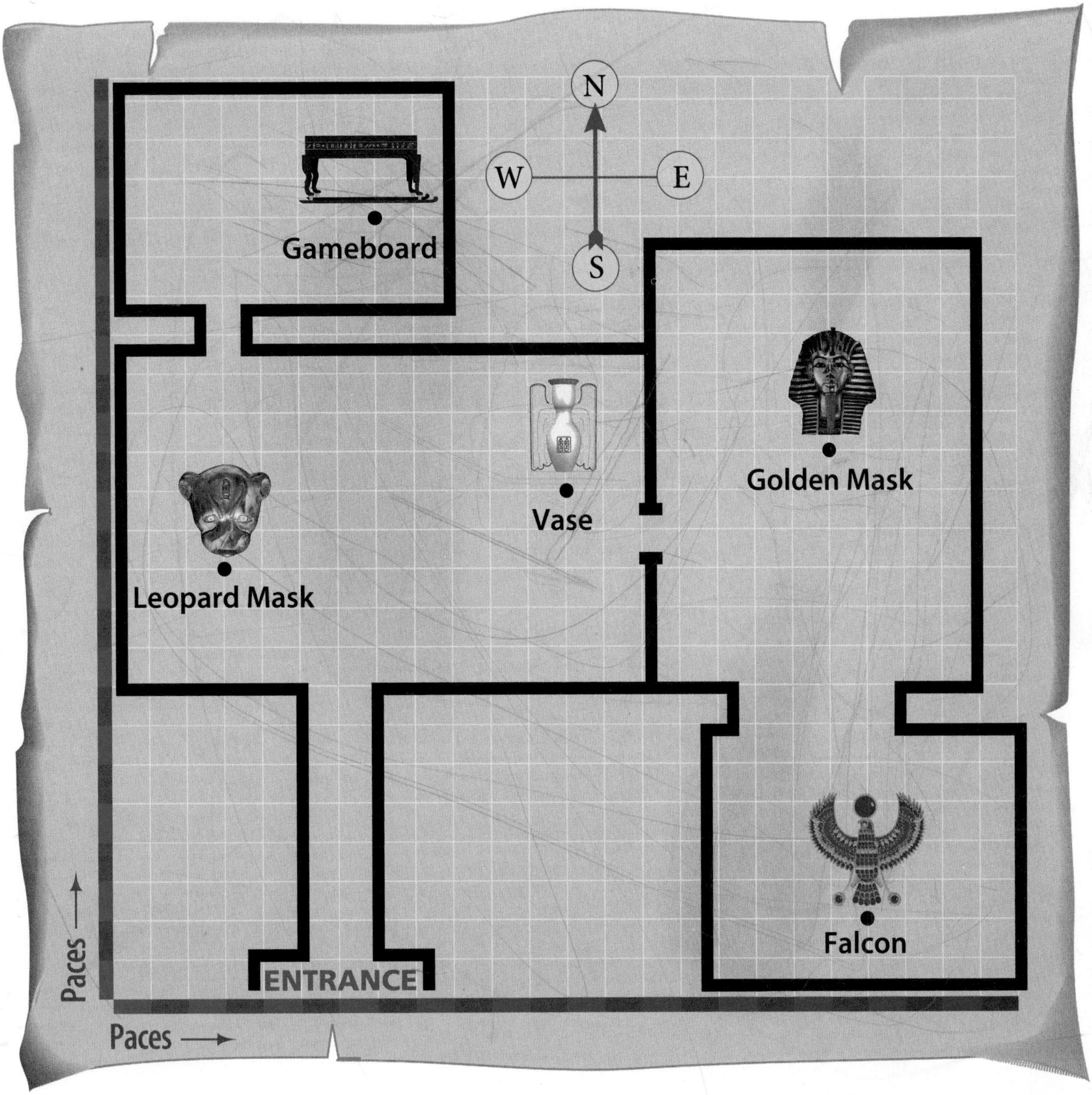

N
W
E
S
Gameboard
Golden Mask
Vase
Leopard Mask
Falcon
ENTRANCE
Paces
Paces

What You'll Need

- *grid paper*

# ACTIVITY 2 Inside and Out

**With Your Group** A **coordinate grid** has two perpendicular number lines. You can use it to decide if points are inside, outside, or on a shape.

**1** What is the ordered pair for point *B*? for *C*?

**An ordered pair of numbers tells where a point is on a grid. The ordered pair for point *A* is (1, 5).**

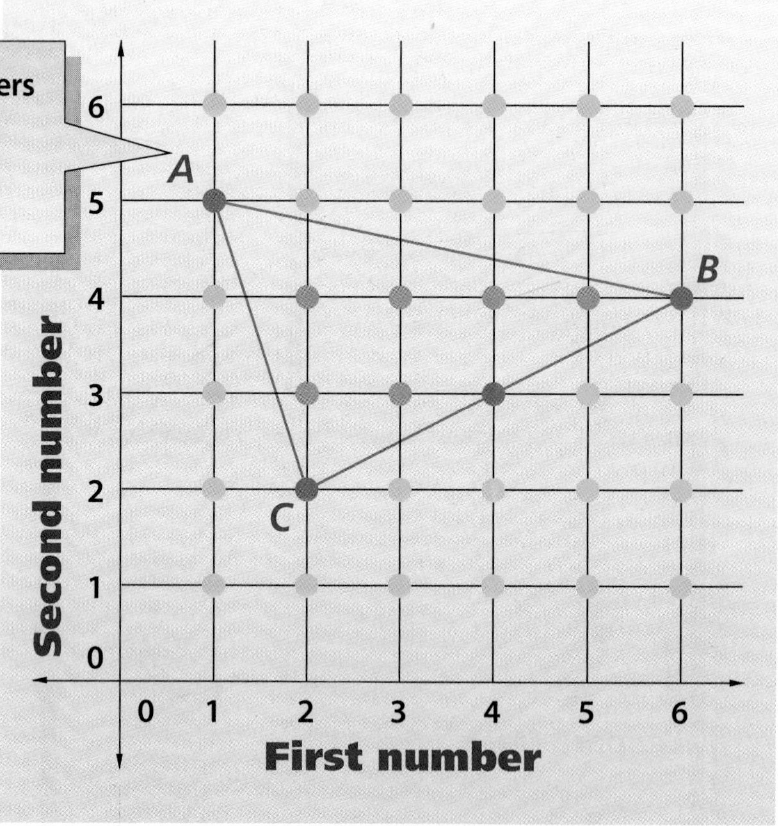

*This map of Egypt has letters on the side and numbers on the bottom. Use them to describe where Cairo, Luxor, and Giza are. Tell how the map is like a coordinate grid and how it is different.*

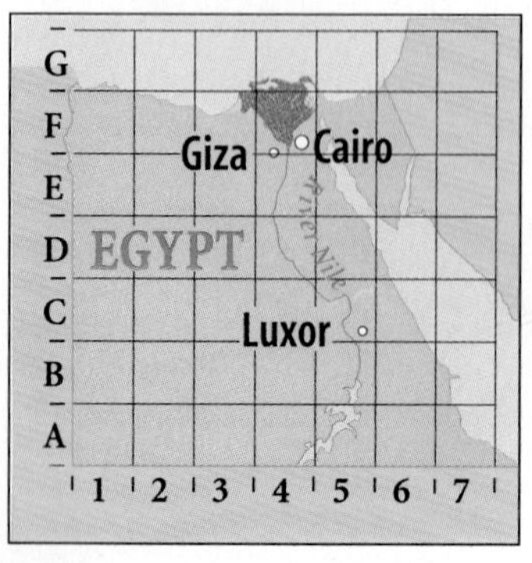


**2** Find the points named by these ordered pairs.

**(3, 2) (4, 5) (4, 3)**

Tell whether each point is inside, outside, or on triangle *ABC*.

**3** Write three other ordered pairs. Do they stand for points inside, outside, or on triangle *ABC?*

ACTIVITY 3

# Point for Point

**With Your Partner** Start with a triangle on a grid. Use your knowledge of ordered pairs to find and score points!

**What You'll Need**

- *grid paper*
- *2 number cubes*

**1** **Each player rolls the cubes, one at a time, to get numbers for an ordered pair. Mark the ordered pairs on the grid.**

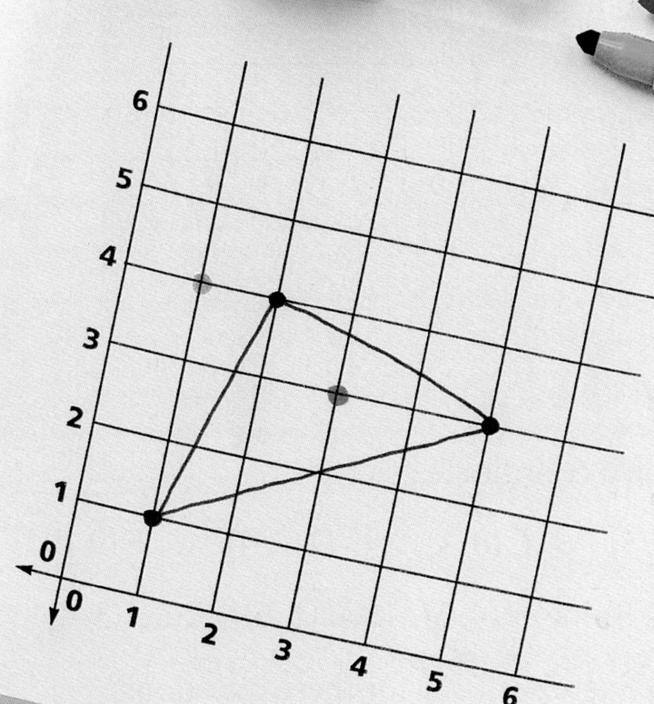

*Draw a triangle, a square, and a rectangle on a coordinate grid. Mark the ordered pairs for the vertexes of each shape.*

**2** **Use the chart to find your score.**

| Location | Score |
|---|---|
| Outside | 1 |
| Inside | 2 |
| On | 3 |

**3** **The first player to get 10 points wins.**

**What You'll Need**

- *grid paper*
- *ruler*

*Think of a way to help you remember which number in an ordered pair is first. Share your idea with other groups.*

# ACTIVITY 4 Mystery Shapes

**With Your Partner** Choose a quadrilateral. Draw it on a grid. Label the vertexes *A*, *B*, *C*, and *D*. Make a code for your picture with ordered pairs. Trade codes. Can you draw each other's shape?

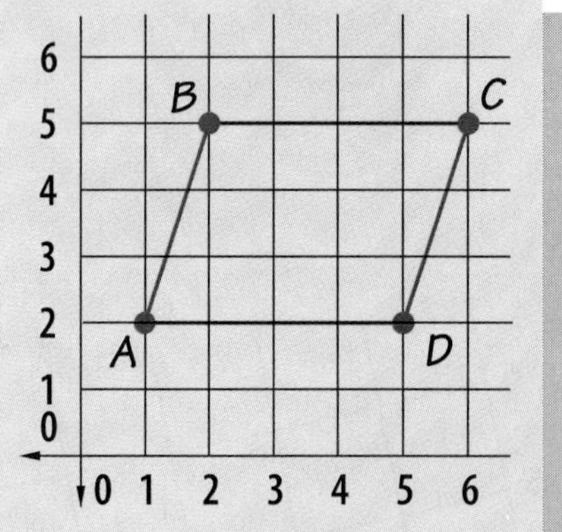


Do You Remember?

## Try It!

Mark these points on a coordinate grid.

1. *A* (2, 1) 2. *B* (5, 3) 3. *C* (8, 1) 4. *D* (7, 4) 5. *E* (9, 6)
6. *F* (6, 6) 7. *G* (5, 8) 8. *H* (4, 6) 9. *I* (1, 6) 10. *J* (3, 4)

Use the points from Exercises 1–10 for these questions.

11. Connect the points in order. Connect *J* to *A*. What shape did you make?
12. Name an angle greater than a right angle.
13. Sketch a line of symmetry for the shape.
14. Name points you can connect to make a pentagon.

**Think About It**

15. Describe two other shapes you can make by connecting some of points *A*–*J*.

# Similar Shapes

**H**ow can a coordinate grid help you compare shapes?

## ACTIVITY 1 Growing Rectangles

**With Your Partner** On grid paper, draw a small rectangle with the lower left corner at (0, 0).

**What You'll Need**
- *grid paper*
- *ruler*

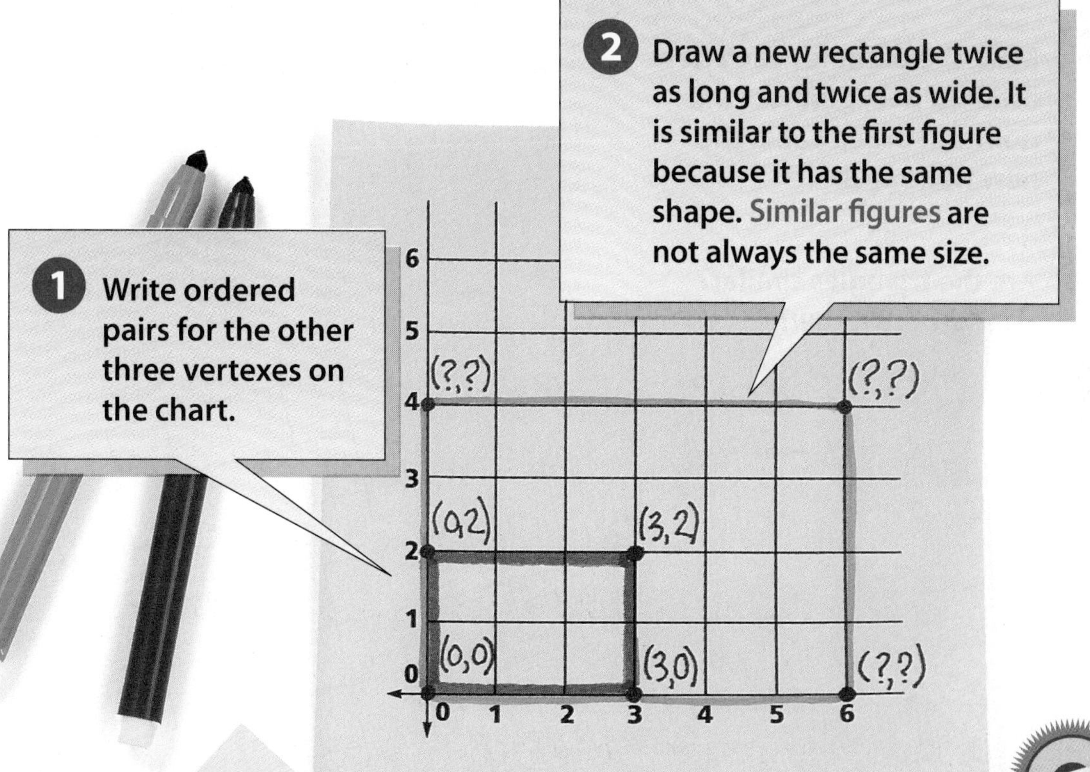


3 **Write the ordered pairs for the new vertexes. What do you notice?**

**REASONING AND PROBLEM SOLVING**

*What if you double only one of the numbers in an ordered pair? Try it with Activity 1.*

What You'll Need

- *2 sheets of grid paper*
- *ruler*

*Tracing the shapes and comparing them can help you tell if they are similar.*

## ACTIVITY 2 Shaping Up

**With Your Group** Ordered pairs can help you draw similar figures.

1. **Draw a small triangle on a coordinate grid. Label the vertexes *S*, *Y*, and *K*. A sample is shown below.**

2. **List an ordered pair for each vertex. Double the numbers in each ordered pair.**

3. **Mark the point for each new ordered pair. Connect the points in order. Label the new triangle *BIG*.**

4. **Are the triangles similar? How do you know?**

**5** **On a different grid, draw a small triangle. Use these ordered pairs: (2, 2) (4, 3) (3, 1).**

**6** **Triple each number in the ordered pairs. What are the new ordered pairs? Draw the new shape.**

**7** **Describe how you could make the shape in Step 5 smaller.**

✔ **Self-Check** *Draw a figure similar to that in Step 6, but smaller. Tell how you know the figures are similar.*

Do You Remember?

# Try It!

Mark these points on a coordinate grid.

**1.** *P* (1, 3) **2.** *Q* (3, 6) **3.** *R* (1, 6) **4.** *W* (0, 0)

**5.** *X* (6, 0) **6.** *Y* (6, 3) **7.** *Z* (0, 3)

Draw each shape on the same grid.

**8.** triangle *PQR* **9.** rectangle *WXYZ*

**10.** a larger shape similar to triangle *PQR*

**11.** a larger shape similar to rectangle *WXYZ*

**12.** a smaller shape similar to rectangle *WXYZ*

**Think About It**

**13.** Study the triangles you drew for Exercises 8 and 10. Which angles are the same size? Explain in writing.

# Secret Sign

Egyptian artists knew how to use grids. First they made sketches on a small grid. Then they drew a large grid on a pyramid wall. They copied their sketches onto the wall one square at a time.

You can use grids to make a flag or banner for a treasure-hunting club.

1. **Think** of a symbol for your flag, such as the key shown here. Pick a name or initials to go with it. You might combine the name and symbol.

2. **Draw** your design on one sheet of $\frac{1}{4}$-in. grid paper. Use letters that are seven squares tall and seven squares wide.

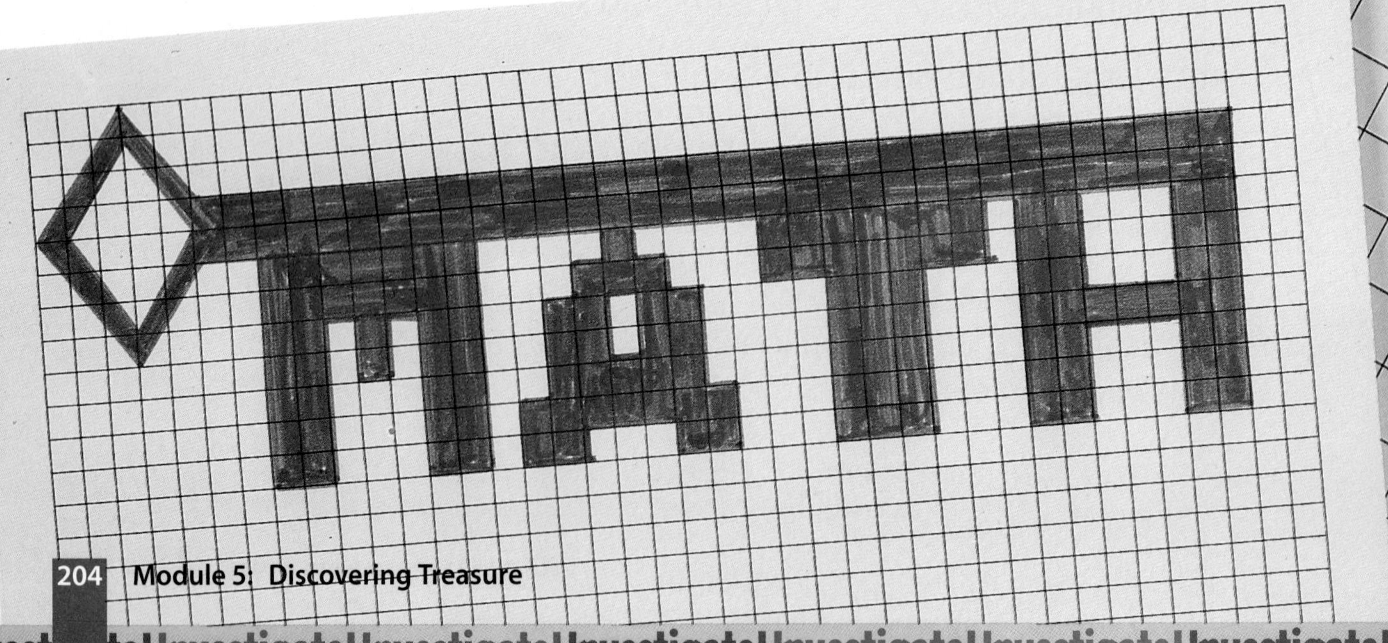

3 **Decide** how to make your design larger. What size squares will you use? You might tape pieces of grid paper together to make one large sheet. Draw and color your design.

4 **Explain** how you made the larger design. Did you draw bigger squares on $\frac{1}{4}$-in. grid paper?

## Ask Yourself

- ☐ What do you want the flag to say about your club?
- ☐ How will the materials affect how large you can make your sign?
- ☐ How can a grid help you design your flag and make your sign?
- ☐ Will people far away be able to read your flag?
- ☐ When people see your sign, will they recognize your club?

SECTION B Exploring Money

# LESSON 3 Counting Money

*Spanish coins like these were made in Mexico, Peru, and Bolivia. They were sent back to Spain in ships. Sometimes the ships sank, leaving gold and silver coins on the ocean floor.*

Sunken treasure can make you think of gold and silver coins. You might have some coins that you found on the way to school or keep in a bank.

## ACTIVITY 1 Counting Coins

**With Your Partner** How much money do you have? To find out you will need to count coins.

1. Take five play coins from a bag of quarters, dimes, nickels, and pennies. Which coins would you count first? Why?

**Here's one way:**

25, 30, 40, 41, 42

2. What is the value of your five coins? Write the total value two ways.

**Here are two ways to write 42 cents.** 42¢ or $.42

**3** Choose other groups of five coins. Use a chart to record each group of coins.

| Quarters 25¢ | Dimes 10¢ | Nickels 5¢ | Pennies 1¢ | Total ¢ | Total $ |
|---|---|---|---|---|---|
| 1 | 1 | 2 | 1 | 46¢ | $.46 |
| 1 | 2 | 1 | 1 | 51¢ | $.51 |
| | | | | | |
| | | | | | |

**4** Which five coins have the smallest value?

**5** Which five coins have the largest value?

**6** Can you find five coins that have a total value of 30¢? Explain your answer.

ACTIVITY OPTION

*Choose three or four coins without showing your partner. Tell your partner the number of coins and their total value. See if your partner can guess the coins.*

✓ Self-Check *An item costs $.60. You give the clerk $1. You get change back in dimes. How many dimes do you get?*

## Activity 2 How Many Coins?

**With Your Partner** A number sentence can help you describe how many coins you have.

1. Choose dimes or nickels. Grab a handful. Don't show your partner the coins.
2. Tell your partner the type of coins you have and their total value.
3. Ask your partner to figure out how many coins you have. How can thinking of missing factors help?

**How many nickels make 35¢?**

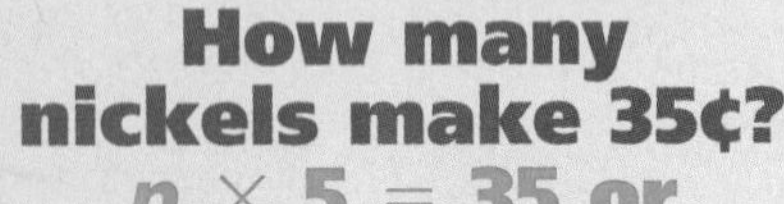

**$n \times 5 = 35$ or $35 \div 5 = 7$**

Do You Remember?

## Try It!

Find the total value. Write the amount in two ways.

1. 4 dimes and 12 pennies
2. 3 quarters and 7 nickels
3. 3 nickels and 6 dimes
4. a quarter, a dime, and 4 nickels
5. 2 dollars, 1 quarter, 8 pennies, and 3 dimes

Find the missing factor. Think of dimes or nickels.

6. $5 \times n = 15$
7. $10 \times k = 70$
8. $c \times 5 = 30$
9. $r \times 10 = 90$
10. $5 \times f = 50$
11. $w \times 10 = 40$

### Think About It

12. Look again at Exercise 4. Think of trading. How could you have the same amount of money but fewer coins? Explain.

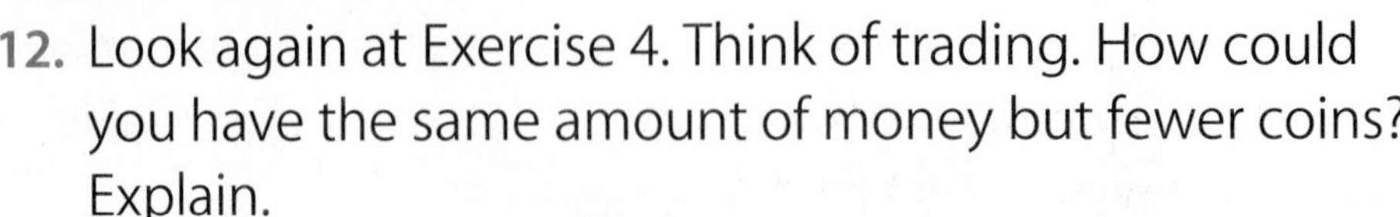

# Count Your Change

## Activity 1 Making Change

**With Your Partner** Suppose you work at the school store. Someone pays more than an item costs. You need to count out change. Count from the cost to the amount paid.

1. Your partner buys the item shown and gives you $1.00. Count out the change. What is the total amount of change?

2. Your partner buys an item for $1.09 and gives you $1.25. Which three coins would you give in change? How would you count?

3. How would you make change from $1.00 for each of these amounts?

   81¢ 64¢ 27¢

4. Tell how you would make change from a $10 bill for these amounts.

   $7.75 $9.01 $3.64

*In Your Journal* *Suppose you don't have quarters, but you have plenty of dimes. How would you count differently for question 1?*

Exercises and Problems

# Treasured Coins

Imagine that your class collects coins. You are buying some supplies for your collection. Use play money to help you answer each question. Use as few coins as possible.

Rubbing Alcohol $0.79

**1** **You buy a toothbrush to clean your coins. What coins and bills should you get back from $5.00?**

**2** **You buy 2 sticks of wax to make rubbings of your coins. You give the clerk a $5 bill. What should your change be?**

**3** **What is the total cost of the magnifying glass and the rubbing alcohol?**

$1.89

**4** **You buy the items in Exercise 3. You pay $2.75. What coins should you get back?**

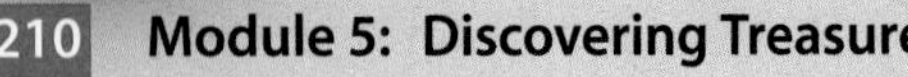

$0.10

5 You buy two pieces of paper and two sticks of wax. You pay $2.50. What coins should you get back?

6 You use $10.00 to pay for the book and pencil. How much change should you get?

2 for $1.29

7 You use $10.05 to pay for the items in Exercise 6. Do you think you will get any coins back? Explain.

$ 5.95

How To Show Coins

8 Choose three items and find the total cost.

9 For Exercise 8, tell what coins and bills you would use to pay with exact change.

10 You have two $1 bills. Find an item you could buy to get three coins in change. Explain your answer.

# Letters for Numbers

*Draw a clock with hands. Use Roman numerals for numbers. Have your classmates read the time on your clock.*

This silver bar was on a Spanish ship that sank in 1622. Like many sunken treasures, it has capital letters that look like a code. Can you figure out how to read the letters?

## Activity 1 Breaking the Code

### With Your Group

1. This clock uses **Roman numerals.** What number does each letter at the right stand for?

I V X

2. You can arrange Roman numerals to make other numbers. Why do you think the order is important?

XI **means 10 + 1, or 11.**
IX **means 10 − 1, or 9.**

3. What other Roman numerals on the clock use addition? Which use subtraction?

**4** Look for a pattern in the chart. Write Roman numerals for 90 and 900.

| | | | | | | | |
|---|---|---|---|---|---|---|---|
| 4 | IV | 5 | V | 9 | IX | 10 | X |
| 40 | XL | 50 | L | 90 | | 100 | C |
| 400 | CD | 500 | D | 900 | | 1,000 | M |

*The Roman numeral for 60 is LX. Compare this to the numeral for 40. How are they alike? How are they different?*

**5** Roman numerals can show larger values. Look at the example below. Change the Roman numerals below into standard years.

MDCLIV

**1,000 + 600 + 50 + 4 = 1,654**

**MMCV** **MCIX** **MDLII**

## Try It!

Write the number in standard form. Look for patterns.

1. XX 2. VII 3. XXVII 4. II 5. CXXX 6. CXXXII

Write the number of cents.

7. $\frac{1}{10}$ of a dollar
8. $\frac{1}{4}$ of a dollar
9. $\frac{1}{3}$ of 9 nickels
10. $\frac{1}{2}$ of 2 dimes

**Think About It**

11. The Roman system had no zero. Do you think it is easier or harder than our number system? Explain your answer in writing.

Do You Remember?

## Cumulative Review

# Treasure Measures

*For 25 years, a treasure hunter named Mel Fisher searched the Florida coast for a sunken ship called the* Atocha. *When he discovered the ship, Fisher found a treasure worth millions of dollars. Some of that treasure is shown here. Use the picture to answer the questions.*

**1** What fraction of the items in the grid are gold coins?

**2** What fraction of the items in the grid are green gems?

36 in.

**3** Assume that the grid is a square. What is its perimeter?

**4** About how long is one side of a small square of the grid?

**5** One jug holds 25 gal of water. How many quarts does one jug hold?

# Check Your Math Power

6. Describe the two starfish using one of these words: They are ___?___.
symmetric
congruent
similar

7. How many lines of symmetry does the design on the gold plate have?

8. Each air tank holds 45 min of air. How long can the diver stay below? Write your answer in hours.

9. Describe how you could draw a third starfish congruent to the smaller starfish.

10. How might the items in the grid be rearranged so that each grid square holds $\frac{1}{9}$ of the total number of items? Explain.

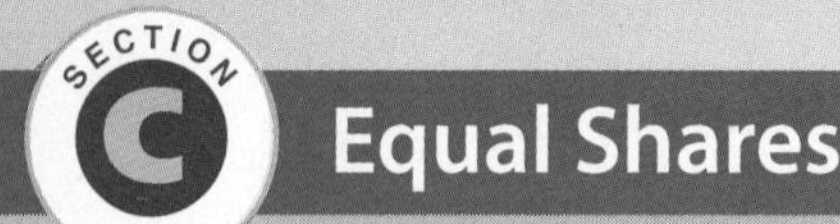

SECTION C Equal Shares

# LESSON 6 Tiny Treasures

LITERATURE

*A young Chinese woman fixes a bird's broken foot. To thank her, the bird drops a watermelon seed into the woman's lap.*

Since it was only a watermelon seed, she threw it into the courtyard. But the next spring, the seed grew into a vine and by summertime there was a big watermelon.

One day, she invited many relatives and friends to celebrate her birthday. At the end of the meal, she took the ripened melon from her garden to share with her guests. But when she opened it, everyone was astonished—the melon was filled with seeds of gold!

From "The Reward from a Sparrow" in *Chinese Folk Tales*, by Louise and Yuan-Hsi Kuo

## ACTIVITY 1 Sharing Seeds

**With Your Group** Suppose the woman shares her gold seeds. You can use counters to show how she would share them among her friends.

1. Three friends share 45 gold seeds. About how many will each friend get? Guess the answer.
2. Use a counter for each seed. Decide how to share them. How many seeds will each friend get?
3. Use counters to find out how five friends could share each amount fairly. Decide what to do with any leftovers.

   **a.** 34 seeds  **b.** 63 seeds  **c.** 87 seeds

**What You'll Need**

- *counters*

*Draw some treasure you might find. Show how to share it with two friends.*

**What You'll Need**

- *base ten blocks*

# Activity 2 Exploring Division

**With Your Class** You can practice sharing with base ten blocks. Suppose you want to share 53 treasures among 4 people. Do you think each person will get more or less than 10?

1. **How can you show 53 blocks with base ten blocks?**

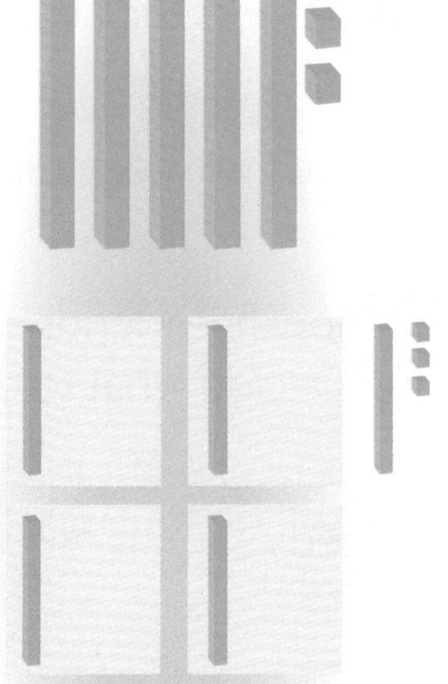

2. **Which will you share first, the tens or the ones? Why? What can you do with the leftover ten?**

3. **How many tens and ones does each person get? Are there any left?**

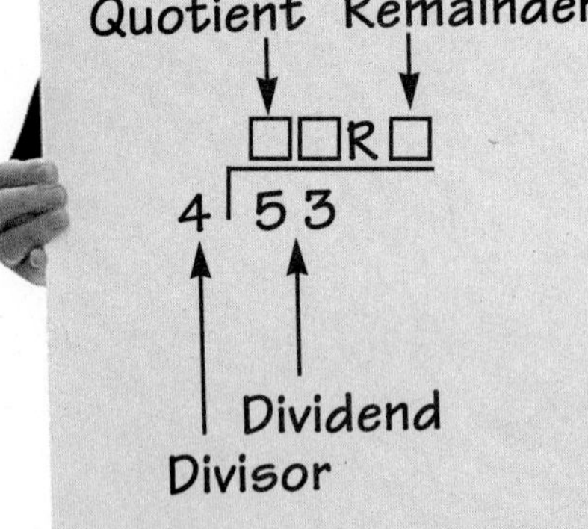


4. **Record the question as division. The quotient is the number of treasures each person gets. The remainder is the number of treasures left.**

*Use base ten blocks to show how 41 pieces of treasure can be shared among 3 people.*

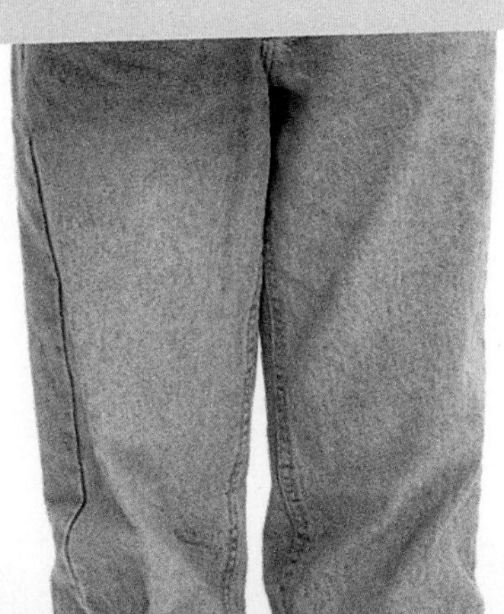

## With Your Partner

**5** Decide whether the quotient will be more or less than ten. Then divide using base ten blocks. Record the quotient and remainder.

✔ **Self-Check** *Use multiplication and addition to check your answers. Are they correct?*

a. **74 ÷ 3** b. **74 ÷ 9** c. **148 ÷ 6**

**6** Discuss your results with other students. Do you see any patterns?

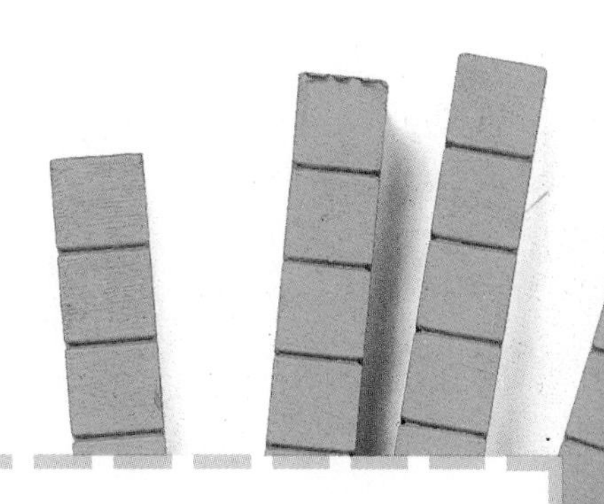

## Try It!

Decide whether each quotient will be greater or less than ten. Then divide. Use base ten blocks.

| | | | |
|---|---|---|---|
| 1. $5\overline{)94}$ | 2. $3\overline{)128}$ | 3. $7\overline{)64}$ | 4. $4\overline{)72}$ |
| 5. $6\overline{)29}$ | 6. $9\overline{)137}$ | 7. $2\overline{)85}$ | 8. $8\overline{)110}$ |

Write >, <, or =.

9. $4 \times 5$ ● $3 \times 6$

10. $6 \times 9$ ● $7 \times 8$

11. $3 \times 9$ ● $5 \times 5$

12. $10 \times 8$ ● $4 \times 20$

### Think About It

13. Can a remainder be greater than the divisor? Can it be greater than the quotient? Explain in writing.

# Treasure Stories

**What You'll Need**

- *base ten blocks*

## Activity 1 How Do You Record?

**With Your Partner** A brother and sister have 79 pieces of treasure. Suppose they share fairly.

1. Estimate whether each person will get more than 10 pieces.

2. You need to divide 79 by 2. Here's one way to start recording the answer. After you subtract the tens, how many are left? Trade the extra tens for ones.

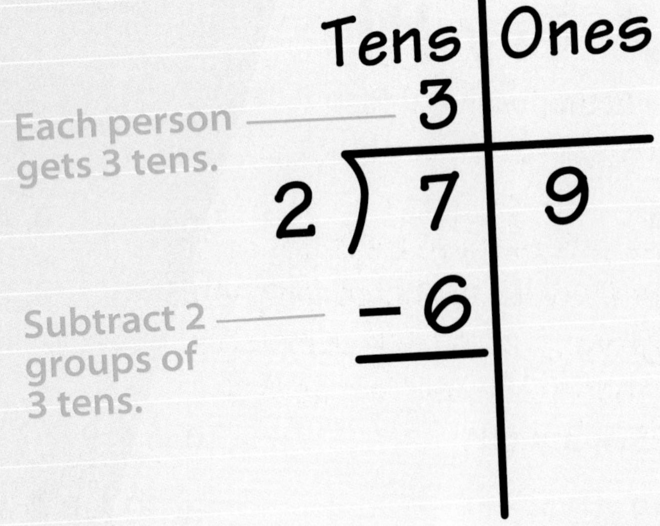

3. How many ones do you have now? How can you record sharing the ones?

4. What do you think you should do with any leftovers? How would you record leftovers?

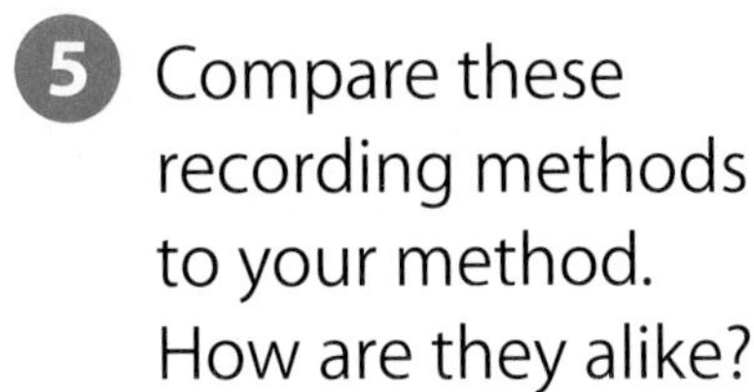

**5** Compare these recording methods to your method. How are they alike?

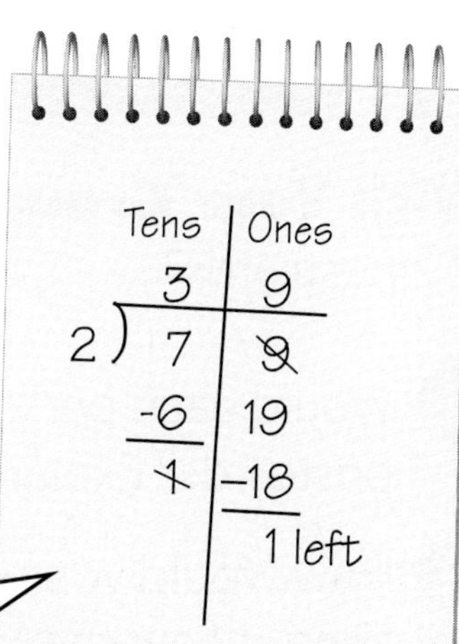


*Harvey's way*

I traded 1 ten for 10 ones. I put all the ones in the ones' column.

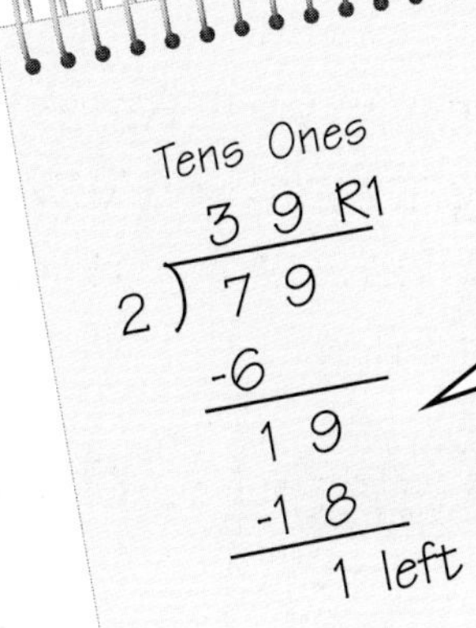


I wrote the number of ones beside the tens I had left. Then I shared all 19 ones.

*Miwa's way*

**6** Choose one of these treasures or one of your own. If you shared fairly with your group, would each person get more than 10 pieces? Divide and record your work.

68 comic books

83 rocks

*In Your Journal* *Suppose two friends find 48 stickers. Use your own way to record how they would share them fairly.*

*You can use base ten blocks to show 352.*

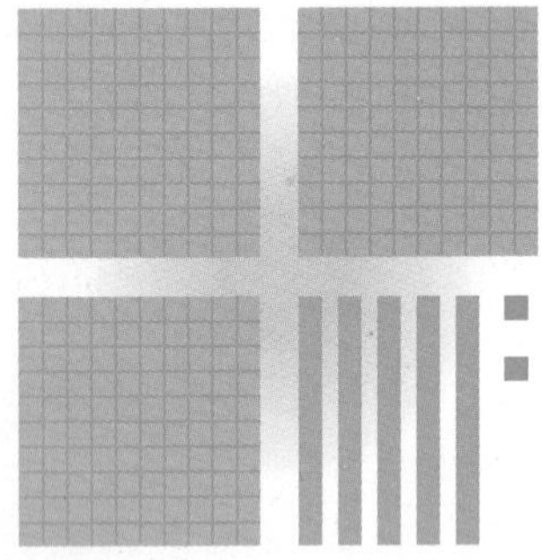

## Activity 2 Hundreds of Treasures

**With Your Group** How could 2 people share 352 postcards?

1. Would each person get more than 100 postcards? Explain your answer.
2. How would you record sharing hundreds? Record how they should share this treasure fairly.

## Try It!

Divide. Write the quotient and remainder. Look for patterns.

1. $2\overline{)55}$
2. $2\overline{)555}$
3. $4\overline{)39}$
4. $4\overline{)390}$
5. $6\overline{)72}$
6. $6\overline{)720}$
7. $9\overline{)74}$
8. $9\overline{)743}$

Find each amount. Look for patterns.

9. $\frac{1}{2}$ of 480
10. $\frac{1}{4}$ of 480
11. $\frac{1}{3}$ of 960
12. $\frac{1}{6}$ of 960

**Think About It**

13. How can you predict the number of digits in a quotient?

# Estimate First

When you divide, try to estimate first. A quick way to estimate is to use numbers that divide easily. These are called **compatible numbers.**

## Activity 1 Compatible Numbers

### With Your Partner

1. Suppose 6 students share 198 toy cars equally. About how many does each student get? Use 180 instead of 198 since 180 divides easily by 6.

$$6\overline{)198} \rightarrow 6\overline{)180}$$

2. For the exercises below, change 198 to a number that is easier to divide. Use the numbers at the right. Estimate your quotient.

a. $9\overline{)198}$ b. $7\overline{)198}$

c. $5\overline{)198}$ d. $8\overline{)198}$

| 160 | 180 |
|---|---|
| 200 | 210 |

3. Find the exact quotients for question 2. Were your estimates high or low? Explain.

*How are the exercises in question 2 alike? How are they different?*

## ACTIVITY 2 Your Treasure

### With Your Partner

Treasure can be old coins or photographs. You can use division to share treasures or to make equal groups. Choose five questions to answer.

1. You buy baseball cards in packages of 8. How many packages do you buy to get 96 cards?

2. You find 99 old coins. Arrange them in groups of 3. How many groups can you make?

3. A can contains 358 old coins. How can two people share the coins equally?

4. A treasure hunt lasted 44 days. How many weeks and days was that?

5. You find 156 photos. If 4 photos fit on one page of an album, how many pages do you need?

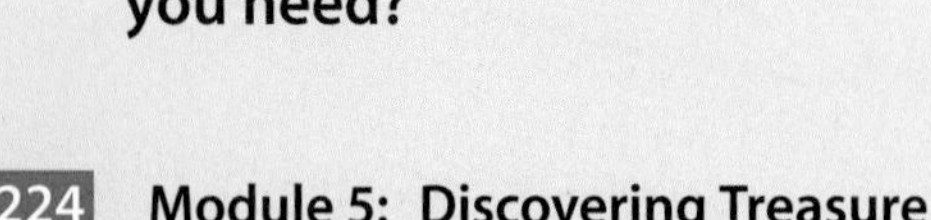

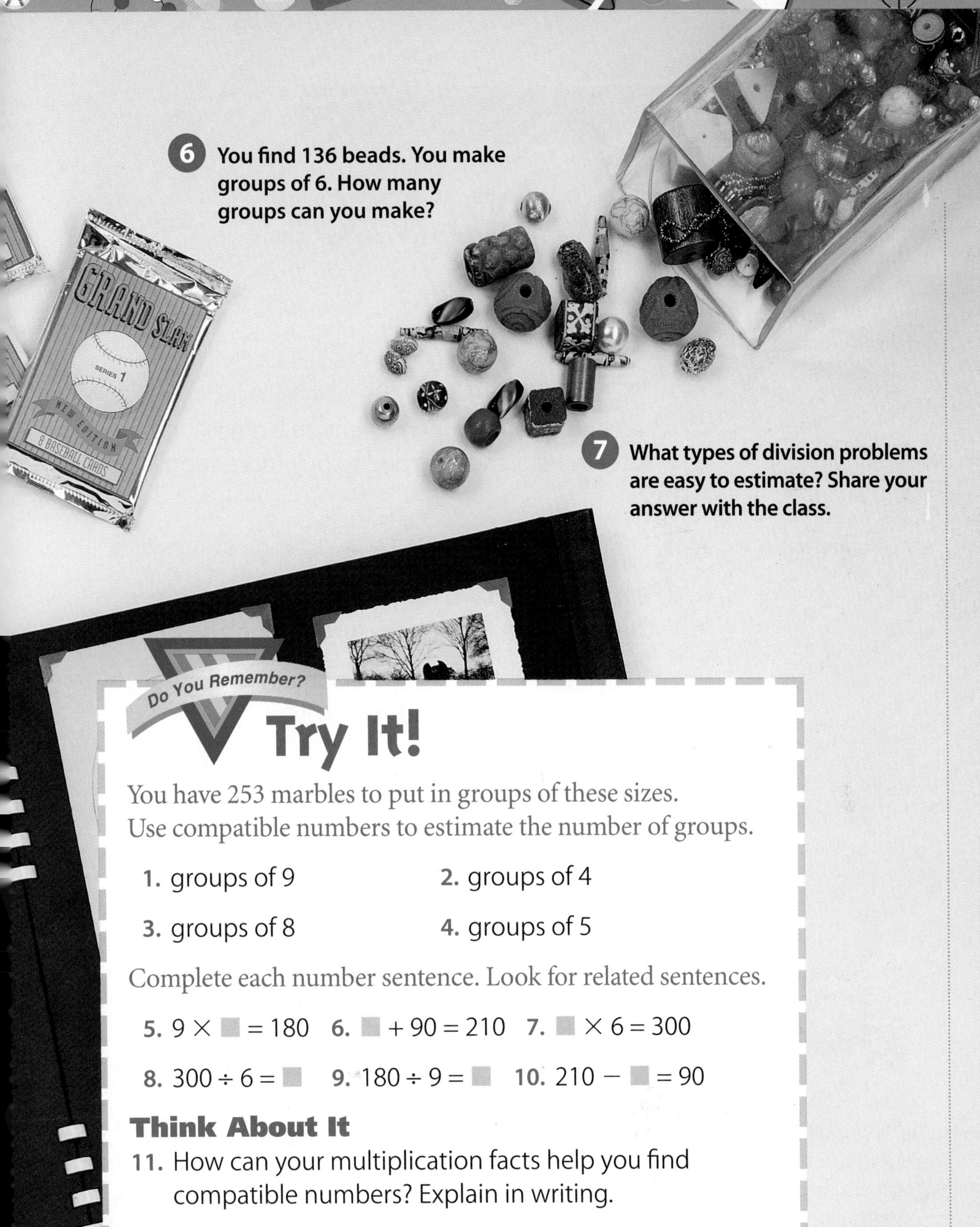


6 You find 136 beads. You make groups of 6. How many groups can you make?

7 What types of division problems are easy to estimate? Share your answer with the class.

Do You Remember?

## Try It!

You have 253 marbles to put in groups of these sizes. Use compatible numbers to estimate the number of groups.

1. groups of 9
2. groups of 4
3. groups of 8
4. groups of 5

Complete each number sentence. Look for related sentences.

5. 9 × ▢ = 180
6. ▢ + 90 = 210
7. ▢ × 6 = 300
8. 300 ÷ 6 = ▢
9. 180 ÷ 9 = ▢
10. 210 − ▢ = 90

### Think About It

11. How can your multiplication facts help you find compatible numbers? Explain in writing.

## Averages and Logic

# Digging for Dinos

**What You'll Need**

- *counters*

Four treasure hunters went on a dinosaur dig. After the dig, they needed to buy more supplies.

## Activity 1 Averaging Expenses

**With Your Group** Use counters to answer the questions. Read the pictograph and chart.

1. How much did each person pay for food? Show this data with counters.
2. Move some counters to make all four stacks the same height. How many dollars does each equal stack show? This is the **average** amount paid for food.

*In Your Journal* *If you had to predict, what do you think the answer to question 2 would be? Solve the problem and check your estimate.*

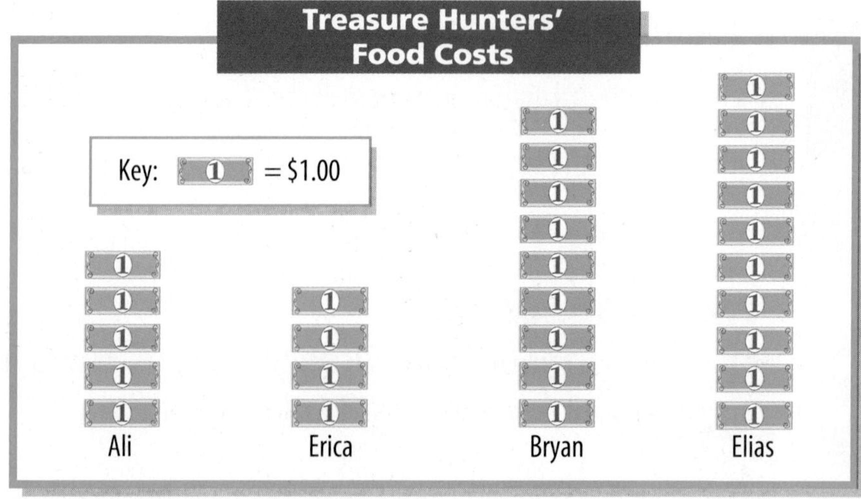

3. The chart shows expenses for digging supplies. Use counters to stand for the amounts.

4. Move counters to make four equal rows or stacks. What is the average of \$7, \$10, \$2, and \$5?

5. Is the average always between the highest and lowest number? Explain your answer.

*In Your Journal* Do you think the average is always a whole number? Why or why not?

What You'll Need

- *paper strips*
- *centimeter ruler*
- *tape*
- *scissors*

# ACTIVITY 2 Unfolding Averages

**With Your Partner** About how long would it take you to find 100 bones at a dinosaur dig? To start, find the average number of bones you could collect in one day.

Dinosaur Bones Found

| | |
|---|---|
| Day 1 | 19 |
| Day 2 | 27 |

1 **Take a strip of paper for each day. On each strip, mark off 1 cm for every bone found that day. Cut to the marked length.**

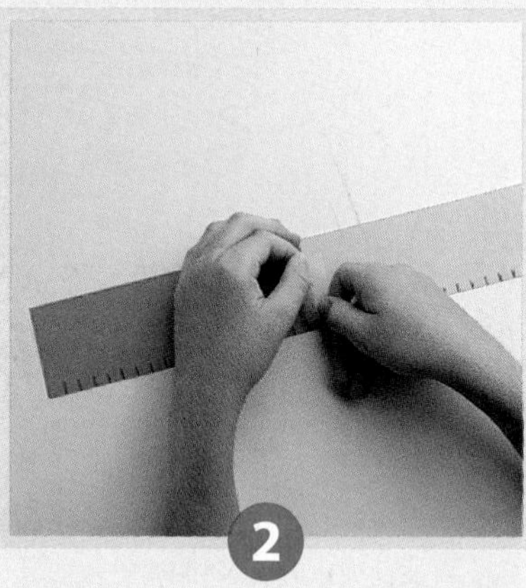

2 **Tape the strips for the two days together without overlapping them. Fold the strips to make two equal parts.**

3 Unfold the strips. Count the centimeters from each end to the crease. This is the average number of bones found each day.

4 Can this average help you predict how many days it will take to find 100 bones? Explain.

*How is folding paper like division?*

Treasure Hunter's Diary

| | Teeth | Eggshells |
|---|---|---|
| Day 1 | 2 | 3 |
| Day 2 | 11 | 10 |
| Day 3 | 9 | 11 |
| Day 4 | 14 | 4 |

*Draw a pictograph that shows the number of teeth found each day. How can you estimate the average by looking at the pictograph?*

5 Suppose you discover this treasure hunter's diary. What is the average number of teeth found each day?

6 Find the average number of eggshells found each day.

## Try It!

Use counters or paper strips to find the average.

1. 6, 10 2. 13, 17 3. \$21, \$35 4. 3, 7, 9, 1

5. 9, 11, 2, 6 6. 7¢, 12¢, 15¢, 10¢

Estimate each quotient. If the estimate is 100 or greater, find the exact quotient and remainder.

7. 570 ÷ 8 8. 923 ÷ 4 9. 471 ÷ 3 10. 609 ÷ 7

**Think About It**

11. Suppose you know the total length of four paper strips. Is that enough information to find the average length? Explain.

# A Step Back in Time

*You can use a calculator, drawings, counters, or paper strips to help you find the average.*

## ACTIVITY 1 Average Footprints

**With Your Partner** Answer these questions about duckbill dinosaur footprints and averages.

1. Look at the data on the front footprints. Can the average of these widths be more than 10 in.? How do you know?

| Front Footprints | | Back Footprints | |
|---|---|---|---|
| Length | Width | Length | Width |
| 5 in. | 8 in. | 18 in. | 24 in. |
| 6 in. | 7 in. | 27 in. | 25 in. |
| 5 in. | 8 in. | 23 in. | 28 in. |
| 6 in. | 10 in. | 24 in. | 24 in. |
| 6 in. | 9 in. | 28 in. | 29 in. |
| 5 in. | 6 in. | | |

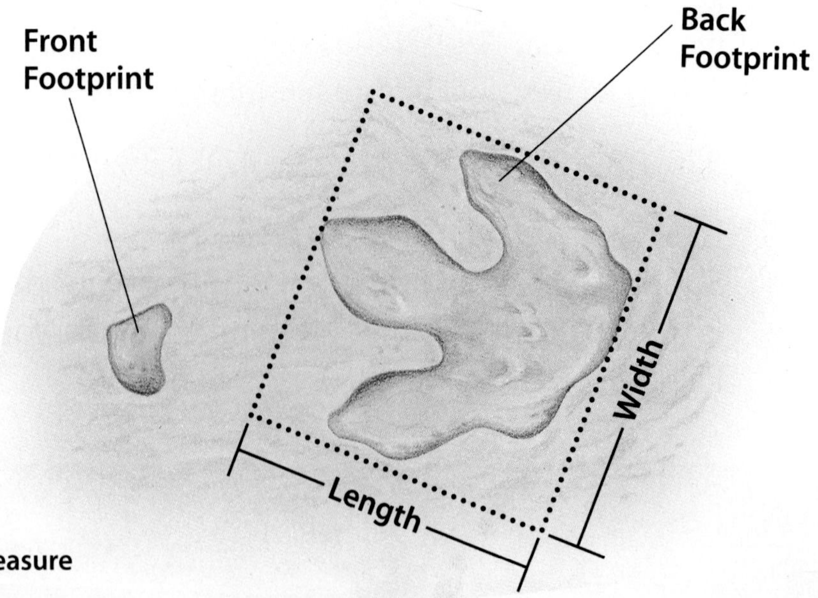

**2** Find the average length of the duckbill's front footprints. Next, find the average width of the front footprints. Record your work. Use the method shown below or your own.

**3** What is the average length of the duckbill's back footprints? Find the average width of the back footprints, too.

**4** For the back footprints, is the length or width usually greater? Explain your answer.

ACTIVITY OPTION

*Measure the footprint lengths of four classmates. Find the average length of the footprints.*

*"I added the footprint lengths. Then I divided by the total number of lengths."*

Do You Remember?

## Try It!

Find the average. Explain any short cuts you use.

1. 11, 11, 11
2. $18, $19, $20
3. 22, 33, 26
4. 10, 30, 50, 70
5. 96, 114
6. 23, 10, 17, 25, 15

Write the missing number so the average is 4.

7. 3, ■
8. 6, ■
9. 7, 2, ■
10. 8, 1, 2, ■

### Think About It

11. Look at your answer to Exercise 2. Is the average of three consecutive numbers always the middle number? Explain.

# Treasure Trek

What You'll Need
- *gameboard*
- *cube labeled 1–6*
- *game pieces*

*Use a calculator to check your answer. If the first number to the right of the decimal point is five or more, round up. If it is less than five, round down.*

## ACTIVITY 1 On Dinosaur Island

**With Your Group** You are hunting treasure on the island. Collect treasure by solving problems. Play in groups of two to four.

1. **Start the Game** Roll the cube. Move a game piece that many spaces.
2. **Solve Problems** If you land on a treasure space, divide the number of treasures by the number you rolled. Find the answer to the nearest whole number.

3 **Find Averages** If you land on a gold space, solve the problem.

4 **Score Points** For each answer you get correct, you receive that number of points to collect.

5 **Finish the Game** Play ends when one person reaches Finish. The highest score wins.

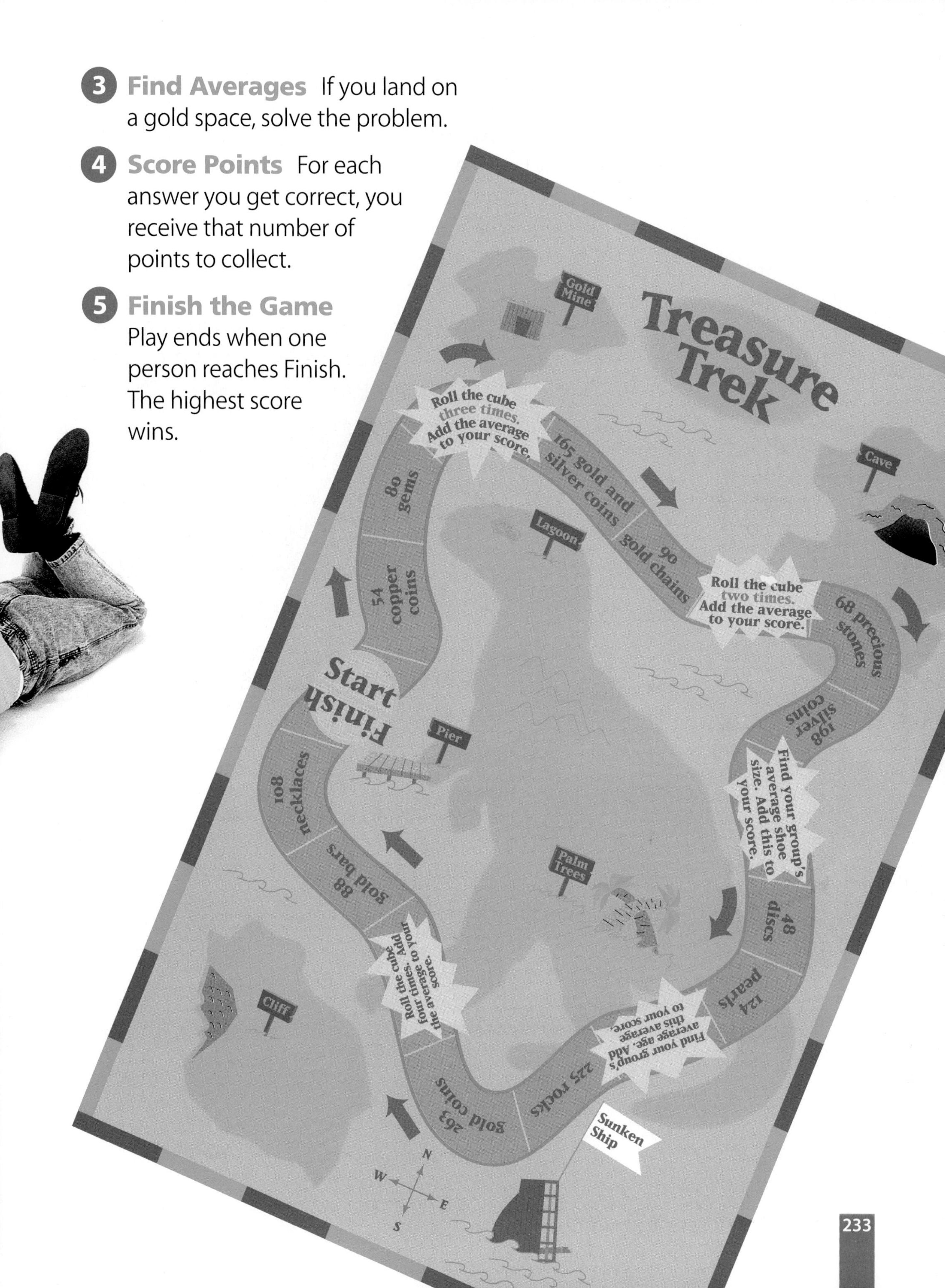

## ACTIVITY 2 A Logical Hunt

**With Your Partner** Look at the map of the Willow Creek area in Montana. At one site, 4,500 bones from 27 dinosaurs were found. Can you find this site from reading the clues below?

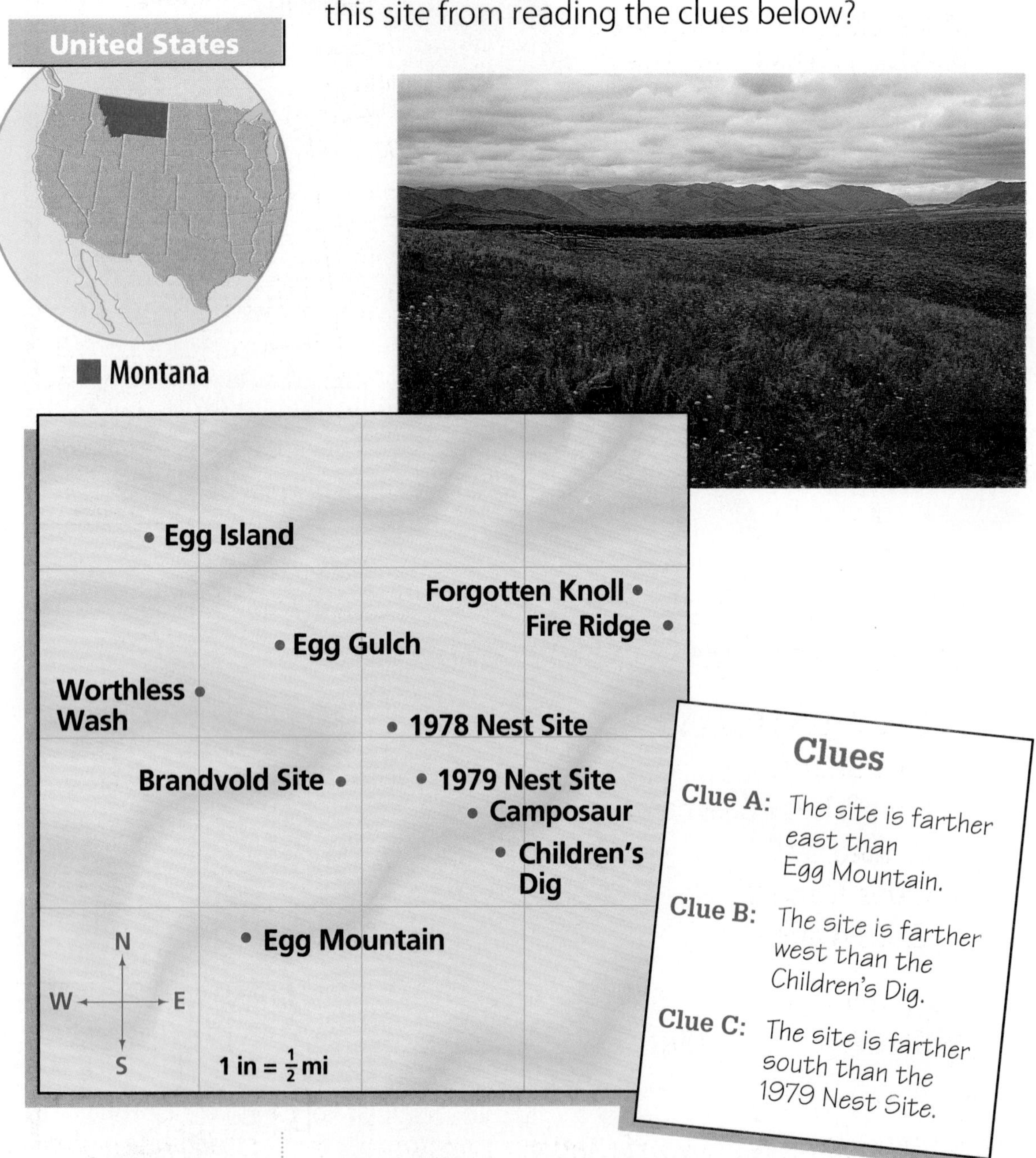


1. What sites can you rule out after reading clue A?

2. Use a chart or your own method to find the site.

3. Look at the map and choose a different site.

4. Write clues for finding the site. Make sure the clues give enough information, but not too much.

5. Trade papers with your partner. Try to solve each other's problem.

## Try It!

Which numbers below fit the given clues?

482 126 583 81 657 217 936 920

1. Clue A: Less than 500
2. Clue B: Odd
3. Clue C: Has no remainder when divided by 9
4. Clues A and B
5. Clues B and C
6. Clues A and C
7. Clues A, B, and C

Which numbers do not fit these clues?

8. Clue A
9. Clue B
10. Clue C

**Think About It**

11. Write about how you found your answer to Exercise 7.

**Self-Check** *Try solving your problem with the clues you wrote. Do they lead you to the site you chose?*

Do You Remember? **Cumulative Review**

# Looking Back

Choose the best answer. Write *a, b, c,* or *d* for each question.

**Use the coordinate grid to answer Exercises 1–4.**

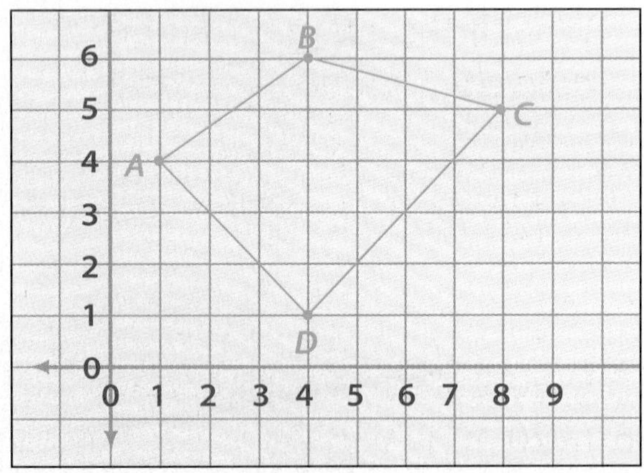


1. What is the ordered pair for point *A*?
   a. (4, 1) b. (1, 4)
   c. (4, 6) d. none of these

2. Name an ordered pair that stands for a point on Figure *ABCD*.
   a. (2, 4) b. (6, 3)
   c. (5, 4) d. none of these

3. Segments *AD* and *CD* are
   a. parallel b. perpendicular
   c. congruent d. none of these

4. Name an ordered pair that stands for a point inside *ABCD*.
   a. (5, 2) b. (6, 3)
   c. (6, 4) d. all of these

**For Exercises 5–7, use these coins.**

5. What amount do the coins show?
   a. $1.76 b. 89¢
   c. $.54 d. $2.14

6. Three people share this amount of money. About how much does each person get?
   a. 90¢ b. 45¢
   c. 30¢ d. 9¢

7. Which shows the same amount as the coins above?
   a. 4 quarters, 9 pennies
   b. 8 dimes, 1 nickel
   c. 17 nickels, 4 pennies
   d. 10 quarters

8. You have \$17.50. You buy three baseball cards for \$3.59 each. How much money is left?
   a. one \$5 bill, two quarters
   b. one \$10 bill, two \$1 bills
   c. four \$1 bills, two quarters
   d. none of these

9. If you buy two cards for \$3.59 each, what change should you get back from \$10.00?
   a. 1 penny, 4 dimes, 3 dollars
   b. 2 pennies, 3 quarters, 2 dollars
   c. 2 pennies, 1 nickel, 2 quarters, 2 dollars
   d. none of these

10. A group of 8 students shares 96 beads fairly. Which number sentence shows how many students are in the group?
    a. $96 \div 8$  b. $8 \div 96$
    c. $96 + 8$  d. $96 - 8$

11. You and three friends share 22 slices of pizza equally. How many slices does each friend get?
    a. between 6 and 7
    b. between 5 and 6
    c. between 7 and 8
    d. more than 8

12. Sixty is the average of 40 and *n*?
    a. 50  b. 80
    c. 2  d. none of these

**Use the chart to answer Exercises 13–14.**

**Treasures Found in a Sunken Ship**

| | Week 1 | Week 2 | Week 3 |
|---|---|---|---|
| Silver bars | 15 | 20 | 37 |
| Gold coins | 56 | 72 | 112 |

13. What is the average number of silver bars found each week?
    a. 65  b. 24
    c. 12  d. none of these

14. What is the average number of gold coins found each week?
    a. 72  b. 16
    c. 112  d. 80

## Check Your Math Power

15. Draw a shape similar to *ABCD* in Exercise 1. Make the sides twice as long. How are the sides and angles of the two shapes alike? How are they different?

16. Your friend has 60¢ in coins. None are pennies. What coins could your friend have? Make a chart to show as many possibilities as you can.

17. For Exercise 17, suppose you know the number of coins. Is this enough information to tell which coins your friend has? Explain your answer.

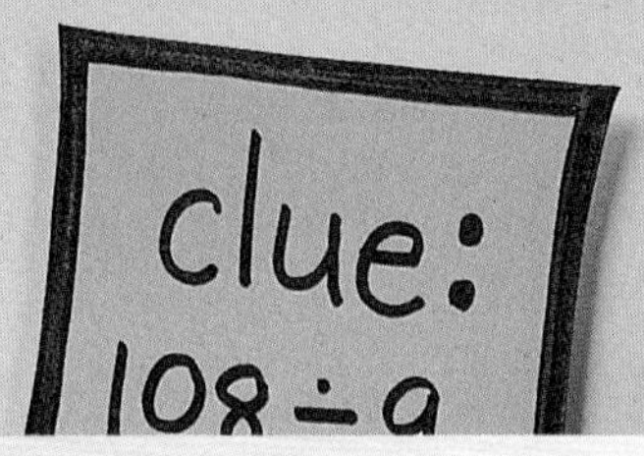

Treasure hunters need at least one key or clue to find a treasure. The Rosetta Stone was such a key. The stone carried a message in three languages. One was Egyptian hieroglyphics, which was a forgotten language. A man named Jean François Champollion looked for patterns in the letters of all three languages. He figured out what the Egyptian symbols stood for. It was like breaking a code! Some codes use math instead of letter patterns. In these investigations, you'll work with codes that use division and multiplication.

***This module shows some of the treasures you might find. Choose an investigation, and you may find more treasure.***

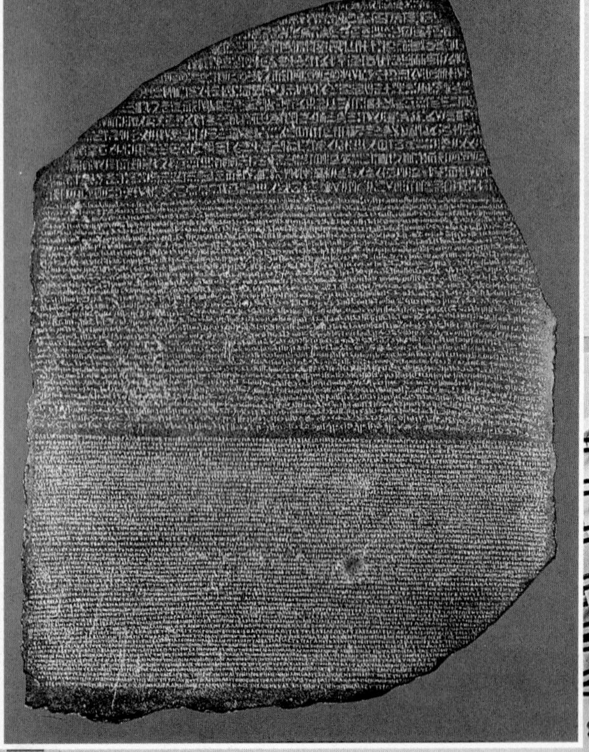

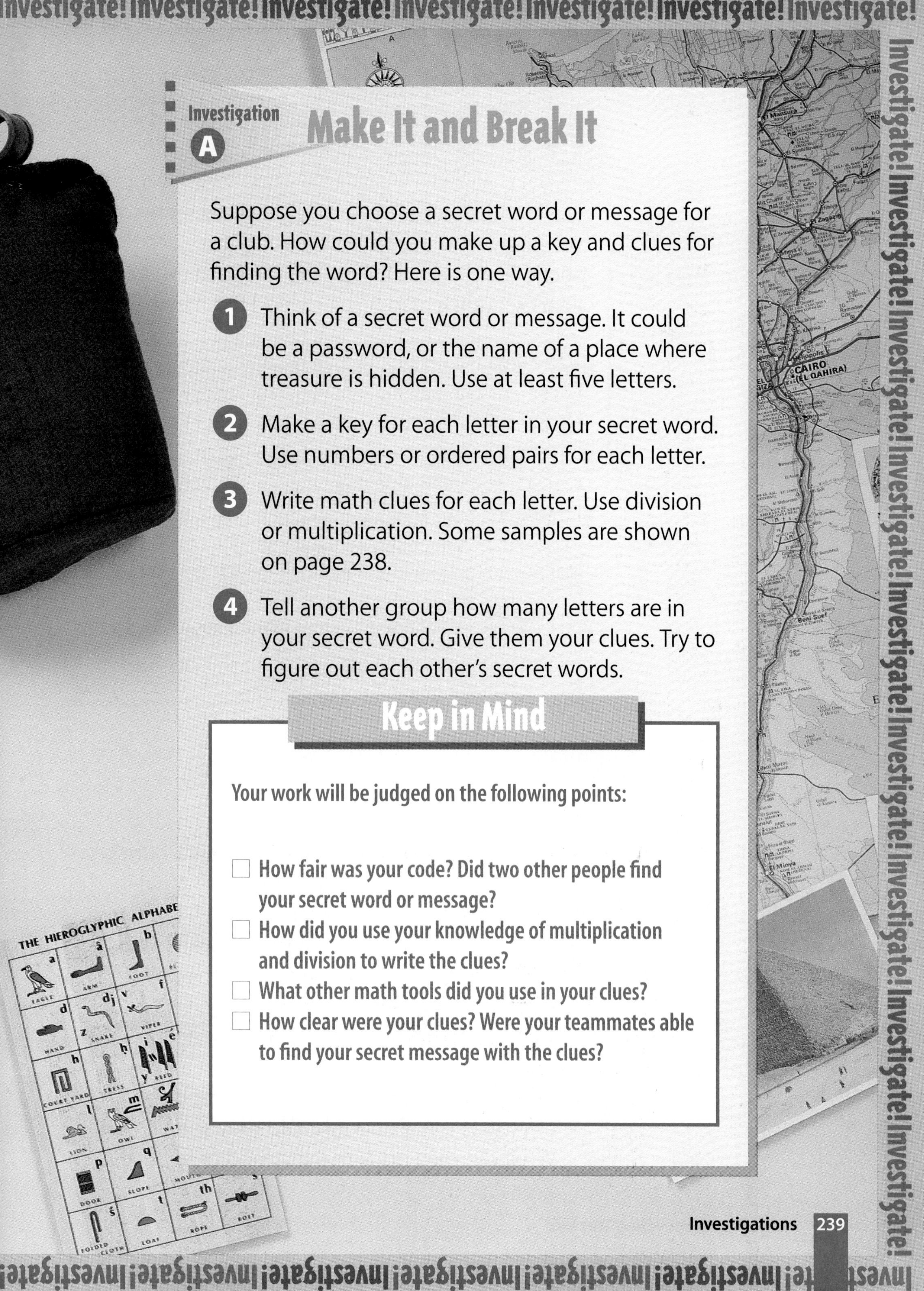

Investigation A

# Make It and Break It

Suppose you choose a secret word or message for a club. How could you make up a key and clues for finding the word? Here is one way.

1. Think of a secret word or message. It could be a password, or the name of a place where treasure is hidden. Use at least five letters.
2. Make a key for each letter in your secret word. Use numbers or ordered pairs for each letter.
3. Write math clues for each letter. Use division or multiplication. Some samples are shown on page 238.
4. Tell another group how many letters are in your secret word. Give them your clues. Try to figure out each other's secret words.

## Keep in Mind

Your work will be judged on the following points:

- ☐ How fair was your code? Did two other people find your secret word or message?
- ☐ How did you use your knowledge of multiplication and division to write the clues?
- ☐ What other math tools did you use in your clues?
- ☐ How clear were your clues? Were your teammates able to find your secret message with the clues?

Investigation B

## Secret Message

Math and logic can help you solve the secret message! Find the letters by using the clues in sections A, B, and D. Copy the letters in the circled spaces. Put them in order to read the message.

**Secret Message**
Fill in the blanks below.

M A T H ① ②
③ ④ ⑤ ⑥
⑦ ⑧
⑨ ⑩ ⑪ ⑫ ⑬ ⑭ ⑮ ⑯

**Clue 1** What item from the tomb is in the border?
_ ⑪ ⑧ _ ③ _ _

**Clue 2** What letter is at point (3, 1) of triangle *SKY*?
⑥

**Clue 3** Pay for ten pencils with four identical coins. What coins are they?
_ ⑭ ⑫ _ ⑦ _ ⑩ ②

**Clue 4** What doesn't belong in the dinosaur borders?
⑨ ⑤ _ _ ① ⑬ ⑮ _ _ ④ ⑯ _

Investigation C

## Exploring Treasures

How is exploring like planning a treasure hunt? Find out. Look for books about exploring a rain forest, Antarctica, or outer space.

- Choose a group of explorers who went on a trip. How much food and supplies did they take? How did they share what they had?
- **Computer Opportunity** On a word processor, write a report about how the explorers shared their supplies for at least three days. Was there enough? Did they share fairly? What did they do with extra food or supplies?

# Decimals in My World

They're everywhere around you! You see numbers like these every day on television, in newspapers, and in stores. These numbers have a special name. In this module you will learn how to use these numbers. You will also discover what they can tell you.

**Measures and Place Value**

**Tenths and Hundredths**

**Comparing Decimals**

**Add and Subtract Decimals**

# Get the Point

THERMOMETER
98.6
C F

1.06

4 cm = 1 km

## 1 Starting Point

Look at the numbers on this page. They have a point between the digits. These are **decimal points.** You might read a number as "two point thirty-eight." What does that number mean?

RADIO HIGHLIGHTS

| | | |
|---|---|---|
| M. | Sports | 88.3 |
| . | Talk | 107.5 |
| | Traffic | 93.7 |
| | News | 88.3 |
| | Public | 95.7 |
| | Rock | 103.5 |
| | Country | 105.5 |
| | Country | 83.7 |
| 12:00 P.M. | Soft Rock | 101.3 |
| 12:30 P.M. | Asian News | 107.7 |
| 1:30 P.M. | Soft Rock | |

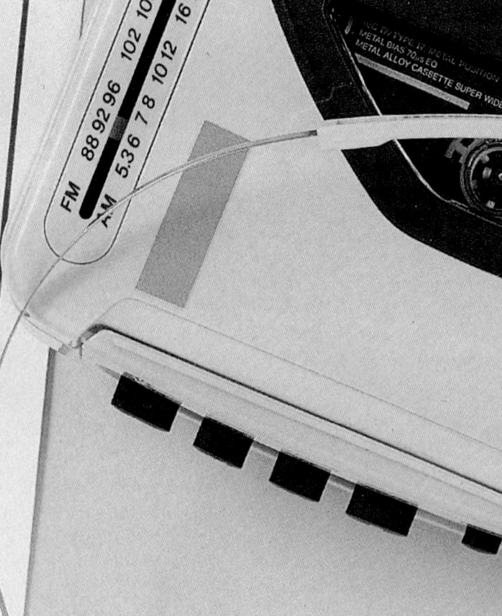


### Word Bank

- centimeter (cm)
- decimal
- decimeter (dm)
- kilometer (km)
- meter (m)

## 2 Scoring Points

Find as many examples as you can of numbers with decimal points. How are the examples you found alike? How are they different?

## 3 Measuring Points

Compare the examples you found. Which ones show measurements? How are the measurements related?

Investigate! Investigate! Investigate! Investigate! Investigate! Investigate! Investigate! Investigate! Investigate! Investigate! Investigate! Investigate! Investigate! Investigate!

### Investigations Preview

Use metric measures, place value, and decimals to predict how far an object will roll downhill. Then invent a new measuring unit.

**Rolling Downhill** (pages 270–271)

How far will a car roll downhill? Does a car roll farther if the hill becomes steeper? Make a model and find out.

**Invent a Measure** (pages 286–288)

Do you think you can improve on a measuring system? Use what you learn about place value and decimals to invent your own measuring unit.

Measures and Place Value

# Meet the Meter!

You have met the inch, foot, and yard. Now you will meet another unit of length, the **meter (m).** A meter is a little longer than a yard.

**What You'll Need**

- *adding machine tape 1 meter long*

## Activity 1 Meter Hunt

**With Your Group** You can use a meter strip to help you hunt for objects a meter long.

1. Look around the classroom for objects that are about 1 m long or 1 m wide. List the objects in your notebook.

2. Decide whether the object is a meter long, greater than a meter long, or less than a meter long. Add your estimates to the chart.

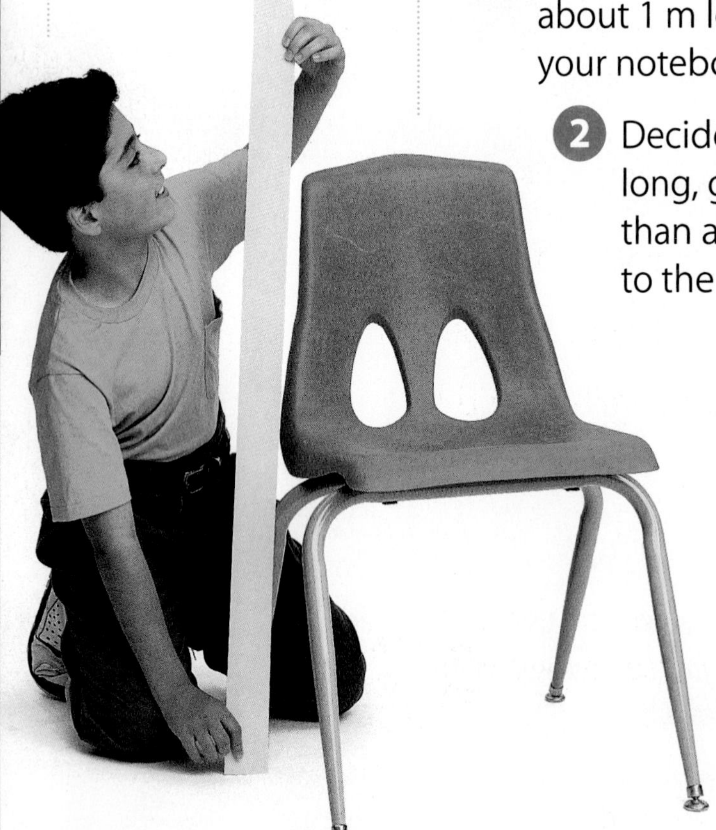

| Item | Length |
|---|---|
| height of chair | less than a meter |
| height of locker | greater than a meter |
| width of desk | less than a meter |

3. Have someone measure the objects with the meter strip. How do the measurements and estimates compare?

4. List five other objects. Trade lists with another group.

5. Estimate the length of each object in meters. Measure the object and compare the measurement with your estimate.

*To measure with your meter strip, line up one end of it with one end of what you want to measure. Then stretch out the meter strip to reach the other end.*

## Try It!

Estimate in meters.

1. your height
2. height of a door
3. length of a baseball bat
4. 2 yards of rope
5. length of your arm from shoulder to fingertip

Draw this shape ▭▭▭▭▭ and shade the fraction.

6. $\frac{1}{5}$ 7. $\frac{2}{5}$ 8. $\frac{1}{10}$ 9. $\frac{2}{10}$ 10. $\frac{3}{5}$

### Think About It

11. What everyday object can you use to help you remember the length of a meter?

**What You'll Need**
- *meter strip from Lesson 1*

## ACTIVITY 1 Smaller Is Better

**With Your Class** The meter strip can be divided into ten equal parts. Each part is called a **decimeter (dm).** What fraction of a meter is a decimeter?

**10 dm = 1 m**

1. Divide your meter strip into ten equal parts as shown.
2. Label the strip to show tenths of a meter.
   a. Which mark would be $\frac{5}{10}$ of a meter?
   b. How many decimeters is $\frac{7}{10}$ of a meter?
3. Measure your Meter Hunt items again. Record the lengths in tenths of a meter. Use the chart you used for the Meter Hunt.
4. Which measurement was closer to the length of the object? Explain.

*$\frac{1}{10}$ m = 1 dm*

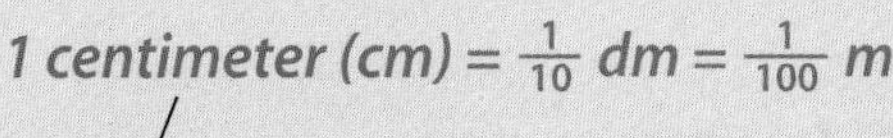


## ACTIVITY 2 A Closer Look

**With Your Group** A decimeter can also be divided into ten equal parts. Each part is called a **centimeter (cm).** What fraction of a decimeter is a centimeter?

**10 cm = 1 dm**

1. Divide the decimeter at one end of your meter strip into ten equal parts. Use the yellow strip on this page to help you.
2. Imagine you divided your whole meter strip into centimeters. How many centimeters would there be? Explain.

**■ cm = 1 m**

3. Measure the line segments. Write your measurement as a fraction of a meter.

**Measure the three horizontal segments. Are you surprised?**

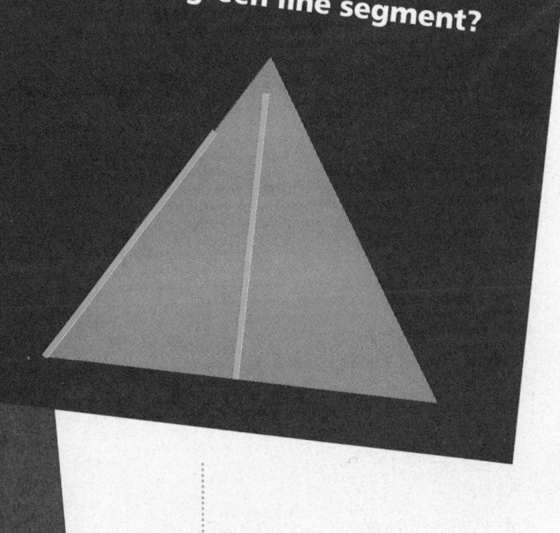


**What You'll Need**

- *meter strip*

*Did you estimate the lengths of the segments before you measured them? How do the measurements of the line segments compare?*

### What You'll Need

- *meter strip*

*Go on a centimeter survey at home too. Find items, measure them, and make a chart of centimeters at home.*

## ACTIVITY 3 Centimeter Survey

**With Your Group** Choose ten objects you find in your classroom. Then make a chart.

1. Measure each item. Work in any order you choose. Use the centimeter end of your meter strip. Record your measurement on the chart.
2. How would you write this measurement as a fraction of a decimeter? Record your answer on the chart.
3. Now try meters. Record your answer as a fraction of a meter.
4. Complete the chart for all ten objects.
5. Which unit worked best for each object?
6. Save your chart for Lesson 3.

| Item | Length in Centimeters | Length in Decimeters | Length in Meters |
|---|---|---|---|
| scissors | 13 cm | $1\frac{3}{10}$ dm | $\frac{13}{100}$ m |
| pencil | | | |

## ACTIVITY 4 Count a Kilometer

**With Your Class** The **kilometer (km)** is useful for measuring long distances.

**1 km = 1,000 m**

**What You'll Need**
- *meter strips*
- *tape*

1. What do you think measures about ten meters? Estimate first. Then tape meter strips together. Find something 10 m long.
2. Think about ten of the 10-m strips. Find something you think is 100 m long.
3. Now think of ten 100-m strips. How many meters long would that be? That's a kilometer!

Do You Remember?

## Try It!

Solve. Which exercises have fractions as answers?

1. 1 m = ▪ dm  2. $\frac{3}{100}$ m = ▪ cm  3. 24 cm = ▪ m
4. 5 dm= ▪ m  5. 20 cm = ▪ dm  6. 60 cm = ▪ m

Write as whole numbers or mixed numbers.

7. $\frac{15}{5}$  8. $\frac{12}{4}$  9. $\frac{4}{3}$  10. $\frac{7}{5}$  11. $\frac{9}{3}$

**Think About It**

12. Look at Exercises 1–6. Write a general rule. How can you tell when the new measure will be a number less than the original one?

LESSON 3

# Decimal Place

*Draw your own number line. Label the tenths as both fractions and decimals.*

In this lesson you'll find out why you can divide a meter into tenths and hundredths.

## ACTIVITY 1 New Neighbors

**With Your Group** Look for patterns.

| Hundreds | Tens | Ones | ? | ? |
|---|---|---|---|---|
| | | | | |

1. Look for a pattern from left to right. What should the place to the right of the ones' place be called? to the right of that place?

2. You know how to write tenths or hundredths as fractions. Now learn to write them as **decimals.** Use your calculator. For each step, write the answer the calculator gives.

   a. **Press 100 ÷ 10 =.**

   b. **Press ÷ 10 =** two more times.

   c. The last number is a decimal fraction. How do you write one tenth as a decimal?

   d. **Press ÷ 10 =** again. How do you write one hundredth as a decimal?

## ACTIVITY 2 Decimals and Meters

**With Your Group** You can use decimals to write tenths or hundredths of a meter.

**1.4 m** one and four tenths meter

**0.75 m** seventy-five hundredths meter

1. How many decimeters long is 1.4 m? How many centimeters long is 0.75 m? Use your meter strips to help you.

2. Read the following measurements aloud. Be sure to say "and" when you read the decimal point.

   **a.** 3.5 m  **b.** 6.7 m  **c.** 7.25 m  **d.** 2.50 m

3. Look again at the measurements you got when you measured classroom items on page 248.

   **a.** Make a new chart. Write the measures as decimals instead of fractions.

   **b.** Work together. Write some ways that you think will make decimals easier to work with than fractions.

**With Your Class** Present your group's thoughts to the class. How many ways did the class think of?

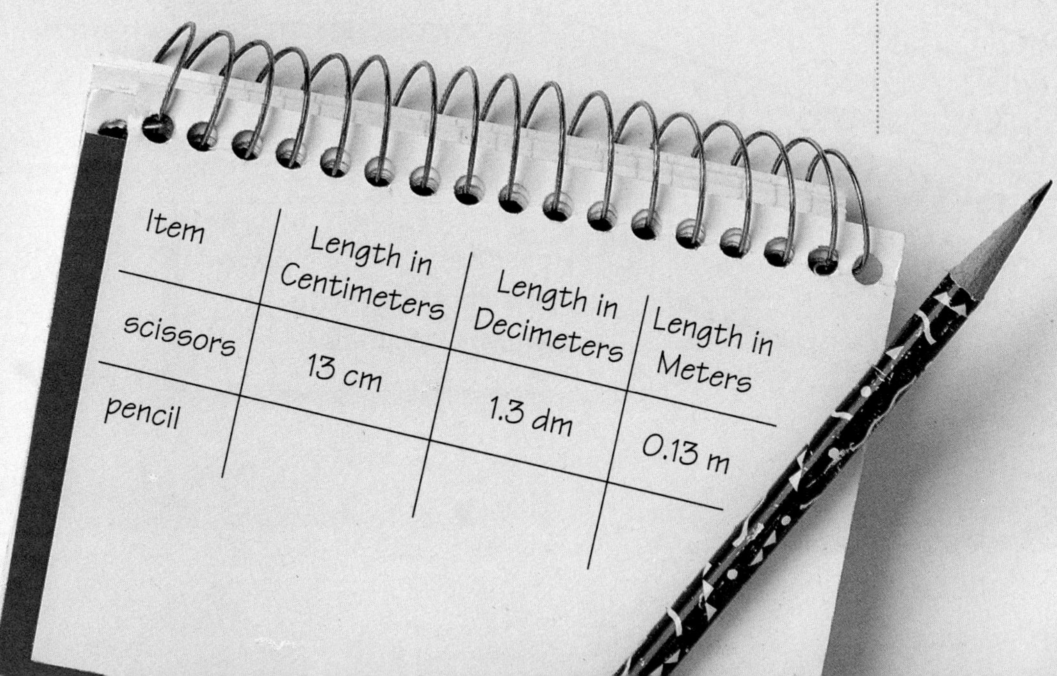

| Item | Length in Centimeters | Length in Decimeters | Length in Meters |
|---|---|---|---|
| scissors | 13 cm | 1.3 dm | 0.13 m |
| pencil | | | |

*Tell how a two-digit number can have a value less than one.*

## ACTIVITY 3 Point It Out!

**With Your Group** Now learn to put any decimal in a place-value chart.

| Tens | Ones | . | Tenths | Hundredths |
|---|---|---|---|---|
| | 7 | . | 9 | |
| | | . | | |
| | | . | | |

1. See how 7.9 is written in the place-value chart.

2. Make a place-value chart. Write 8.2 and 6.23 in it.
   a. Which number is greater? How do you know?
   b. How does using a place-value chart help?

number of states in the United States
price of a gallon of milk
one thousand, two hundred ten
your height in meters
two and six tenths
number of days in the year
number of buildings on your block

3. Make another place-value chart. Write the numbers shown in the notebook in your place-value chart.

4. How does making a place-value chart help you compare decimals?

## ACTIVITY 4 What's My Number?

**On Your Own** Solve the number puzzles. Put the digits in the right places.

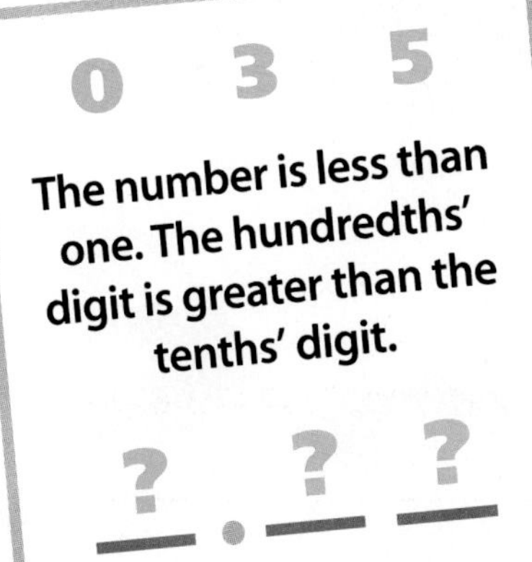


8 2 5

**The number is less than 50. The tens' digit is three less than the tenths' digit.**

? ? . ?

**With Your Partner**

Talk about how you solved the puzzles.

*Make up your own number puzzles for a classmate to solve.*

## Try It!

Are the measurements the same? If not, rewrite one of them.

1. $1\frac{3}{10}$ m and 1.03 m
2. 23 cm and 0.23 m
3. 4 dm and 0.04 m
4. $2\frac{3}{100}$ m and 2.3 m

Write fractions as decimals and decimals as fractions.

5. 0.6
6. 0.45
7. 0.63
8. 1.7
9. $\frac{3}{10}$
10. $\frac{24}{100}$
11. $1\frac{5}{10}$
12. $2\frac{3}{100}$

**Think About It**

13. How do the numbers in Exercises 5 and 9 compare?

# How Big, Really?

Copy the numbers from the notebook. For each question, place a decimal point in the measurement so the measurement makes sense.

1. How long is the guitar?
2. How wide are the sunglasses?
3. How long is the basketball court?
4. How far is it from one end of the court to the center?
5. How long is the line of shoes?

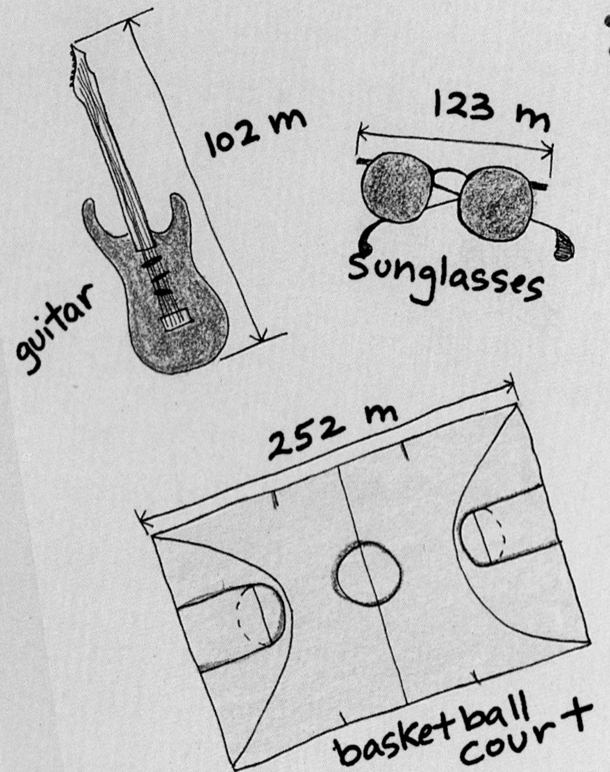

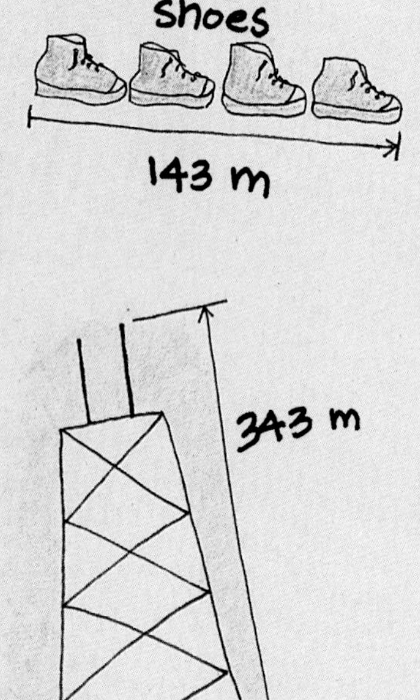

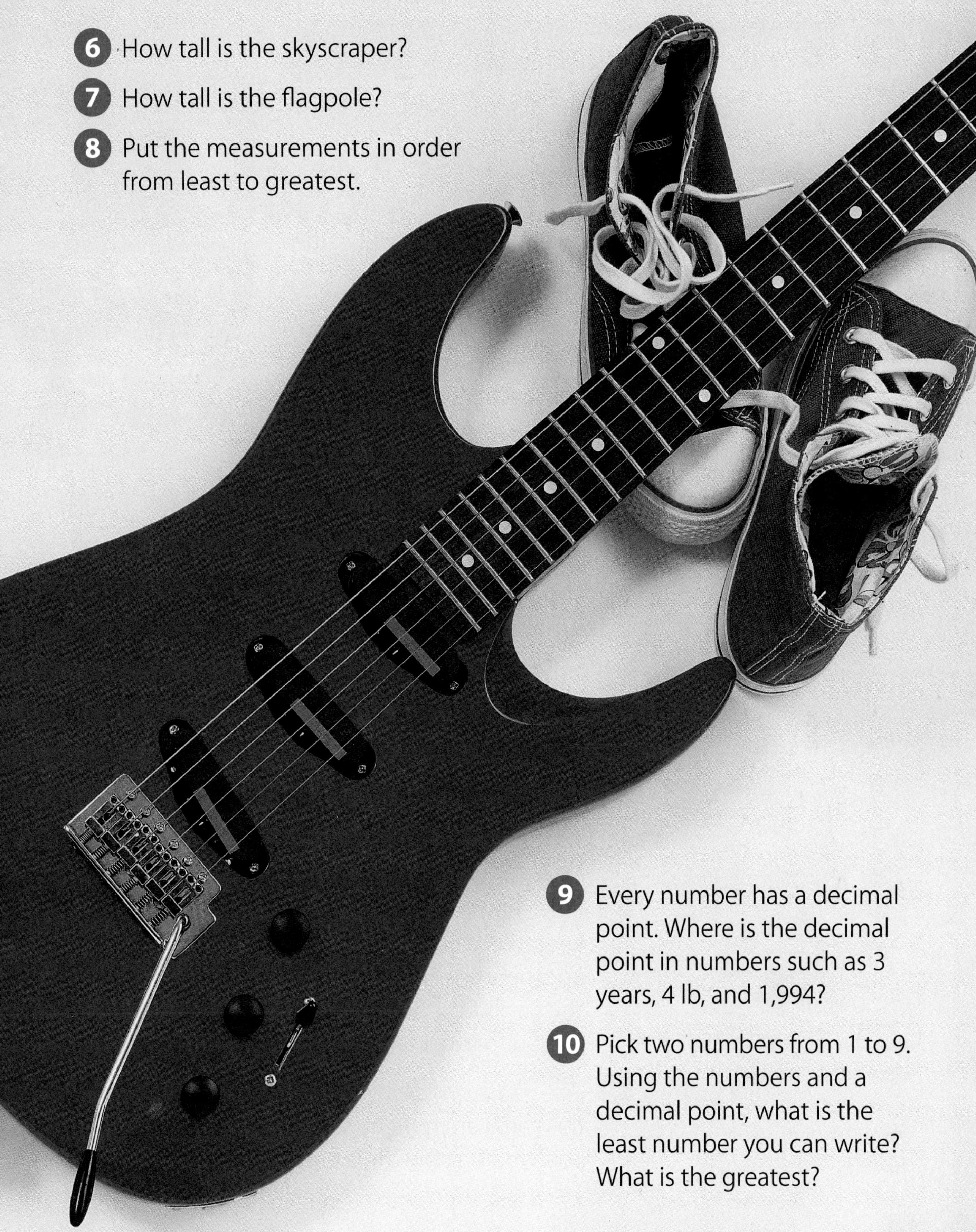

6. How tall is the skyscraper?

7. How tall is the flagpole?

8. Put the measurements in order from least to greatest.

9. Every number has a decimal point. Where is the decimal point in numbers such as 3 years, 4 lb, and 1,994?

10. Pick two numbers from 1 to 9. Using the numbers and a decimal point, what is the least number you can write? What is the greatest?

# Lesson 4 Tenths in Action

You've learned two ways to write one tenth, 0.1 and $\frac{1}{10}$. Now play some matching games to sharpen your skills!

## Activity 1 Tenths Match

**What You'll Need**
- *index cards*

### With Your Partner

Can you find a fraction and a decimal that name the same number? Play Tenths Match.

1. Make cards like the ones shown.
2. Lay the cards face down. Take turns picking two cards.
3. If the numbers match, keep the pair and take another turn. If not, put the cards face down and let your partner take a turn.
4. The game ends when all the cards are matched. See who has the most cards.

*Pick another eight pairs of decimals and fractions. Write them on cards. Now you have more games to play!*

# ACTIVITY 2 Battle of the Tenths

**With Your Partner** Choose one of these games to play. Try to get the most cards.

1. Use the same cards. Mix them up. Make two equal stacks of cards, one for you and one for your partner.
2. Turn over the top card from your stack. Compare the card with your partner's card.

**What You'll Need**
- *index cards from Activity 1*

*How can you rewrite the rules for Game A or Game B using <, >, and =?*

### Game A

- The player whose card shows a number that is less gets to keep both cards.
- If the numbers are equal, the winner of the next round takes all four cards.
- Play until all the cards are gone.

### Game B

- The player whose card shows a greater number takes both cards.
- If the numbers are equal, the winner of the next round takes all four cards.
- Play until all the cards are gone.

**What You'll Need**
- *tenths' squares*

## Activity 3 Decimal Shapes

**With Your Partner** For this activity you will need some squares marked off into tenths.

1 **Shade one tenth of a tenths' square. Name the shaded area two ways.**

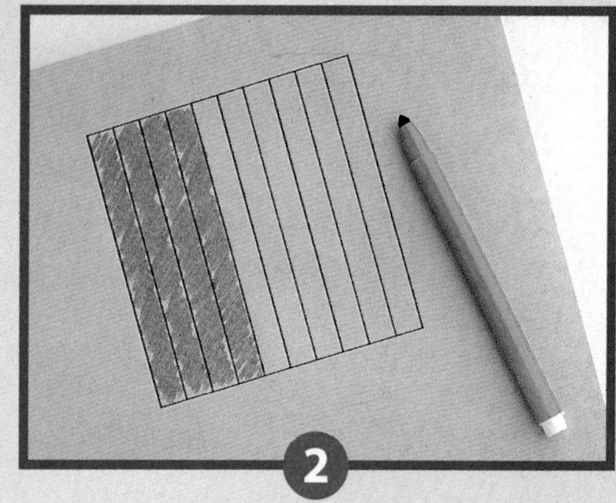

2 **Shade 0.4 of the square. Name it as a fraction.**

3 Take turns shading and naming tenths with your partner.

**a.** $\frac{5}{10}$ **b.** 0.2 **c.** $\frac{7}{10}$ **d.** $1\frac{4}{10}$

**e.** Shade $\frac{20}{10}$. What other name can you write?

**What You'll Need**
- *hundredths' squares*

*What other shapes could you draw to show tenths? Try drawing some and then show them to your partner.*

## Activity 4 Shaping Hundredths

**With Your Partner** This activity will help you show an area that is $\frac{1}{100}$ of a whole.

1 Use some hundredths' squares. Shade one small square. How do you know that the shaded area is a hundredth of the whole?

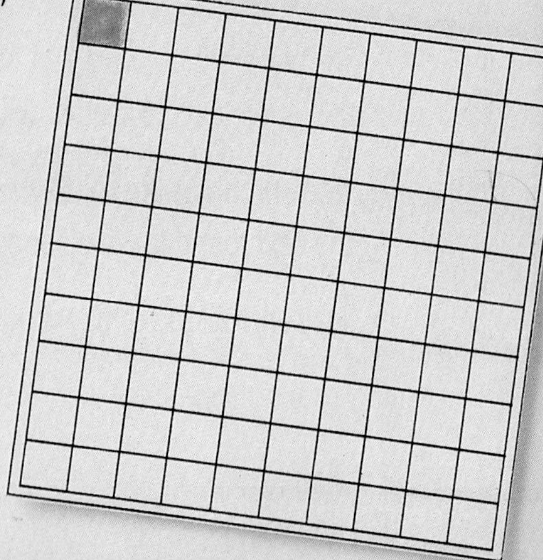

**2** Shade and name these hundredths.

a. $\frac{20}{100}$  b. 0.70  c. 0.25

**3** Shade 0.75. How many tenths are shaded? How do you know?

**4** Write three decimals in hundredths. Show each on a hundredths' square. Trade squares. Have your partner match each area with its name.

**5** Which is greater, 0.6 or 0.06? Use drawings to explain your thinking.

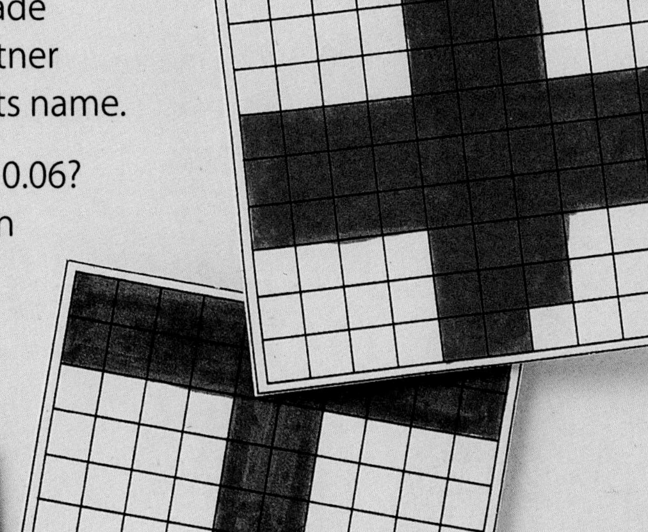

Do You Remember?

## Try It!

Write each fraction as a decimal.

1. $\frac{3}{100}$  2. $\frac{30}{100}$  3. $\frac{3}{10}$  4. $\frac{30}{10}$

5. $\frac{5}{100}$  6. $\frac{50}{100}$  7. $\frac{5}{10}$  8. $\frac{50}{10}$

Write each measurement as a decimal part of a meter.

9. 2 cm  10. 2 dm 5 cm  11. 32 cm

12. 1 m 35 cm  13. 10 dm 35 cm  14. 3 m 5 cm

**Think About It**

15. What pattern do you see in Exercises 1–8? Explain.

# Ordering Decimals

## ACTIVITY 1 Get in Order

**With Your Class** Make a decimal line-up!

1. Everyone write a decimal between 0 and 2 on a sheet of paper or card. Write the decimal in tenths.

2. Line up in order, least to greatest.

3. Now each person should write a decimal in hundredths. Line up, least to greatest.

**With Your Group** Look at the numbers your group wrote.

4. Write four number sentences that compare tenths. Use >, <, or =. Then write four number sentences that compare hundredths.

**0.3 < 0.9** **1.24 > 0.36**

ACTIVITY 2

# Round Decimals

**With Your Group** Think about a decimal line-up on a number line.

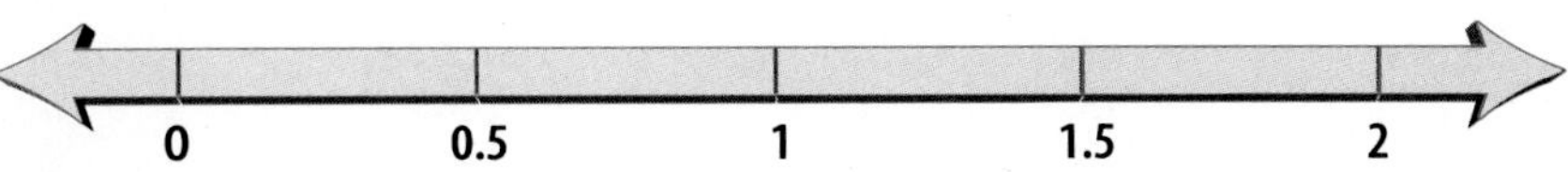


1. Would you place 0.2 closer to 0 or to 1?
2. Which whole number is 1.6 closer to?
3. Use your group's decimals in tenths from Activity 1. Tell whether the numbers round to 0, 1, or 2.
4. A halfway number like 1.5 is not closer to 1 than 2. People usually agree to round up. What would 1.5 round to? 4.5?

*In Your Journal* *Tell how rounding helps you estimate.*

Do You Remember?

## Try It!

Order each group from least to greatest.

1. 2.8  2.3  1.9  1.5
2. 6  5.8  5.9  6.1
3. 0.7  0.4  2.9  0
4. 4.1  4.0  3.90  0.38

Which numbers round to 3? Which round to 20?

5. 2.7
6. 3.4
7. 2.1
8. 3.5
9. 20.3
10. $1\frac{3}{4}$
11. $2\frac{1}{2}$
12. 22
13. 18.2
14. 24

### Think About It

15. In Exercises 1–4, which did you compare first, ones or tenths? Explain in writing.

Do You Remember?

## Cumulative Review

# Chinatown

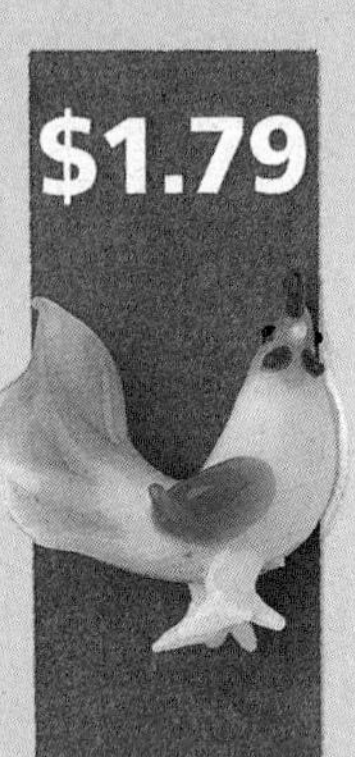

In some neighborhoods people celebrate their common culture. People in many cities welcome the Chinese New Year with a dragon parade.

1. **You have two dollars. How much more do you need to buy both statues on the left?**

2. **If the coins below are added to the coins near the wallet, how much money will there be altogether?**

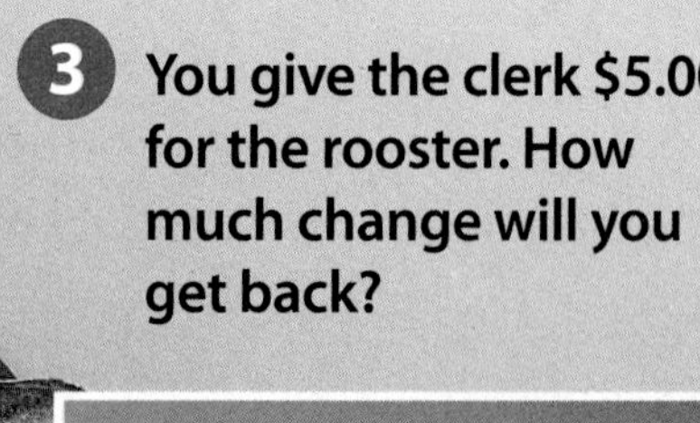

3. **You give the clerk $5.00 for the rooster. How much change will you get back?**

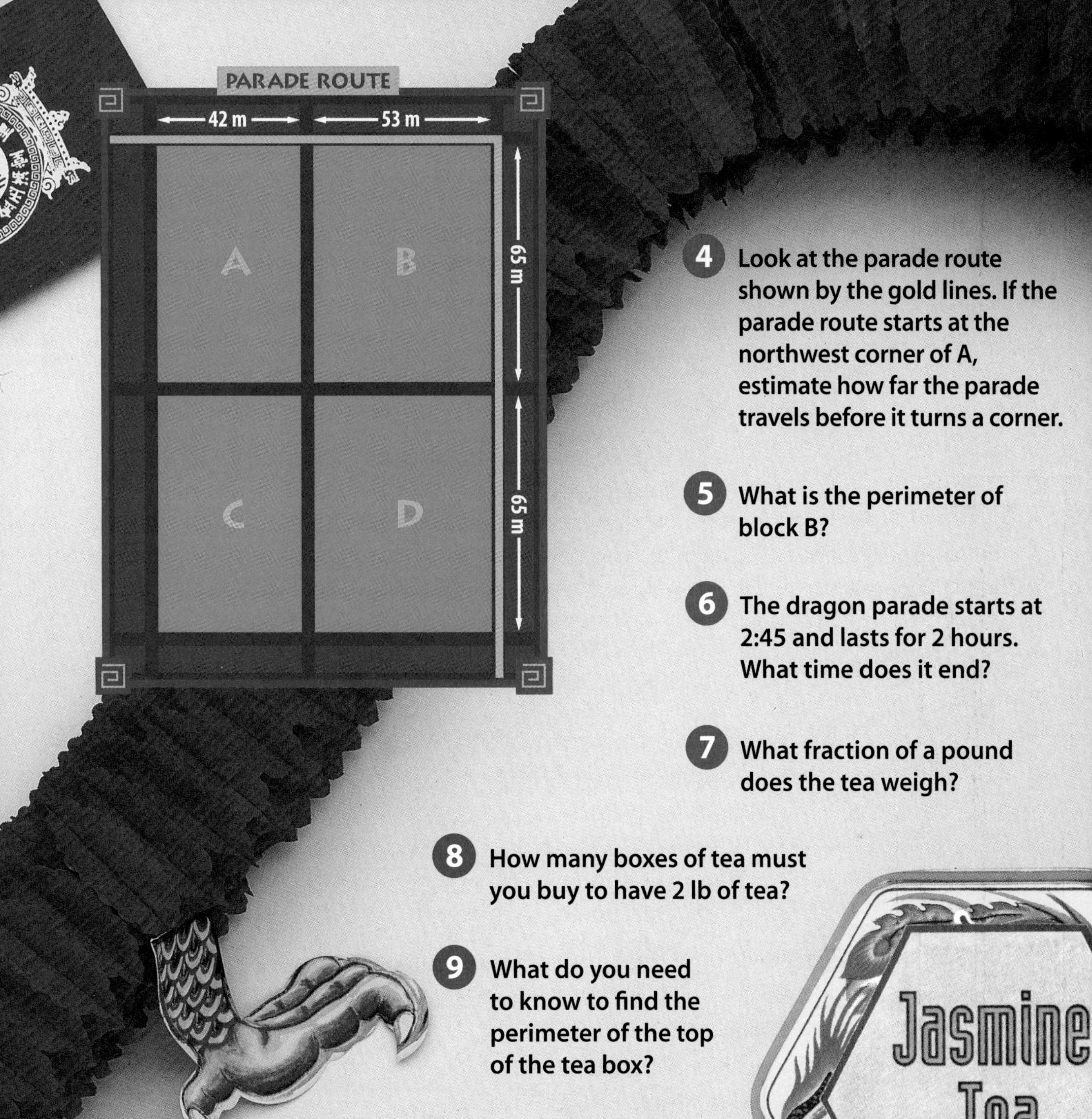


4 Look at the parade route shown by the gold lines. If the parade route starts at the northwest corner of A, estimate how far the parade travels before it turns a corner.

5 What is the perimeter of block B?

6 The dragon parade starts at 2:45 and lasts for 2 hours. What time does it end?

7 What fraction of a pound does the tea weigh?

8 How many boxes of tea must you buy to have 2 lb of tea?

9 What do you need to know to find the perimeter of the top of the tea box?

## Check Your Math Power

10 A parade starts at 2:45. You want to be there at least half an hour before it starts. You also have two things to do before the parade. Make up two things to do and estimate the time they would take. What time should you leave home for the parade?

## Comparing Decimals

# Parts and Parts

You know how to find tenths and hundredths. Now learn how they work together.

### Activity 1 How Much Space?

**With Your Group** Compare the tenths and hundredths that make up the square below.

**What You'll Need**
- *Tracing Tool or tracing paper*

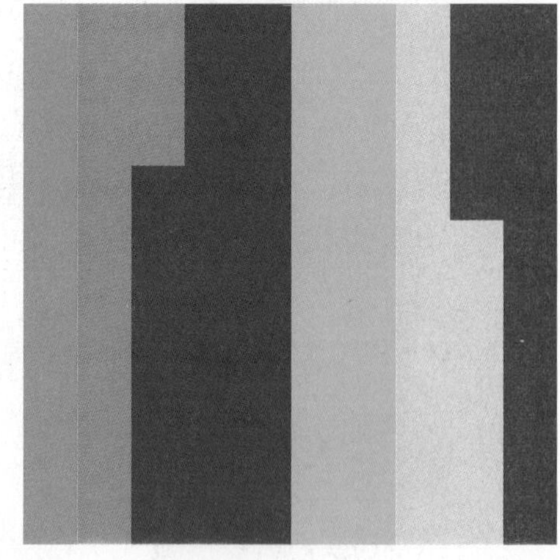

1. Look at the blue part of the square. What part of the whole is it? Trace it or use the tenths' square of your Tracing Tool to find out.
2. Now measure the blue part with a hundredths'-square grid. Write the number of hundredths as a decimal.
3. Compare. Complete this number sentence.
4. Write a number sentence to compare the tenths and hundredths shown in green.

0.1 ● 0.10

? ● ?

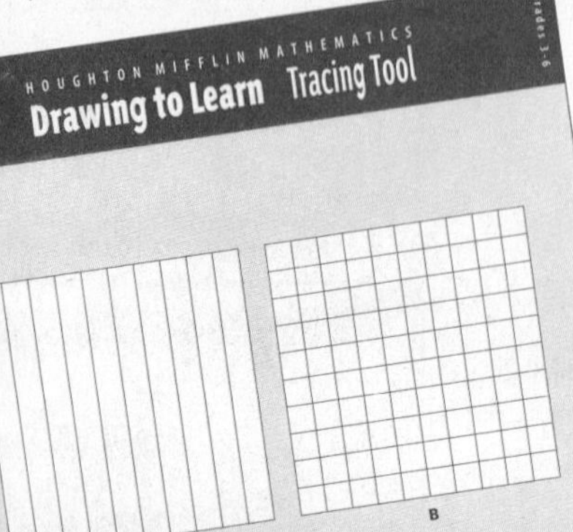

5. Now look at the red part. It is 0.14 of the whole. How many tenths are red? Use your Tracing Tool or tracing paper for help. Complete the sentence below.

6. Repeat the activity for the yellow, purple, and orange sections.

| | | | | | |
|---|---|---|---|---|---|
| **red** | **14 hundredths** | = | ■ **tenths** | ■ **hundredths** |
| **yellow** | ■ **hundredths** | = | ■ **tenths** | ■ **hundredths** |
| **purple** | ■ **hundredths** | = | ■ **tenths** | ■ **hundredths** |
| **orange** | ■ **hundredths** | = | ■ **tenths** | ■ **hundredths** |

## Activity 2 Calculator Country

**With Your Partner** You can also use your calculator to count tenths and hundredths.

**Enter 0.01 + 0.01.**

1. Press = until you reach 25 hundredths.
2. Guess what the numbers will be before you see them.
3. Write the numbers as they appear. How did the numbers change when you added 0.01 to 0.09? Explain.

**Enter 0.85 + 0.01.**

4. Press = until you reach 1.
5. Tell how the number changed when you added 0.01 to 0.99. Share your ideas with your class.

*Enter a number less than 10 on your calculator. Enter + 0.05. Before you press = each time, guess the next number.*

**What You'll Need**

- *index cards*

## ACTIVITY 3 Make a Match

**With Your Partner** Make a card for each decimal shown. Pick one of the following games to play. The object of each is to match tenths and hundredths.

### Concentration

- Lay the cards face down.
- Turn two cards over. Read the decimals aloud.
- If they match, keep the pair. Play again.
- If you have no match, turn the cards face down and end your turn.
- See who can make more matches.

### Go Fish!

- Each of you gets five cards. The rest go face down in a pile.
- Take turns asking for a card to match one in your hand.
- Your partner must give it to you if possible. If not, then pick one from the pile.
- When you make a match, lay down your cards face up.
- Try to make the most matches.

| 4.8 | 3.7 | 1.1 | 0.30 |
|---|---|---|---|
| 0.9 | 2.2 | 3.1 | 1.10 |
| 0.4 | 2.20 | 4.80 | 0.60 |
| 0.20 | 2.5 | 3.70 | 1.8 |
| 0.3 | 3.10 | 0.90 | 0.40 |
| 0.2 | 1.80 | 0.6 | 2.50 |

**What matches can you find in these cards?**

ACTIVITY 4

# Time to Compare

## With Your Partner

1. How does knowing $0.2 = 0.20$ help you compare the cards shown on the right?

2. Use the cards from Activity 3. Order them from least to greatest. Decide what to do with cards that are equal.

3. Compare. Use $<$, $>$, or $=$.

   a. 0.5 ● 0.90 b. 1.8 ● 1.10

   c. 0.7 ● 0.24 d. 0.35 ● 0.6

4. Write a general rule to compare decimals in tenths and hundredths.

**Self-Check** *Why is it helpful to change tenths to hundredths when you have tenths and hundredths to compare?*

## Try It!

Order each group from least to greatest.

1. 0.6, 0.4, 0.8, 0.27
2. 50.5, 0.5, 5.0, 0.05
3. 0.6, 0.45, 0.8, 0.1
4. 0.32, 3.2, 3.02, 32.0

Find the missing numbers.

5. $\frac{3}{10} + \frac{4}{10} = n$
6. $\frac{5}{10} - \frac{2}{10} = n$
7. $\frac{9}{10} - n = \frac{4}{10}$
8. $\frac{2}{10} + n = \frac{9}{10}$
9. $1\frac{4}{10} + \frac{6}{10} = n$
10. $\frac{12}{100} + \frac{5}{100} = n$

### Think About It

11. What is the pattern you see in Exercise 2? Explain in writing.

# Money Sense

You can use what you've learned about decimals to make you smarter about money!

## Activity 1 Decimal Dollars

**With Your Class** Find out how money and decimals are related.

1. Copy the place-value chart. Choose any three decimals and write them in your chart.

| | Ones | . | Tenths | Hundredths |
|---|---|---|---|---|
| a. | | | | |
| b. | | | | |
| c. | | | | |

2. Now write the decimals as money. Use a dollar sign ($) and a decimal point. Show the dollars, dimes, and pennies.

| | Dollars | . | Dimes | Pennies |
|---|---|---|---|---|
| a. | | | | |
| b. | | | | |
| c. | | | | |

3. How is writing money amounts like writing decimals? How is it different? Share your ideas.

**On Your Own** Use the pictures on the next page. Copy and complete the chart.

*Draw a chart that shows one penny as a fraction of a dollar and as a decimal part of a dollar. Include a nickel, a dime, a quarter, and a half dollar in your chart.*

**Orange**  10¢ 10¢ 10¢ 1¢ 1¢ 1¢ 1¢

**Peppers**  25¢ 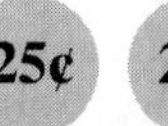 25¢ 25¢  1¢ 1¢

**Cheese**  THE UNITED STATES OF AMERICA ONE DOLLAR 25¢ 25¢ 25¢ 25¢ 5¢ 10¢

**Peanut**  1¢ 1¢

| Item | Dollars | | | |
|---|---|---|---|---|
| | Ones | . | Tenths | Hundredths |
| Peanut | | | | |
| Orange | | | | |
| Peppers | | | | |
| Cheese | | | | |

## Try It!

Write using a dollar sign and decimal point.

1. 7¢
2. 29¢
3. 5¢
4. 189¢
5. four hundred dollars
6. 4 nickels, 2 pennies

Use mental math.

7. $99 + 18$
8. $199 + 35$
9. $47 + 8$
10. $200 - 75$
11. $2 \times \$.99$
12. $3 \times 49$

### Think About It

13. Why is a decimal system of money a good idea?

Investigation

# Rolling Downhill

Rolling objects roll downhill. They will coast to a stop on their own. Do you think you can find a pattern to help you predict how far an object will roll as a hill becomes more and more steep?

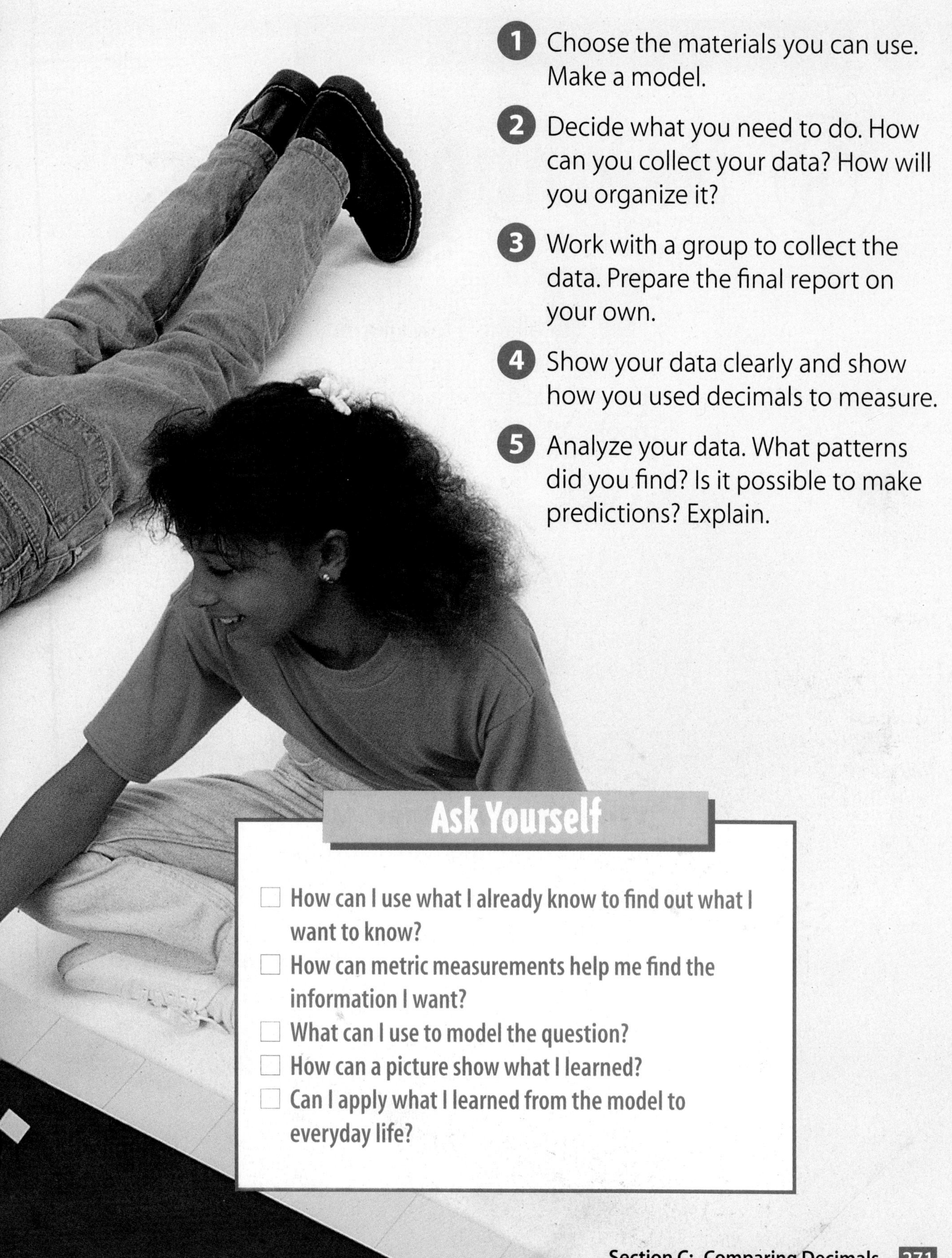

1. Choose the materials you can use. Make a model.
2. Decide what you need to do. How can you collect your data? How will you organize it?
3. Work with a group to collect the data. Prepare the final report on your own.
4. Show your data clearly and show how you used decimals to measure.
5. Analyze your data. What patterns did you find? Is it possible to make predictions? Explain.

## Ask Yourself

- ☐ How can I use what I already know to find out what I want to know?
- ☐ How can metric measurements help me find the information I want?
- ☐ What can I use to model the question?
- ☐ How can a picture show what I learned?
- ☐ Can I apply what I learned from the model to everyday life?

SECTION D

## Add and Subtract Decimals

LESSON 8

# Neighbor Walks

Walking a few kilometers a day is good for your health. Suppose you walk from the bank to the market and then to the bookstore. How far have you walked?

0.5 km

What You'll Need

- *tenths' squares*
- *crayons or markers*

### ACTIVITY 1 Tenths and Tenths

**With Your Partner** Make some tenths' squares. Color them to help you add decimals.

1. Find the sum 0.5 + 0.3. Color each addend. Then write the sum.

$$\begin{array}{r} 0.5 \\ +\ 0.3 \\ \hline ? \end{array} \qquad \begin{array}{r} \frac{5}{10} \\ +\ \frac{3}{10} \\ \hline \end{array}$$

How can thinking of fractions help?

2. Now find these sums.

a. $0.4 + 0.1 = n$ b. $0.2 + 0.4 = n$

0.3 km

**3** How are these additions similar? Add to find out.

a. 0.8 + 0.2 　 b. 0.7 + 0.3

✓ **Self-Check**
*Estimate the totals before you find the sums. Then check your answer against your estimate.*

**4** Add to find sums greater than 1.

a. 1.4 + 0.8 　 b. 0.7 + 1.9 　 c. 1.7 + 2.4 　 d. 2.3 + 4.8

**5** Write two additions with tenths. Trade with your partner and find the sums.

Do You Remember?

## Try It!

Add. What do you notice about the sums?

1. 0.5 +0.4 　 2. 0.3 +0.6 　 3. 0.2 +0.7 　 4. 0.8 +0.1

Estimate. Find sums greater than 2.

5. 0.6 +0.6 　 6. 0.9 +0.9 　 7. 1.3 +0.8 　 8. 2.1 +0.1

Write using decimals and place value.

9. two $1 bills, 3 quarters 　 10. 4 quarters, 7 dimes

### Think About It

11. Look at the addends and sums for Exercises 1–4. What other tenths add up to the same sum? Explain in writing.

What You'll Need
- *tenths' squares*

# Activity 2 Find the Difference

**With Your Group** Now you know how to add decimals. Get ready to subtract!

1. **Shade, color, or outline $\frac{8}{10}$ on your tenths' square.**

2. **Cross out $\frac{2}{10}$. How many tenths are left?**

3. **Complete the number sentence.**
   $0.8 - 0.2 = n$

4. **Find the difference. Use decimal squares.**
   a. $0.6 - 0.2 = n$
   b. $0.7 - 0.1 = n$
   c. $0.9 - n = 0.4$

**On Your Own** Use tenths' squares or mental math to find these differences.

*In Your Journal* Tell how you know that $2 = \frac{20}{10}$

**1** Subtract.

a. 1.7 − 0.3

b. 2.6 − 1.5

**2** Trade a one for tenths and subtract.

a. 1.3 − 0.5

b. 2.6 − 1.8

c. 2.0 − 0.4

d. 3.2 − 2.5

**3** Write two subtraction sentences using tenths. Trade sentences with another group member and complete them.

## Try It!

Subtract. What do you notice about the differences?

1. 0.5 − 0.4
2. 0.6 − 0.5
3. 0.7 − 0.6
4. 1.8 − 1.7

Estimate. Find differences less than 1.

5. 1.4 − 0.4
6. 1.6 − 0.8
7. 3.2 − 2.1
8. 3.2 − 2.3

Solve.

9. 2.4 − ■ = 0.4

10. 1.3 − ■ = 1.1

**Think About It**

11. Write three more sentences that have the same differences as Exercises 1–4. What pattern do you see?

# Lesson 9 Going for Gold

## LITERATURE

*At the 1960 Olympics, Wilma Rudolph won the 100-m and 200-m races. But her greatest event was the relay race.*

The crowd gasped. Wilma had to stop dead to get the baton. Jutta Heine, anchor woman for the German team, raced into the lead. Wilma set after her. Her long, fluid strides seemed to burn up the track. She was running at a speed no one could believe. She pulled up even with the German girl. They fought it out, stride for stride. The crowd was on its feet screaming with excitement. In the last split second, Wilma thrust ahead. The United States team had won! *Wilma had her third gold medal.* It was the first time in the history of the Games that an American woman had won three gold medals for running.

From *Golden Girls: True Stories of Olympic Women Stars*
by Carli Laklan

Races like Wilma's are measured in tenths or hundredths of seconds. Can you snap your fingers in a fraction of a second? Try it and find out.

**With Your Partner** Have your partner measure how long you take to snap your fingers ten times. Is it less than ten seconds? If so, then each snap takes less than a second.

## ACTIVITY 1 More Hundredths

**With Your Partner** Adding hundredths is a lot like adding tenths. Try it!

### What You'll Need

- *hundredths' square*
- *crayons or markers*

**1** Color the addends on your hundredths' square to find the sum 0.54 + 0.34.

Think of fractions:

$$\frac{54}{100} + \frac{34}{100}$$

$$\begin{array}{r} 0.54 \\ +\ 0.34 \\ \hline ? \end{array}$$

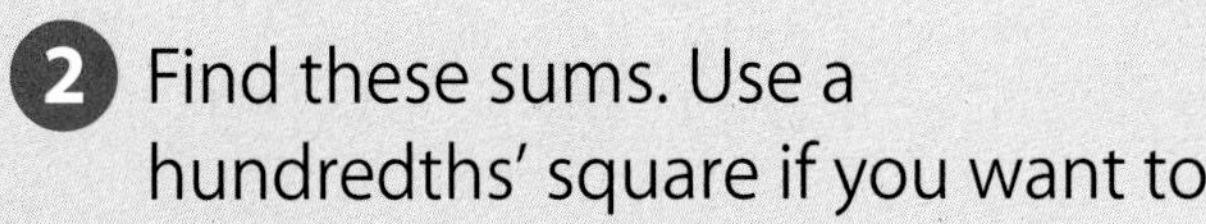

**2** Find these sums. Use a hundredths' square if you want to.

a. $\begin{array}{r} 0.52 \\ +\ 0.48 \\ \hline \end{array}$ b. $\begin{array}{r} 0.42 \\ +\ 0.49 \\ \hline \end{array}$

**3** Now add tenths and hundredths.

a. $\begin{array}{r} 0.80 \\ +\ 0.18 \\ \hline \end{array}$ b. $\begin{array}{r} 1.60 \\ +\ 0.34 \\ \hline \end{array}$ c. Why does it help to write a zero in the hundredths' place?

*Shade squares on a hundredths' square to show why it helps to write a zero in the hundredths' place in Exercise 3.*

✓ **Self-Check** *Did you use rounding to help estimate?*

## ACTIVITY 2 Estimation Time

**With Your Partner** Sometimes you don't want to find an actual sum.

1. Describe two times when you would want to estimate sums.
2. Discuss how to estimate. Find estimated sums.

a.
$$\begin{array}{r} 4.27 \\ +3.93 \\ \hline \end{array}$$

b.
$$\begin{array}{r} 2.06 \\ +5.97 \\ \hline \end{array}$$

c.
$$\begin{array}{r} 7.06 \\ +4.38 \\ \hline \end{array}$$

d.
$$\begin{array}{r} 10.54 \\ +21.34 \\ \hline \end{array}$$

## Try It!

By estimating tell which sums are greater than 2. Find only those actual sums.

| 1. | 2. | 3. | 4. |
|---|---|---|---|
| $\begin{array}{r} 0.43 \\ +0.34 \\ \hline \end{array}$ | $\begin{array}{r} 0.27 \\ +0.72 \\ \hline \end{array}$ | $\begin{array}{r} 1.43 \\ +0.37 \\ \hline \end{array}$ | $\begin{array}{r} 2.01 \\ +0.01 \\ \hline \end{array}$ |

| 5. | 6. | 7. | 8. |
|---|---|---|---|
| $\begin{array}{r} 1.23 \\ +0.5 \\ \hline \end{array}$ | $\begin{array}{r} 1.46 \\ +0.6 \\ \hline \end{array}$ | $\begin{array}{r} 1.32 \\ +0.69 \\ \hline \end{array}$ | $\begin{array}{r} 0.63 \\ +1.40 \\ \hline \end{array}$ |

Write in decimal form and add.

9. 2 dollars 75¢ and 1 dollar 49¢
10. 43¢ and 64¢
11. 62¢ and 89¢

**Think About It**

12. Order the sums you found for Exercises 1–8 from least to greatest.

# Less Hundredths

Now that you know how to add hundredths, you can find out how to subtract them too!

## ACTIVITY 1 Take It Away!

**With Your Partner** You are ready to subtract hundredths. Use your hundredths' square to help you.

**What You'll Need**
- *hundredths' square*

1. Use a hundredths' square to show 0.75.

2. Cross out 0.22. How many hundredths are left? Record your answer.

3. Find the differences. You may want to use a hundredths' square.

a. $\begin{array}{r} 0.43 \\ -0.12 \\ \hline \end{array}$ b. $\begin{array}{r} 0.50 \\ -0.25 \\ \hline \end{array}$

c. $\begin{array}{r} 0.67 \\ -0.35 \\ \hline \end{array}$ d. $\begin{array}{r} 0.29 \\ -0.18 \\ \hline \end{array}$

*Cut up a hundredths' square. Use its pieces to explore subtracting decimals.*

**What You'll Need**

- *hundredths' square*

*In Your Journal* Explain why you can trade one tenth for ten hundredths.

**On Your Own** Use a hundredths' square or mental math to find these differences.

**1** Find each difference. You may need to trade tenths for hundredths.

a. 1.75 − 0.83

b. 2.68 − 1.59

c. 5.45 − 3.52

| Tia | Kamal |
|---|---|
| 3.62 | 3.62 |
| −1.3 | −1.30 |

**2** Would you use Tia's way or Kamal's way to find the difference? Why?

$3.62 - 1.3 = n$

**3** Solve for *n*.

a. $2.54 - 1.64 = n$

b. $4.74 - 3.9 = n$

c. $4.08 - n = 2.4$

**4** Solve for *n*.

## ACTIVITY 2 Guess Again

**With Your Partner** Use your calculator to play a hundredths' game.

**Enter 0.95 − 0.05.**

1. Count out loud as you press = until you get to 0.75.
2. Before you press = again, your partner must tell what the next number will be.
3. Your partner gets a turn after naming three numbers correctly. The game is over when you reach 0.

**Enter 0.36 − 0.04.**

4. Repeat Steps 1–3.

*How is trading one tenth for ten hundredths like trading a dime for ten pennies?*

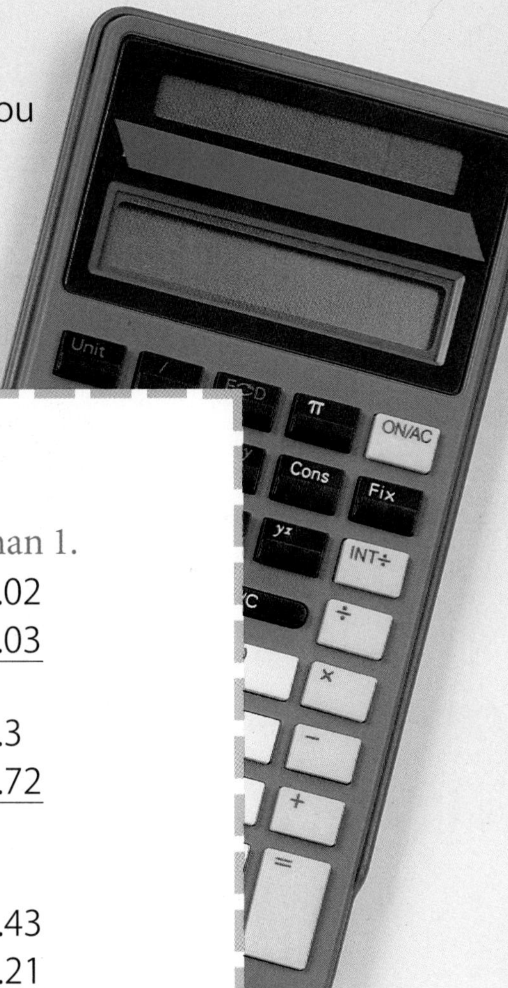

## Try It!

Estimate. Find only the actual differences less than 1.

1. 0.95 − 0.05
2. 0.43 − 0.21
3. 1.62 − 0.41
4. 6.02 − 5.03
5. 9.47 − 8.98
6. 4.3 − 0.21
7. 1.44 − 0.3
8. 2.3 − 1.72

Subtract.

9. \$1.43 − .27
10. \$2.59 − .39
11. \$0.83 − .49
12. \$3.43 − 2.21

### Think About It

13. Write Exercises 3–5 as subtraction of mixed numbers. Which do you prefer, subtracting decimals or mixed numbers? Explain in writing.

# Block Party

You and your neighborhood friends can make a game of adding and subtracting decimals. Have fun while you learn! Be the first to put your counters on five blocks across or down.

**What You'll Need**
- *gameboard*
- *counters*

## Activity 3 Think Ahead

**On Your Own** Think about ways you can place your counters. Decide on a plan. Use estimation to help you play the game.

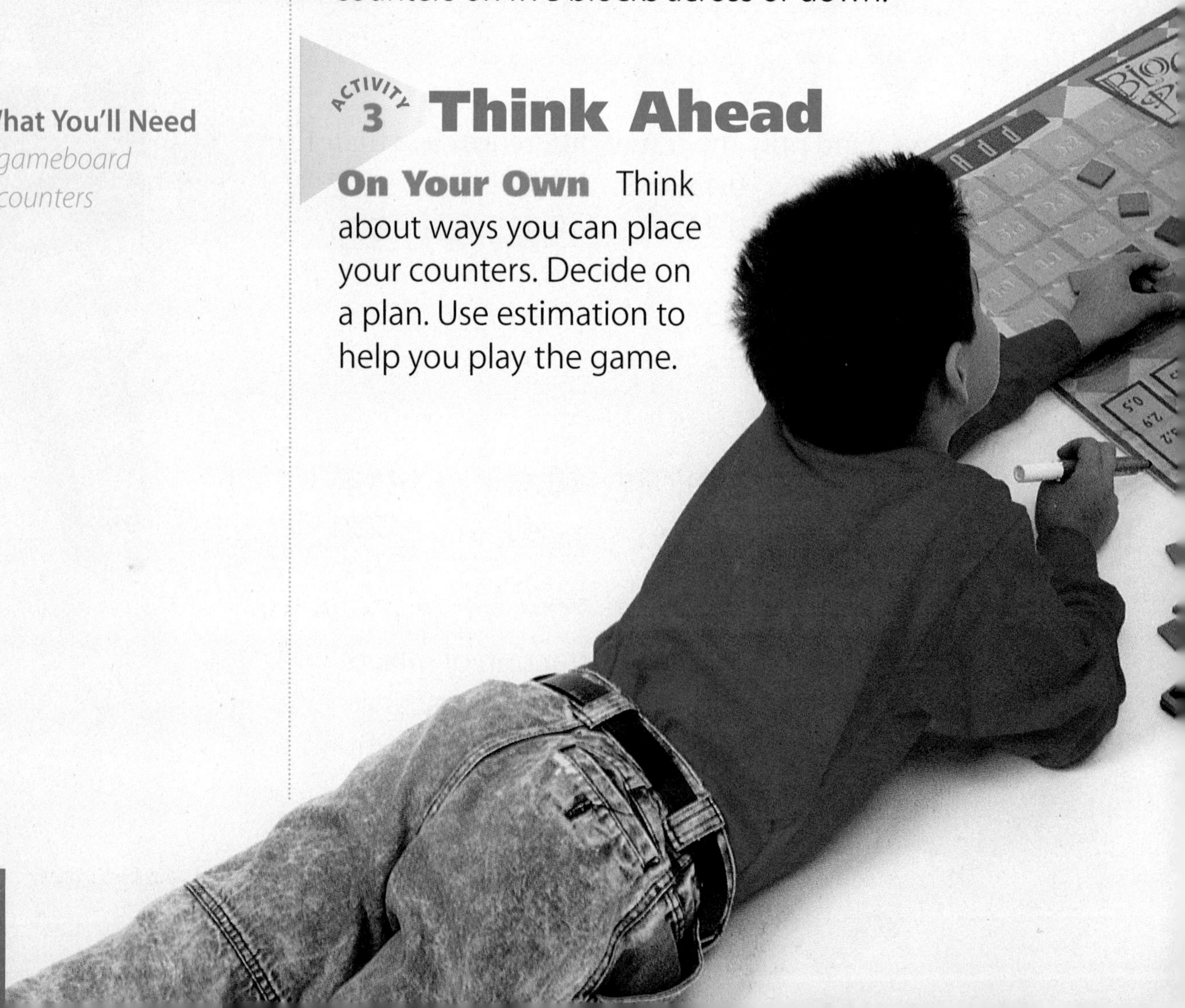

## Addition Game

Choose one decimal from column A and one from column B. Find the sum on the gameboard. Place a counter on the block. End your turn.

## Subtraction Game

Choose one decimal from column C and one from column D. Subtract one from the other. Find the difference on the gameboard. Place a counter on the block. End your turn.

## Try It!

Which exercises have about the same estimated answers? Estimate to make matches.

1. $4.7 - 2 = n$
2. $6.35 - 4.2 = a$
3. $0.9 + 1.3 = n$
4. $9.7 + 3.86 = c$
5. $25.1 + 25.2 = n$
6. $6.3 + 8.15 = n$
7. $8.1 - 4.99 = a$
8. $5.06 - 2.9 = x$
9. $2 \times 24 = n$

### Think About It

10. Explain how you estimated in Exercises 1–9.

Do You Remember? **Cumulative Review**

# Looking Back

**Choose the right answer. Write *a, b, c* or *d* for Exercises 1–16.**

1. Which number has a 3 in the tenths' place?

   a. 43.0　　b. 721.30
   c. 97.03　　d. 34.27

2. Which number has the 7 in the hundredths' place?

   a. 77.28　　b. 752.19
   c. 9.76　　d. 46.57

3. Which measurement is the same as 4 m 7 cm?

   a. 47 m　　b. 4.7 m
   c. 4.07 m　　d. 0.47 m

4. Sayad read 8 books, Darius read 6, and Mohammed read 7. What is the average number of books read?

   a. 14　　b. 7
   c. 21　　d. 3

5. What is true of the figure below?

   a. It has 3 faces.
   b. The shape is a triangle.
   c. Three faces are rectangles.
   d. Three faces are triangles.

6. Which number sentence is true?

   a. $4.6 > 8.27$
   b. $6.3 < 2.45$
   c. $7.4 = 7.40$
   d. $0.8 < 0.02$

7. Which is 7.04?

   a. seven and four hundredths
   b. seven tenths and four hundredths
   c. seven and four tenths
   d. seven and forty hundredths

**Use these squares to answer Exercises 8–10.**

a. 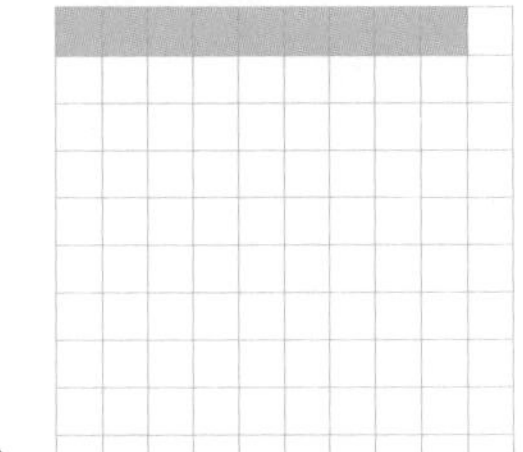

b. 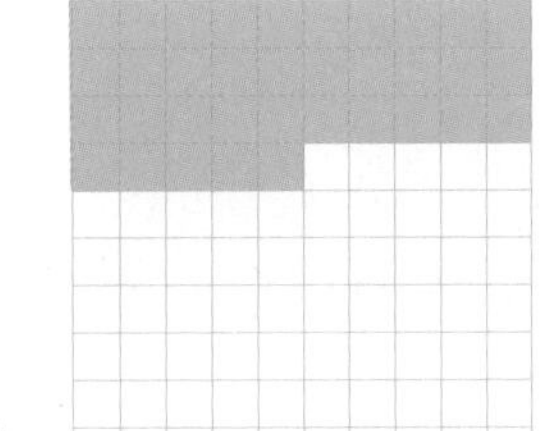

c. 

d. 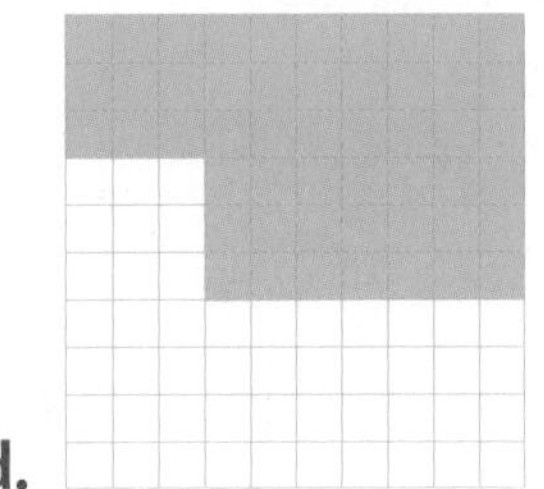

8. Which shows 0.35 shaded?

9. Which shows 0.7 shaded?

10. Which shows 0.09 shaded?

11. Which is ordered from least to greatest?

    a. 10.54, 9.96, 9.92, 10.82
    b. 9.92, 9.96, 10.54, 10.82
    c. 10.82, 10.54, 9.96, 9.92
    d. 9.96, 9.92, 10.82, 10.54

12. Which is the sum of 5.5 + 3.8?

    a. 8.13 b. 9.3
    c. 1.7 d. 5.88

13. Which is the difference of 14.7 − 4.06?

    a. 10.74 b. 18.76
    c. 2.59 d. 10.64

## Check Your Math Power

14. What's the greatest amount of money you can have with five coins if only two coins are alike?

15. Look at the three digits below. The greatest digit is in the tenths' place. The digit in the ones' place is $\frac{1}{4}$ of the greatest number. What number is in the hundredths' place? Make more riddles with the digits.

16. Make up one addition and one subtraction number sentence using two of these fractions. Write them as decimals.

    $\frac{2}{10}$ $\frac{42}{100}$ $\frac{7}{10}$ $\frac{9}{100}$

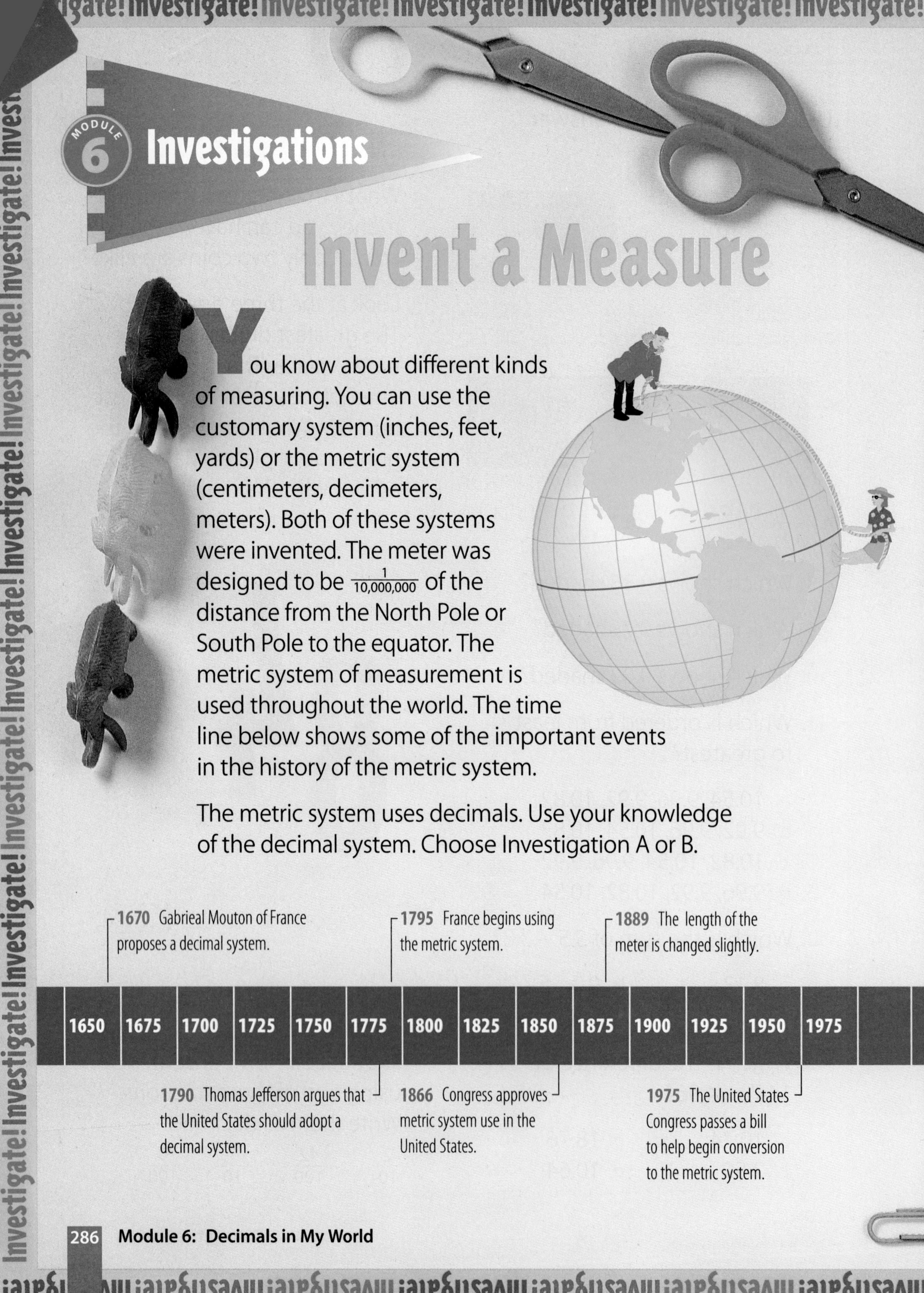

MODULE 6 **Investigations**

# Invent a Measure

You know about different kinds of measuring. You can use the customary system (inches, feet, yards) or the metric system (centimeters, decimeters, meters). Both of these systems were invented. The meter was designed to be $\frac{1}{10,000,000}$ of the distance from the North Pole or South Pole to the equator. The metric system of measurement is used throughout the world. The time line below shows some of the important events in the history of the metric system.

The metric system uses decimals. Use your knowledge of the decimal system. Choose Investigation A or B.

**1670** Gabrieal Mouton of France proposes a decimal system.

**1790** Thomas Jefferson argues that the United States should adopt a decimal system.

**1795** France begins using the metric system.

**1866** Congress approves metric system use in the United States.

**1889** The length of the meter is changed slightly.

**1975** The United States Congress passes a bill to help begin conversion to the metric system.

| 1650 | 1675 | 1700 | 1725 | 1750 | 1775 | 1800 | 1825 | 1850 | 1875 | 1900 | 1925 | 1950 | 1975 |
|---|---|---|---|---|---|---|---|---|---|---|---|---|---|

Investigation A

# Be Mr. Mouton!

1. **Investigate** what it takes to create a new system of measurement.
2. **Choose** a new unit. A sneaker or a pencil might be a good one. Name larger and smaller units too. Your new system should use decimals.
3. **Measure** several objects with your new units. Compare your system with the metric system. Do you think yours is better? not as good? Why?
4. **Write** a report to explain your system. If you like, pretend to write a letter to Congress explaining why you think your system is a good idea.

## Keep in Mind

Be sure to do the following things in your report.

- ☐ Tell why you chose your basic unit. Tell what you chose not to use as a base and why.
- ☐ Describe any problems your system might have. Explain whether it's easy to remember and easy to use.
- ☐ Tell why you think your system is useful. Make a list or use drawings to help you.
- ☐ Tell how you can use decimals with your measurements.

## Investigation B: Standard Measure

Little children mix up dimes and pennies. They often think that because pennies are larger they are worth more than dimes. Investigate the possibility of new coin sizes that little children will not confuse.

1. **Analyze** several possibilities. What are some advantages and disadvantages of each possibility?

2. **Pretend** to write a letter to someone in the U.S. Mint. Propose a change that you think would be a good idea and tell why. Show that you understand the decimal system and the use of decimals in metric measurement.

## Ongoing Investigation: How Much Is a Million?

How many items has your class collected so far? Based on the size of your collection, do you think you will have enough storage space for a million? Use what you've learned to design an ideal storage space for your collection. Use drawings, words, and numbers to describe your design.

# Multiplying Our Resources

Students all over the world are concerned about natural resources like water and trees. People are finding ways to use less paper and water every day. You can get involved.

Multiplying and Dividing by Ten

Multiplying by Multiples of Ten

Multiplying by Two-Digit Numbers

Section D

Dividing by Multiples of Ten

# Multiplying Our Resources

## Resource Alert

### 1 Make Sketches

Look around your classroom, home, and neighborhood. Do you see resources being wasted? Draw pictures to show how wasting resources happens.

### 2 Collect Data

Read all about it. How can we save our resources? Pay special attention to numbers. How do they help you understand the information? What questions do you have about how numbers are used?

### Word Bank

- Associative Property
- degree Celsius (°C)
- degree Fahrenheit (°F)
- Distributive Property
- gram (g)
- liter (L)
- mean
- median
- mode
- range

## 3 Share the Data

Help others learn about saving resources. Post information on a bulletin board. Think of other ways to inform your family and neighbors.

### Investigations Preview

You'll explore how to use your math skills to help save water, paper, and other resources.

*Every Drop Counts* (pages 310–311)

How much water is used in your home, school, or neighborhood? Knowing about liters, milliliters, and multiplication can help you invent a way to save water.

*Strength in Numbers* (pages 334–336)

What could a "green" group do to save resources in your community? Your multiplication and division skills will help you map out a savings plan.

# Multiplying and Dividing by Ten

## Lesson 1 How Much Water?

*Draw a bar graph of water use in different countries. How does the graph help you compare your country to others?*

Do people in the United States use a lot of water? How can numbers help you find out?

### Activity 1 Compare Water Use

**With Your Class** Look at the map. It shows the amount of water used per person each day in different countries. Measure water with a metric unit called a **liter (L).** It is almost the same as a quart.

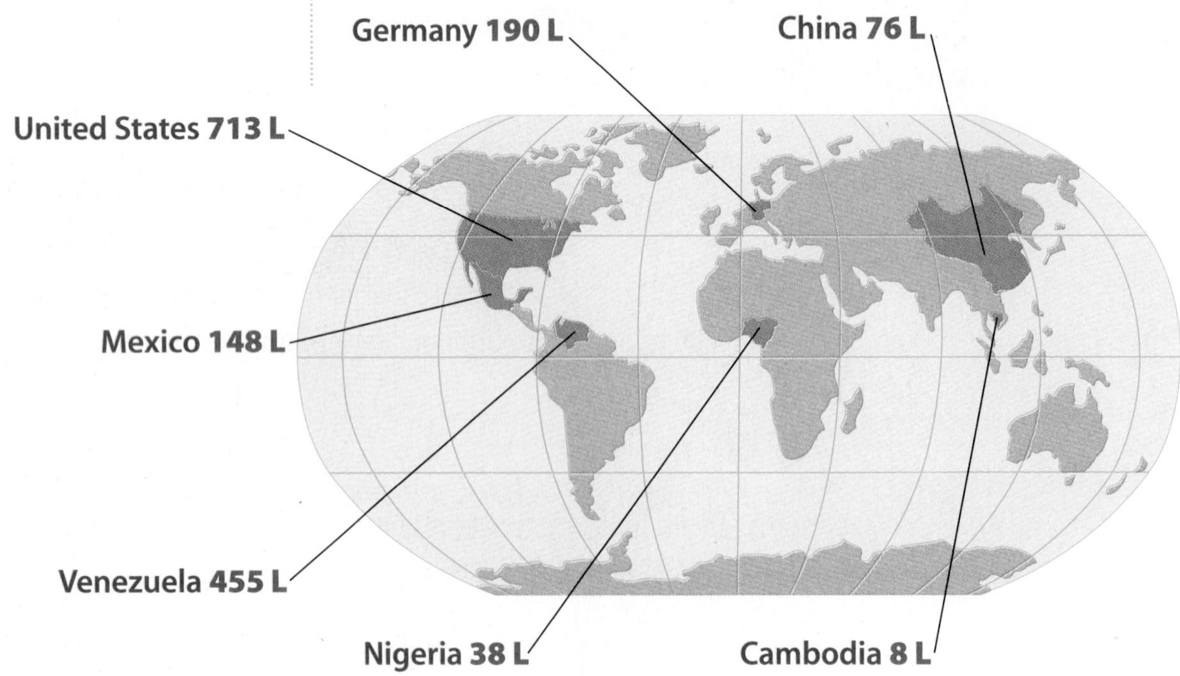

*If you have a computer spreadsheet program, you can use it to order and compare the water-use data.*

1. List the countries in order from lowest water use to highest.
2. Now compare how much water people in different countries use. How can you tell if a number is high or low? If you know where the middle is, you can decide if a number is high or low.
3. One kind of middle is the **mean.** You already know how to find the mean number of liters used. You add up the number of liters used. Then you divide by the number of countries. Find the mean for the water-use map.
4. Another kind of middle is the **median.** Look at your ordered list. The number in the middle of an ordered list is the median. What is the median for your ordered list of water use?

**On Your Own** Practice making a list in order. List all the ways you use water. Then put the items in a new order. Start with the activities that use the most water. How did you decide on your order?

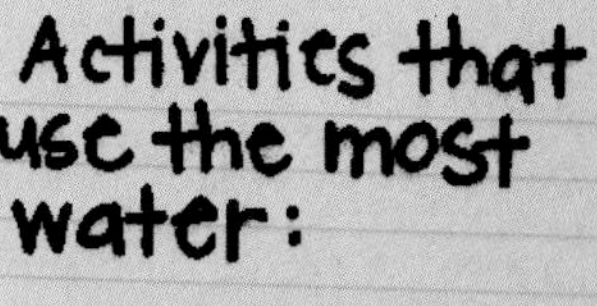

### What You'll Need

- *1 clear container*
- *waterproof marker*
- *measuring spoon*
- *small paper cup*
- *water*
- *other containers to hold water and measure*

## Activity 2 Using Liters

**With Your Group** Mark a container you can use for measuring water. Small amounts of water are measured in **milliliters (mL).**

**1,000 mL = 1 L**

1. A teaspoon holds about 5 mL of water. A tablespoon holds about 15 mL. Use your spoon to see how many milliliters your small cup can hold.

2. **Use your cup to add water to your container. Every time you add water, mark how many milliliters have been added so far. Make a longer mark for each liter. How many milliliters and liters does your container hold?**

*Find containers marked to show the liters and milliliters they hold. Line them up and compare them. Use them to estimate the liters held by unmarked containers.*

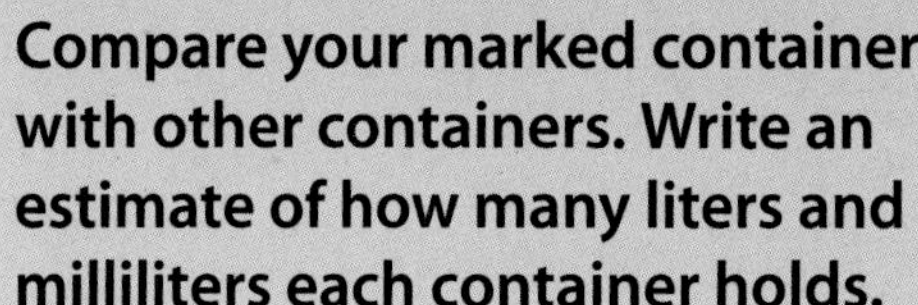

**3** Compare your marked container with other containers. Write an estimate of how many liters and milliliters each container holds.

**4** Use your marked container to measure the water that other containers hold. Record your results.

**5** Compare your estimates with your actual measurements. How accurate were your estimates?

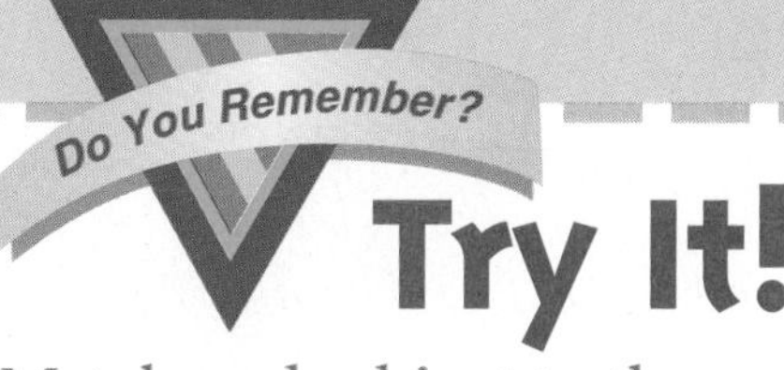


## Try It!

Match each object to the amount that you think would fill it.

**1.** milk pitcher **2.** bathtub **3.** swimming pool
**4.** bucket **5.** eyedropper **6.** juice glass

**a.** 11 L **b.** 2 L **c.** 100 L **d.** 11,000 mL
**e.** 180 mL **f.** 5 mL **g.** 5,000 L **h.** 2,000 mL

Change the measure to meters, using a decimal.

**7.** 10 dm **8.** 1 m 1 dm **9.** 3 cm **10.** 8 dm **11.** 100 cm

### Think About It

**12.** Did the results of Activity 2 help you answer Exercises 1–6? Explain.

# Lesson 2 Down the Drain

**What You'll Need**

- *base ten blocks*

## Activity 1 Lost Liters

**With Your Class** Do you leave the water running while you wash your face and hands? During that time you waste about 10 L of water.

1. How many liters are lost if you wash once a day for 5 days? 7 days? 10 days? Write a number sentence to show each answer. What pattern do you see?

**✓ Self-Check** *Once you know the pattern, it's easy to multiply any number by ten. Can you do it faster in your head than on a calculator?*

2. What could you do to find out how much water gets wasted in 14 days?

3. Use base ten blocks to help you multiply the amount for 14 days. How many rows of ten would you need? What trades can you make to find the product?

**With Your Partner** Pick one of these activities. Take turns giving each other numbers to multiply by ten. After the activity, write a rule that tells how to multiply by ten.

4. Set up base ten blocks. Have your partner write down the multiplication factors and product shown by your blocks.

5. Find the product in your head while your partner uses a calculator. Switch roles. Which way is faster?

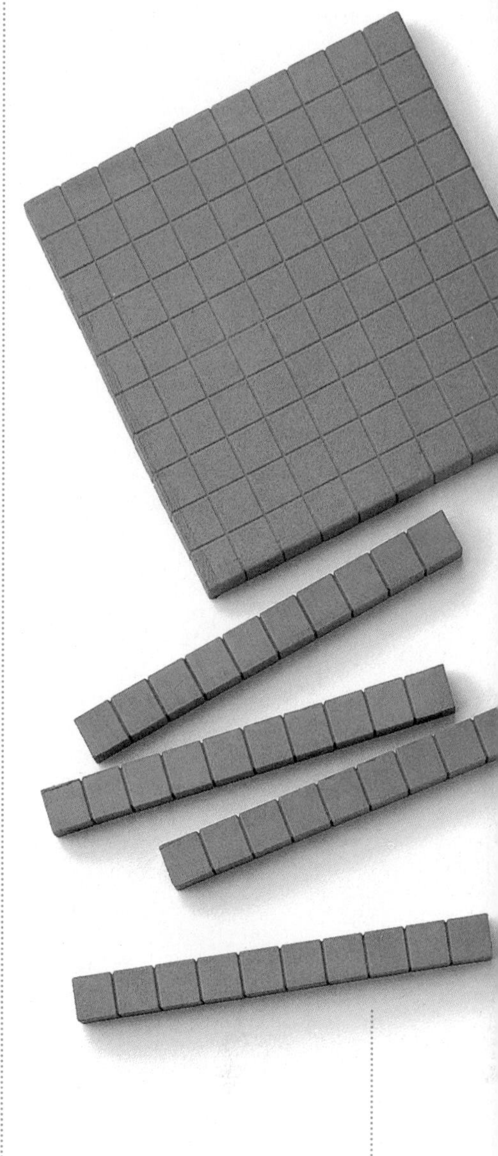

*Using base ten blocks makes it easy to multiply by ten. How could you use base ten blocks to multiply by 100?*

*In Your Journal* Describe what happens to the place value of digits in the chart below.

# Activity 2 Sinkhole!

**With Your Class** Do you leave water running while you wash dishes? Doing so sends about 100 L of water down the drain. How much water is wasted if you do dishes this way 14 times?

1. The **Associative Property** lets you regroup to multiply.

$$100 \times 14 = (10 \times 10) \times 14 = 10 \times (10 \times 14)$$

Use the Associative Property and multiplication by 10 to find the product of $100 \times 14$.

2. Copy and complete the place-value chart. What patterns do you see?

Do You Remember?

## Try It!

Make a multiplication table to show each number multiplied by 5, 10, and 100. Describe the patterns you find.

**1.** 5 **2.** 54 **3.** 543 **4.** 2 **5.** 23 **6.** 230

Find the number for each variable.

**7.** $234 \div 2 = y$ **8.** $3 \times m = 654$ **9.** $t \div 5 = 78$
**10.** $216 \div p = 8$ **11.** $r \times 4 = 716$ **12.** $k \times 20 = 400$

**Think About It**

**13.** Look at answers to Exercises 1–6. What happens to the digit in the ones' place when you multiply by 100?

# Drop by Drop

LESSON 3

## ACTIVITY 1 Plug the Leaks

**With Your Class** In 10 minutes leaks can waste a lot of water. Division by ten can help you find out how much water is wasted every minute.

1. Suppose a toilet leaks 90 mL in 10 minutes. How much leaks in 1 minute? Why are the missing numbers below the same?

   $10 \times ? = 90$ $\qquad$ $10\overline{)90}$ = ?

2. A leaking faucet can drip 240 mL in 10 minutes. How much water leaks every minute? Is the quotient larger than 10? larger than 20? How does multiplication help?

   $10 \times ? = 240$ $\qquad$ $10\overline{)240}$ = ?

3. A leaky hose can waste 855 mL in 10 minutes. About how much water is wasted in 1 minute?

   $10\overline{)855}$ = ?

*You can use a computer to make a line graph or bar graph showing how much water is wasted by leaks. Why would graphs be a good way to share this information?*

# Activity 2 Water by the Minute

**With Your Partner** Some people don't have enough clean water. Others use more than their share. Follow the steps to find out how much water is used per minute in each of these activities.

1. How can you find out if the amount per minute is more than 100 L? more than 10 L?
2. Copy and complete the chart. Why might you want to round each number to a multiple of ten before dividing?

| Water Used | 10 min | 1 min |
|---|---|---|
| washing dishes | 114 L | |
| in the shower | 226 L | |
| watering grass | 384 L | |

**3** Use the quotient you got from rounding to find the exact quotient. What did you do with the remainders? Which is the better way to write the quotient below for liters of water? Why?

$$10\overline{)362} = 36 \text{ R}2$$

$$10\overline{)362} = 36\tfrac{1}{5}$$

*Suppose you get a remainder that is greater than ten. What does that remainder tell you about your quotient?*

Do You Remember?

## Try It!

Find the largest quotient in the group.

1. a. 302 ÷ 3 b. 302 ÷ 5 c. 302 ÷ 10
2. a. $2\overline{)58}$ b. $7\overline{)58}$ c. $10\overline{)58}$
3. a. 864 ÷ 10 b. $4\overline{)864}$ c. $7\overline{)864}$
4. a. $10\overline{)255}$ b. $10\overline{)355}$ c. 455 ÷ 10

Find the sum. Round the answer to the nearest tenth.

5. 2.35 + 4.06 6. 6.8 + 3.12 7. 4.5 + 5.98
8. 3.57 + 8.3 9. 7.39 + 1.91 10. 8.21 + 5.16

**Think About It**

11. When your divisor gets larger, what happens to your quotient? Write your explanation.

## Multiplying by Multiples of Ten

# Slow the Flow

How much water do you waste? In a year it would probably fill up a swimming pool. How can you cut down your waste of this resource?

### Activity 1 Be a Super Saver!

**With Your Class** This chart shows average amounts of water used for each activity. This information will help you plan how to save water. After you solve problem 1, choose problem 2 or 3 to solve. Then make up more problems using the data on the chart.

| Activity | Water Used |
|---|---|
| Shower (1 min) | 19 L |
| Bath | 113 L |
| Flush toilet | 13 L |
| Wash dishes for 4 people | 30 L |
| Dishwasher | 45 L |
| Wash hands | 8 L |
| Brush teeth | 10 L |

**Self-Check** *See if you understand the meaning of your answer to a problem. Try using the product you get in a sentence about water saving.*

1 How many liters of water would be saved if 20 students each showered 1 minute less a day?

Shower:
19 L per min
x 20 students

20 = 10 x 2

*You know how to multiply $10 \times 19$. How can you use that to solve $20 \times 19$?*

2 How much water would be saved if 40 students each washed dishes in the sink instead of using the dishwasher?

Dishwasher:
45 L per min
x 40 students

Hand-washing dishes:
30 L per min
x 40 students

3 How much water would be saved if 40 students each showered 1 minute less a day? How much water would they save in 30 days?

*How much is 2,000 L of water? Draw a picture of something that would hold 2,000 L. How can what you know about the liter help you?*

## ACTIVITY 2 High-Water Marks

**On Your Own** How could a class save about 2,000 L of water a day? Make a plan for the class.

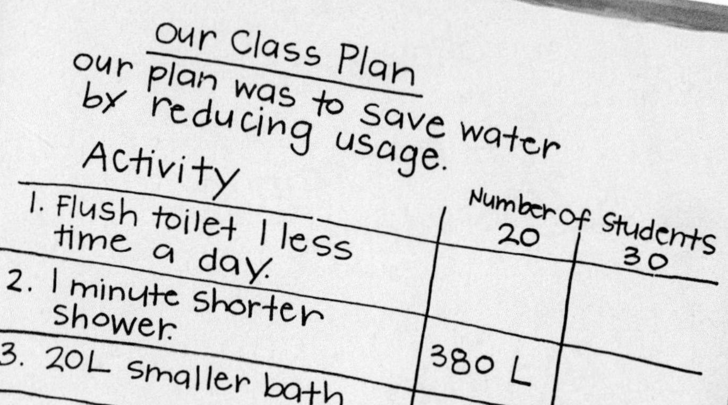


### Do You Remember?

## Try It!

Find the product. How many groups of ten are in it?

1. $48 \times 20$
2. $35 \times 50$
3. $33 \times 60$
4. $60 \times 13$
5. $80 \times 55$
6. $100 \times 25$

Find the differences that are less than one.

7. $4.34 - 4.06$
8. $6.8 - 5.12$
9. $4.05 - 3.82$
10. $8.17 - 6.3$
11. $7.9 - 6.91$
12. $10.25 - 9.18$

**Think About It**

13. How would you find the number of groups of ten in $3{,}000 \times 23$?

# Pool Your Savings

It would be tough to find out exactly how much water a group uses. How can you get a good idea?

*Design water-conservation posters or write commercials for saving water. Use data on this page to show how water can be saved.*

## ACTIVITY 1 Making Estimates

**With Your Class** If everyone joins to save water, a lot can be saved. Estimate how much water can be saved.

1. Look at the students' water-saving goals below. How did they estimate their savings?
2. Make another estimate of each student's savings. Are your estimates closer to the exact products? Use your calculator to find out.

What You'll Need

- *gameboard*
- *cube labeled 1–3*
- *spinner with multiples of ten 20–60*
- *game pieces*

## ACTIVITY 2 Flow Factors

**With Your Group** Water travels through hundreds of kilometers of pipeline to reach you. As you play this game, you'll be tracking water used and saved along the pipeline.

1. **Make** a tally sheet. Your group starts with 20,000 L of water in the pipeline.
2. **Roll** the cube. Move your marker the number of spaces you roll. You can move ahead or back. The space tells an amount of water used or saved. Spin the spinner to get a number of days.

3. **Multiply** the amount of water by the number of days. The product is the total amount of water saved or used. Each of you should do the multiplication on your own. Show your work in your notebook.
4. **Share** your product with the rest of your group. Do you agree? If not, check each other's work until you agree.
5. **Change** your tally sheet. Add the amount of water saved to the total in the pipeline. Subtract the amount of water used.
6. **Repeat** Steps 2–5 until you reach the end. Compare your group's tally sheet with the sheets of other groups. Which group has the most water left in the pipeline? Check that the results are correct.

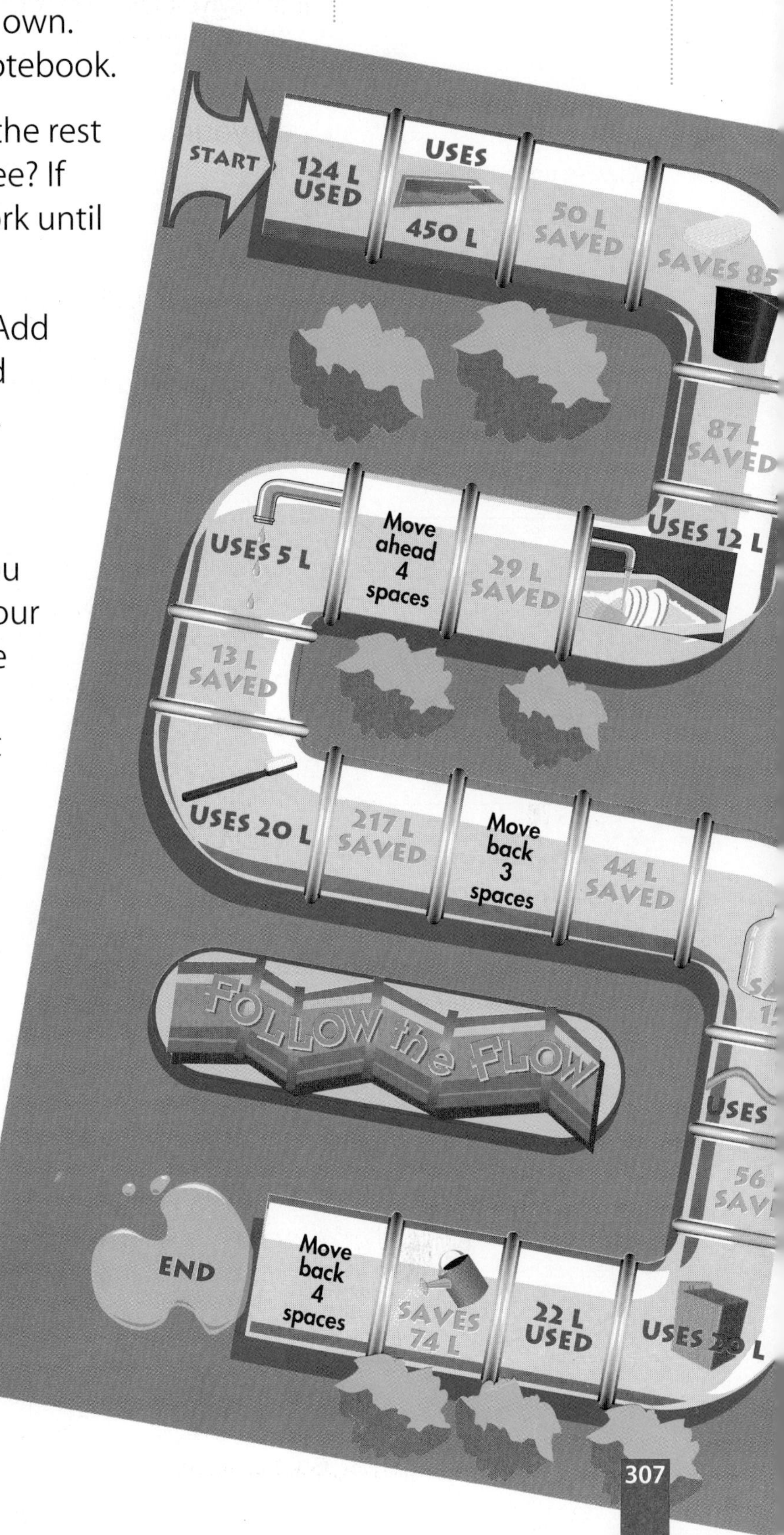

What You'll Need

- *4 cubes labeled 1–6*

REASONING AND PROBLEM SOLVING

*How do you know how many digits are in your answer?*

## ACTIVITY 3 A Group Effort

**With Your Group** List six ways that the people in this neighborhood are using water wisely. Skip-count by 500 to get a different water-saving goal for each way. Play this game for each goal on your list.

**1** **Roll four number cubes to get four digits.**

**2** **On your own, use the digits to make up two factors for a multiplication. The factors tell how many people are saving water and how many liters each saves.**

**3** **Estimate each person's product. Find the estimate closest to the water-saving goal for this game.**

**4** **What would happen in this game? The goal is 1,000 L, and you roll 3, 4, 6, and 2. Which estimate is closest to the goal?**

| People | Savings | Estimate |
|---|---|---|
| 32 | 46 L | 30 × 50 = 1,500 L |
| 42 | 36 L | 40 × 40 = 1,600 L |
| 23 | 46 L | 20 × 50 = 1,000 L |
| 346 | 2 L | 300 × 2 = 600 L |

ACTIVITY OPTION

*Use the four digits you roll to make the largest product possible. The winner is the person who saves the most water.*

Do You Remember?

## Try It!

Which pair of factors would you use to estimate? Why?

| | | |
|---|---|---|
| **1.** 43 × 68 | **a.** 40 × 60 | **b.** 40 × 70 |
| **2.** 76 × 27 | **a.** 70 × 20 | **b.** 80 × 30 |
| **3.** 310 × 72 | **a.** 310 × 70 | **b.** 300 × 70 |
| **4.** 24 × 26 | **a.** 20 × 20 | **b.** 20 × 30 |
| **5.** 89 × 47 | **a.** 90 × 50 | **b.** 80 × 40 |

Which numbers have 5 or 10 as a factor?

**6.** 40 **7.** 695 **8.** 506 **9.** 817 **10.** 1,740

### Think About It

**11.** Write a sentence or two explaining how you would estimate 25 × 25.

Investigation

# Every Drop Counts

Can you think of a way to save water in your home, school, or neighborhood? Help people use less water but still get the water they need.

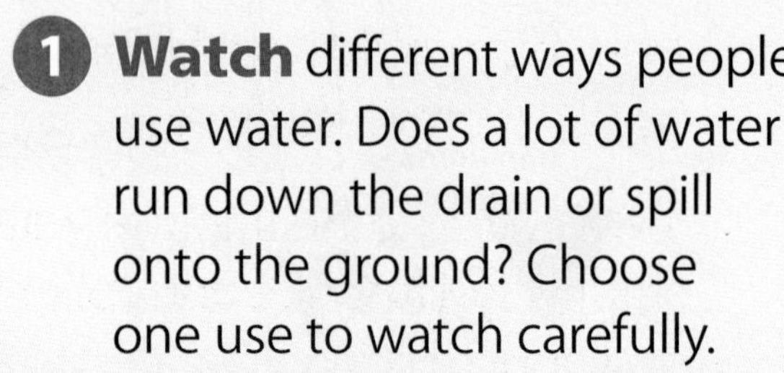

1. **Watch** different ways people use water. Does a lot of water run down the drain or spill onto the ground? Choose one use to watch carefully.
2. **Measure** how much water flows out each time someone uses water this way. What if it's more than your measuring container can hold? Figure out the water use in a day, week, month, and year.

3. **Experiment** to find a way of saving water in the activity. Figure out the amount of water your way could save in a day, week, month, and year.

4. **Persuade** others to use water your way. Describe your plan in a report.

## Ask Yourself

- ☐ What do you know about measuring water usage?
- ☐ What's your plan for finding reasonable measurements?
- ☐ How are you recording your measurements?
- ☐ Did you compare the amount of water used without the water saver with the amount used with the water saver?
- ☐ How can you show others that your aid really works?

Do You Remember? **Cumulative Review**

# Rain Forest Math

As trees are cleared away in rain forests, millions of people and animals lose their homes. Some of these people are working to save their forests. Find out more as you answer these questions.

## Vanishing Forest

**About 100 acres of rain forest get cleared each minute.**

1. How many acres of rain forest get cleared each hour?
2. How many acres of rain forest get cleared in a day?
3. Suppose $\frac{1}{3}$ of a 12-acre section of rain forest is burned to make room for farming. How many acres are left?
4. Thunderstorms may occur more than 200 days a year in the rain forests. The yearly rainfall in three cities near the South American rain forests are 84 cm, 146 cm, and 178 cm. What is the average yearly rainfall for these cities?

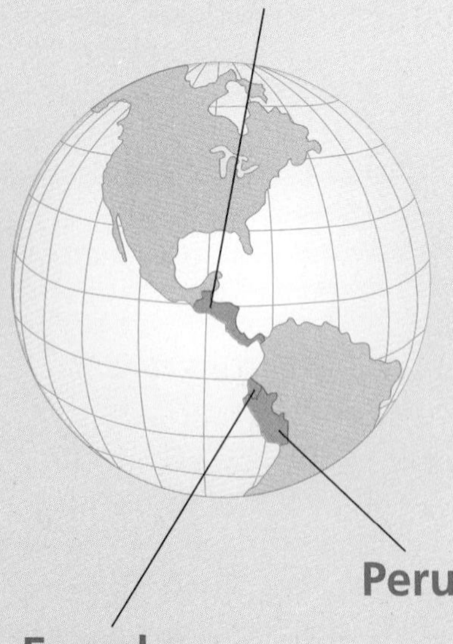

## Farmers in Central America Save Rain Forest and Raise Iguanas.

Iguanas are large lizards that live in the rain forest. A 1-acre iguana farm can produce 200 lb of meat each year.

5 Suppose 5 lb of iguana meat makes 2 family dinners. How many dinners can be produced each year on 1 acre? on 55 acres?

6 How many acres of iguana farm would provide dinner for 720 families?

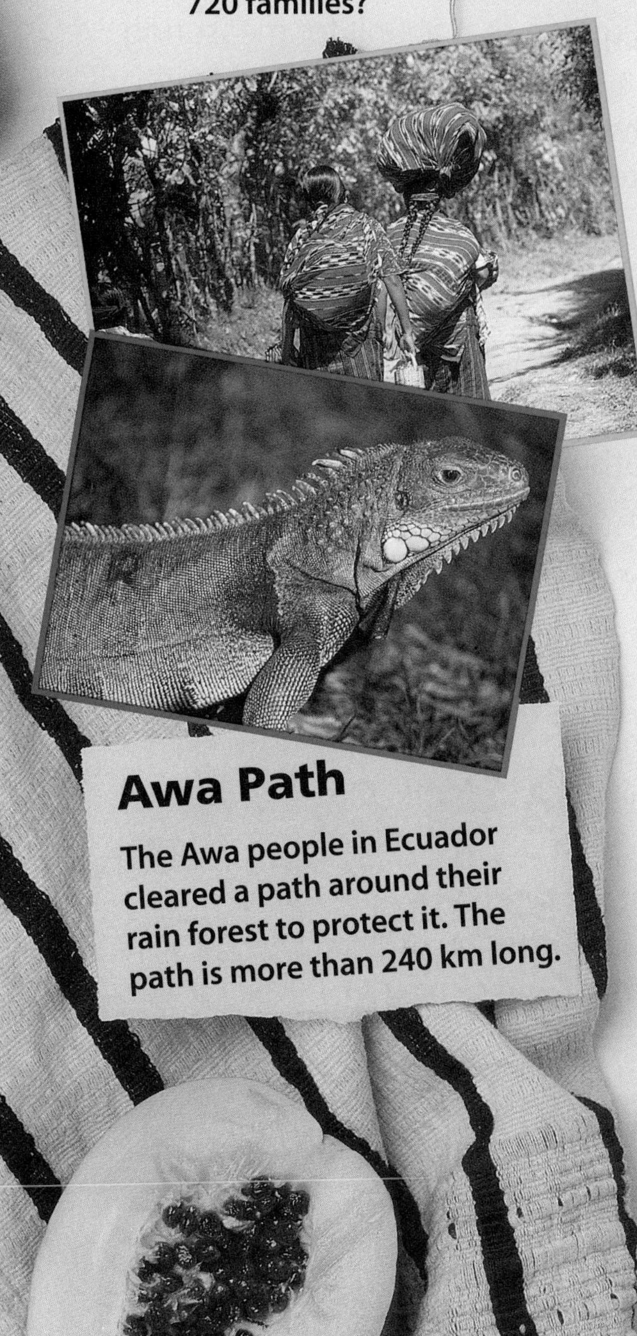

## Aguaje Prices

Teresa lives near the Amazon River in Peru. She collects aguaje fruit from the rain forest to sell in the city. She could sell a large bag of fruit for 4.95 soles, a medium bag for 3.73 soles, and a small bag for 2.19 soles.

7 How much could Teresa earn by selling 1 bag of each size?

8 Would Teresa earn more by selling 2 large bags and 1 small bag or by selling 3 medium bags? How much more?

## Awa Path

The Awa people in Ecuador cleared a path around their rain forest to protect it. The path is more than 240 km long.

## Check Your Math Power

9 Teresa sold all her bags and earned about 150 soles. How many of each size might she have sold? Use estimation.

10 What are some rectangular areas that could be protected with a perimeter of 240 km? What would be the largest possible area?

# Lesson 6 Paper Poll

*An average family of four uses about 1,044 kg of paper a year. That's almost the weight of a car. What else might be this heavy?*

The **kilogram (kg)** is a metric unit for measuring mass. The mass of a thing is often described as its weight. A pile of newspapers 8 cm high has a weight (mass) of about 1 kg. One kilogram is about 2 lb.

## Activity 1 Heavyweights

**With Your Group** Do one of these exercises. Then make up an exercise about the data on the notebooks. Let another group find the answer.

1. **How much would 1 tree weigh? How much would 60 trees weigh?**

2. **How many trees get cut down for Sunday papers in 10 weeks? How many are cut down in 30 weeks? in 50 weeks?**

ACTIVITY 2

# Measuring Paper

**With Your Group** A smaller unit for measuring mass is the **gram (g).** There are 1,000 g in 1 kg. The mass of a large paper clip is about 1 g.

**What You'll Need**

- *wire clothes hanger*
- *scissors*
- *2 paper cups*
- *large paper clips*
- *paper samples*

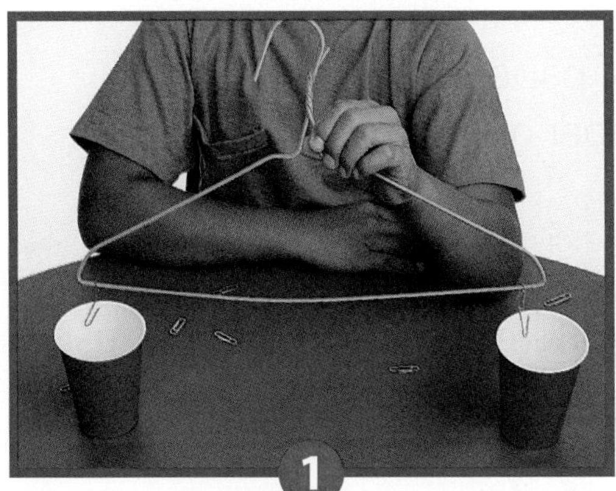

1

**Build a balance scale like the one above.**

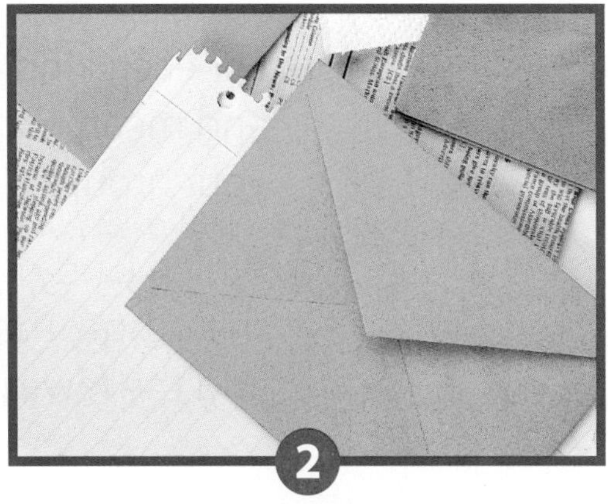

2

**Collect pieces of at least four different kinds of paper.**

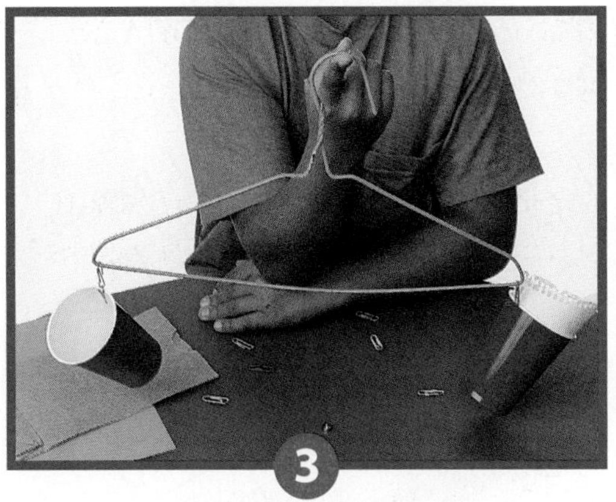

3

**Compare the paper, using your scale. Which paper is heaviest? How many grams is the mass of each paper? Record your findings.**

4

**List the masses of the papers from heaviest to lightest.**

*A pencil's mass is about 10 g. How many pencils make up 1 kg?*

*Use grid paper to graph the amount of paper you use. Show findings from your chart.*

## Activity 3 Paper Survey

**With Your Group** Make a chart like the one on the left below. It should show the kinds of paper you use. How does your monthly paper use compare with other people's? Find out by doing Exercises 1–3 in any order. Do Exercise 4 last.

1. For each kind of paper, find the median and mean number of grams per person in your group.

2. Which kind of paper is used the most? Find the **range,** the difference between the most and the fewest grams per person.

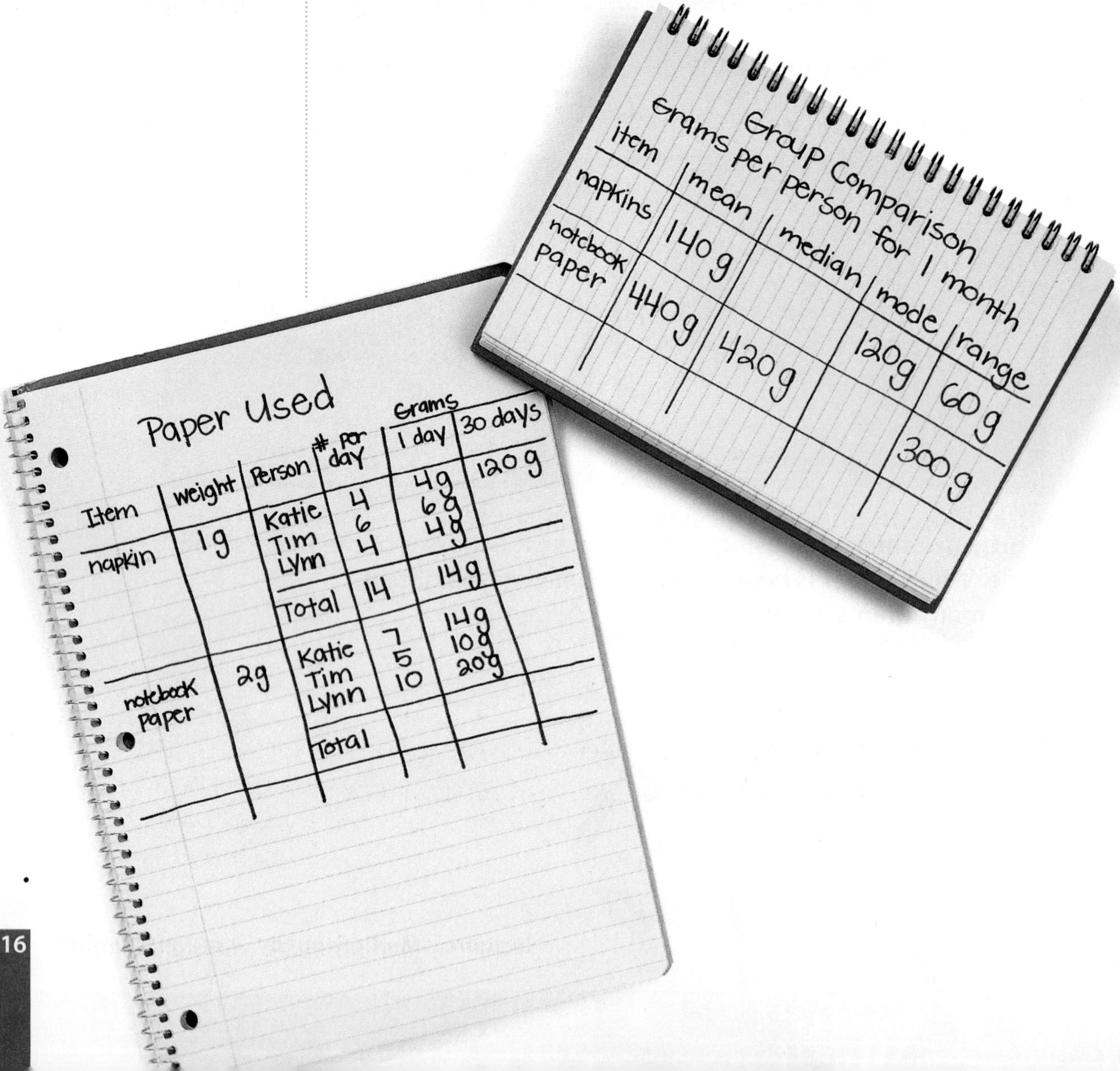

Paper Used

| Item | weight | Person | # per day | Grams 1 day | Grams 30 days |
|---|---|---|---|---|---|
| napkin | 1g | Katie | 4 | 4g | 120g |
| | | Tim | 6 | 6g | |
| | | Lynn | 4 | 4g | |
| | | Total | 14 | 14g | |
| notebook paper | 2g | Katie | 7 | 14g | |
| | | Tim | 5 | 10g | |
| | | Lynn | 10 | 20g | |
| | | Total | | | |

Group Comparison
Grams per person for 1 month

| item | mean | median | mode | range |
|---|---|---|---|---|
| napkins | 140 g | | 120g | 60 g |
| notebook paper | 440 g | 420 g | | 300 g |

3. For which kind of paper is each person's use about the same? Find the **mode,** the amount most often used.

4. How does your group's monthly paper use compare with other groups'?

## Try It!

Change grams to kilograms and kilograms to grams.

**1.** 3 kg　　**2.** 6,000 g　　**3.** 8 kg

**4.** 4 kg　　**5.** 5,000 g　　**6.** 10 kg

Use the masses in Exercises 1–6. Change grams to kilograms. Then find the following.

**7.** mean　　**8.** median　　**9.** mode　　**10.** range

**11.** Estimate the greatest product. Prove it.

**a.** $150 \times 4$　　**b.** $35 \times 10$　　**c.** $18 \times 30$

### Think About It

**12.** A gram can be divided into 1,000 equal units. Guess the name of the units. How can the metric system help you?

# LESSON 7 The Big Pileup

✔ **Self-Check** *If an exact product is greatly different from a reasonable estimate, what might you do?*

Each person in the United States uses about 21 kg of paper a month. How can estimation and multiplication help you find out how much paper people use?

## ACTIVITY 1 Estimating

**On Your Own** Use what you know about rounding to help you estimate products.

1. Copy and complete the estimates in the notebook. What do they tell you about the exact product of 24 × 21? Pick the estimate you think is closest to the exact product. Be ready to tell why you think so.

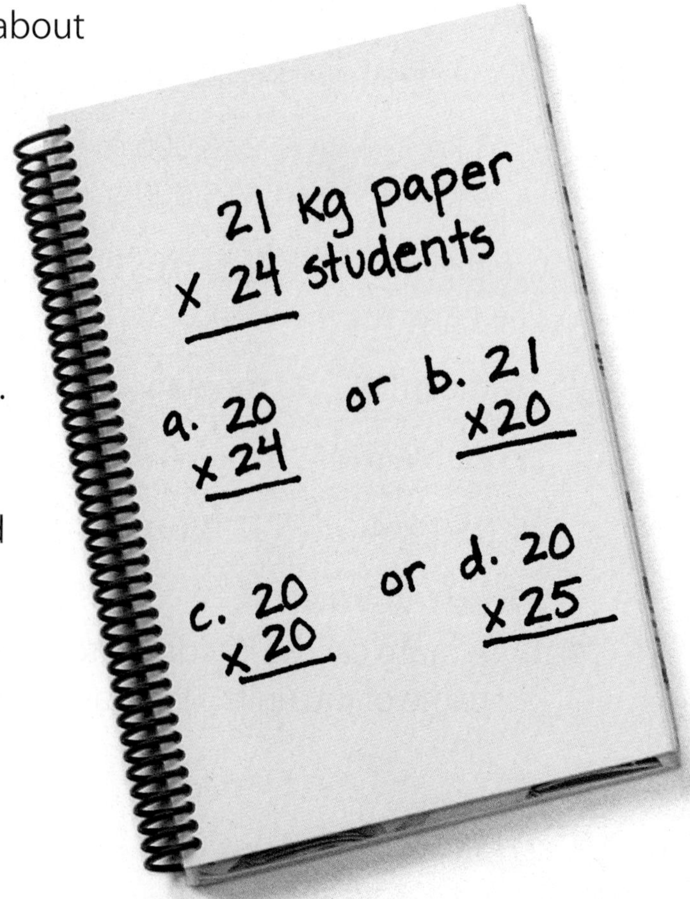


2. Estimate the following. How much paper would 38 students use? How much would 42 people use? What would 55 people use? Compare your estimates with those of two classmates.

## ACTIVITY 2 Getting Closer

**With Your Group** Sometimes you need a close answer. You can multiply the exact numbers without rounding.

1. A class has 24 students. Suppose each student uses about 36 sheets of looseleaf paper per month. How much notebook paper would the class use in a month? Think of 24 stacks of 36 sheets each. How could you rearrange the stacks for easier multiplication?

2. Copy and complete the chart below. First round the factors to estimate each product. Then find an answer by multiplying the exact numbers. Record each easier multiplication you use to get the final answer.

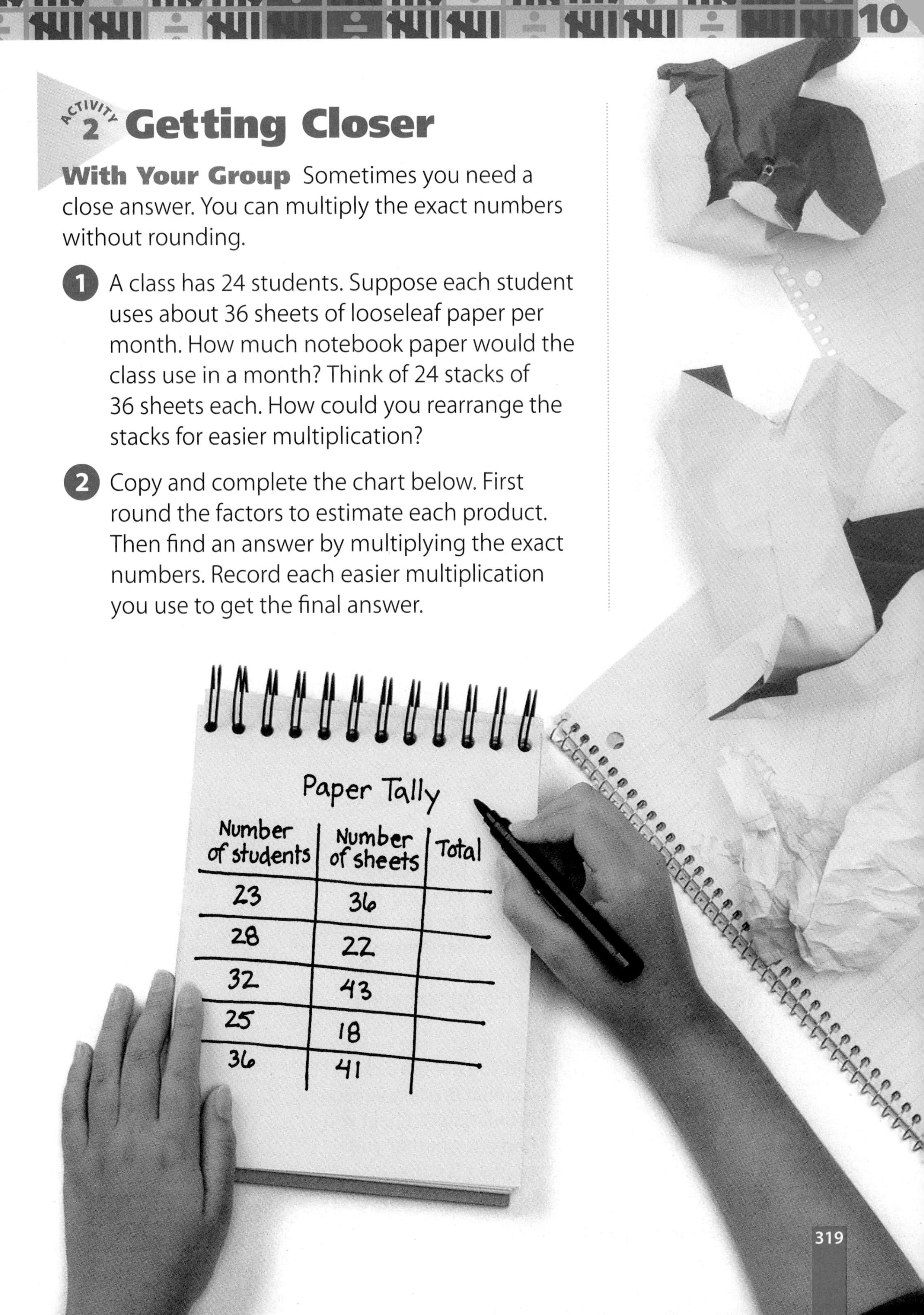

Paper Tally

| Number of students | Number of sheets | Total |
|---|---|---|
| 23 | 36 | |
| 28 | 22 | |
| 32 | 43 | |
| 25 | 18 | |
| 36 | 41 | |

# More Multiplication

**With Your Group** You can find products in more than one way.

**1** **Does each of the ways written in the notebook lead to the same product? What pattern do you see?**

**2** **Because of the Distributive Property, a multiplication can be split into smaller steps.**

A family throws away 12 kg of trash a day. How much do they throw away in 45 days?

a. $12 \times 40 + 12 \times 5$

b. $12 \times 20 + 12 \times 20 + 12 \times 5$

c. $12 \times 30 + 12 \times 10 + 12 \times 5$

Packaging makes up 28 kg of the family's trash each week. How much packaging is thrown out in 52 weeks?

**3** **Use the Distributive Property to help you answer the question on the smaller notebook. Write different versions of the multiplication.**

**4** **Did you get the same product in every version? Estimation can help you find out whether your product is correct.**

*Sketch an array for multiplying a pair of two-digit numbers that aren't multiples of ten. Show a way to rearrange the array to find the product.*

# ACTIVITY 4 Brown-bagging It!

**With Your Group** Explain how the product in the notebook below was calculated. See if you can use this way to multiply. How many paper bags do your families use?

*See page 394 in the Tool Kit to review the steps in multiplying by a two-digit factor.*

**1 Find out the total number of bags your families use per week. How many bags would be used in 13 weeks? 28 weeks? 52 weeks?**

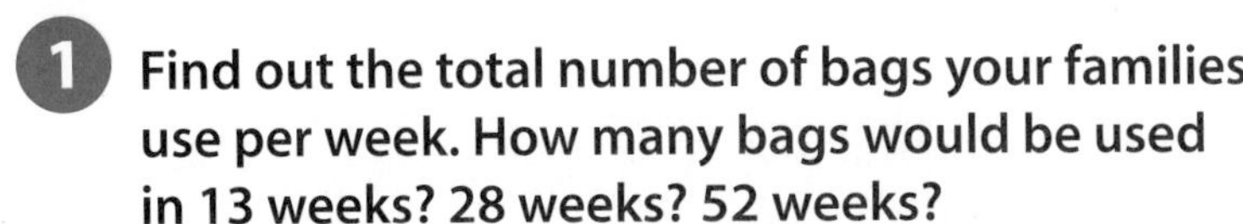

53 bags a week
× 13 weeks
159
+530
689 bags

**2 How many trees were cut down to make your group's paper bags for a year?**

One tree makes 700 paper bags.

Do You Remember?

## Try It!

Complete parts a and b. Describe how you can use the answers to find the answer to part c.

| | a. | b. | c. |
|---|---|---|---|
| 1. | a. $60 \times 32$ | b. $8 \times 32$ | c. $68 \times 32$ |
| 2. | a. $9 \times 59$ | b. $3 \times 59$ | c. $12 \times 59$ |
| 3. | a. $30 \times 15$ | b. $3 \times 15$ | c. $27 \times 15$ |
| 4. | a. $90 \times 516$ | b. $2 \times 516$ | c. $88 \times 516$ |

Find $\frac{3}{4}$ of the number.

5. 24 6. 40 7. 64 8. 88 9. 516 10. 800

### Think About It

11. Explain two ways to change a factor and make it easier to multiply. Write your answer.

Lesson 8

# Tree Releaf

LITERATURE

*Walter didn't recycle. He dropped trash outside. One night in a dream he saw what could happen to the world if everyone was as thoughtless as he. Walter saw a polluted, treeless world.*

The future he'd seen was not what he'd expected. Robots and little airplanes didn't seem very important now. He looked out his window at the trees and lawns in the early morning light, then jumped out of bed.

He ran outside and down the block, still in his pajamas. He found the empty jelly doughnut bag he'd thrown at the fire hydrant the day before. Then Walter went back home and, before the sun came up, sorted all the trash by the garage.

A few days later, on Walter's birthday, all his friends came over for cake and ice cream. They loved his new toys: the laser gun set, electric yo-yo, and inflatable dinosaurs. "My best present," Walter told them, "is outside." Then he showed them the gift that he'd picked out that morning—a tree.

After the party, Walter and his dad planted the birthday present.

From *Just a Dream*
by Chris Van Allsburg

- Why was the tree Walter's favorite present?
- List all the reasons you can for planting trees.

| Kids | each Plants | total |
|---|---|---|
| 20 | 100 | |
| 20 | 10 | |
| 20 | 50 | |
| 20 | | |
| | | 240 |

## ACTIVITY 1 Tree Musketeers

**With Your Group** Walter might want to join the Tree Musketeers, a national group that plants trees. Suppose Walter's local group of 20 members wants to plant 240 trees. Each member gets the same number of trees. How many trees will each member have to plant?

1. What ways can you think of to answer this question? Can multiplication help?
2. Fill in the chart. Will each person have to plant 100 trees? at least 10 trees? at least 50 trees?
3. Use the chart to find the exact answer. Then finish filling in the chart.

*In Your Journal*
*Explain how you used multiplication to solve the division problem.*

*Guess-and-check helps you do a division exercise. Guess the quotient. Multiply it by the divisor. Check how close the product is to the dividend. Try to make the next guess even closer.*

## Activity 2 P-R-R-R Plan

**With Your Class** How can you save trees? One good plan is to precycle, reuse, reduce, and recycle paper. A class of 30 students set a goal to precycle a total 670 g of paper each day. Each student will precycle the same amount. How much will each student need to precycle?

$$30\overline{)670}$$

**Paper Saving Goals**

5,432 g ÷ 10 students
6,312 g ÷ 60 students
906 g ÷ 50 students
7,214 g ÷ 90 students
487 g ÷ 30 students
618 g ÷ 20 students
8,484 g ÷ 80 students
1,701 g ÷ 40 students
92 g ÷ 10 students
540 g ÷ 70 students

1. Would each student precycle at least 10 g? at least 100 g? Why don't you have to think about 1,000 here?

$$30 \times 100 = ?$$
$$30 \times 10 = ?$$

2. Use the multiplications to help you guess the quotient.

3. Look at the Paper-Saving Goals. Write which divisions you think have two-digit quotients. Check your answers.

## Activity 3 Reuse

**With Your Group** On slips of paper write ideas for reusing paper. On the back of each slip write a three-digit number. The number will stand for kilograms in a neighborhood paper-reuse drive. For each slip choose any multiple of 10 between 10 and 90. It stands for the number of families in the neighborhood. How much paper will each family have to save? One example is shown below.

*Why are multiples of ten easier than other numbers for starting guess-and-check? Watch for a pattern. What way of changing the dividend helps you make the best guesses?*

1. How do you know if your quotient has two digits ?

$$40 \times 10 = ?$$
$$40 \times 100 = ?$$

2. How can you use multiplication to decide what digit goes in the tens' place?

$$40 \times ? = 800$$
$$40 \times ? = 1{,}200$$

3. How does knowing the tens' digit help you guess the whole quotient?

# ACTIVITY 4 Reduce

**With Your Class** Reducing the amount of paper you and your friends use by 883 kg could save about 17 trees. If 30 of you each wanted to save the same amount, how much paper would you each need to save?

$30\overline{)883}$

1. **How many digits are in the quotient?**

   **30 × 10 = ?**
   **30 × 100 = ?**

2. **What digit goes in the tens' place? How can you use multiples of ten to help you decide?**

   **30 × 30 = ?**
   **30 × 20 = ?**

3. **How many more 30's are in 283?**

   **30 × 8 = ?**
   **30 × 9 = ?**

4. **What is the best way to show the remainder? How much less paper would 20 students need to use to save 674 kg?**

✓ **Self-Check** *How can you check a division exercise? Remember that multiplication and division are inverse operations.*

## Activity 5 Tick-Tack-Toe Game

**With Your Partner** Who can recycle the most paper per day? For each game fill in three-digit numbers on a grid to show kilograms recycled.

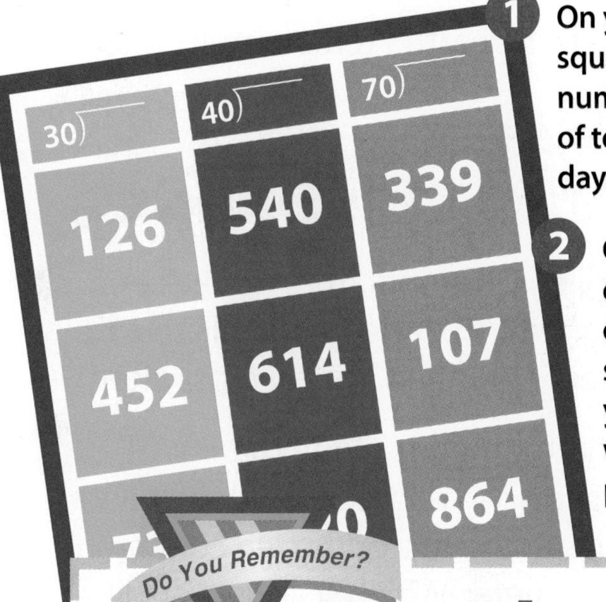


1. On your turn mark a square. Divide that number by the multiple of ten (the number of days) above it.

2. Check each other's quotients. Stop when one player marks three squares in a row. Add your quotients to see who recycled the most paper per day.

**What You'll Need**

- *grid paper*

*Can you think of ways to recycle paper in your classroom? Make a chart and track your progress for a month.*

Do You Remember?

## Try It!

Predict the digit in the quotient's tens' place when 986 is divided by the following. Then divide.

**1.** 10 **2.** 20 **3.** 30 **4.** 40 **5.** 50

Divide.

**6.** $30\overline{)4,123}$ **7.** $30\overline{)753}$ **8.** $30\overline{)927}$

Find the products greater than 1,000.

**9.** $24 \times 32$ **10.** $40 \times 52$ **11.** $88 \times 31$
**12.** $51 \times 12$ **13.** $65 \times 19$ **14.** $78 \times 11$

### Think About It

**15.** What happens to the quotient when the divisor increases? when the dividend increases?

# LESSON 9 Hot and Cold

**T**rees help keep the earth's temperature within a comfortable range.

What You'll Need
- *thermometer*

## ACTIVITY 1 Cooler in the Shade

**With Your Group** Temperature is measured in **degrees Fahrenheit (°F)** or **degrees Celsius (°C).** In the United States Fahrenheit is used most often.

1. Look at the thermometers. Write the temperature shown in degrees Fahrenheit and degrees Celsius at the top of the red column on each thermometer. Which scale is more like metric units, such as centimeters? Why?

Water freezes at 32°F (0°C).
Water boils at 212°F (100°C).

2 Compare temperatures in bright sun and in shade. What difference do trees make in air temperature?

3 Measure the temperature of several different locations in your school.

4 Make a chart to record your findings. Find the mean, median, mode, and range of the temperatures on the chart.

Temperature Recordings
closet 65°F
playground 74°F
bathroom 70°F
shelf 60°F

*Anders Celsius developed the Celsius scale in 1742. He proposed 100° for the freezing point of water and 0° for the boiling point. Why do you think these temperatures were later reversed?*

## Try It!

Pick all the temperatures that make sense for each item.

| | | |
|---|---|---|
| **1.** snowball | **2.** hot chocolate | **3.** sun |
| **4.** classroom | **5.** hot radiator | **6.** swimming pool |

| | | | |
|---|---|---|---|
| **a.** 31.9°F | **b.** 20.3°C | **c.** 130.6°F | **d.** 5,500.7°C |
| **e.** 0°F | **f.** 67°F | **g.** 0.5°C | **h.** 9,900°F |

Find the quotients greater than 30.

| | | |
|---|---|---|
| **7.** $683 \div 10$ | **8.** $20\overline{)808}$ | **9.** $40\overline{)152}$ |
| **10.** $60\overline{)958}$ | **11.** $962 \div 30$ | **12.** $746 \div 20$ |

### Think About It

**13.** What do you think a temperature of $-5$°F means?

## Exercises and Problems

# A Weighty Issue

Your friend's school is holding a newspaper-recycling drive. Choose eight out of these ten problems to solve.

**1** **It takes 1 tree to make about 50 kg of newspaper. Copy the chart below. About how many trees' worth of newspaper did each class collect? Complete the second column on the chart.**

**2** **The class with the greatest number of kilograms per student gets a prize! Complete the last column to find out who wins.**

| Number of Students | Number of trees | Total Kg collected | Kg per Student |
|---|---|---|---|
| 30 1st graders | | 4,020 | |
| 20 2nd graders | | 1,940 | |
| 50 3rd graders | | 8,250 | |
| 40 4th graders | | 8,640 | |
| 60 5th graders | | 9,480 | |

**3** **An 8-cm stack of newspaper weighs 1 kg. How high a stack could the winning class make? How high a stack did they collect per person?**

**4** **What is the range of the total kilograms collected? What is the median number of kilograms collected?**

**5** **What is the mean number of students in a class?**

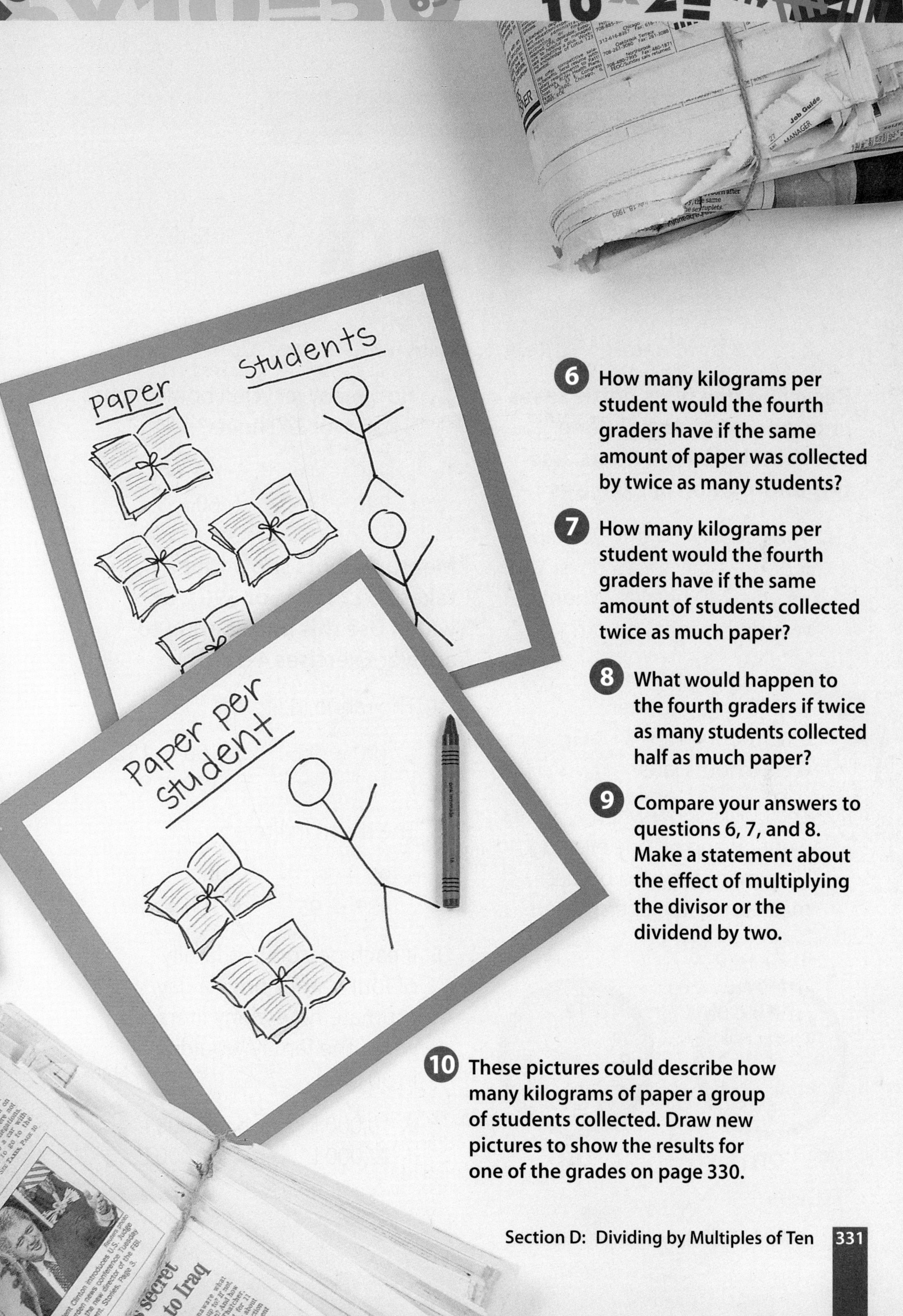


6 How many kilograms per student would the fourth graders have if the same amount of paper was collected by twice as many students?

7 How many kilograms per student would the fourth graders have if the same amount of students collected twice as much paper?

8 What would happen to the fourth graders if twice as many students collected half as much paper?

9 Compare your answers to questions 6, 7, and 8. Make a statement about the effect of multiplying the divisor or the dividend by two.

10 These pictures could describe how many kilograms of paper a group of students collected. Draw new pictures to show the results for one of the grades on page 330.

Do You Remember? **Cumulative Review**

# Looking Back

Choose the right answer. Write *a, b, c,* or *d* for each question.

**Recycling one glass bottle saves enough energy to light one 100-watt bulb for 4 hours. Use this information in Exercises 1–3.**

1. Your goal is to light 10 bulbs 5 hours a day for 15 days. You recycle 240 bottles. When would the lights go off?

   a. 21 hours sooner
   b. 210 hours sooner
   c. 21 hours later
   d. 210 hours later

2. The clocks show when 12 lights went on and off one evening. How many recycled bottles make up for the energy used?

   a. 7 b. 6 c. 1 d. 4

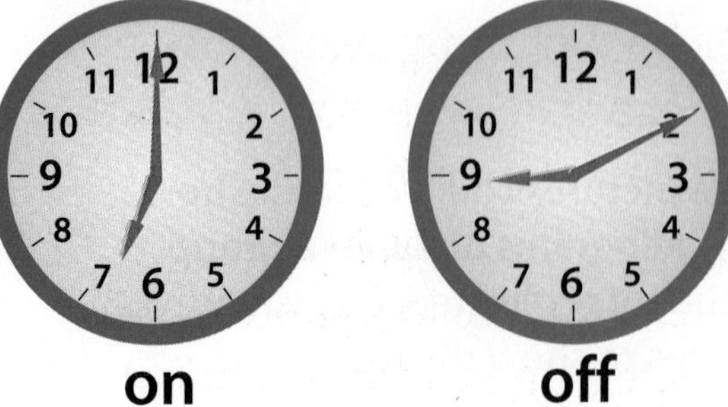


3. How many recycled bottles light 3 bulbs for 240 hours?

   a. $240 \div 4$ b. $60 \div 4$
   c. $240 \div 3$ d. $60 \times 3$

**Measurements show that a bath takes 95 L, 152 L, or 190 L of water. Use this information to answer Exercises 4–6.**

4. The range in liters is

   a. $190 - 95$ b. $190 - 152$
   c. $152 - 95$ d. $190 + 95$

5. The mean in liters is

   a. $95 \div 3$ b. $437 \div 3$
   c. $437 \div 95$ d. $190 \div 3$

6. If each person in a family of four bathes once a day, estimate how many liters of water the family would use in 30 days.

   a. 19,000 L b. 18,000 L
   c. 12,000 L d. 22,000 L

7. Write five numbers with the same mean and median.

8. A cow drinks 11 L of water to produce 4 L of milk. How much water does the cow need to produce 320 L?

   a. $8 \times 10$ L  b. $320 \div 11$ L
   c. $80 \times 11$ L  d. $320 \div 4$ L

**Use the above diagram to answer Exercises 9–11.**

9. A stalk needs 100 L of water to grow tall. How much water is needed for 3 acres?

   a. 30,000 L  b. 300,000 L
   c. 100,000 L  d. 3,000 L

10. How many acres should be planted to get 1,650 bushels?

    a. $1,650 \div 11$  b. $1,650 \times 11$
    c. $1,650 \div 33$  d. $1,650 \div 100$

11. If an acre's yield is 10 bushels different from the average, what is the range of possible yields?

12. In a year a tree can change about 4,000 g of carbon dioxide into oxygen. How many kilograms is that in 6 months?

    a. 2 kg  b. 24 kg
    c. 8 kg  d. 10 kg

13. In 30 years 6,500 square kilometers of the Para forest in Brazil have been cleared. If the cutting continues, about how many square kilometers of forest will be cleared in the next 5 years?

    a. 5,000  b. 3,000
    c. 8,000  d. 1,000

## Check Your Math Power

**Use the data to write your own problems and solve them.**

14. Every 900 kg of paper that is recycled saves 17 trees and 26,000 L of fresh water.

15. To produce 1 L of gasoline, 70 L of water are needed.

16. Offices throw away enough paper in a year to form a wall 4 m high from Los Angeles to New York City. Assume the wall is 4,000 km long and 10 cm wide (the width of a brick).

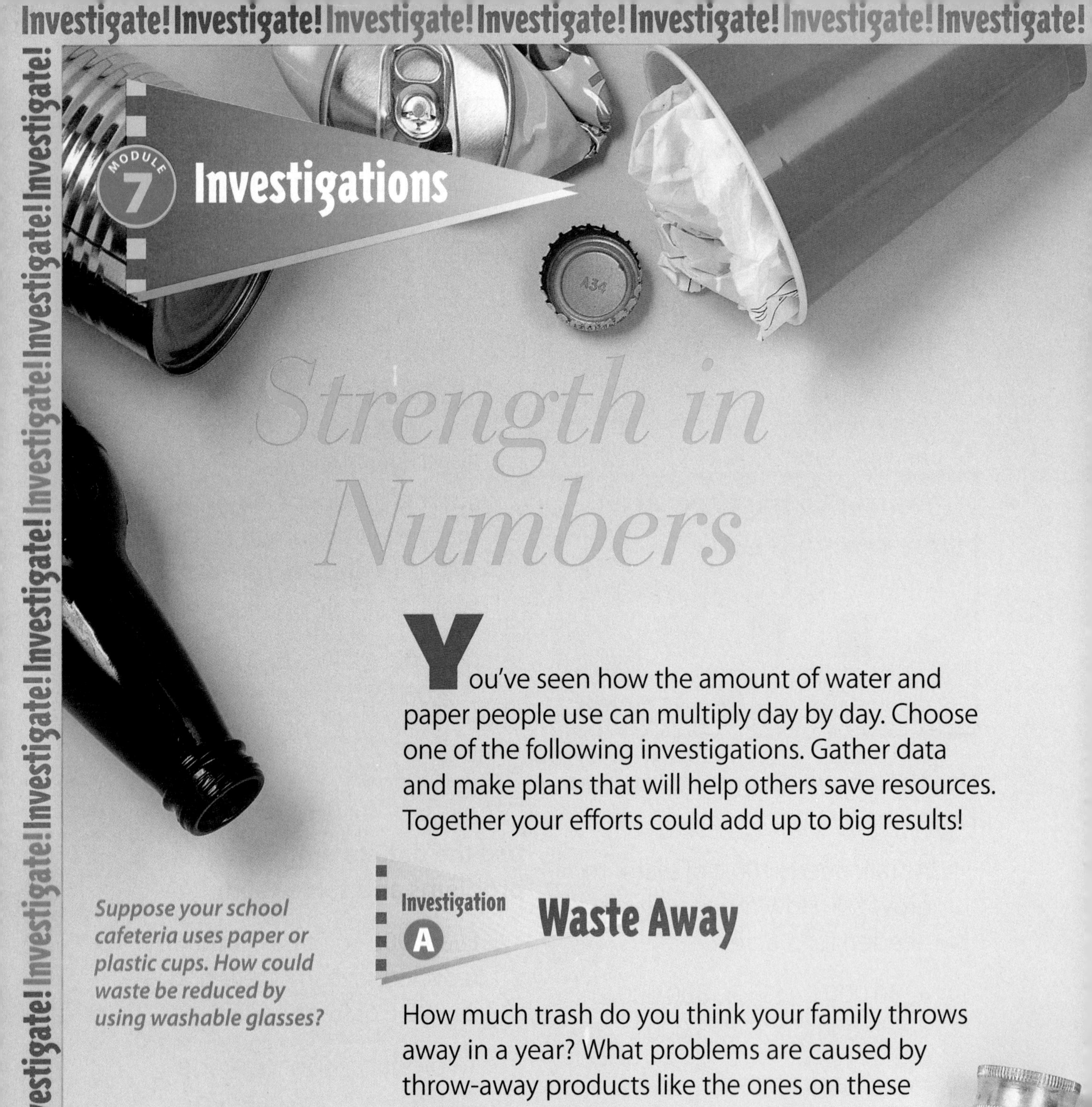

# Module 7 Investigations

# Strength in Numbers

You've seen how the amount of water and paper people use can multiply day by day. Choose one of the following investigations. Gather data and make plans that will help others save resources. Together your efforts could add up to big results!

## Investigation A Waste Away

How much trash do you think your family throws away in a year? What problems are caused by throw-away products like the ones on these pages? Try to reduce the use of one item in your home, school, or community.

*Suppose your school cafeteria uses paper or plastic cups. How could waste be reduced by using washable glasses?*

*Some families agree to fill a bucket to wash their cars instead of using a hose. How much water could be saved?*

1. Select a product or resource that gets thrown away after use. Estimate how many units of the product your group's families use in a day, a week, and a year.
2. Measure use of the product. You can't measure every bit. Why is it enough to measure a few examples?
3. Record your measurements. How many units of the product do your families use in a day?
4. Predict results for a week and a year. How do your predicted results and estimates compare?
5. Set a goal for reducing the amount of the product that gets thrown away. To reach that goal, how much would each family member have to save in a week? in a year? How would members' habits have to change?

Paper Cups
How many are used in our cafeteria?

| Number per day used | Trash | | |
|---|---|---|---|
| | grams per day | grams per wk. | grams per yr. |

## Keep in Mind

**Your report will be judged by how well you do the following things.**

- ☐ Use what you know about the process of measurement to get your data.
- ☐ Use multiplication and division to set up your plan.
- ☐ Convince your class the plan will work.

*What if families started using cloth diapers instead of disposable ones? How much would waste be reduced in your area?*

## Investigation B: Recycle

Plan a way to save trees by recycling paper.

- Pick a kind of paper that can be recycled in your community. How much of that paper gets thrown away by your class in a day? in a week? in a year?
- Set a recycling goal. To reach that goal, how much would each class member have to recycle per day? per week? per year? How would the paper be collected for recycling?

### Computer Option

You can set up a computer spreadsheet to help you organize data. Spreadsheets allow you to use the computer to multiply and divide quickly. If you enter data for a day's use, you can program the computer to calculate use for a week and a year. Try different recycling goals to see the results. You can also print out your spreadsheet. Pass out copies to classmates.

## Investigation C: Picture It!

Find out about buying recycled paper. Make a poster to share information with your class. How many trees could be saved in a year by your class? by your school? What would recycled paper cost per person for a week? a month? a year? How much more or less would it cost than paper that isn't recycled?

# Lucky Summer

Summer is coming. Maybe you're already looking forward to the months ahead. Think about what plans you would like to make for the summer. Which of those plans is the most likely to happen? Which is the least likely? Do any of your summer plans seem impossible?

# Summer Fun

## 1 Days of Summer

The calendars shown here are filled with ideas for summer fun. Which of these things will you probably do? Which will you probably not do? Are there any that you'll do for sure? Are there any that seem impossible?



## 2 Fun Ideas

Think of three ideas for summer fun. One idea should be likely to happen, one should be unlikely to happen, and one impossible. Explain why each idea is likely, unlikely, or impossible.

### Word Bank

- equally likely
- experimental probability
- outcome
- percent
- probability
- ratio
- tree diagram
- trial

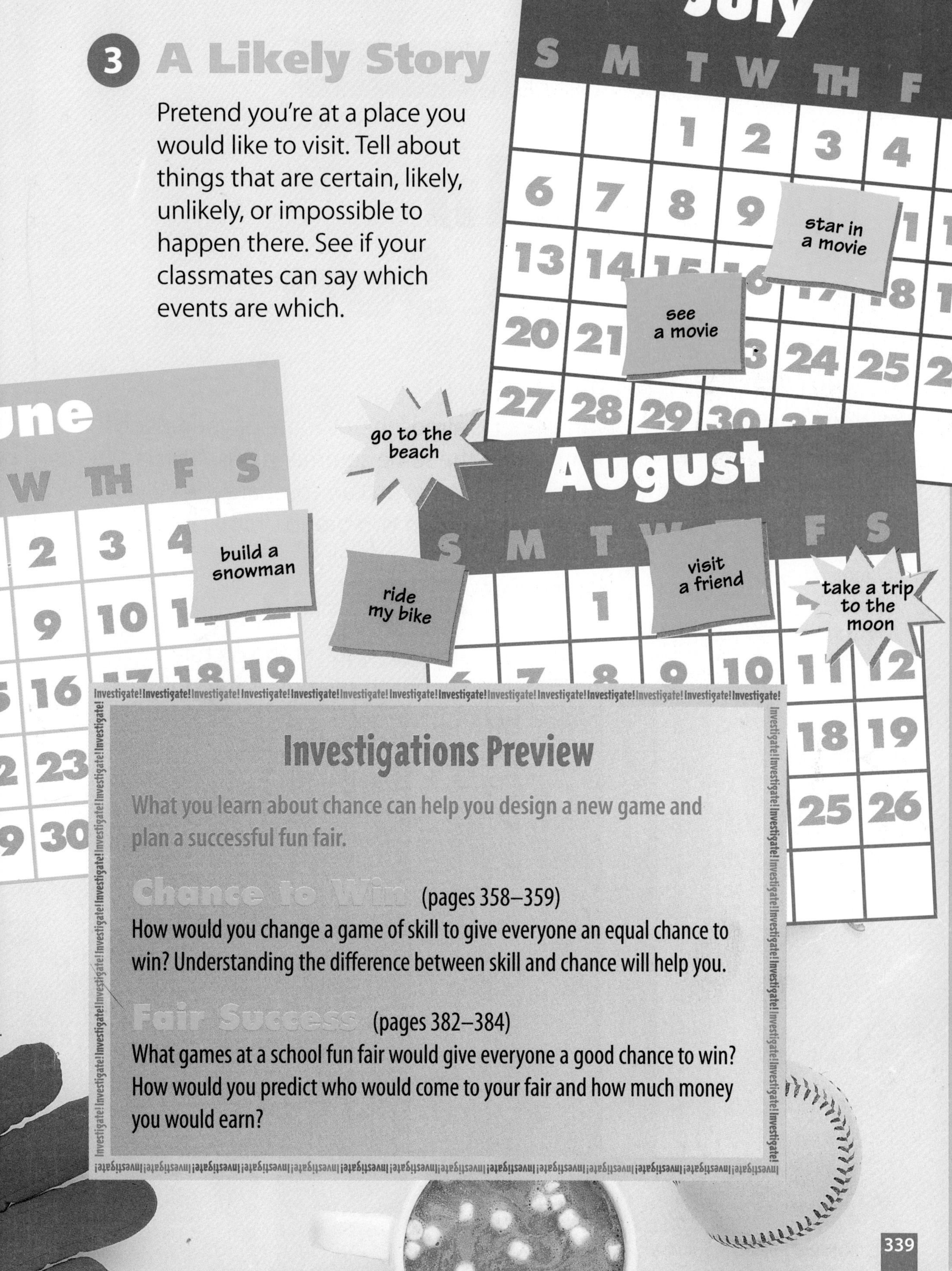


## 3 A Likely Story

Pretend you're at a place you would like to visit. Tell about things that are certain, likely, unlikely, or impossible to happen there. See if your classmates can say which events are which.

## Investigations Preview

What you learn about chance can help you design a new game and plan a successful fun fair.

### Chance to Win (pages 358–359)

How would you change a game of skill to give everyone an equal chance to win? Understanding the difference between skill and chance will help you.

### Fair Success (pages 382–384)

What games at a school fun fair would give everyone a good chance to win? How would you predict who would come to your fair and how much money you would earn?

# LESSON 1 Fun in the Sun

*Draw a simple picture to show the ratio of beach swimmers to pool swimmers in your group. How does the picture help you understand what a ratio is?*

Summer is almost here! Some of your friends probably have the same summer plans. Others have different plans. You can compare the number of people or things in two groups with a **ratio.**

## ACTIVITY 1 Splish Splash

**With Your Group** Look at the pictures below. The ratio of beach swimmers to pool swimmers is 2 to 1. How can you tell? Discuss the other ratios and what they mean.

**beach to pool swimmers**
**2 to 1**

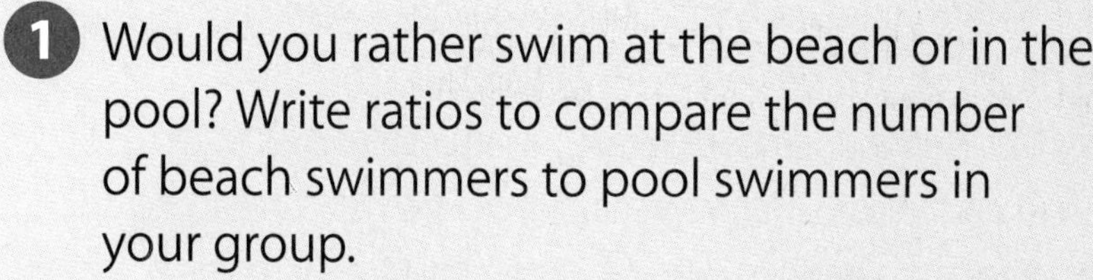

1. Would you rather swim at the beach or in the pool? Write ratios to compare the number of beach swimmers to pool swimmers in your group.

2. Write some secret ratios that compare the places or ways students in your group like to swim. For example, compare how many like the backstroke to how many prefer the crawl.

3. Play a guessing game with other groups. On your turn, divide your group to show one of your secret ratios. Other groups try to guess what your ratio is comparing. They can ask you ten yes-or-no questions.

*Writers try to answer the questions who, what, when, where, why, and how. These questions can help you make up your own ratios and guess other group's ratios.*

**pool swimmers out of all swimmers**
**2 out of 3**

**girls to boys**
**2 to 1**

**boys to girls**
**1 to 2**

**girls out of all swimmers**
**2 out of 3**

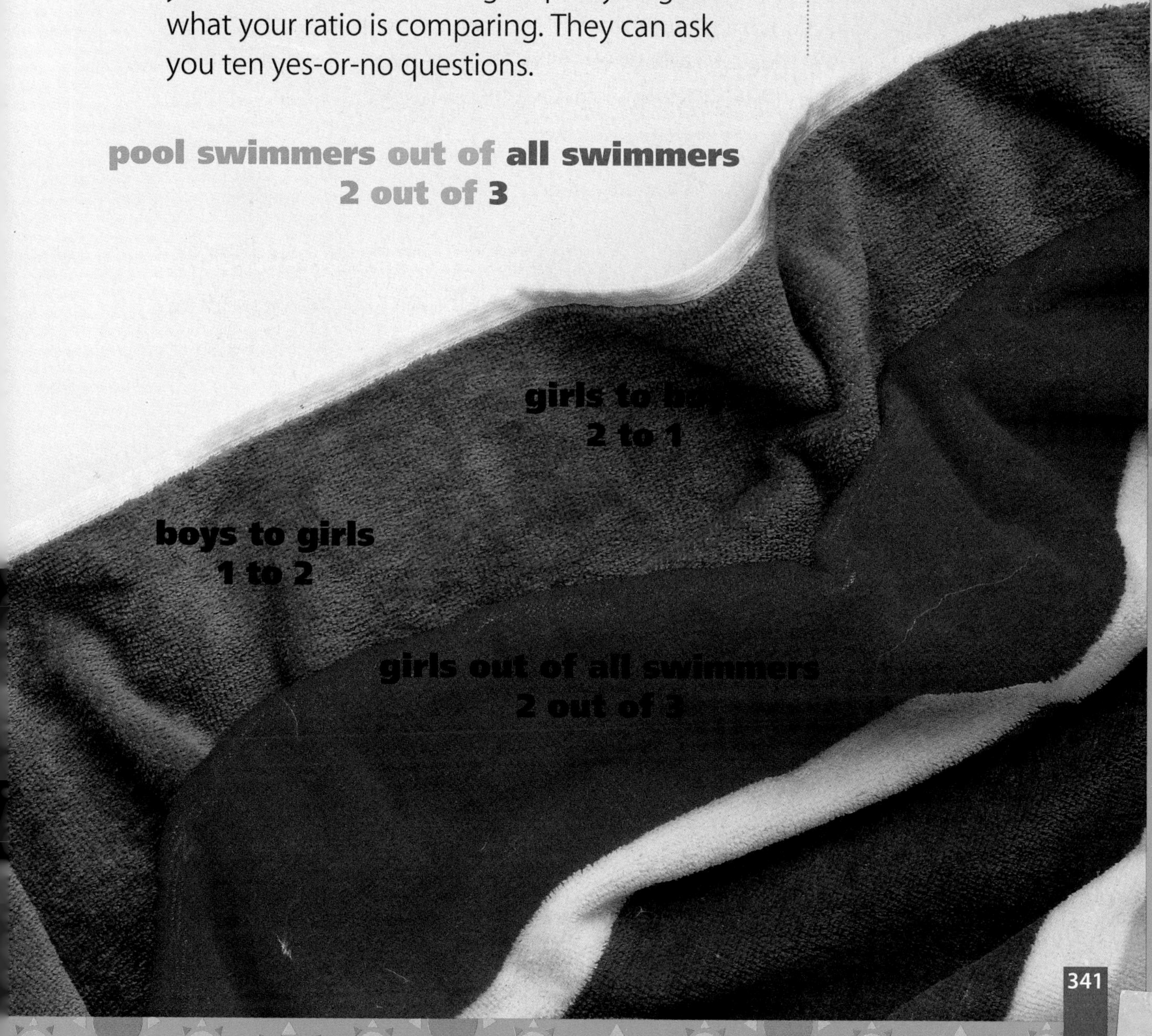

# ACTIVITY 2 Summertime Ratios

**With Your Partner** This summer scene is full of ratios. How would you write a ratio to compare the number of cups to the number of pitchers on the lemonade stand?

**1** **Look at the lemonade stand. Suppose you double the number of cups and pitchers. How many of each would there be? Sketch a picture to show the new ratio of cups to pitchers.**

**2** **When you doubled the numbers, the ratio stayed the same. On your sketch, circle each set to show you still have 3 cups for every 1 pitcher. The ratios "3 for every 1" and "6 for every 2" are equal ratios.**

Self-Check

*How can you use multiplication to see if all the ratios in your table are equal?*

**3** **List ten ratios you find on these pages.**

**4** **Choose two ratios from your list. Draw pictures to show the numbers of each ratio growing 2, 3, 4, 5, and 6 times greater. Circle the sets to show that each ratio is equal to the ratio you started with.**

**5** **Make tables of the equal ratios you drew in Exercise 4. Discuss with your class any patterns you see.**

| Cups | 3 | 6 | ? | ? | ? | ? |
|---|---|---|---|---|---|---|
| Pitchers | 1 | 2 | 3 | 4 | 5 | 6 |

*To find mean temperatures, have your partner read the temperatures aloud while you use a calculator to add them.*

# ACTIVITY 3 Weather or Not?

**On Your Own** Finding weather ratios can help you choose the best summer activity for a given place. The calendars on these pages show the kind of weather you can expect in three towns.

**JULY in Mayport, Florida**

| | | | | | | |
|---|---|---|---|---|---|---|
| 1 80° | 2 82° | 3 85° | 4 78° | 5 72° | 6 69° | 7 69° |
| 8 79° | 9 82° | 10 95° | 11 95° | 12 82° | 13 78° | 14 85° |
| 15 71° | 16 70° | 17 82° | 18 95° | 19 102° | 20 105° | 21 95° |
| 22 88° | 23 79° | 24 88° | 25 85° | 26 85° | 27 82° | 28 68° |
| 29 82° | 30 96° | 31 98° | | | | |

**JULY in Portland, Oregon**

| | | | | | | |
|---|---|---|---|---|---|---|
| 1 74° | 2 75° | 3 68° | 4 69° | 5 71° | 6 69° | 7 68° |
| 8 68° | 9 70° | 10 72° | 11 68° | 12 68° | 13 67° | 14 66° |
| 15 67° | 16 68° | 17 68° | 18 70° | 19 72° | 20 71° | 21 69° |
| 22 69° | 23 72° | 24 70° | 25 69° | 26 77° | 27 85° | 28 71° |
| 29 73° | 30 74° | 31 69° | | | | |

Portland, Oregon

Florida

1. What weather is best for swimming? bicycling? playing indoors?
2. Write ratios about the weather in each town.
   - Find the ratio of sunny days to days of the month.
   - Find the ratio of rainy days to days of the month.
   - Find the median or mean temperature.
   - Think of one other weather ratio to find.

*Why might someone choose an activity different from the one you chose for a town?*

**3** Compare ratios for the three towns. Which ratios help you choose the town with the best weather for swimming? bicycling? playing indoors? Why?

**4** Choose the best activity for each town. Write a report about how you made your choices. Tell which ratios you compared.

## Try It!

Write the ratio. Next make a table to compare groups 2, 3, and 4 times as large.

1. ▢ wheels to 1 bicycle
2. 1 ft to ▢ in.
3. 1 L to ▢ mL
4. 1 m to ▢ cm
5. 1 car to ▢ wheels
6. 1 m to ▢ dm

Use estimation to complete. Write $>$, $<$, or $=$.

7. $3 \times 221$ ● 900
8. $2 \times 3{,}997$ ● 8,000
9. $8 \times 88$ ● 641
10. $7 \times 498$ ● 3,500
11. $5 \times 8{,}668$ ● 43,500

**Think About It**

12. Write how you can check to see if two ratios are equal.

# Summer Surveys

## ACTIVITY 1 Percent Sense

**With Your Class** Suppose you asked 100 students your age the best place to spend a summer afternoon. You might get answers like the ones you see on the color cards.

1. One way to show answers is in a **percent (%)**, a ratio that means "for every hundred." Explain why each of the expressions below shows that 43 out of 100 students chose the beach.

   **43 out of 100**

   $\frac{43}{100}$ **0.43** **43%**

2. Write each of the other responses as a percent, a fraction, and a decimal.
3. What percent liked to stay indoors? What percent liked to go outside?
4. How many students your age might choose a movie if you surveyed 200? 300? 500? Would the percent change? Why or why not?

10
Chose the movies

16
Chose the library

## ACTIVITY 2 Summer Plans

**With Your Class** Survey 100 people about their summer plans. Use at least one question from this page. Use other questions you think of.

1. Predict how many people out of 100 will give each answer. Write your predictions as percents.
2. To survey 100 people in all, how many people should each of you survey? How can you make sure no one is surveyed twice?
3. Take the survey. Count the number of people who gave each answer. Write the number as a percent. How close were your predictions?

*In Your Journal*
*Describe how you made predictions for your survey. How would your predictions change if you were going to survey only adults? only students?*

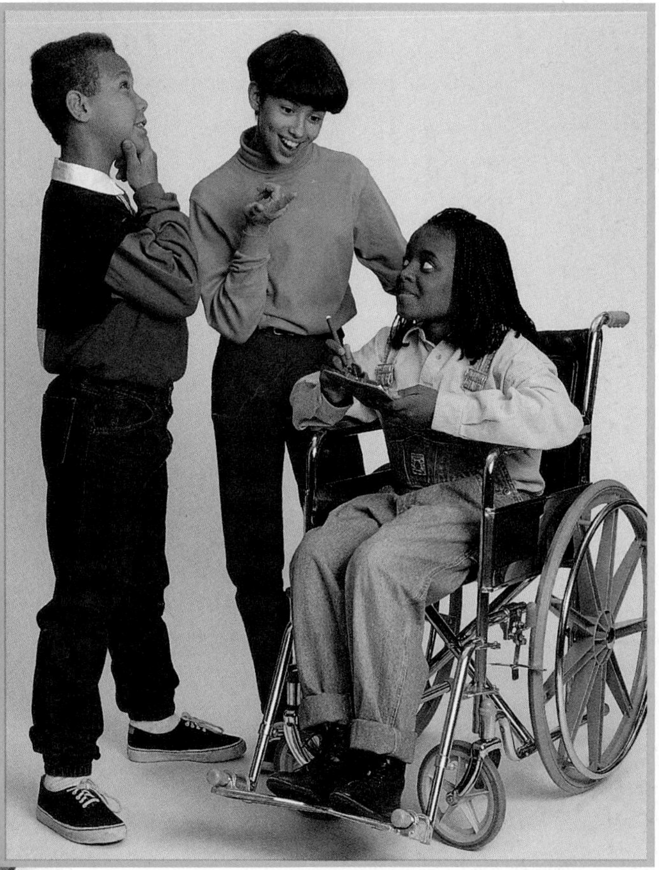

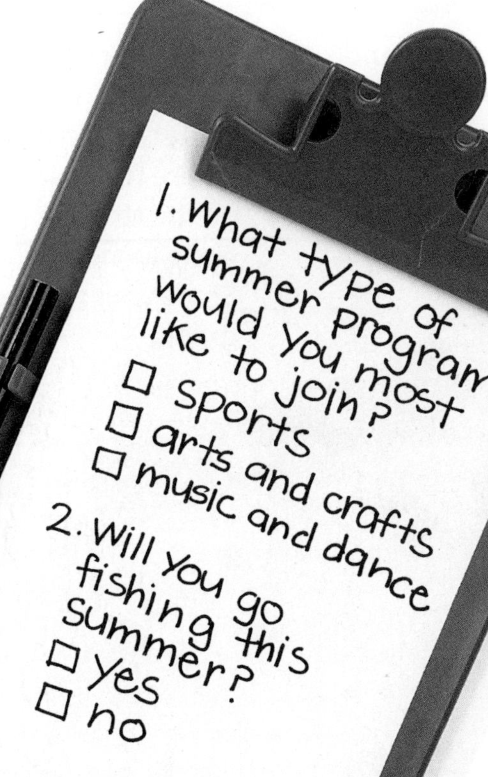

**What You'll Need**

- *1-m strip of adding machine tape marked in centimeters*
- *crayons or markers*
- *tape*
- *large sheet of paper*

## Activity 3 Roll Call

**With Your Group** Choose one survey question. Write the percent of people who gave each answer. You can make a circle graph to show the percents, just as you did for fractions.

1. What percent does the whole 1-m strip represent? Why? Explain how you would shade your strip to show 15%, 25%, and 60%.

2. **Shade the strip to show the percent who gave each answer. Use a different color for each percent.**

3. **Tape the strip end to end. Place it in a circle on a large sheet of paper.**

4. **Mark the circle's center. Draw a line from the center to each point where two colors meet on the strip. Shade the circle to match the strip. Share your finished graph.**

*Try drawing the same circle graph without the shaded strip. How does the shaded strip help you make your graph more exact?*

**With Your Partner** The parts of a circle have names. Look at your circle graph. Read these clues about the names. Write what you think each name means. Label the parts on your graph.

5 The **circumference** of your circle graph is 1 m. Label the circumference.

6 The line you drew to mark each percent is a **radius.** Label a radius.

7 One radius meeting another in a straight line makes a **diameter.** Label or draw a diameter.

*Color a string of 100 macaroni shells to show the percents in your survey. How would you estimate the percents if you had only 10 shells?*

## Try It!

A survey asked 100 people to name their favorite summer fruit. Match each percent below with its part of the circle graph.

1. peaches: 40%
2. plums: 20%
3. nectarines: 15%
4. raspberries: 10%
5. cherries: 10%
6. grapes: 5%

Write the percent as a fraction in lowest terms.

7. 20% 8. 10% 9. 40% 10. 15% 11. 5%

**Think About It**

12. If you surveyed more people, would you need more circle graphs to show their answers? Why or why not?

# Lesson 3 Chances Are

What games and sports will you play this summer? What might happen in those games? Numbers can describe **probability,** the chance that something will happen.

## Activity 1 Believe It or Not

**With Your Class** Use what you know to decide the probability of predictions A – E on these pages.

1. Which predictions have a good chance of happening? Which have no chance? Which have about the same chance of happening as not happening?
2. Think of a way to score the probability of a prediction really happening. Write a number as the score for each prediction.

**A.** Swimming goggles will protect your eyes from the chlorine in the pool.

**B.** The right shoes will help you run faster than ever before.

**C.** Your favorite player will break a record this year.

**With Your Partner** Discuss the probability of each prediction. Agree on a way to score it.

3. Write each prediction again in two ways. One way should be more likely to happen. The other way should be less likely to happen.

4. Give each rewrite a probability score. Be ready to tell others how you chose the scores.

REASONING AND PROBLEM SOLVING

*Suppose you gave a prediction a low probability. If the prediction comes true, does that mean you were wrong about its probability? Why or why not?*

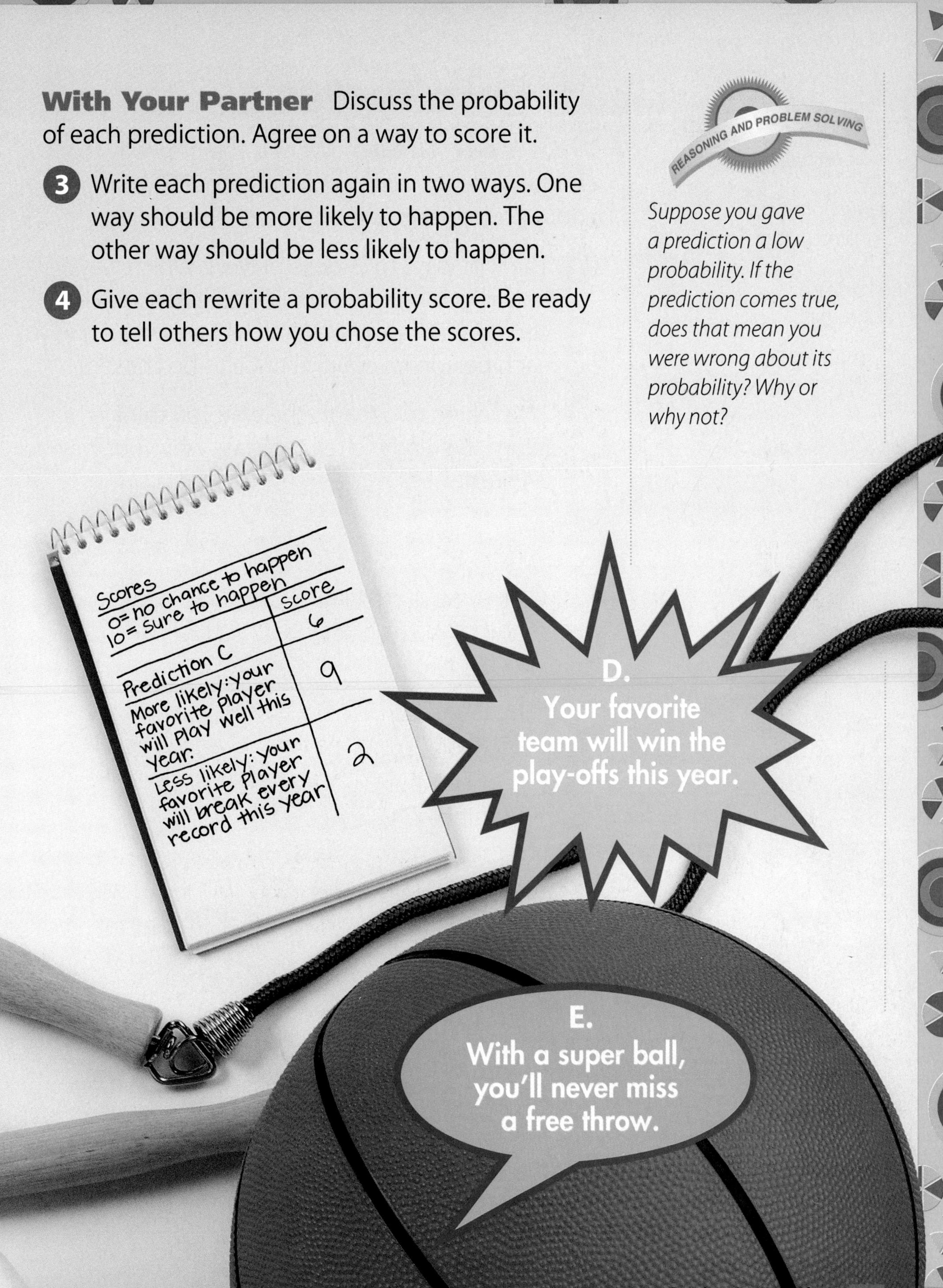

*Illustrate a set of instructions for the fairest way to pick a team. How would the drawings help someone understand the instructions?*

## Activity 2 Fair Teams

**With Your Group** What is the best way to choose sides for a class kickball game? Thinking about probability can help you choose fairly.

1. Think of ways to choose players. Which ways would give one person a better chance to be chosen than another? Which ways would give each person an equal chance to be chosen?

2. Try picking two teams the way you think is fairest. Be ready to tell the class why your way is fairest.

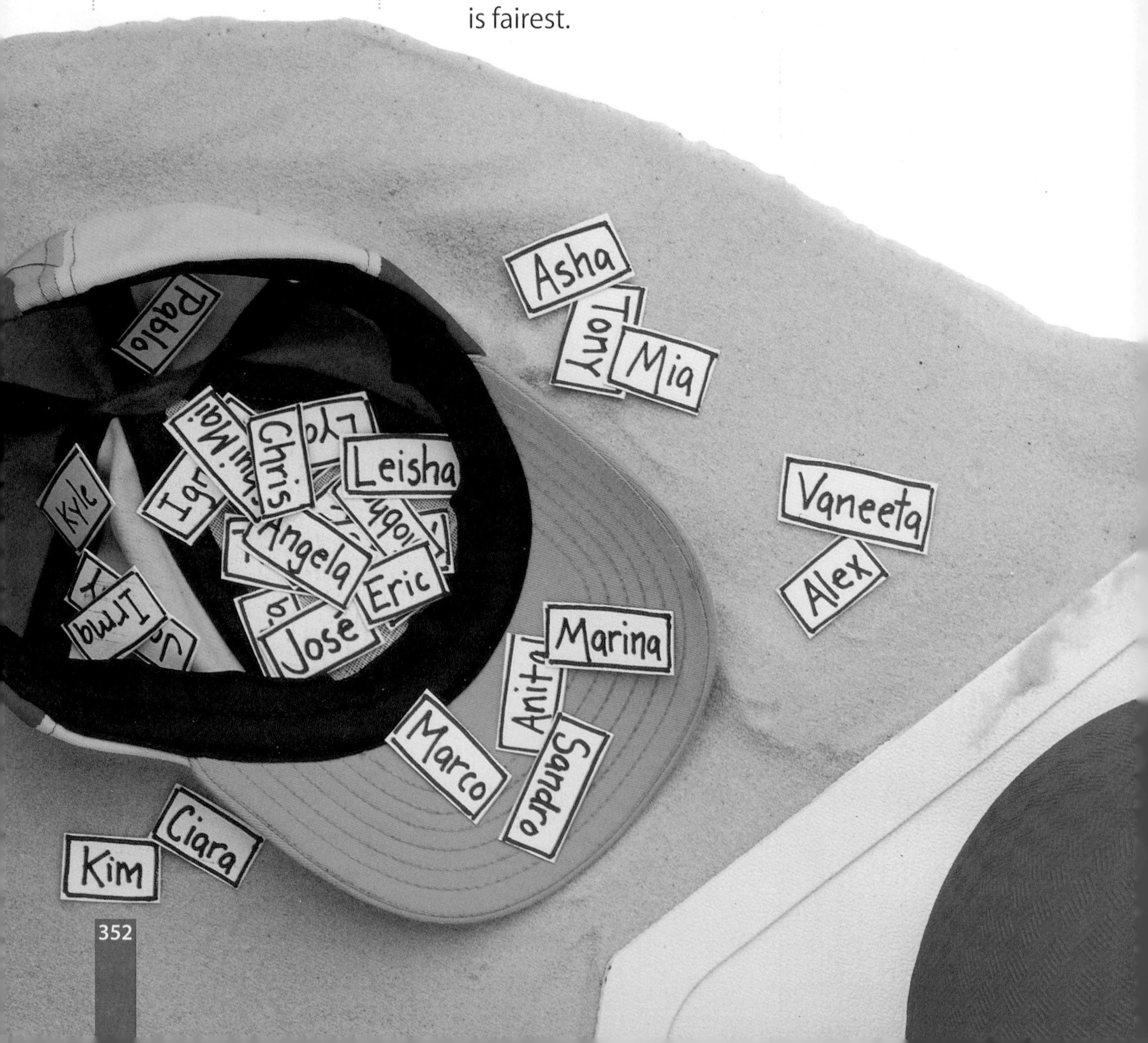

# ACTIVITY 3 Chance or Skill?

**With Your Partner** A player's skill changes the probability of winning some games. In other games a player wins mostly by chance.

1. Copy the chart below. Add five more games to it. Write whether chance or skill is more important in winning each game. Be ready to tell why you think so.

2. Compare the games. How likely are you to win if you practice more than the other players? How likely if you're much older or younger than they are?

| GAME | Win by chance or skill? |
|---|---|
| 1. Basketball | |
| 2. War card game | |
| 3. Tick-tack-toe | |
| 4. Scissors, paper, stone | |

*In Your Journal* *What rule changes would give everyone a more equal chance to win at kickball? Explain how your rules would make the game more fair.*

## Try It!

What is the probability of seeing these items in your neighborhood? Write *likely* or *unlikely*.

1. 2 dogs
2. 3 cows
3. 15 buses
4. 1 bike
5. 12 cars
6. 48 windows

Multiply only if the product has a 4 in the ones' place.

7. $24 \times 26$
8. $18 \times 42$
9. $54 \times 61$
10. $12 \times 82$

**Think About It**

11. Which items in Exercises 1–6 have about the same chance of being seen in most places? Why?

# Try, Try Again

Test some games. The test results tell you the **experimental probability** of winning.

**What You'll Need**
- *Fraction Tool or circle shape and ruler*
- *paper clip*

## ACTIVITY 1 Spinner Game

**With Your Class** Two things that have the same chance of happening are **equally likely.** Are you equally likely to spin a win on the two spinners? Why or why not? See if you're right.

1. **Copy** each spinner with your Fraction Tool. You can spin a paper clip held by a pencil.

**Spinner A**

win | lose

**Spinner B**

win | lose

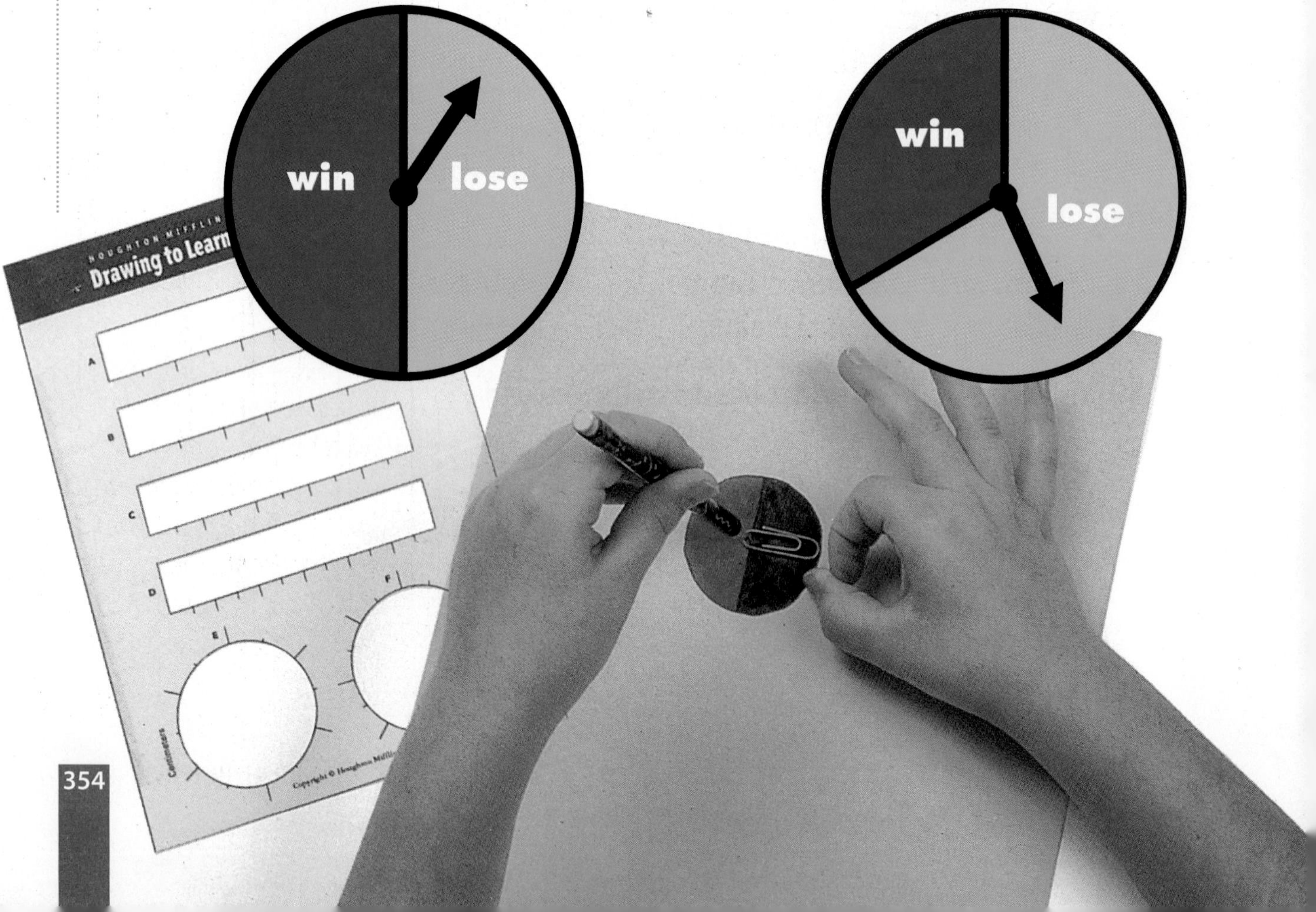

| Our Predictions | |
|---|---|
| Spinner A | Spinner B |
| 5 wins out of 10 spins | 3 wins out of 10 spins |
| ? wins out of 20 spins | ? wins out of 20 spins |
| ? wins out of 30 spins | ? wins out of 30 spins |

**Our Results**

| Spins | Spinner A Win | Spinner A Lose | Spinner B Win | Spinner B Lose |
|---|---|---|---|---|
| 𝍸𝍸 | 𝍸 I | IIII | III | 𝍸 II |

| Experimental Probability of Winning | Spinner A | Spinner B |
|---|---|---|
| after 10 spins | 6 out of 10 | ? out of 10 |
| after 20 spins | ? out of 20 | ? out of 20 |
| after 30 spins | ? out of 30 | ? out of 30 |

**2** **Predict** how many wins you'd spin in 10 tries on each spinner. Make equal ratios to predict every 10 spins. Predict up to 100 spins.

**3** **Spin** each spinner 100 times. Record the result of each spin on a chart.

**4** **Compare** the experimental probabilities you found for your predictions after every 10 spins. Change your predictions if you wish.

**5** **Share** your results with another group after 100 spins. Discuss these questions.
- Which spinner do you think is fairer? Why?
- How can you tell by looking at a spinner whether parts are equally likely to be spun?

**6** **Draw** a spinner with four parts that are equally likely to be spun. Use your Fraction Tool.

✓ **Self-Check** *Stop after every 10 spins. See whether the number of wins is close to what you predicted. If not, use the experimental probability you found to make an equal ratio for the next 10 tries.*

### What You'll Need
- *1 play coin*
- *toothpick*
- *1 cube labeled 1–6*

## Activity 2 Test Your Luck

**With Your Group** Choose at least two of the experiments on these pages.

- Make a prediction. Make 10 **trials,** or tries, to answer the question. Record the **outcomes,** or results.
- How often did you get the outcome you wanted? Write the experimental probability you found in these 10 trials.
- Predict the results of 10 more trials. Test your prediction. Record the outcomes of all 20 trials.
- Continue predicting and testing up to 100 trials.

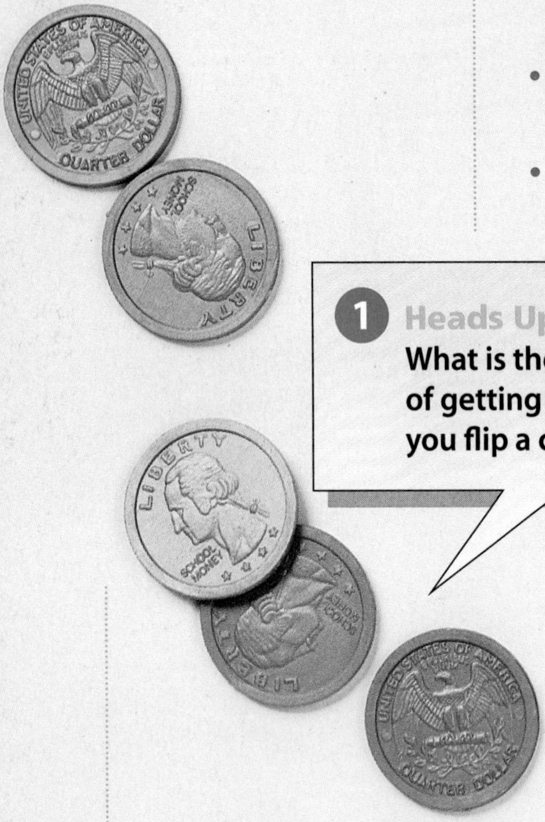

**1 Heads Up**
**What is the probability of getting heads when you flip a coin?**

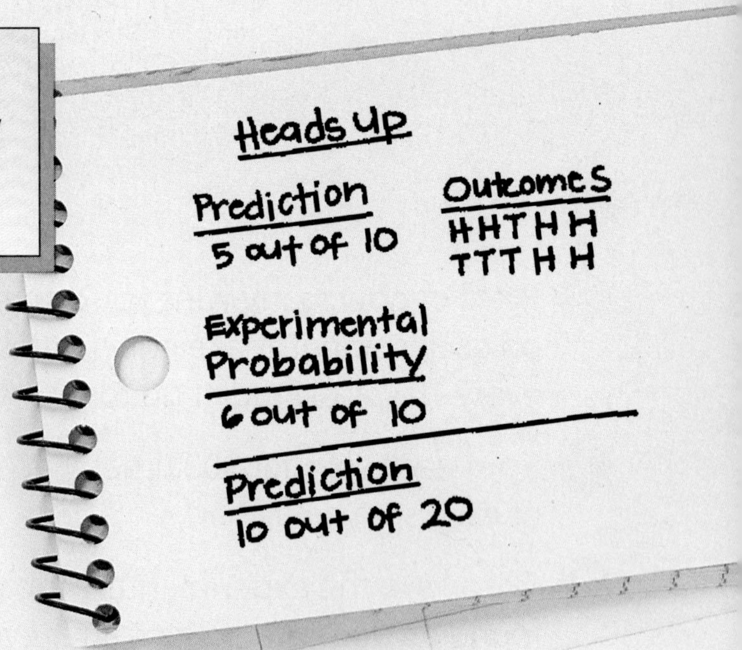

Heads up
Prediction
5 out of 10
Outcomes
HHTHH
TTTHH
Experimental Probability
6 out of 10
Prediction
10 out of 20

**2 Between the Lines**
**Drop a toothpick on a sheet of lined paper. What is the probability the toothpick won't touch any lines?**

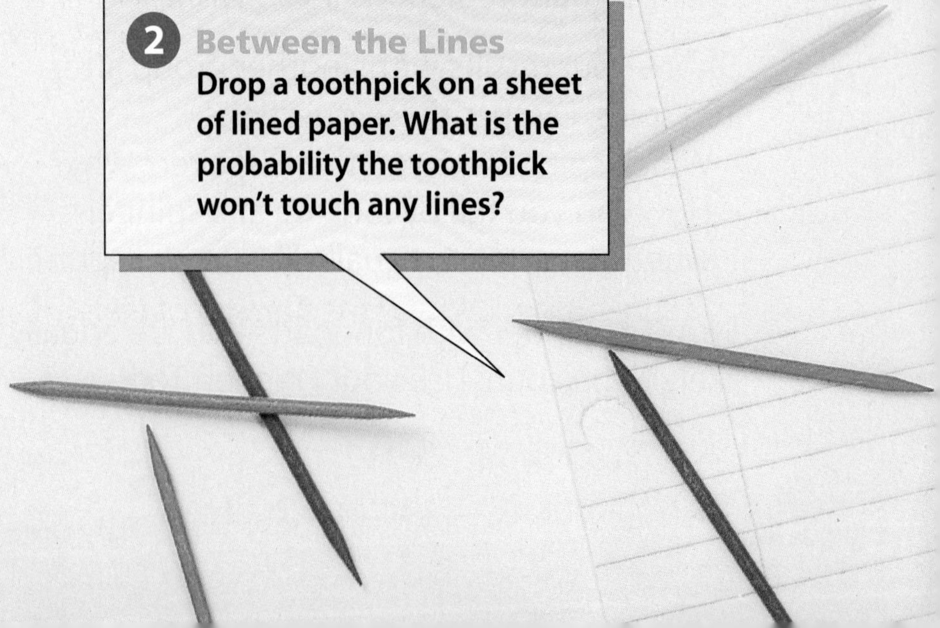

**ACTIVITY OPTION**

*After you finish an experiment, try a second one. Use two coins, cubes, toothpicks, or a different target. How does the experimental probability change?*

## 3 On Target

**What is the probability of your placing a pencil's eraser on the "1" space while your eyes are closed?**

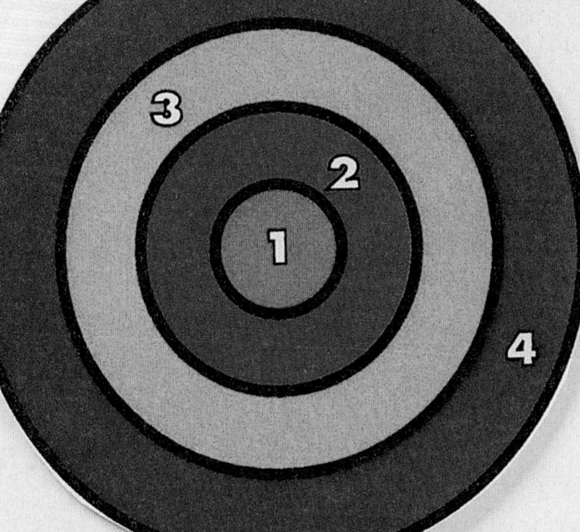

*You can use a computer graphing program to create a bar graph and a circle graph that show probabilities of different outcomes in a game. Which kind of graph works better?*

## 4 High Roller

**What is the probability of rolling 6 on a number cube?**

Do You Remember?

# Try It!

Write the experimental probability of flipping heads (H).

1. H H H H T
2. H H T T
3. H T H T
4. T T T T
5. H H T H
6. H H T H H T T T H
7. H T
8. H T H H T H
9. H H T T H T

Write each fraction in simplest terms.

10. $\frac{3}{15}$
11. $\frac{5}{50}$
12. $\frac{15}{100}$
13. $\frac{80}{200}$

### Think About It

14. Write how you found the number of trials in Exercises 1–9.

Investigation

# Chance to Win

What if your favorite sport became a game of chance instead of skill? You'd have a chance to beat any player in the world!

1. Think about your favorite sport and its rules. What do different players do? What results can come from their actions?

2. Create a game of chance that has some of the same rules and plays as your sport. Make spinners, number cubes, or cards for your game. As you play, change the game pieces and rules. Try to make the game more fair and more fun.

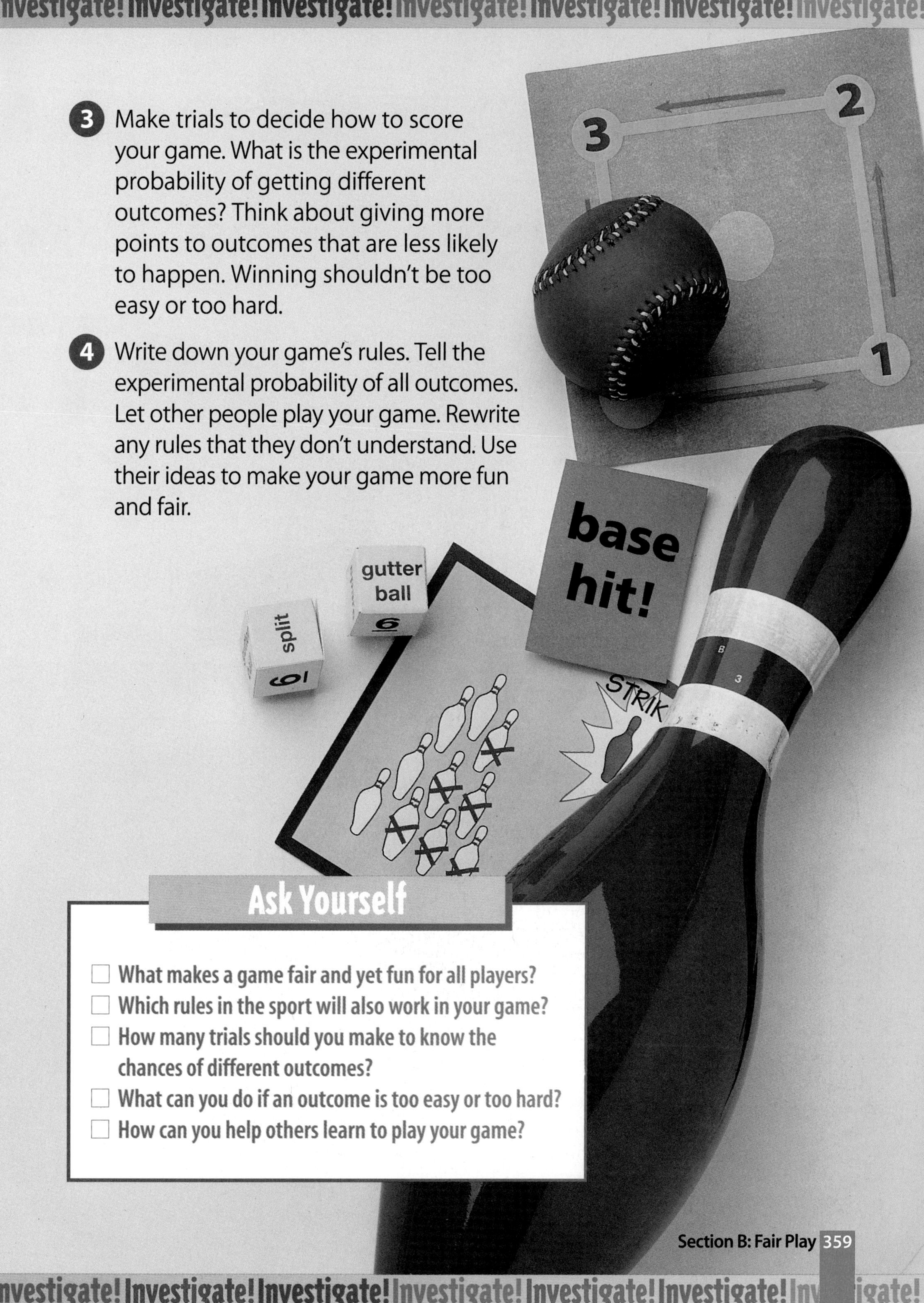


3. Make trials to decide how to score your game. What is the experimental probability of getting different outcomes? Think about giving more points to outcomes that are less likely to happen. Winning shouldn't be too easy or too hard.

4. Write down your game's rules. Tell the experimental probability of all outcomes. Let other people play your game. Rewrite any rules that they don't understand. Use their ideas to make your game more fun and fair.

## Ask Yourself

- ☐ What makes a game fair and yet fun for all players?
- ☐ Which rules in the sport will also work in your game?
- ☐ How many trials should you make to know the chances of different outcomes?
- ☐ What can you do if an outcome is too easy or too hard?
- ☐ How can you help others learn to play your game?

Do You Remember? **Cumulative Review**

# County Fair

The county fair is open. As you visit each attraction, solve the problems.

## Roller Coaster

**1** a. The roller coaster seats 36 people. How many cars might there be? how many people in each car? List the possibilities. Which are most likely?

b. A ride on the roller coaster lasts $2\frac{1}{2}$ minutes. Before each ride it takes 30 seconds to change passengers. How many can ride in 1 hour?

## Spin-the-Wheel

**2** Everyone gets to spin the wheel. Which prize is a player most likely to win? Why do you think so?

**3** Do you think more than 50% will win a whistle? Why or why not?

**4** You try once. Is the chance that you will win a bear closer to 5%, 25%, 50% or 75%?

**5** You watch 25 people spin. You see 20 win a whistle, 4 win a yo-yo, and 1 win a bear. If 100 people spin, estimate how many will win each prize.

## Whirl-Away

**6** The cars spin as they go around a track. A car spins 11 times in 70 seconds. How many spins does it make during the $3\frac{1}{2}$-minute ride?

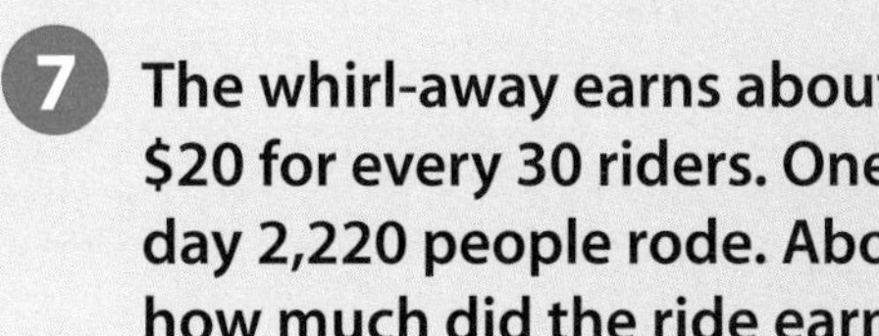

**7** The whirl-away earns about \$20 for every 30 riders. One day 2,220 people rode. About how much did the ride earn?

## Ferris Wheel

**8** The Ferris wheel is full. You count 2 people in each of 18 seats. The Ferris wheel fills up 42 times a day. How many people can ride in a week?

**9** Your ride takes 10 minutes. You have to wait twice that long before each ride. How many times could you ride in $2\frac{1}{2}$ hours?

County Fair Ferris Wheel \$.55

County Fair Whirl-Away \$.65

County Fair Roller Coaster \$.75

# Check Your Math Power

## Time to Go

**10** Your watch says 4:20 P.M. You have to meet your group back at the roller coaster at 5:30 P.M. You have \$3.65 in your pocket. What rides can you go on with the time and money you have left?

- It takes 45 seconds to walk between different rides.
- Before each turn you wait twice as long as the ride takes.

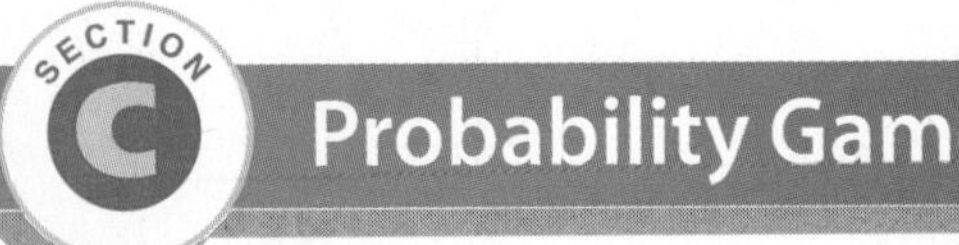

# LESSON 5 Is It Possible?

DRAWING TO LEARN

*How can you use your Fraction Tool to help you draw a number line?*

LITERATURE

Crossing the River *is an African folktale.*

Once there was a man who had to take a wolf, a goat, and a cabbage across a river. But his boat was so small it could hold only himself and one other thing. The man didn't know what to do. How could he take the wolf, the goat, and the cabbage over one at a time, so that the wolf wouldn't eat the goat and the goat wouldn't eat the cabbage?

From *Stories to Solve: Folktales from Around the World*
Retold by George Shannon

## ACTIVITY 1 On the Line

**With Your Class** Copy the diagram below. It will help you use probabilities to finish the story.

| 0 | | 1 |
|---|---|---|
| **impossible** | **possible** | **certain** |
| Man takes two things at a time. | Man takes wolf across first. | Goat eats cabbage. |

1. The man can never do some things. Why does it make sense that an **impossible event** has a probability of 0?

2. **Certain events** have a probability of 1. If the man takes the wolf first, what is the probability that the goat will eat the cabbage?

3. What two other things can the man take across first? List them on your number line. Also list what is certain to happen to the items left.

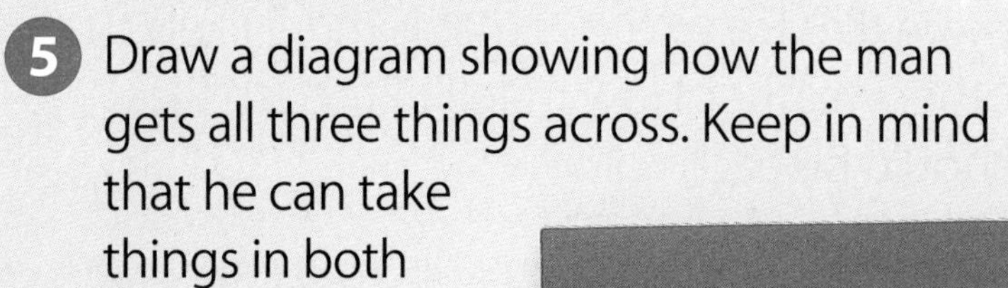

4. What is the man most likely to take across first? Is the probability closer to 0 or 1? Why?

5. Draw a diagram showing how the man gets all three things across. Keep in mind that he can take things in both directions.

*Suppose an event has a probability halfway between 0 and 1. What fraction of the time is it likely to happen? How could you write the probability?*

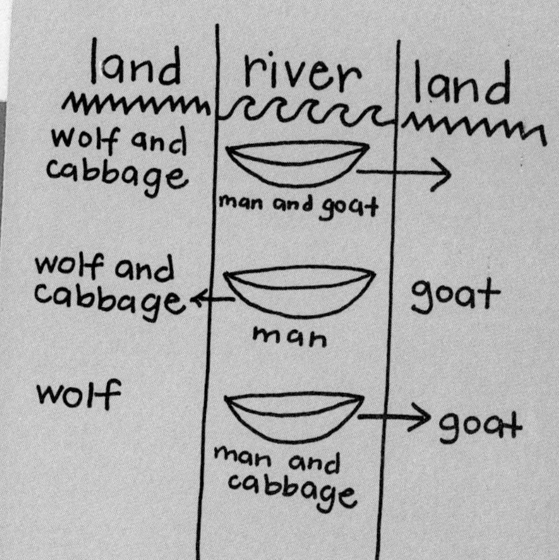

### What You'll Need

- *10 color tiles*
- *bag to hold tiles*

# ACTIVITY 2 Rain, Rain, Go Away

**With Your Group** Discuss the summer weather in your part of the country. How often is a day sunny? cloudy? rainy?

1. Is the chance of a sunny day closer to 0 or to 1? Is 0 or 1 closer to the chance of a cloudy day? a rainy day?

2. Do a probability test. Put ten color tiles in a bag.
   - Choose one color for each kind of weather: sunny, cloudy, and rainy.
   - Choose the number of tiles for each color. Use more tiles for weather that is more likely than other weather. How many of the ten tiles should be each color?

3. Without looking, pull one tile from the bag. Record the result. Put the tile back into the bag.

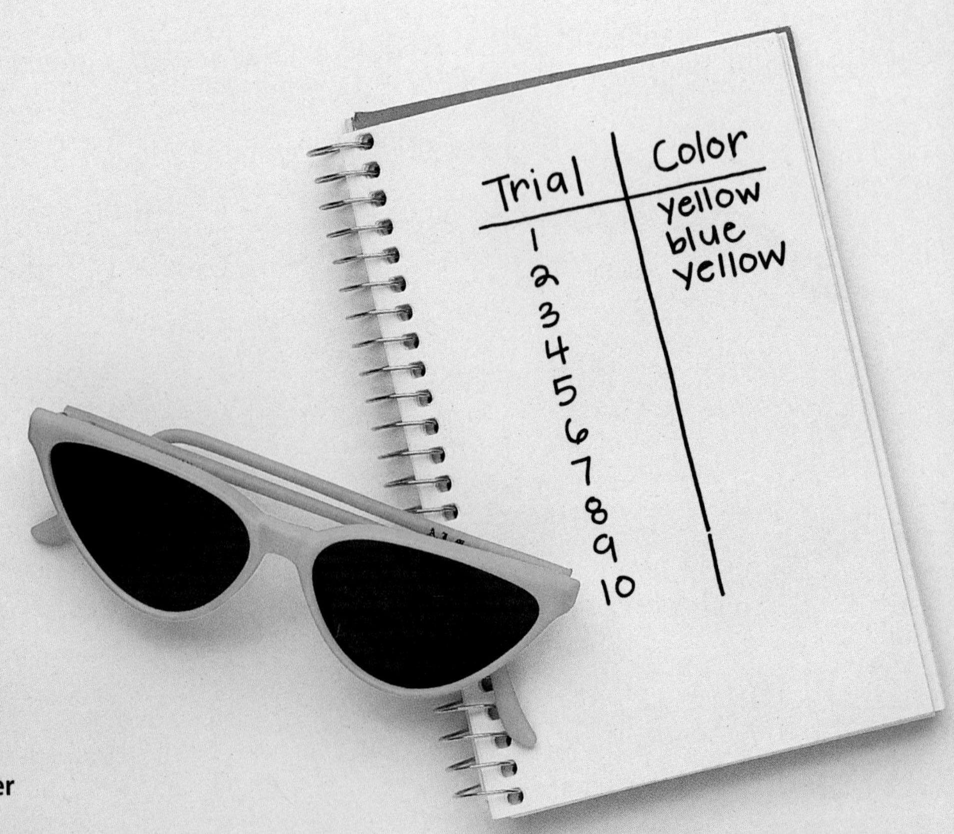

*A weather report may predict a 30% chance of rain. Do you think the probability of rain is closer to 0 or 1? Why?*

4 Make nine more trials. Write the results.
   a. sunny to total
   b. cloudy to total
   c. rainy to total

5 Was the probability of sunny weather closer to 0 or to1? cloudy weather? rainy weather?

*Use the tenths' square on your Tracing Tool. Show the results of your ten trials.*

Do You Remember?

## Try It!

Tell whether each probability is closer to 0 or 1.

1. 2 out of 10
2. 3 out of 5
3. 3 out of 9
4. 1 out of 5
5. 3 out of 3
6. 6 out of 6

Complete each number sentence.

7. $3 \times 27 = ■$
8. $■ \times 3 = 180$
9. $34 \times 155 = ■$
10. $■ \times 5 = 235$
11. $20 \times ■ = 400$
12. $210 \times ■ = 4{,}200$

**Think About It**

13. Which probabilities in Exercises 1–6 are certain? Why?

# Games Galore

What You'll Need
- *markers*
- *tagboard*
- *scissors*

## Activity 1 Go Fish!

**With Your Partner** Make a set of playing cards for a rainy-day game. A set should have three kinds of underwater animals with six cards of each kind. Number the cards of each kind 1 through 6. Read the rules on the left.

1. Look at the players' cards for their first turn. With ten cards in the pile, is the chance of getting the matching 4 closer to 0 or 1? Explain.
2. Pass out cards to begin a game. What card do you need? Is your chance of getting the card closer to 0 or 1? Why?
3. Describe a time when your chance of getting a card is about $\frac{1}{2}$.

### Go Fish! Rules

1. Each player gets four cards.
2. The rest of the cards go face down.
3. Take turns asking for a card. Try to get three cards with the same number.
4. If your partner has the card you ask for, he or she must give it to you. If not, you must go fish for a face-down card. When you get three matching cards lay them down.
5. Play ten rounds. Get as many sets of three cards as you can.

Go Fish! Rules

*In Your Journal* What part of Go Fish! is a game of chance? How does understanding probability help you play?

4. Write answers to these questions before each turn. Which card will you ask for? Is the chance you'll get it closer to 0, $\frac{1}{2}$, or 1? Why do you think so?
5. Take ten turns each. Share with the class how your predictions changed as you played.

## Activity 2 Your Turn

**With Your Partner** Choose a card game like War or Concentration. Or create a new game that can be played with color tiles, number cubes, or spinners. Players should use prediction and probability to help them win.

1. Write clear directions for your game.
2. Trade games with another pair of partners. Read the directions, then play the game.
3. Write about the game after you play it. Was the game easy to play? Why are well-written directions important?

**What You'll Need**

- *cubes labeled 1–6*
- *spinners*
- *color tiles*

# Chance ADVENTURE

**What You'll Need**
- *2 cubes labeled 1–6*
- *gameboard*
- *game pieces*

## ACTIVITY 3 Play the Game

**With Your Group** Have an adventure indoors. Try to be first to land on the treasure trunk. The path is full of probabilities. Think before you take a chance! Follow these directions on each turn.

1. Roll two number cubes.
2. Choose one of the numbers you rolled. Try to roll it again with only one cube. You get as many tries as the other number you rolled. For example, suppose you first roll 4 and 2. Then you can choose four tries to roll 2 or two tries to roll 4.

**✓ Self-Check**
*Rushing ahead may cause you to fall behind. Look at the gameboard before deciding what number to try to roll and move.*

3. Before you roll again, write a prediction. How many tries will it take you to roll your number?

4. Keep these points in mind as you move along the path.
   - Move ahead the number of spaces you roll on the cube.
   - Move only if you roll your number in the tries allowed.
   - If your prediction is correct, move ahead an extra space.
   - If you don't roll your number, move back one space.

**ACTIVITY OPTION**

*Play the game again. This time if you predict correctly, take another turn. To land on the treasure trunk, you must roll the exact number of spaces needed.*

# Combinations

Women of the Twana nation in the state of Washington play a game with beaver teeth. They toss teeth that have carvings on one side. Scoring depends on how the teeth land. You can play this game with your partner, using coins or "beaver teeth" you make from cardboard.

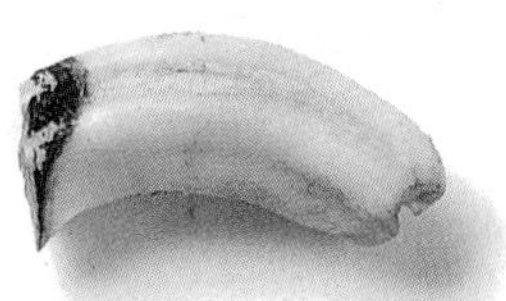

## Predict

1. Suppose you want only one out of four pennies to show heads. Is the probability of that happening closer to 0 or 1? Explain.
2. Will the chance of tossing one tail be the same as tossing one head? How do you know?
3. In how many different combinations could the four coins land?
4. Sketch the combinations.

## Play

5. Toss four coins 20 times. Record the results of each trial.
   a. Write ratios to compare the number of times each combination was tossed to the total number of trials.
   b. Repeat for 20 more trials. What is the new ratio for each combination in 20 trials?

### Think

6. Which combination did you toss most often?

7. Why did that happen?

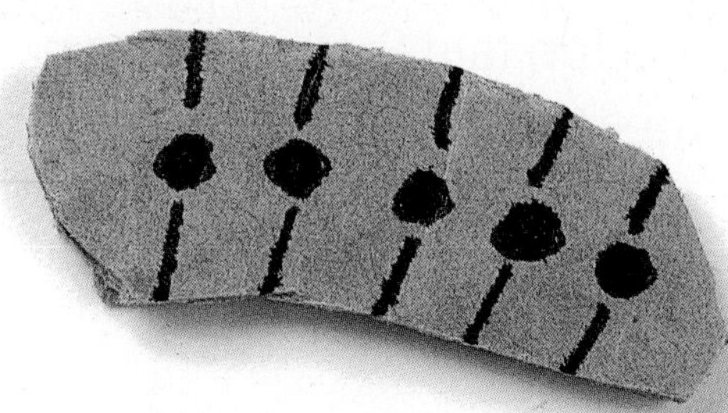

8. Draw a number line. Mark 0, $\frac{1}{2}$, and 1. Mark where you think the probability of tossing each combination should be. Use your ratios to help you.

9. Explain why you placed each combination where you did.

10. Which combination of coins should be worth the most points? Why do you think so?

# Lesson 7 Fun Fair

Get ready for a fun fair! Probability can help you plan games that are fun for everyone.

**What You'll Need**

- *1 cube with color labels*

## Activity 1 Floating Ducks

**With Your Class** In this game six toy ducks each have a different color on the bottom. What's the probability of guessing a duck's color? You can write the ratio as a fraction.

$$\text{Probability} = \frac{\text{number of outcomes you choose}}{\text{number of possible outcomes}}$$

$$\frac{\text{1 purple duck}}{\text{6 ducks}} \qquad \text{Probability} = \frac{1}{6}$$

1. Choose six possible outcomes for a duck's color. How do you know that any outcomes you choose will have a probability between 0 and 1?

2. Choose one outcome. What is the probability a duck has that color? How do you know?

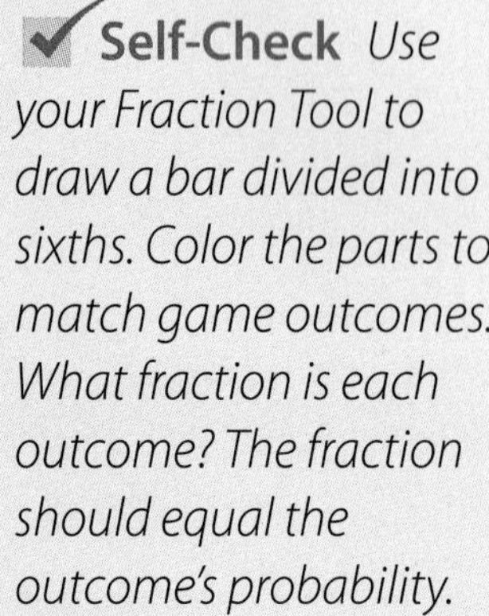

✓ **Self-Check** *Use your Fraction Tool to draw a bar divided into sixths. Color the parts to match game outcomes. What fraction is each outcome? The fraction should equal the outcome's probability.*

**With Your Group** You probably don't have six ducks to test this game. Instead use a cube that has the same six colors as the ducks. Try guessing the color you will roll on the cube.

*Use your Fraction Tool to draw a spinner with six equal parts. Find the probability of guessing the color you will spin. Why should you get the same probability as guessing the color on the cube? Test your spinner.*

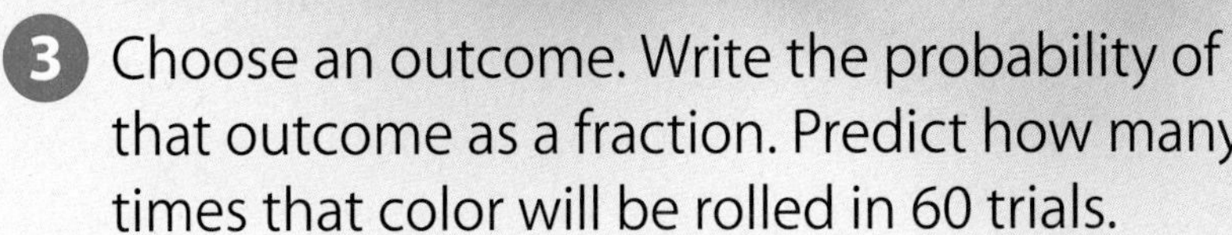

3. Choose an outcome. Write the probability of that outcome as a fraction. Predict how many times that color will be rolled in 60 trials.

   Repeat Step 3 for each possible outcome.

4. Experiment to test the probabilities you wrote. Record your results to share with the class.

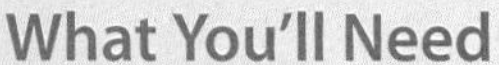

**What You'll Need**

- *box for "pond"*
- *paper clips*
- *construction paper*
- *crayons or markers*
- *magnet*
- *string*
- *ruler*

# Activity 2 Fishing Game

**With Your Group** Plan and test this game. Without looking into the fish pond, players try to catch some paper fish. A player can get a prize by catching a certain color fish.

**1 Plan the Game** Decide the number of fish. Plan how many fish will be each color. Which colors get prizes? Make a chart that shows the probability of catching each color fish.

**2 Make the Game** Make each fish and use a paper clip for its mouth. For a fishing pole tie a magnet on a string to a ruler. Use a big box for the pond. Predict how many fish of each color you will each catch in ten turns.

| color | probability |
|---|---|
| blue | |
| red | |
| purple | |
| green | |
| pink | |
| yellow | |

**TOOLS AND TECHNIQUES**

*What if you had 2 red fish in a pond of 100 fish? How would you express the probability as a decimal? as a percent? Use your calculator to help you.*

**3 Play the Game** Take a turn and record the result. Then throw the fish back. After ten turns each, see if the results match your predictions.

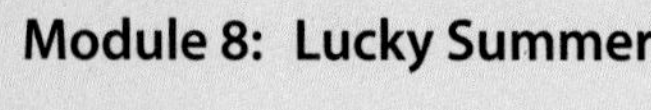

**4 Share Your Game** Trade games with another group. Play their game. Test the probabilities they predicted.

Discuss students' responses.

Do You Remember?

## Try It!

What is the probability of catching each color fish on these two pages? Write the probability as a fraction in simplest terms.

1. red
2. purple
3. blue
4. yellow
5. pink
6. green

Write the mixed number as a fraction.

7. $1\frac{5}{8}$
8. $3\frac{1}{3}$
9. $5\frac{1}{2}$
10. $2\frac{1}{4}$

### Think About It

11. Which color fish in Exercises 1–6 are you least likely to catch? most likely to catch? How do you know?

# LESSON 8 Winning Ways

A player may get more than one try in a fun-fair game. What is the chance of winning?

## ACTIVITY 1 Treasure Chest

**With Your Class** Reach into the chest two times. If you choose two matching paper coins, you win.

**What You'll Need**
- *30 slips of paper*
- *bag or box with cover*

1. Mark ten slips of paper *P* for pennies and mark ten *D* for dimes. On the first try you could get a penny or a dime. The second try could also be a penny or a dime.

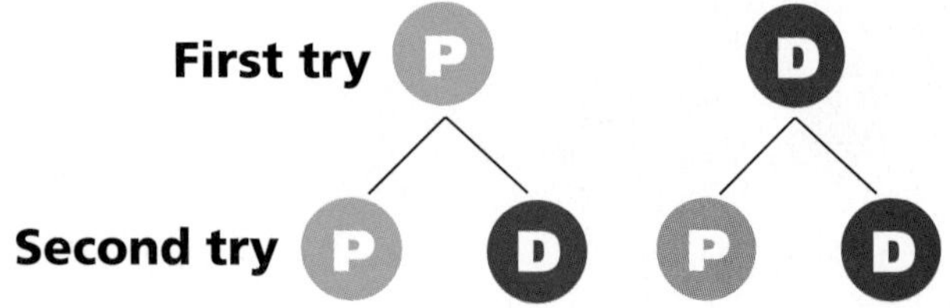


a. How does this **tree diagram** show that the probability of getting two pennies is $\frac{1}{4}$?
b. Why is the probability of getting two dimes also $\frac{1}{4}$?
c. What is the probability of winning the game? How do you know?

2. Predict how many times you would win in 60 trials. Make 60 trials to check your prediction.

*Think of a new Treasure Chest game. The order of choosing coins should affect your chance of winning.*

**3** What if you added ten slips of paper marked *N* for nickels? How would the probability of winning change? Copy and complete this tree diagram. Make a prediction and do 60 trials.

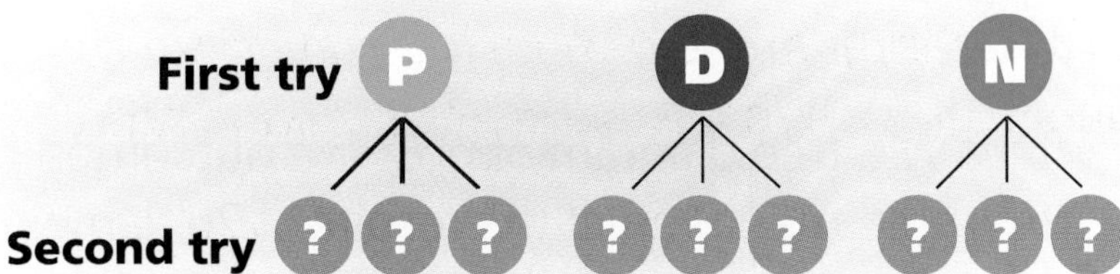


**4** Prizes could be given for the value in cents of two coins chosen. Copy and complete the chart below. Use your tree diagram to find the probability of choosing each amount. Test your predictions.

**DRAWING TO LEARN**

*Make up rules for a Treasure Chest game with three tries. Draw a tree diagram of outcomes. What is the probability of winning? Test your prediction.*

| Amount of 2 coins | Probability |
|---|---|
| a. 15¢ | |
| b. 10¢ | |
| c. 11¢ | |
| d. 2¢ | |

## What You'll Need

- *3 play coins*
- *2 or more containers of different sizes*

# ACTIVITY 2 Lucky Toss

**With Your Group** You get three tries to toss a coin into a container. The more times you get the coin in, the better the prize. Test the game by doing Exercises 1 and 2. Then choose either Exercise 3 or Exercise 4.

1. **Draw** a tree diagram of possible outcomes for three tries. Predict the results of 20 games. How many times would you get 3 coins in? 2 coins in? 1 coin in?

2. **Test** your prediction. Toss from 3 ft away. Record the results of 20 trials. How do the results compare with your prediction?

3. **Change** the game. Use a container of a different size. Maybe toss from closer in or farther away. Make a prediction and test your game. How did the results change? Share your game with another group.

*In Your Journal* *How might a player's age affect the chances of winning the Lucky Toss? What changes would give all players the same chance to win?*

**4** **Toss** a coin three times. Draw a tree diagram and find the probability of getting three heads. Make a prediction and do 20 trials. Compare the results with the chance of winning the Lucky Toss.

*Suppose you roll a number cube two times. What is the probability of getting the same number each time? Draw a tree diagram of outcomes. Make a prediction and do 60 trials.*

Do You Remember?

## Try It!

Draw a tree diagram to show the results of two spins. Write the probability.

40 10 30 20

1. each number less than 30
2. 10 and 20
3. same number twice
4. two 10's
5. two even numbers
6. one odd and one even

Use number pairs on the tree diagram to find the following.

7. the least product
8. the greatest product
9. the range of products
10. the least sum

### Think About It

11. Are the spinner probabilities more like the ones for the Treasure Chest game or for the Lucky Toss game? Explain your answer in writing.

Do You Remember? Cumulative Review

# Looking Back

Choose the right answer. Write *a, b, c,* or *d* for each question.

**You have 360 players. There are 120 boys and 240 girls. Each team should have the same number of girls and the same number of boys on it. Use this information for Exercises 1–3.**

1. Who should be on each team if there are 20 teams?

   a. 14 girls and 7 boys
   b. 7 girls and 14 boys
   c. 12 girls and 6 boys
   d. 6 girls and 12 boys

2. Who should be on each team if there are 30 teams?

   a. 8 girls and 4 boys
   b. 4 girls and 8 boys
   c. 5 girls and 10 boys
   d. 10 girls and 5 boys

3. The price of 10 team T-shirts is $54. How much do shirts for all the players cost?

   a. $540 b. $19,440
   c. $3,600 d. $1,944

**You make summer punch with 1 L ginger ale, 2 L lemonade, and 3 L orange juice. Use this information for Exercises 4–6.**

4. What is the ratio of lemonade to ginger ale?

   a. 1 L to 2 L b. 1 L to 3 L
   c. 2 L to 1 L d. 3 L to 2 L

5. You use 500 mL ginger ale for punch. How many milliliters of lemonade should you use?

   a. 1,000 mL b. 1 mL
   c. 500 mL d. 2 mL

6. How much orange juice and lemonade do you need with more ginger ale? Copy and complete the table below.

| You Need | Liters | | | | |
|---|---|---|---|---|---|
| Ginger ale | 1 | 2 | 3 | 4 | 5 |
| Lemonade | 2 | | | | |
| Orange juice | 3 | | | | |

**You asked 100 students how they like to get around in the summer. You found that 12 like roller skating, 37 like cycling, 10 like walking, and 41 like riding in a car. Use this information for Exercises 7–9.**

7. What percent like to get around on wheels?

   a. 37% b. 10%
   c. 90% d. 22%

8. What percent like a good way to exercise?

   a. 59% b. 10%
   c. 41% d. 0%

9. How many chose roller skating? Write your answer as a percent, a decimal, and a fraction.

**Choose 1 out of 4 tiles from a bag. The gold tile scores 3 points. The blue scores 2 points. The green scores 1 point. The white scores 0 points. Put the tile back before choosing again. Use the following answers for Exercises 10–12.**

a. $\frac{1}{4}$ b. $\frac{3}{4}$

c. $\frac{15}{16}$ d. $\frac{6}{16}$

10. What is the chance that you will score points on the first try?

11. What is the chance of scoring at least 1 point in two tries?

12. What is the chance that you will score exactly 3 points in two tries?

**In a bag of marbles, 4 are yellow, 2 are blue, 1 is red, and 1 is green. Which area or areas on the graph show the probability of drawing each color?**

13. green

14. blue

15. red

16. yellow

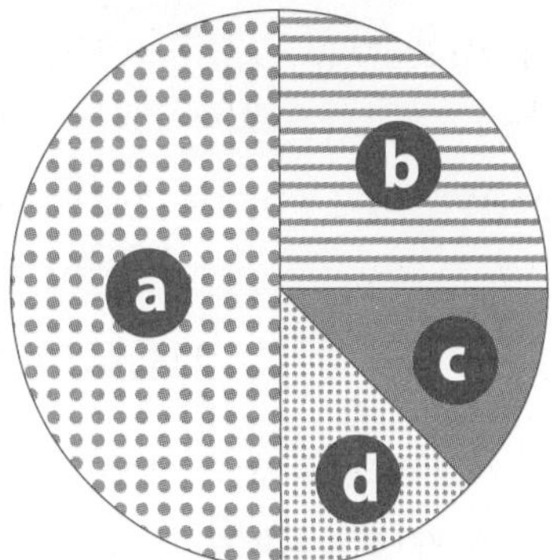


## Check Your Math Power

**To play a game, you spin a spinner twice. Your chance of winning is $\frac{1}{9}$ Use this information for Exercises 17–19.**

17. Write game rules and draw a spinner. Make a tree diagram for all possible outcomes after two spins.

18. How can you make the game harder to win?

19. How can you make it easier to win without changing the spinner or number of spins?

MODULE 8 Investigations

# Fair Success

Every day people use probability to plan special events. Suppose you were going to plan a school fun fair. Predicting probabilities could help improve your chances for success.

## Investigation A Fair Play

Invent a game for the fair. It should give people a fair chance to win. It should also earn money for your school. Make the game with things that are easy to find. Try using rubber balls, paper plates, pennies, dried beans, coffee cans, or soup cans.

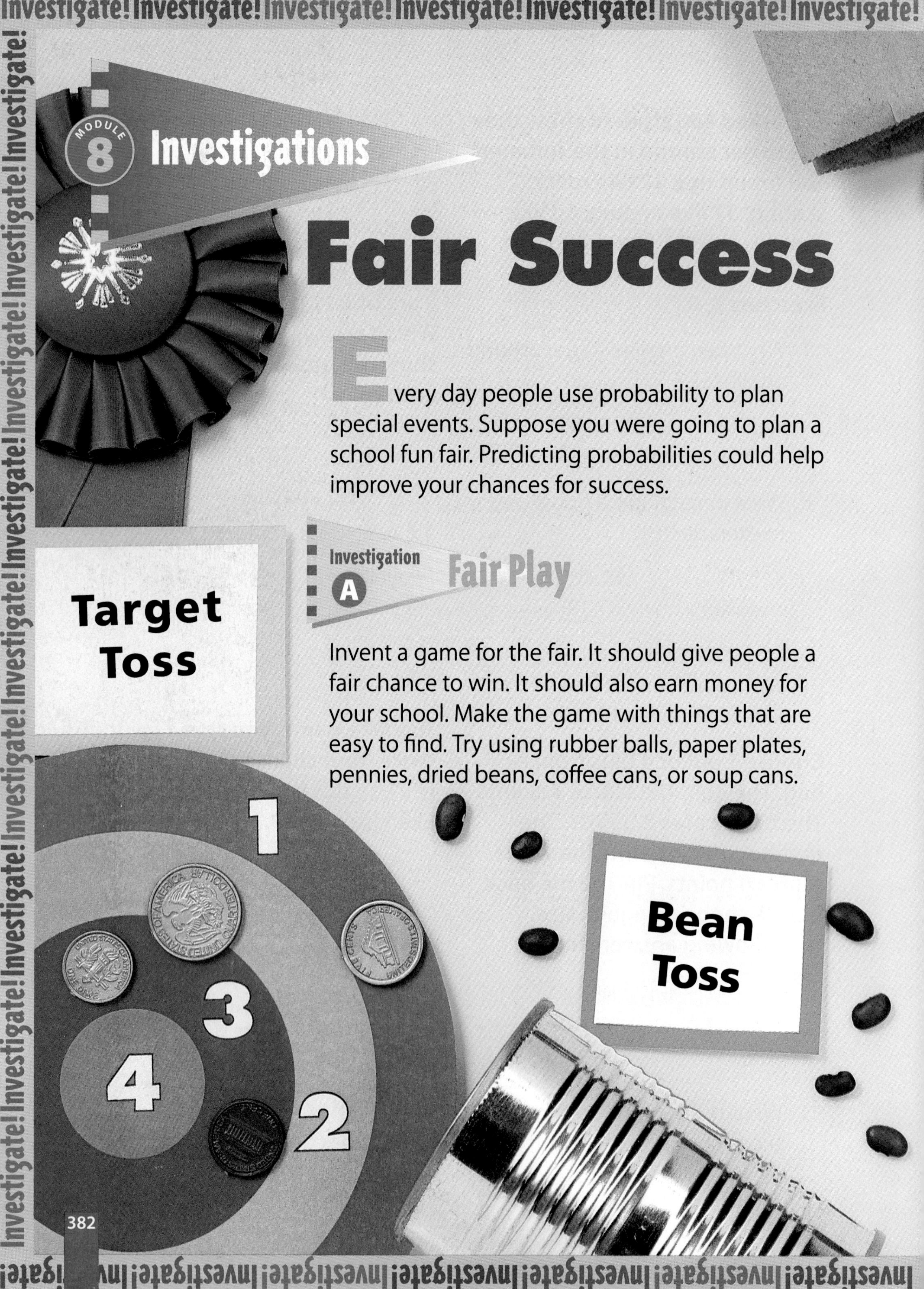

1 **Test** your game. Is it too hard or too easy? What are the chances to win a prize?

2 **Choose** prizes that will make people want to play. How much should a ticket cost? You need to pay for the prizes and still earn money.

3 **Survey** classmates. Ask them if they would play your game at a fair. If so, how many times would they probably play?

4 **Use** survey answers to figure out how much you would earn if 100 people came to the fair. What if 200 came? 400? 800? 1,000? Make a table to show your predictions.

5 **Write** a description of your game. Explain how you used probability to test it. Tell why it would be a good game for the fair.

## Keep in Mind

Your report will be judged on the following points.

- ☐ Can you explain how you used probability to test your game ?
- ☐ Is there a fair chance to win? Are the prizes fair?
- ☐ Can you show that your game would earn money?
- ☐ Is your prediction table clear and accurate ?

## Investigation B Take Me Out to the Fair

You might want to predict how many students from each grade would come to your fair. How many teen, adult, and preschool family members would come with them? Plan how you would make these predictions.

1. How could a survey help you? Would you need to survey the whole school? Would you survey people in different grades? How many people?
2. What questions would you ask? Show how you would use the answers to predict the number coming in each age group.
3. How could your predictions help you plan games? Think of other ways your predictions could help you plan the fair.

## Ongoing Investigation How Much Is a Million?

It's time to make your final count of the items you've collected. How close to a million did you come? Work with your classmates to prepare a report on your collection. Be sure to include

- a graph or other visual that shows the growth of your collection
- your prediction about how much more time you would need to reach a million
- any advice you would give next year's fourth graders about how to do their investigation

# Tool Kit

## Contents

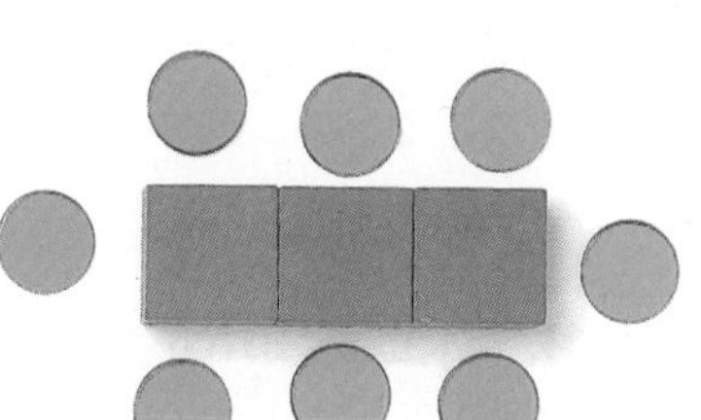

## Problem Solving Strategies



## Computation Tools

## Technology



## Data Collection

## Drawing to Learn



## Measurement



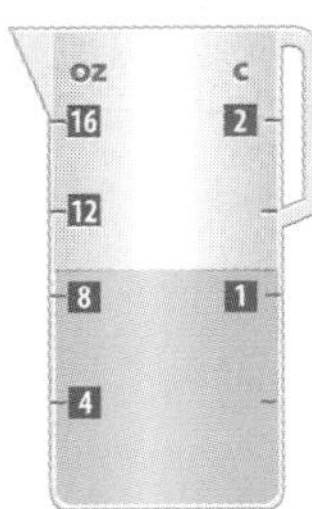

# Ways to Solve Problems

On the next few pages, you'll find different strategies, or ways, for solving math problems. Learning these strategies will give you a powerful set of problem solving tools.

**Problem**

**You have square tables for a party. Only one person can sit comfortably on each side. What is the greatest number of people you can seat at 1, 2, 3, 4, 5, and 6 tables if you want the tables to touch on at least one side?**

## Draw a Picture or a Diagram

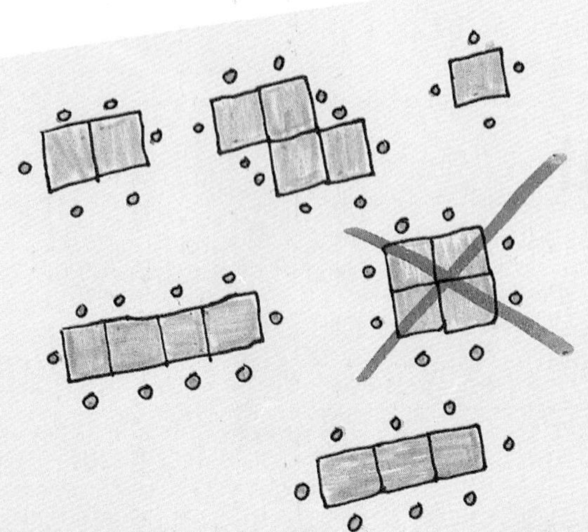

Drawing a picture or diagram can help you solve many problems. You will probably find it helpful to draw a picture when a problem asks you to arrange objects, work with shapes, or compare varying measurements in a space. (See Drawing to Learn on pages 406–407.)

## Build a Model or Act It Out

Making a model with objects is another way to find solutions to a problem about arrangements. In this case, you could use blocks to show tables and counters to show chairs. You could move the blocks and counters all sorts of ways to find the best arrangements.

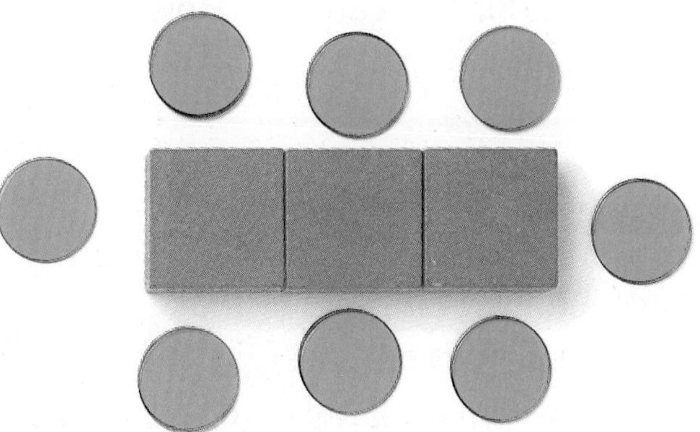

## Use a Pattern

You may find a pattern when you are trying to solve some problems. If you do, use the pattern to predict numbers without doing extra calculations. Drawing a picture or making a table can also help you discover the pattern.

**Steps**

1. **Work through the first several steps of the problem. Drawing a picture often helps.**
2. **Write the numbers in a table and look for a pattern.**

| Tables | 1 | 2 | 3 | 4 | 5 | 6 |
|---|---|---|---|---|---|---|
| Chairs | 4 | 6 | 8 | 10 | | |

Pattern: Add 2 chairs for each table.

3. **Use the pattern to complete the table.**

| Tables | 1 | 2 | 3 | 4 | 5 | 6 |
|---|---|---|---|---|---|---|
| Chairs | 4 | 6 | 8 | 10 | 12 | 14 |

# Tool Kit

## Problem Solving Strategies

**Problem**

**What is the least number of coins you can use to make 35 cents? What is the greatest number of coins you can use? How many different ways can you make 35 cents?**

## Organize Information

Some problems require you to make combinations or arrange data. In these cases, it helps to organize your information in a list, table, chart, or graph. On the next two pages, you'll see ways to make a list and a table. For an example of a graph, see Data Collection on pages 404–405.

**Write a List** Making a list is one way to organize your information. Write down all the possibilities.

**First I'll list all the ways to make 35¢ using just one quarter. Then I'll write all the ways to make 35¢ using 3 dimes.**

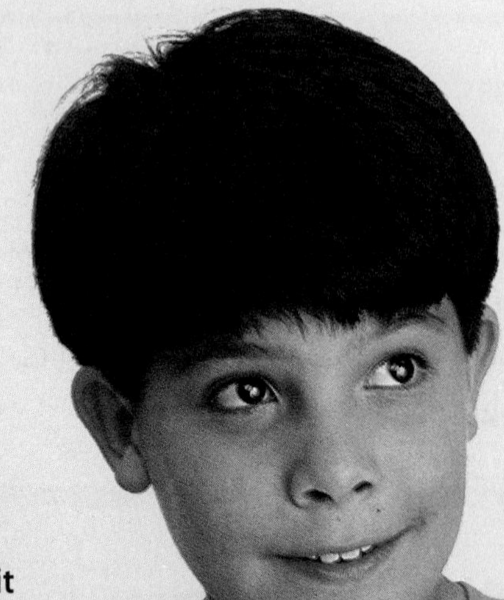

Ways to Make 35¢

1 quarter, 1 dime
1 quarter, 2 nickels
1 quarter, 10 pennies
1 quarter, 1 nickel, 5 pennies
3 dimes, 1 nickel
3 dimes, 5 pennies

**Make a Table or Chart** If you find yourself writing the same words again and again, organize your information into a table. Making a table will save you time and space. The categories in your table will be the words you are repeating. Writing a title for the table helps make your purpose clear.

You can use a table to quickly answer questions like these:

- Which combination uses the most coins?
- Which combination uses the most nickels?

Write a title that describes the data.

Label the columns in your table.

**Ways to Make 35¢**

| Quarters | Dimes | Nickels | Pennies |
|---|---|---|---|
| 1 | 1 | | |
| 1 | | 2 | |
| 1 | | | 10 |
| 1 | | 1 | 5 |
| | 3 | 1 | |
| | 3 | | 5 |
| | | | |

# Tool Kit

## Problem Solving Strategies

**Problem**

**A sporting goods store usually sells bats for $8.95. Now they're on sale for $6.98. If balls cost $4.95, how many bat-and-ball sets can you buy with $120?**

## Use a Simpler or Related Problem

Some problems seem hard because they involve lots of data or large numbers. Unnecessary data also makes problems difficult to solve. In such cases, working a simpler or related problem can show you how to work through the original problem.

**Steps**

| | | | |
|---|---|---|---|
| **1. Cut out words and numbers you don't need. (In this case, it doesn't matter that bats *used* to sell for $8.95.)** | **2. Create a simpler problem using "easy" numbers.** | **3. Solve the simpler problem.** | **4. Use that method to work through the first problem.** |

***Simpler Problem:***
**Bats cost $3; balls cost $2. How many sets can I get for $15?**

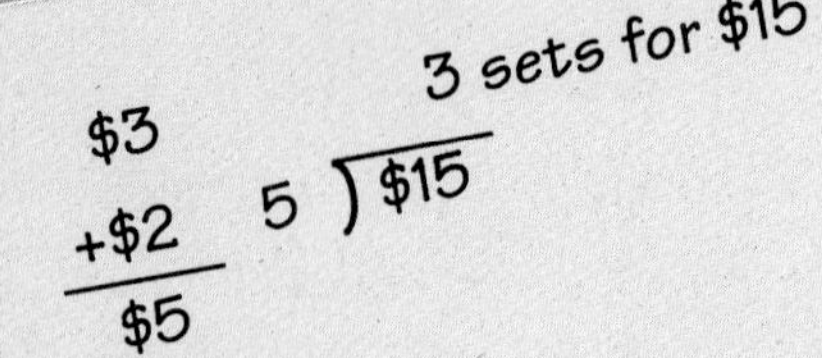


First Problem:
$6.98
+$4.95
$11.93
about $12 for one set

12 ) $120
10 sets for $120

**Problem**

**Find two numbers whose sum is 135 and whose difference is 21. What are they?**

## Guess and Check

Guess and Check is a strategy that helps you plunge right into a problem. First make a guess at an answer. Then check to see if it works. Use that information to decide if your next guess should be lower or higher.

**Steps**

| Steps | |
|---|---|
| **1. Make a guess.** | How about 100 and 35? |
| **2. Check it out to see if it works.** | $100 + 35 = 135$<br>But $100 - 35 = 65$ |
| **3. Use your guess to make a better guess.** | The numbers must be closer to one another. Maybe it's 70 and 65: $70 + 65 = 135$. But $70 - 65 = 5$. |
| **4. Keep trying until you get the answer that works.** | 78 and 57?<br>$78 + 57 = 135$<br>$78 - 57 = 21$! |

# Tool Kit

## Computation Tools

# Computing by Steps

Use this part of the Tool Kit to review ways to add, subtract, multiply, and divide. You'll find methods for computing with paper and pencil as well as "in your head."

## Paper and Pencil

These methods are helpful whenever you are using paper and a pencil to compute large numbers.

### Addition: Trading Ones

1. Add the ones. Trade if needed.

```
   1
   38
 + 14    (12)
 ----
    2
```

2. Add the tens.

```
   1
   38
 + 14
 ----
   52
```

### Addition: Trading Tens and Ones

1. Add the ones. Trade if needed.

```
    1
   376
 +  55    (11)
 -----
     1
```

2. Add the tens. Trade if needed.

```
   11
   376
 +  55    (13)
 -----
    31
```

3. Add the hundreds.

```
   11
   376
 +  55
 -----
   431
```

## Subtraction: Trading Tens

1. Look at the ones. Trade if needed.

```
 5 13
 6̸ 3̸
− 1 4
-----
```

4 > 3. A trade is needed.

2. Subtract the ones.

```
 5 13
 6̸ 3̸
− 1 4
-----
    9
```

3. Subtract the tens.

```
 5 13
 6̸ 3̸
− 1 4
-----
  4 9
```

## Subtraction: Trading Tens and Hundreds

1. Trade if needed. Subtract the ones.

```
   3 15
 3 4̸ 5̸
− 1 9 6
-------
      9
```

2. Trade if needed. Subtract the tens.

```
    13
 2 3̸ 15
 3̸ 4̸ 5̸
− 1 9 6
-------
    4 9
```

9 tens > 3 tens. A trade is needed.

3. Subtract the hundreds.

```
    13
 2 3̸ 15
 3̸ 4̸ 5̸
− 1 9 6
-------
  1 4 9
```

## Addition: Decimals

1. Line up the decimal points so you will be adding "like" quantities.

```
   5.74
  23.88
+ 10.70
-------
```

2. Add the hundredths and rename.

```
      1
   5.74
  23.88
+ 10.70
-------
      2
```

3. Add the tenths and rename.

```
   2  1
   5.74
  23.88
+ 10.70
-------
     32
```

4. Add the whole numbers. Place a decimal point in the answer.

```
  1 2  1
   5.74
  23.88
+ 10.70
-------
  40.32
```

# Tool Kit

## Computation Tools

### Subtraction: Decimals

1. Change whole numbers to decimals. Line up the decimal points.

```
  18.00
-  5.83
```

18 is 18.00

2. Trade if needed. Subtract the hundredths.

```
   7 910
  18.00
-  5.83
      7
```

3. Trade if needed. Subtract the tenths.

```
   7 910
  18.00
-  5.83
     17
```

4. Subtract the whole numbers. Place the decimal point.

```
   7 910
  18.00
-  5.83
  12.17
```

### Adding and Subtracting Fractions: Same Denominators

1. See if the denominators are the same.

$\frac{4}{5} - \frac{1}{5}$

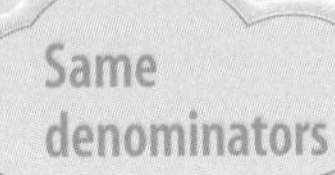


2. Subtract the numerators. Write the difference over the common denominator.

$\frac{4}{5} - \frac{1}{5} = \frac{3}{5}$

### Multiplying by a 1-Digit Factor

1. Multiply the ones. Rename if necessary.

```
      1
  1,482
     ×6
      2
```

$6 \times 2 = 12$

2. Multiply the tens. Rename if necessary.

```
     41
  1,482
     ×6
     92
```

$6 \times 8 = 48$
$48 + 1 = 49$

3. Multiply the hundreds. Rename if necessary.

```
  2 41
  1,482
     ×6
    892
```

$6 \times 4 = 24$
$24 + 4 = 28$

4. Multiply the thousands.

```
  2 41
  1,482
     ×6
  8,892
```

$6 \times 1 = 6$
$6 + 2 = 8$

## Multiplying by a 2-Digit Factor

❶ Multiply by the ones.

```
  46
× 25
----
 230
```

5 × 46

❷ Multiply by the tens.

```
  46
× 25
----
 230
 920
```

2 tens × 46

❸ Add.

```
   46
 × 25
-----
  230
+ 920
-----
1,150
```

## Dividing by a 1-Digit Divisor

❶ Decide how many digits are in the quotient.

```
   _ _
7)534
```

The first digit is in the tens' place.

❷ Estimate the first digit.

```
   7
7)534
```

❸ Multiply to find the number of tens shared. Subtract to find the tens left.

```
   7
7)534
 - 49
    4
```

4 tens

❹ Trade the tens for ones. Share the ones.

```
   76
7)534
 - 49
   44
 - 42
    2
```

7 × 6

# Tool Kit

## Computation Tools

### Mental Math

Doing computation mentally can be faster than writing numbers down. Here are some strategies you can use for mental math.

#### Counting On or Counting Back

When you add or subtract with small numbers, you can count ahead or count back to find the answer mentally.

**Add: 48 + 3**

Start with 48 and count on.

Think:
48 . . . 49, 50, 51

**Subtract: 59 − 3**

Start with 59 and count back.

Think:
59 . . . 58, 57, 56

#### Adding by Endings

When you add numbers mentally, use an addition fact with the same digits in the ones' place.

**38 + 7 = ?**

8 + 7 = 15
This sum ends in a 5.

38 + 7 must
end in a 5 too.

## Grouping for Tens

When you have several numbers to add, make groups of tens first.

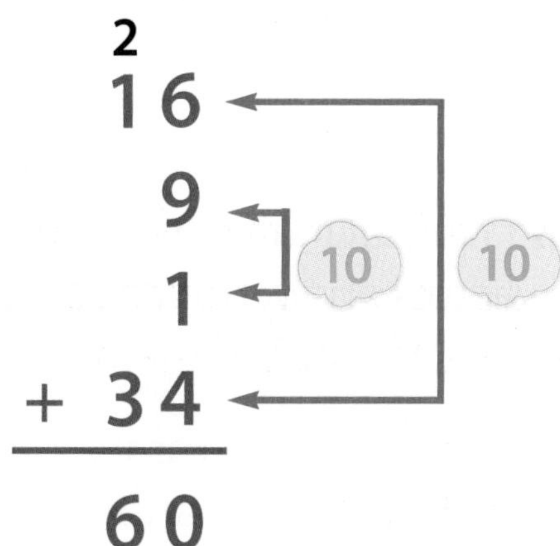


First group for tens in the ones' place. Then add all of the tens.

## Compensation

When you add or subtract, changing one number to a rounded number can make solving easier. Then change your answer to compensate.

$22 + 59 = n$

$22 + 60 = 82$

$82 - 1 = 81$

**Add 1** to 59 to get 60. **Subtract 1** from the answer to compensate.

$22 + 59 = 81$

## Breaking Apart Numbers

You can break apart numbers so that they are easier to use mentally.

**Add**

$64 + 23$

$64 + (20 + 3)$ Break apart 23.

$(64 + 20) + 3$

$84 + 3 = 87$

# Tool Kit

## Computation Tools

### Estimation

Estimation is using mental math to get an answer that's close to the actual answer but not exact. When is it helpful to estimate?

- When an exact answer isn't necessary
- When you want to know if your answer is reasonable
- When there is no way of getting an exact number

Here are four estimation strategies.

**Rounding**

You can make a number simpler to work with mentally by rounding it.

| *Rounding to nearest 100* | | *Rounding to nearest 10* | |
|---|---|---|---|
| 122 → | 100 | 42 → | 40 |
| 375 → | 400 | 87 → | 90 |
| 889 → | 900 | 364 → | 360 |

**Rounding to Estimate Products**

To get a quick multiplication estimate, round the factors.

$$19 \times 665$$

$$\downarrow \qquad \downarrow$$

$$20 \times 700 = 14{,}000$$

### Front-End Estimation

Use front-end estimation to quickly add money amounts.

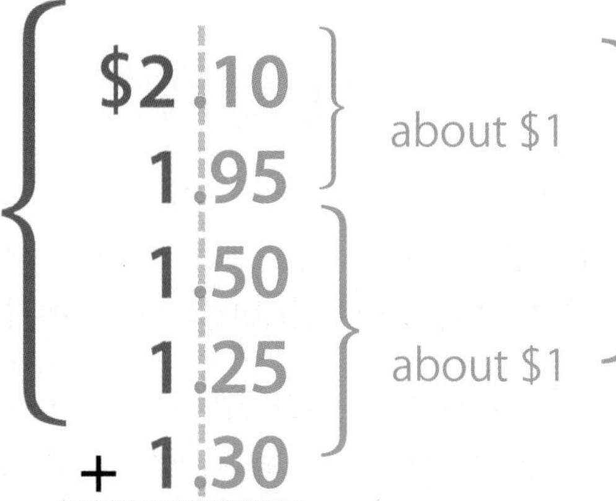


First group dollars. You get $6.

Then group the cents by dollars. You get about $2.

$6.00 + about $2.00 = about $8.00

### Compatible Numbers

Compatible numbers are numbers that are easy to compute. You can use compatible numbers to estimate division.

$23\overline{)95}$

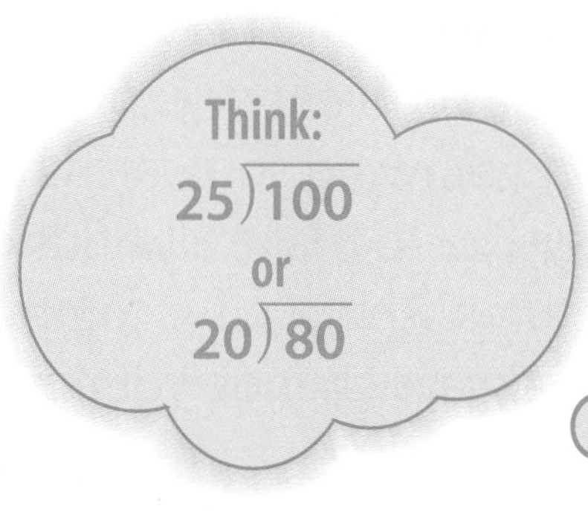


Quotient: about 4

# Electronic Tools

Computers and calculators can help you solve problems, calculate numbers, and present work. The trick is in knowing how and when to use them.

## Computer

Computers can help you collect, organize, and analyze large amounts of data. With different kinds of software, you can create diagrams, charts, tables, graphs, and pictures.

**Software** Software programs are the instructions that tell a computer what to do. Drawing programs, spreadsheets, word processing packages, and computer games are all software.

**Drawing Programs** Pictures can help you solve a problem or explain an idea. Using drawing software is a fun and easy way to make all kinds of pictures. And on the computer you can always change your picture.

**Drawing Software Uses:**

- draw pictures
- make patterns
- illustrate stories
- create floor plans

**Spreadsheets/Graphs** Spreadsheet programs are very useful when you are working with lots of numbers. Spreadsheets have columns and rows, like a table. You can enter your own numbers or have the computer calculate them for you. Then you can sort, rearrange, and even graph your information.

> **Spreadsheet Uses:**
> - organize budgets
> - make tables
> - draw graphs

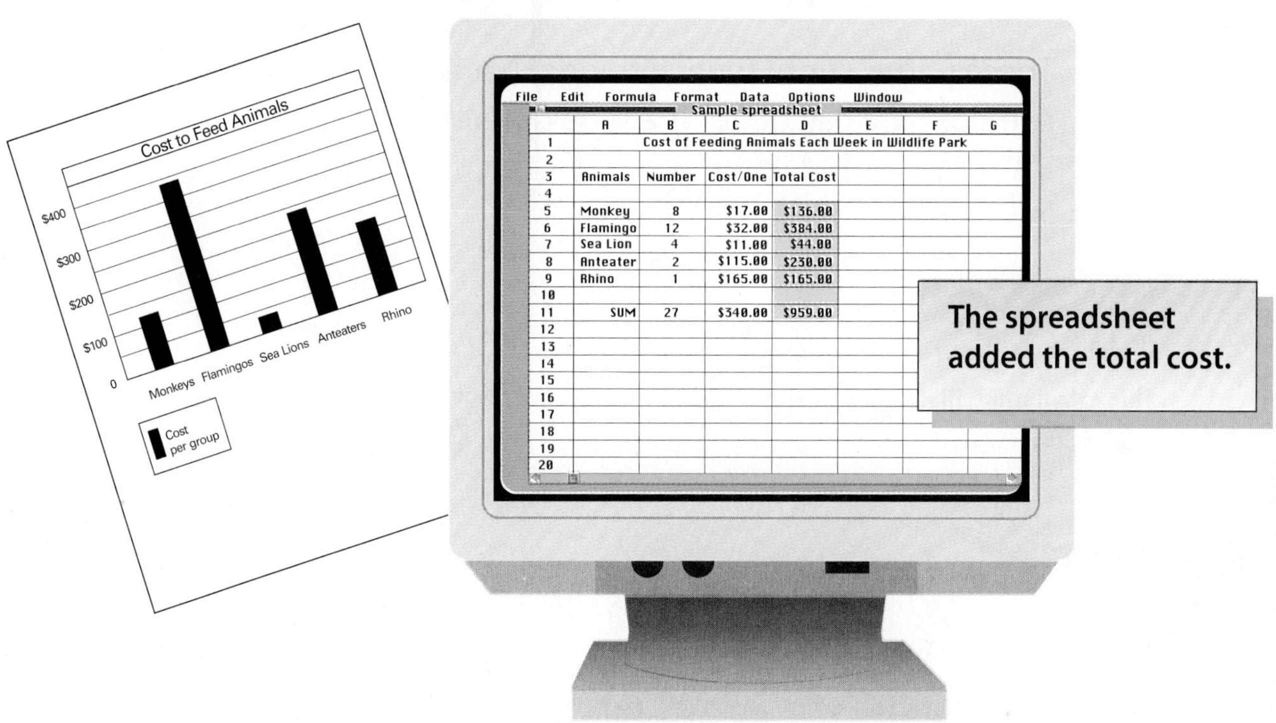


| | A | B | C | D | E | F | G |
|---|---|---|---|---|---|---|---|
| 1 | Cost of Feeding Animals Each Week in Wildlife Park | | | | | | |
| 2 | | | | | | | |
| 3 | Animals | Number | Cost/One | Total Cost | | | |
| 4 | | | | | | | |
| 5 | Monkey | 8 | $17.00 | $136.00 | | | |
| 6 | Flamingo | 12 | $32.00 | $384.00 | | | |
| 7 | Sea Lion | 4 | $11.00 | $44.00 | | | |
| 8 | Anteater | 2 | $115.00 | $230.00 | | | |
| 9 | Rhino | 1 | $165.00 | $165.00 | | | |
| 10 | | | | | | | |
| 11 | SUM | 27 | $340.00 | $959.00 | | | |
| 12 | | | | | | | |
| 13 | | | | | | | |
| 14 | | | | | | | |
| 15 | | | | | | | |
| 16 | | | | | | | |
| 17 | | | | | | | |
| 18 | | | | | | | |
| 19 | | | | | | | |
| 20 | | | | | | | |

**Databases** With database software you can organize large amounts of data, including words, dates, and numbers. A database is a great place to put survey results because it can sort through all the answers in the survey. For example, for this survey, the database can search for how many boys have pet hamsters or what kind of pet is owned by the most students.

> **Database Uses:**
> - record survey data
> - group data into categories

| | Name | Male/Female | Age | Pets |
|---|---|---|---|---|
| 1 | Mark Ellis | M | 11 | dog parrot |
| 2 | Sue Linn | F | 12 | fish |
| 3 | Reggie Brown | M | 10 | dog |
| 4 | Cassie Houston | F | 12 | dog cat |
| 5 | Rosa Rodriguez | F | 12 | hamster |
| 6 | | | | |
| 7 | | | | |
| 8 | | | | |
| 9 | | | | |
| 10 | | | | |
| 11 | | | | |
| 12 | | | | |
| 13 | | | | |
| 14 | | | | |
| 15 | | | | |

# Tool Kit

## Technology

### Calculator

These pages show several things that a calculator can do. Each calculator is a little different. Read the instructions that come with your calculator to learn how to use it.

| | Examples: |
|---|---|
| **Division**<br>This calculator will divide and show the remainder. | $173 \div 15$<br>173 [INT÷] 15 [=] [11 Q 8 R] |
| **Fractions**<br>This calculator will compute with fractions. | $\frac{1}{2} \times \frac{2}{3}$<br>1 [/] 2 [×] 2 [/] 3 [=] [2/6] |
| **Parentheses**<br>This calculator will perform multiple calculations in the order you want. | $2 \times (4 + 5)$<br>2 [×] [(] 4 [+] 5 [)] [=] [18] |
| **Memory**<br>This calculator will store numbers and operations in memory. | $3 + (6 \times 2) + (6 \times 2) + (6 \times 2)$<br>3 [+] [(] 6 [×] 2 [)] [M+]<br>[+] [MR] [+] [MR] [=] [39] |
| **Decimals**<br>This calculator will calculate decimals. | $1.25 + 3.72$<br>1 [.] 25 [+] 3 [.] 72 [=] [4.97] |

## 1 Memory

**M+** Stores the number on the display in memory, or adds the displayed number to any value already in memory

**M–** Subtracts the displayed number from memory

**MR** Displays the value stored in memory

**x⇄M** Exchanges the number on the display with the number in memory

## 2 Clearing

**ON/AC** Clears the memory, display, and operation

**Backspace** Clears the last digit entered

**CE/C** Clears the last value entered

**CE/C** **Backspace** Clears the display but not the memory

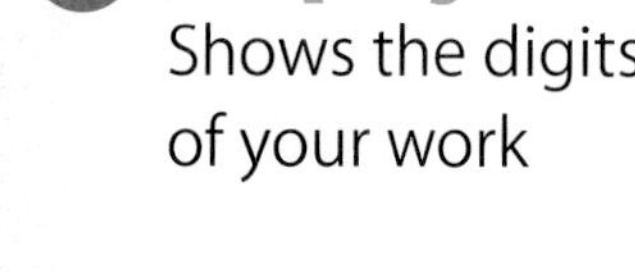

## 3 Display

Shows the digits of your work

## 4 Repeats

**=** Can be used to repeat an operation with the same number:

4 **+** 2 **=** 6

**=** 8

**=** 10

Technology

# Working with Data

Data refers to facts of all kinds. Numbers, statistics, dates, and responses to interviews are all examples of data. Here are some steps to help you plan and organize data at several stages.

## Eight Steps to Good Data Collection



### 1 Begin with a Question

Choose a question that you can answer by collecting data from several people or sources.

### 2 Plan Your Strategy

Choose a way to collect data. Where will you go for information? What kind of data are you likely to collect? How can you share it?

### 3 Collect and Record the Data

This could be as simple as a few tally marks in response to a question or as complex as making several graphs.

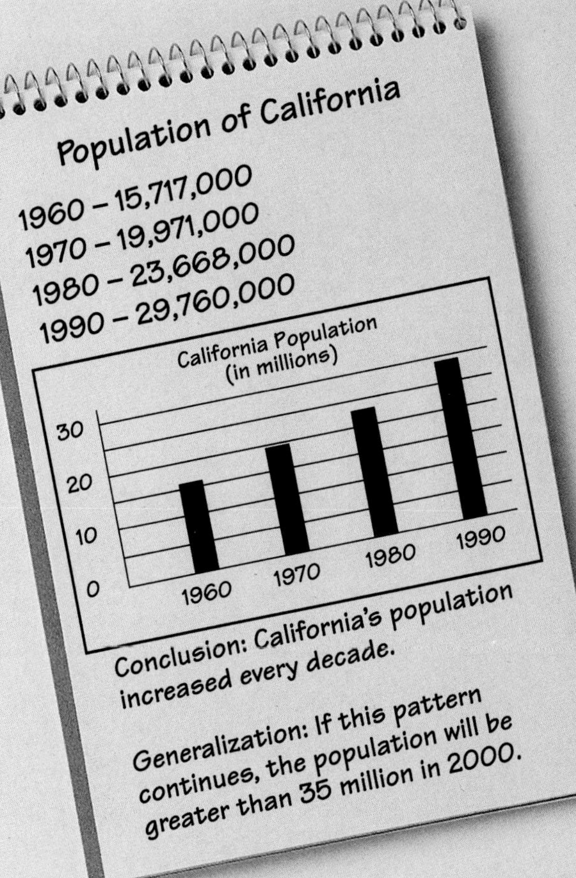


## 4 Organize the Data

Review and arrange your data. What's the best way to categorize your data?

## 5 Represent Your Data

What's the best way to display your data? A table? A chart? A graph? Now you're ready to share your results.

## 6 Draw a Conclusion

What does the data tell you about your original question? Does it describe something? Does it allow you to make comparisons?

## 7 Use Your Conclusion

You may be able to use your conclusion as a basis for a prediction, generalization, or decision.

## 8 Look Back/Look Ahead

As you look over the results of your data collection, you may want to begin the process again with a related or refined question. Or you may wish to test the theory you developed.

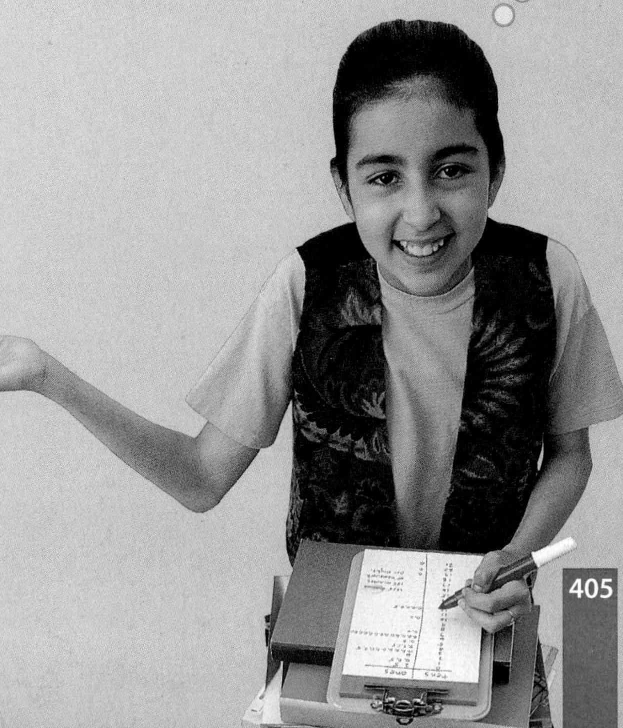

# Drawing as a Math Tool

Drawing can help you discover, understand, and share key concepts in math. Use your Drawing to Learn tools to make a variety of precise shapes and measurements.

## Drawing to Discover

Drawing can lead to discovery. For example, if you draw what you know about a problem, you often find the solution. If you draw a chart, you can see how groups of numbers relate. And drawing helps you discover your own creative ideas about math.

As you draw, patterns appear that you might not have noticed otherwise.

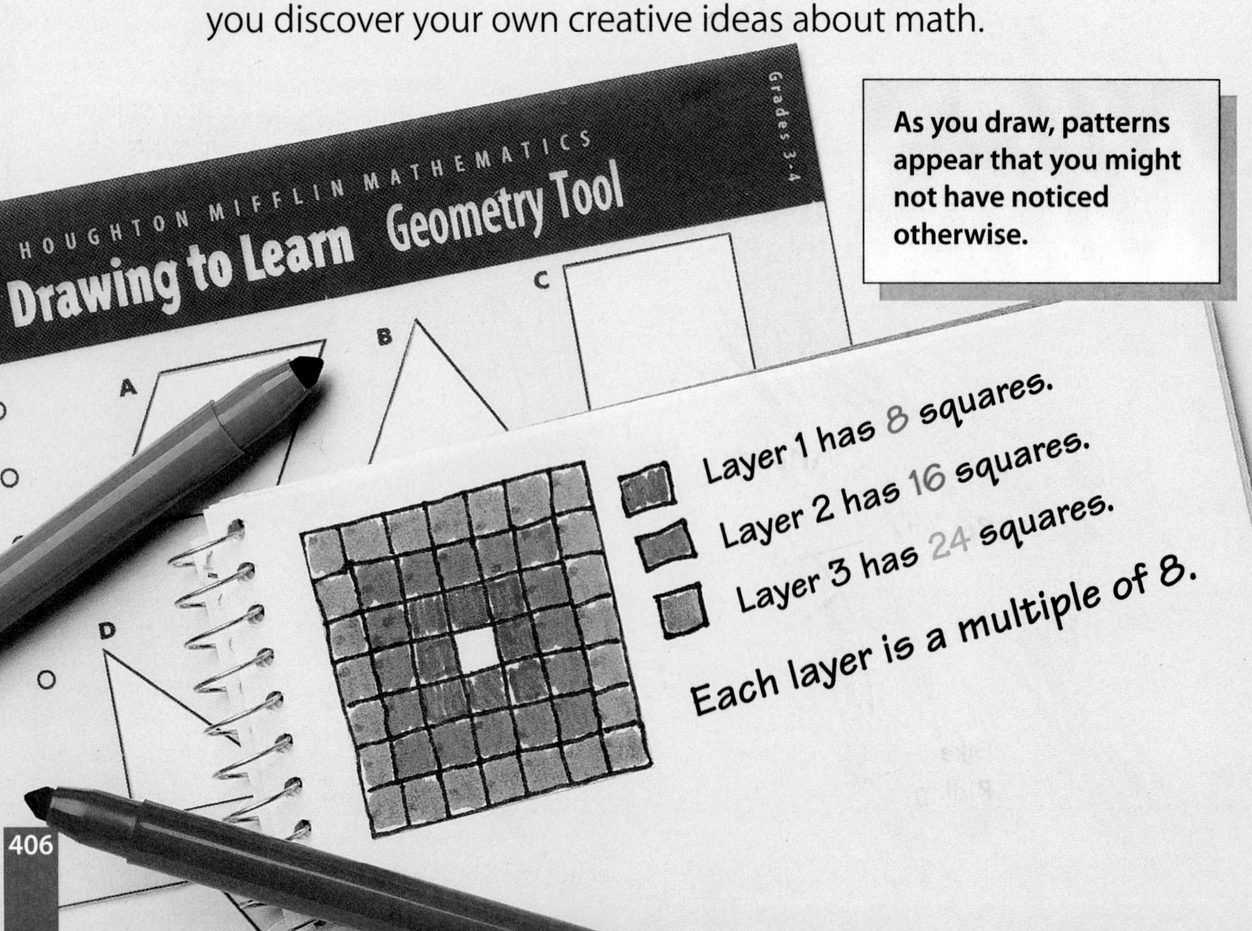

## Drawing to Understand

To simplify the steps of a process, pick up a pencil and start to draw. Drawing can also help you understand key concepts in math, including the basic computations of adding, subtracting, multiplying, and dividing.

You can use drawing to create your own system for understanding a key math concept.

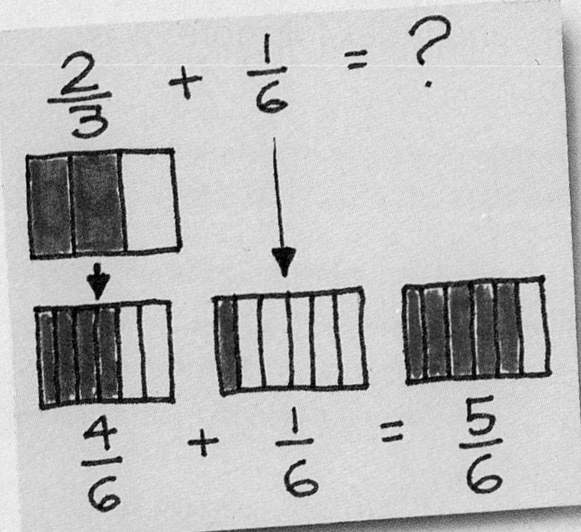


## Drawing to Share

Pictures, diagrams, graphs—all these are visual ways to share information. You can pack a great deal of data into a drawing.

People can point to your graph and ask questions or give feedback.

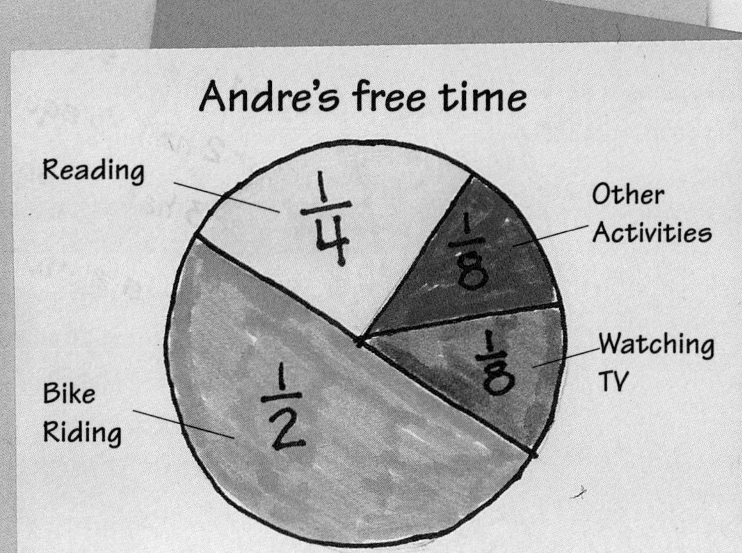

# Measurement Tools

The charts on this page identify common measures. Check the glossary and index for more information on specific terms.

| | Customary | Metric |
|---|---|---|
| Length | 1 foot (ft) = 12 inches (in.)<br>1 yard (yd) = 3 feet (ft) or 36 inches (in.)<br>1 mile (mi) = 5,280 feet (ft) | 1 centimeter (cm) = 10 millimeters (mm)<br>1 decimeter (dm) = 10 centimeters (cm)<br>1 meter (m) = 10 decimeters (dm)<br>1 kilometer (km) = 1,000 meters (m) |
| Capacity | 1 cup (c) = 8 fluid ounces (fl oz)<br>1 pint (pt) = 2 cups (c)<br>1 quart (qt) = 2 pints (pt)<br>1 gallon (gal) = 4 quarts (qt) | 1 liter (L) = 1,000 milliliters (mL)<br>1 kiloliter (kL) = 1,000 liters (L) |
| Mass/ Weight | 1 pound (lb) = 16 ounces (oz)<br>1 ton (t) = 2,000 pounds (lb) | 1 gram (g) = 1,000 milligrams (mg)<br>1 kilogram (kg) = 1,000 grams (g) |
| Temperature | *Fahrenheit*<br>freezing point = 32° F<br>boiling point = 212° F | *Celsius*<br>freezing point = 0° C<br>boiling point = 100° C |

| Time |
|---|
| 1 minute (min) = 60 seconds (s) |
| 1 hour (h) = 60 minutes (min) |
| 1 day = 24 hours (h) |
| 1 week = 7 days |
| 1 year = 52 weeks |

# Module 4.1 Section A

## a For use with Lesson 1 (pages 4–9)

Use your reasoning skills to answer *true* or *false*.

1. A square is not a rectangle.
2. A triangle can sometimes be a parallelogram.
3. Polygons always have four sides.
4. Some parallelograms have right angles.
5. Squares are parallelograms.
6. Polygons can have just two sides.
7. The difference of 43 and 12 is 31.
8. The sum of 27 and 2 is 25.
9. The first even number after 3 is 4.

## b For use with Lesson 2 (pages 10–13)

Use the shapes to answer the questions.

a.  b. c.  d. e. f.

10. How many lines of symmetry does each shape have?
11. Which shapes are congruent?
12. Which congruent shapes are flips of one another?
13. Which shapes have parallel sides?
14. Which of the shapes below cannot be made by cutting shape **a** from a paper folded once?

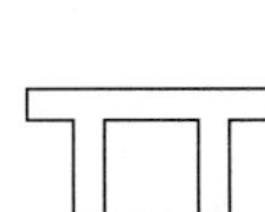 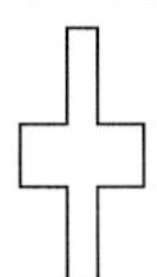 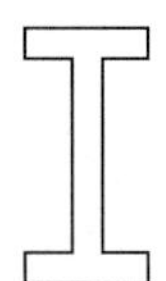 

Write two numbers that have the following things.

15. a difference of 10
16. an even difference
17. a sum of 30
18. an odd sum

# Module 4.1 Section B

## a For use with Lesson 3 (pages 14–17)

Use the drawing to solve.

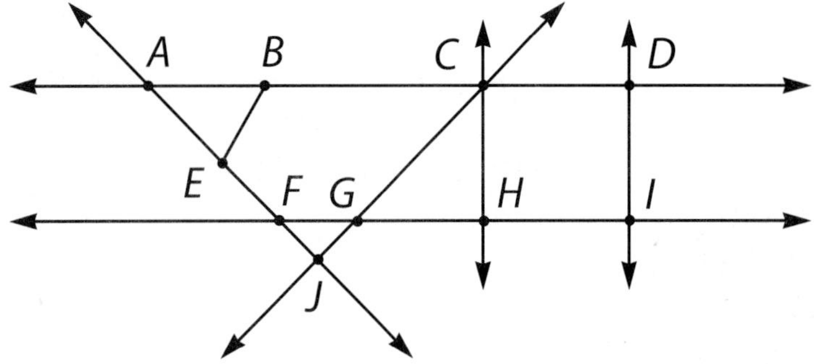


1. Name four points on line *AD*.
2. Name rays that have point *G* as an endpoint.
3. Name two lines that are parallel.
4. Would you call *BE* a ray, a line, or a line segment?
5. Name at least three triangles.

## b For use with Lesson 4 (pages 18–21)

Use the drawing to solve.

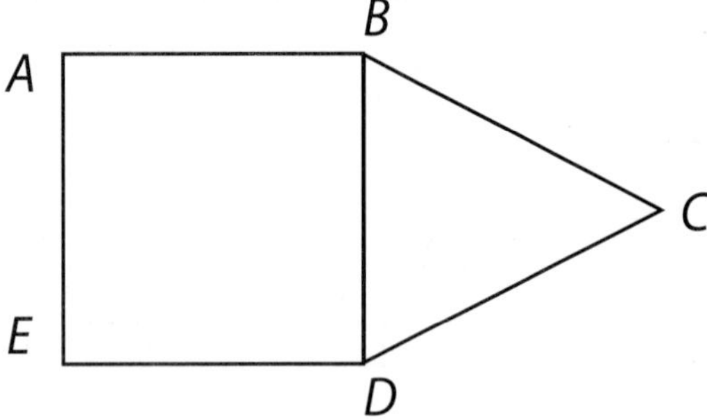


6. Name the triangle.
7. Name the square.
8. Name the pairs of parallel sides.
9. Name the right angles.

# Module 4.1 Section C

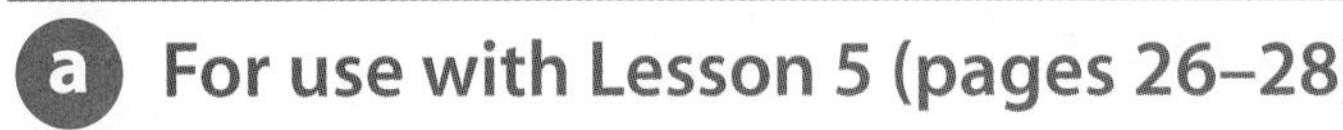

## a For use with Lesson 5 (pages 26–28)

Draw these rectangles. Record the area of each in square units. Then record the perimeter.

1. 3 units by 2 units
2. 4 units by 3 units
3. 5 units by 5 units
4. 5 units by 2 units
5. Which areas are multiples of 3?
6. Which areas are multiples of 5?
7. Which perimeters are multiples of 7?
8. Which perimeters are multiples of 5?

## b For use with Lesson 6 (pages 29–32)

Answer these questions about this figure. Its bottom face is a square.

9. What is the name of this solid?
10. How many faces does it have?
11. How many faces are triangles?
12. How many edges does it have?
13. How many vertexes does it have?

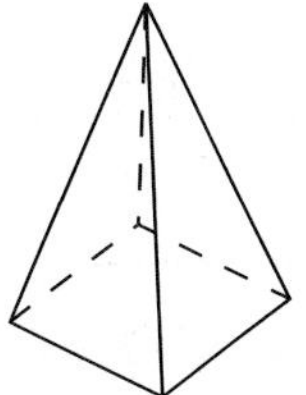

## c For use with Lesson 7 (pages 33–35)

Use these nets to answer the questions.

a. 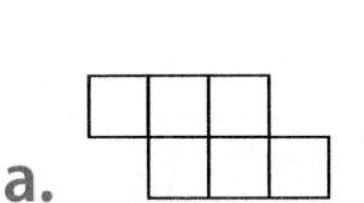 b. 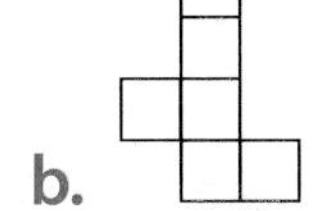 c. 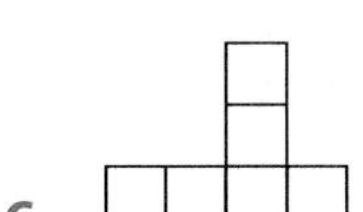 d. 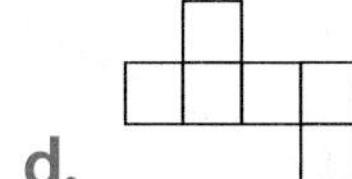 e. 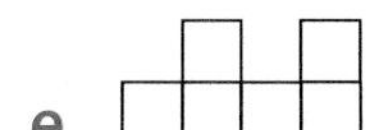

14. Which of these figures will make a cube?
15. Draw a turn of Figure **e.**
16. Draw a flip of Figure **a.**
17. Find the area of each figure.
18. Find the perimeter of Figure **a.**

# Module 4.1 Section D

## a For use with Lesson 8 (pages 36–39)

Use boxes A through D to answer the questions. Suppose box A is just large enough to hold a basketball.

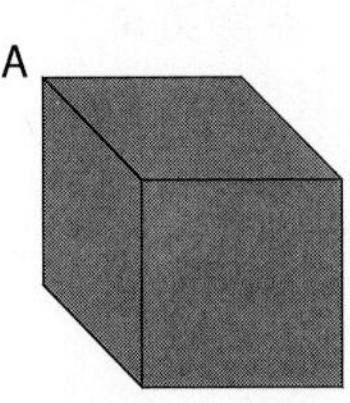

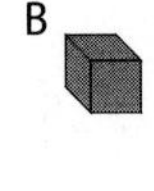

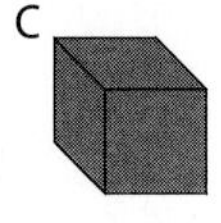

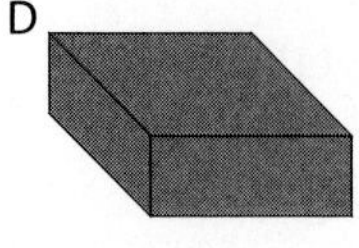


1. Order the boxes from the smallest to the largest volume.
2. If box B holds 200 raisins, estimate how many raisins box C would hold.
3. Estimate which of these objects fits into box B.
   a. a postage stamp  b. a lamp shade  c. a hairbrush
4. Estimate which of these objects fits into box D.
   a. a loaf of bread  b. a shirt  c. a basketball
5. Estimate how many of box D could fit into box A.
6. Draw a net for box C.
7. What do all of the boxes have in common?
   Make a list.

## b For use with Lesson 9 (pages 40–43)

How many blocks would it take to build each group of blocks?

8. 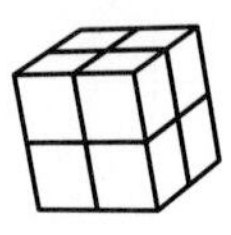

9. 

10. 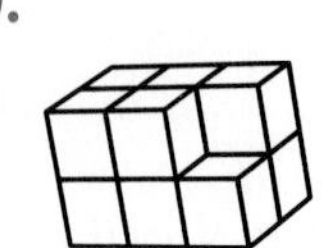

11. 

12. 

13. 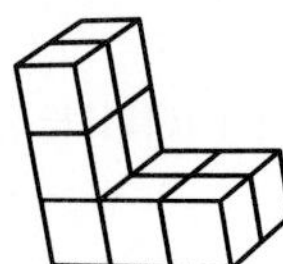

14. 

15. 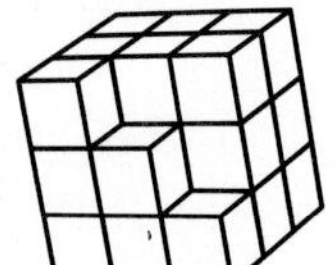

16. 

# Module 4.2 Section A

## a For use with Lesson 1 (pages 52–56)

Write each number in standard form.

1. 4 thousands, 2 hundreds
2. 3 hundreds, 6 ones
3. 9 hundreds, 5 tens, 8 ones
4. 6 thousands, 8 ones
5. 9 hundreds, 4 tens, 7 ones
6. 3 thousands, 7 tens

Write the number of thousands, hundreds, tens, and ones in each number.

7. 8,452
8. 904
9. 3,005
10. 2,040
11. 4,599
12. 701

## b For use with Lesson 2 (pages 57–59)

Use >, <, or = to compare the numbers.

13. 212,700 ● 1 million
14. 45,907 ● 304 thousand
15. 56 thousand ● 56,428
16. 789 thousand ● 789,000
17. 43 million ● 430,000,000
18. 27,844 ● 278 thousand
19. 19 million ● 19,000
20. 343 thousand ● 343,000
21. 246,800 ● 28 thousand
22. 400 thousand ● 395,000

## c For use with Lesson 3 (pages 60–61)

Write a reasonable estimate.

23. people in a movie theater
24. rungs on a ladder
25. quarters in a pocket
26. channels on television
27. pages in a dictionary
28. eyelets on a shoe
29. fingers in a classroom
30. leaves on a tree

# Module 4.2 Section B

## a For use with Lesson 4 (pages 62–67)

Write each time in a different way.

1. 4 minutes
2. 200 seconds
3. 100 minutes
4. 1,000 seconds
5. 10 minutes
6. 100 seconds
7. 11 minutes
8. 150 seconds
9. In Exercises 1–8 write the times in order from least to greatest.

## b For use with Lesson 5 (pages 68–71)

What day is it?

10. If today is Wednesday, what day is tomorrow?
11. If today is Sunday, what day was yesterday?
12. If Friday is the tenth, what day is the thirteenth?
13. If Tuesday is the ninth, what day is seven days later?
14. What day is two days before Friday?
15. What day is a week before Saturday?
16. What day is two weeks from Sunday?

Write the time as 1 hour 30 minutes later.

17. 8:00 A.M.
18. noon
19. 3:45 A.M.
20. 2:45 P.M.
21. 5:30 P.M.
22. 7:15 A.M.
23. midnight
24. 9:45 P.M.
25. 12:01 A.M.
26. 6:19 P.M.

# Module 4.2 Section C

## a For use with Lesson 6 (pages 74–77)

Write each measurement in feet and inches.

1. 30 in.
2. 44 in.
3. 2 yd 2 ft 2 in.
4. 11 yd 10 in.
5. 100 in.
6. 67 in.
7. 85 in.
8. 122 in.
9. 2 yd 6 in.
10. 3 yd 5 ft
11. 6 ft 14 in.
12. 1 yd 1 ft 1 in.

Find the perimeter for each rectangle.

13. 4 ft by 5 ft
14. 11 in. by 1 ft 3 in.
15. 7 ft by 2 yd
16. 8 in. by 2 ft
17. 10 in. by 1 yd
18. 9 ft by 5 ft
19. 3 yd by 10 ft
20. 4 ft by 1 in.

## b For use with Lesson 7 (pages 80–81)

Round to the nearest ten. Then round to the nearest hundred.

21. 567
22. 404
23. 39
24. 891
25. 743
26. 909
27. 355
28. 68
29. 365
30. 275
31. 351
32. 538

What numbers, when rounded to the nearest ten, could have given the following?

33. 170
34. 400
35. 80
36. 550
37. 710
38. 580
39. 600
40. 890
41. 1,230

# Module 4.2 Section D

## a For use with Lesson 8 (pages 82–85)

Estimate. Write $>$, $<$, or $=$ to make each sentence true.

1. $568 + 387$ ● 900
2. $799 - 221$ ● 100
3. $57 + 68$ ● 140
4. $437 + 688$ ● 1,200
5. $43 + 39$ ● 70
6. $666 - 475$ ● 300
7. $95 - 48$ ● 50
8. $456 + 764$ ● 1,200

## b For use with Lesson 9 (pages 86–88)

**472 638 28 398 560 71 183**

Choose two of the numbers above that have the given sum.

9. 655
10. 99
11. 1,198
12. 709
13. 958
14. 1,110

Choose two of the numbers that have the given difference.

15. 567
16. 74
17. 155
18. 610
19. 377
20. 166

## c For use with Lesson 10 (pages 89–91)

Indicate whether you need an exact number or an estimate.

21. Is $10 enough to buy four items in the grocery store?
22. What change will you get from your $10 bill?
23. Are there enough students to require three or four buses?
24. How long is it until lunch time?
25. How many miles is it to the next exit?
26. How many stamps must you buy?
27. How many days is the book overdue?
28. How many yards of fabric are needed to make the pattern?

# Module 4.3 Section A

## a For use with Lesson 1 (pages 100–103)

Find the product.

| | | |
|---|---|---|
| 1. $5 \times 6$ | 2. $7 \times 9$ | 3. $8 \times 4$ |
| 4. $5 \times 7$ | 5. $8 \times 8$ | 6. $3 \times 9$ |
| 7. $7 \times 6$ | 8. $7 \times 8$ | 9. $9 \times 9$ |
| 10. $4 \times 7$ | 11. $9 \times 8$ | 12. $4 \times 9$ |
| 13. $8 \times 6$ | 14. $7 \times 7$ | 15. $8 \times 5$ |

## b For use with Lesson 2 (pages 104–107)

Find the product.

| | | |
|---|---|---|
| 16. $4 \times 9$ | 17. $5 \times 5$ | 18. $2 \times 9$ |
| 19. $6 \times 6$ | 20. $9 \times 8$ | 21. $4 \times 4$ |
| 22. $7 \times 3$ | 23. $6 \times 8$ | 24. $5 \times 3$ |
| 25. $2 \times 7$ | 26. $9 \times 9$ | 27. $8 \times 8$ |
| 28. $8 \times 7$ | 29. $7 \times 7$ | 30. $9 \times 3$ |

Write two factors that have these products.

| | | |
|---|---|---|
| 31. 27 | 32. 54 | 33. 81 |
| 34. 15 | 35. 40 | 36. 49 |
| 37. 72 | 38. 35 | 39. 30 |
| 40. 48 | 41. 63 | 42. 64 |
| 43. 16 | 44. 42 | 45. 45 |
| 46. 56 | 47. 25 | 48. 28 |

# Module 4.3 Section B

## a For use with Lesson 3 (pages 110–112)

Find the missing factors or products.

1.

| Input | 0 | 5 | | | 20 |
|---|---|---|---|---|---|
| Output | 0 | 15 | 30 | 45 | |

2.

| Input | 2 | | 6 | | 9 |
|---|---|---|---|---|---|
| Output | 18 | 27 | 54 | 63 | |

3.

| Input | 56 | | 40 | 32 | |
|---|---|---|---|---|---|
| Output | 7 | 6 | 5 | | 2 |

Find the quotient.

4. $72 \div 8$
5. $30 \div 6$
6. $16 \div 8$
7. $40 \div 5$
8. $63 \div 7$
9. $21 \div 7$
10. $20 \div 4$
11. $48 \div 6$
12. $54 \div 9$
13. $35 \div 7$
14. $27 \div 3$
15. $36 \div 9$
16. $56 \div 7$
17. $36 \div 4$
18. $63 \div 9$

## b For use with Lesson 4 (pages 113–119)

Find the quotient and remainder.

19. $43 \div 8$
20. $29 \div 7$
21. $11 \div 9$
22. $54 \div 6$
23. $46 \div 4$
24. $36 \div 5$
25. $55 \div 8$
26. $17 \div 3$
27. $27 \div 4$
28. $30 \div 9$
29. $57 \div 7$
30. $74 \div 8$

# Module 4.3 Section C

## For use with Lesson 5 (pages 122–127)

Find the product.

1. $12 \times 5$
2. $15 \times 6$
3. $13 \times 5$
4. $21 \times 8$
5. $43 \times 4$
6. $11 \times 7$
7. $55 \times 5$
8. $37 \times 6$
9. $19 \times 3$
10. $25 \times 8$
11. $20 \times 7$
12. $34 \times 8$

## b For use with Lesson 6 (pages 128–131)

Rewrite the factors using the Commutative Property of Multiplication. Then find the products.

13. $3 \times 5 \times 7$
14. $35 \times 4$
15. $2 \times 4 \times 9$
16. $16 \times 6$
17. $28 \times 7$
18. $33 \times 4 \times 2$
19. $6 \times 7 \times 8$
20. $30 \times 4$
21. $10 \times 3 \times 8$
22. $20 \times 7 \times 2$
23. $5 \times 8 \times 2$
24. $9 \times 10 \times 8$

Find the product.

25. $2 \times 3 \times 5$
26. $3 \times 4 \times 2$
27. $2 \times 3 \times 4$
28. $2 \times 2 \times 2$
29. $5 \times 2 \times 6$
30. $3 \times 5 \times 6$
31. $5 \times 5 \times 2$
32. $4 \times 1 \times 9$
33. $3 \times 3 \times 3$
34. $6 \times 6 \times 6$
35. $5 \times 4 \times 2$
36. $1 \times 8 \times 7$
37. $5 \times 2 \times 9$
38. $4 \times 4 \times 4$
39. $9 \times 2 \times 4$
40. $3 \times 3 \times 6$
41. $10 \times 2 \times 3$
42. $6 \times 4 \times 3$
43. $3 \times 8 \times 2$
44. $1 \times 1 \times 6$
45. $8 \times 2 \times 2$
46. $9 \times 1 \times 9$
47. $4 \times 3 \times 5$
48. $6 \times 9 \times 3$

# Module 4.3 Section D

## a For use with Lesson 7 (pages 132–135)

Find a possible date for the following birthday numbers.

1. 81
2. 33
3. 96
4. 25
5. 58
6. 112
7. 200
8. 310
9. 150
10. 99

## b For use with Lesson 8 (pages 136–139)

Draw and label rectangles having the following areas.

11. 32 square units
12. 40 square units
13. 1 square unit
14. 21 square units
15. 50 square units
16. 42 square units
17. 10 square units
18. 72 square units

Use the area and the length to find the width.

19. 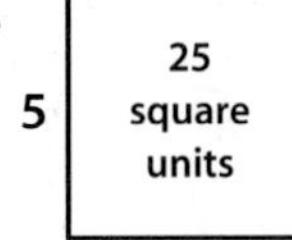


20. 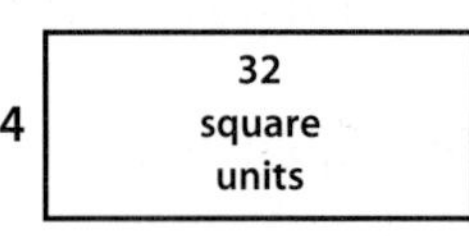


21. 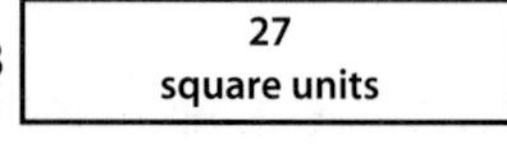


22. 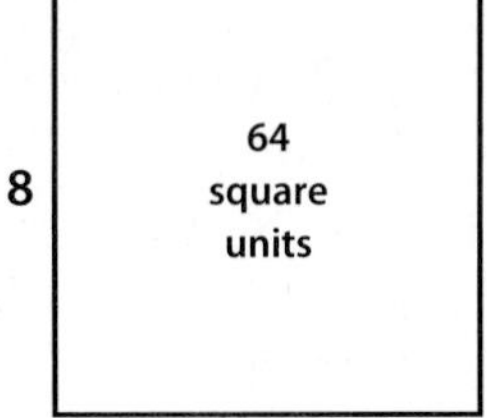


23. 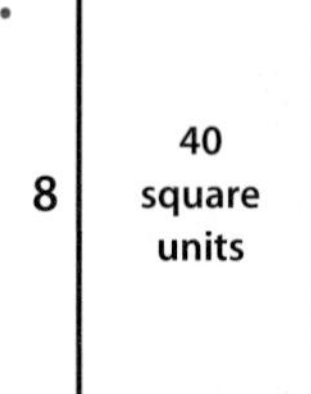


24. 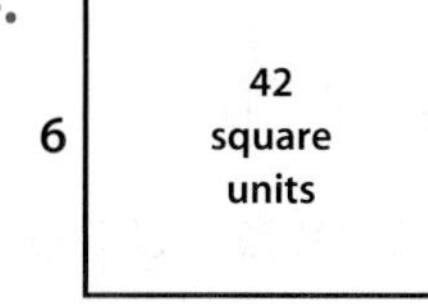

# Module 4.4 Section A

## a For use with Lesson 1 (pages 148–150)

Draw a circle. Shade the fraction.

1. $\frac{1}{4}$
2. $\frac{3}{4}$
3. $\frac{1}{2}$
4. $\frac{1}{8}$
5. $\frac{3}{8}$
6. $\frac{1}{3}$
7. $\frac{2}{3}$
8. $\frac{5}{8}$

## b For use with Lesson 2 (pages 151–153)

Draw a shape. Then shade the fraction.

9. $\frac{1}{4}$
10. $\frac{1}{6}$
11. $\frac{1}{10}$
12. $\frac{2}{3}$
13. $\frac{3}{4}$
14. $\frac{5}{10}$
15. $\frac{7}{16}$
16. $\frac{3}{5}$

## c For use with Lesson 3 (pages 154–156)

Use the picture to write an equivalent fraction in simplest form.

17. $\frac{6}{8} = \frac{3}{■}$ 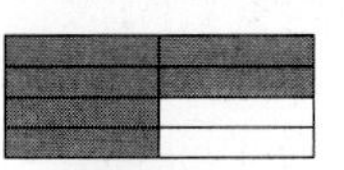

18. $\frac{6}{10} = \frac{■}{■}$ 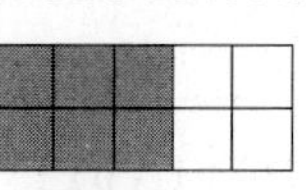

19. $\frac{3}{6} = \frac{1}{■}$ 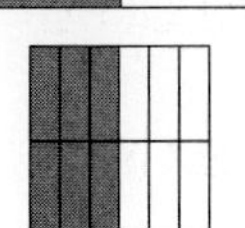

20. $\frac{2}{6} = \frac{1}{■}$ 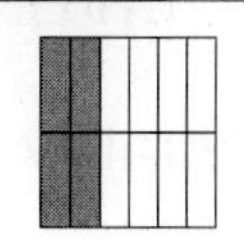

## d For use with Lesson 4 (pages 157–159)

Compare the fractions. Write $>$, $<$, or $=$.

21. $\frac{7}{10}$ ● $\frac{3}{10}$
22. $\frac{5}{12}$ ● $\frac{7}{12}$
23. $\frac{1}{4}$ ● $\frac{1}{8}$
24. $\frac{1}{2}$ ● $\frac{7}{14}$
25. $\frac{2}{3}$ ● $\frac{5}{6}$
26. $\frac{2}{5}$ ● $\frac{3}{10}$
27. $\frac{1}{100}$ ● $\frac{2}{10}$
28. $\frac{1}{3}$ ● $\frac{2}{6}$
29. $\frac{1}{2}$ ● $\frac{5}{10}$

Find the missing number.

30. $\frac{1}{2} = \frac{■}{10}$
31. $\frac{3}{4} = \frac{6}{■}$
32. $\frac{5}{5} = \frac{■}{■}$
33. $\frac{22}{24} = \frac{11}{■}$
34. $\frac{2}{3} = \frac{4}{■}$
35. $\frac{4}{8} = \frac{■}{■}$

# Module 4.4 Section B

## a For use with Lesson 5 (pages 162–163)

Match the object with its most reasonable length.

| | |
|---|---|
| 1. lunch bag | a. $31\frac{1}{2}$ in. |
| 2. shoelace | b. $1\frac{1}{2}$ in. |
| 3. paper clip | c. 18 in. |
| 4. school bus | d. $20\frac{1}{2}$ ft |
| 5. baseball bat | e. $178\frac{1}{4}$ ft |
| 6. playground | f. $9\frac{1}{2}$ in. |

Write the measure you would use for each. Write *inches, feet,* or *miles.*

7. notebook
8. library table
9. bicycle path
10. pencil
11. car length
12. computer screen

## b For use with Lesson 6 (pages 164–167)

Write the amount two other ways.

13. 2 qt
14. 2 gal
15. 2 c
16. 16 oz
17. 9 pt
18. $2\frac{1}{2}$ gal

Name a container for which the given measure is a reasonable estimate of its capacity.

19. 10 oz
20. 5 gal
21. 2 qt
22. 20 gal
23. 1 pt
24. 1 gal

Complete each number sentence.

25. 2 t = ▢ lb
26. 20 oz = ▢ lb
27. 2 lb = ▢ oz
28. 1 t 400 lb = ▢ lb

# Module 4.4 Section C

## a For use with Lesson 7 (pages 170–173)

Write the fraction for the part of the given set.

| pencil | notebook | ruler | eraser |
|---|---|---|---|
| chalk | pen | marker | math book |

1. part of the set you can write with
2. part of the set with only 5 letters
3. part of the set that begins with the letter *b*
4. part of the set that is made of paper
5. part of the set that you find in school
6. part of the set that is about 1 ft long

## b For use with Lesson 8 (pages 174–177)

The circle graph shows the result of a survey of 40 people. How many people chose each kind of TV show?

7. comedy
8. sports
9. movies
10. quiz shows

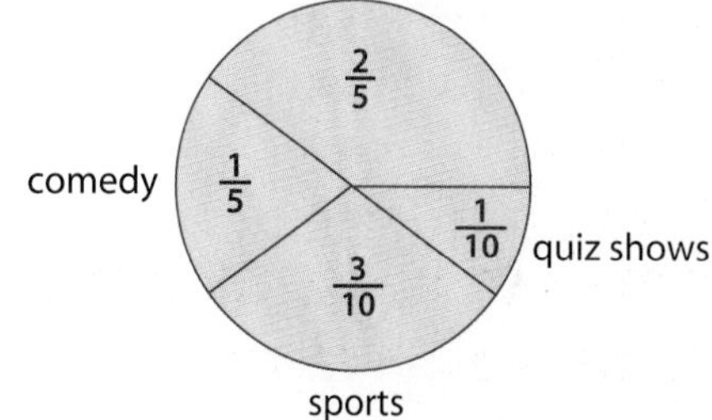


The circle graph shows the choice of musical instruments by 120 students. How many chose each instrument?

11. violin
12. piano
13. drums
14. guitar

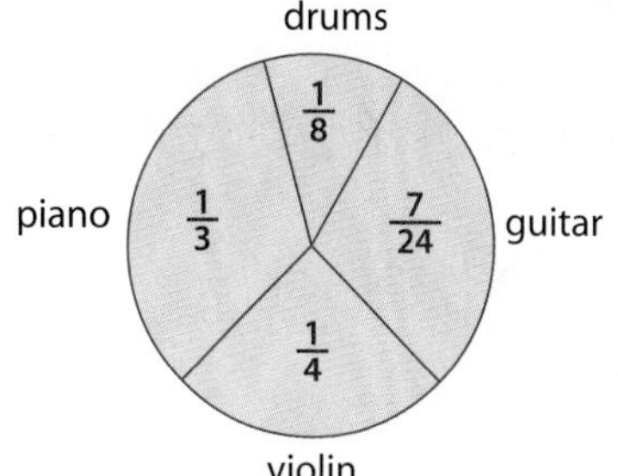

# Module 4.4 Section D

## a For use with Lesson 9 (pages 178–183)

Find each sum or difference.

1. $\frac{9}{10} - \frac{9}{10}$
2. $\frac{3}{8} + \frac{2}{8}$
3. $\frac{5}{6} + \frac{1}{6}$
4. $1 - \frac{5}{6}$
5. $\frac{2}{3} - \frac{1}{3}$
6. $\frac{2}{3} + \frac{2}{3}$
7. $5 + \frac{3}{8}$
8. $2 - \frac{1}{3}$
9. $\frac{3}{8} + \frac{3}{8}$
10. $\frac{2}{5} + \frac{1}{5}$
11. $\frac{3}{10} + \frac{5}{10}$
12. $\frac{1}{2} + 0$

## b For use with Lesson 10 (pages 184–187)

Find the difference.

13. $12\frac{1}{2} - 9$
14. $18\frac{3}{4} - 6$
15. $10\frac{1}{4} - 1$
16. $15\frac{7}{8} - 7$
17. $20\frac{1}{4} - 20$
18. $16\frac{1}{2} - 10$
19. $17\frac{3}{4} - 12$
20. $18\frac{1}{8} - 11$
21. $12 - 2\frac{1}{4}$

Compare the sums or differences. Write >, <, or =.

22. $\frac{2}{3} + 2$ ● $\frac{3}{4} + 2$
23. $2 + \frac{1}{2}$ ● $3 - \frac{1}{2}$
24. $1\frac{1}{2} - \frac{3}{4}$ ● $\frac{3}{4}$
25. $1\frac{1}{8} + \frac{7}{8}$ ● $2\frac{1}{2} - 2$
26. $2\frac{3}{4} + 1\frac{1}{4}$ ● $4\frac{1}{2}$
27. $3\frac{1}{5} - \frac{4}{5}$ ● $3$
28. $2 + \frac{3}{4}$ ● $2\frac{3}{4}$
29. $5 - \frac{3}{4}$ ● $5 - \frac{1}{2}$
30. $1\frac{1}{8} - \frac{3}{8}$ ● $\frac{1}{2} + \frac{1}{2}$
31. $4\frac{3}{8} + \frac{1}{8}$ ● $4\frac{5}{8} - \frac{1}{8}$
32. $5\frac{2}{3} + \frac{2}{3}$ ● $4\frac{1}{2} + \frac{1}{2}$
33. $3\frac{3}{4} - \frac{1}{2}$ ● $2 + \frac{3}{4}$
34. $4\frac{1}{2} + 2\frac{3}{4}$ ● $5 + \frac{7}{8}$
35. $6\frac{3}{4} - 2\frac{3}{4}$ ● $4\frac{1}{2} + \frac{3}{8}$

# Module 4.5 Section A

## a For use with Lesson 1 (pages 196–200)

Plot the following ordered pairs.

1. (0, 0) 2. (1, 4) 3. (2, 0) 4. (3, 4)

5. (7, 0) 6. (7, 4) 7. (3, 0)

8. Name the polygon formed by connecting points 1–3.

9. Name the polygon formed by connecting points 4–7.

## b For use with Lesson 2 (pages 201–203)

Plot the ordered pairs and connect the points.

10. (3, 4), (5, 6), (5, 8), (7, 4)

11. (4, 0), (5, 1), (3, 3), (2, 2)

12. (6, 1), (8, 0), (7, 2)

13. (0, 0), (3, 0), (1, 1)

14. (1, 4), (4, 4), (4, 7), (1, 7)

15. (2, 5), (3, 5), (3, 6), (2, 6)

16. Find two shapes in Exercises 10–15 that are similar to each other.

17. Draw a shape similar to 13. Tell how you know it's similar.

18. Write the coordinates of the two similar triangles in the figure.

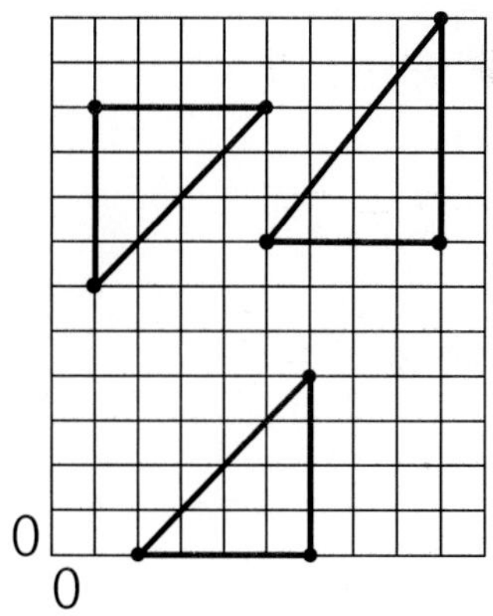

# Module 4.5 Section B

## a For use with Lesson 3 (pages 206–208)

Find two combinations of coins and bills to make each amount. The first combination should have fewer coins and bills than the second combination. For coins use pennies, nickels, dimes, and quarters. For bills use \$1, \$5, \$10, and \$20.

**1.** \$6

**2.** \$8.48

**3.** \$0.19

**4.** \$2.20

**5.** \$0.91

**6.** \$24.45

**7.** \$0.52

**8.** 24¢

**9.** \$9

**10.** \$8.70

## b For use with Lesson 4 (pages 209–211)

Find the change.

**11.** cost: \$2.19; gave: \$5

**12.** cost: \$3.45; gave: \$4

**13.** cost: \$5.11; gave: \$6.01

**14.** cost: \$10.32; gave: \$11

**15.** cost: \$8.18; gave: \$10.03

**16.** cost: \$12.97; gave: \$15

**17.** cost: \$4.44; gave: \$10

**18.** cost: \$5.35; gave: \$6.10

**19.** cost: \$0.93; gave: \$1

**20.** cost: \$32.22; gave: \$40

## c For use with Lesson 5 (pages 212–213)

Write the Roman numerals.

**21.** 33 **22.** 40 **23.** 104 **24.** 88 **25.** 1990

**26.** 440 **27.** 305 **28.** 1776 **29.** 1600 **30.** 2000

Write the number in standard form.

**31.** XVI **32.** XXIII **33.** MC **34.** DCL **35.** CCXX

**36.** CM **37.** LXVIII **38.** XXXIX **39.** XC **40.** LIV

# Module 4.5 Section C

## a For use with Lesson 6 (pages 216–219)

Write the remainders for each example.

1. $41 \div 5$
2. $2\overline{)9}$
3. $3\overline{)20}$
4. $3\overline{)22}$
5. $4\overline{)31}$
6. $43 \div 5$
7. $2\overline{)11}$
8. $9\overline{)37}$
9. $6\overline{)26}$
10. $8\overline{)25}$
11. $8\overline{)51}$
12. $8\overline{)63}$

## b For use with Lesson 7 (pages 220–222)

Estimate the quotient. Then find the quotient and remainder.

13. $44 \div 9$
14. $60 \div 8$
15. $52 \div 7$
16. $87 \div 9$
17. $46 \div 5$
18. $33 \div 7$
19. $53 \div 6$
20. $35 \div 4$
21. $8\overline{)70}$
22. $7\overline{)69}$
23. $8\overline{)50}$
24. $7\overline{)30}$
25. $9\overline{)85}$
26. $5\overline{)46}$
27. $7\overline{)38}$
28. $3\overline{)29}$

Compare the quotients. Write $>$, $<$ or $=$.

29. $5\overline{)41}$ ● $5\overline{)36}$
30. $8\overline{)51}$ ● $6\overline{)51}$
31. $9\overline{)37}$ ● $4\overline{)37}$
32. $3\overline{)13}$ ● $8\overline{)25}$
33. $6\overline{)29}$ ● $6\overline{)39}$
34. $2\overline{)16}$ ● $5\overline{)40}$
35. $8\overline{)32}$ ● $6\overline{)25}$
36. $3\overline{)16}$ ● $4\overline{)20}$
37. $9\overline{)62}$ ● $9\overline{)55}$

## c For use with Lesson 8 (pages 223–225)

Estimate the quotient by using compatible numbers. Then find the quotient and remainder.

38. $6\overline{)117}$
39. $9\overline{)437}$
40. $8\overline{)551}$
41. $7\overline{)500}$
42. $5\overline{)266}$
43. $4\overline{)319}$
44. $6\overline{)472}$
45. $9\overline{)705}$
46. $8\overline{)394}$

# Module 4.5 Section D

## ⓐ For use with Lesson 9 (pages 226–229)

Find the average of each group of numbers.

1. 11, 15, 14, 20
2. 3, 3, 5, 7, 9, 11, 13, 13, 17
3. 7, 8, 16, 18, 31
4. 2, 2, 2, 5, 5, 6, 6
5. 10, 20, 20, 40, 80
6. 100, 50
7. 120, 140, 160
8. 13, 15, 17, 23, 32
9. What number must be added to Exercise 2 to make the average 10?
10. What number must be added to Exercise 6 to make the average 80?

## ⓑ For use with Lesson 10 (pages 230–231)

Find the averages for each group of numbers.

11. $0.50, $1.00
12. 4, 12
13. 100, 200, 300, 400
14. 1, 99
15. 1 quarter, 1 nickel
16. 2 dimes, 2 quarters
17. 2, 10, 15
18. $1, $5, $6

## ⓒ For use with Lesson 11 (pages 232–235)

Use 45, 67, 88, 91, 123, 150, 180, 210, 250, and 402 to answer the following questions.

19. What numbers have 9 as a factor?
20. What numbers have no factors, except 1 and themselves?
21. What numbers can be divided by 3?
22. What numbers have 8 as a factor?
23. What numbers can be divided by 5?
24. What numbers can be divided by 4?
25. What numbers can be divided by 3 and 5?
26. What numbers have 7 as a factor?

# Module 4.6 Section A

## (a) For use with Lesson 1 (pages 244–245)

Write each measurement as a decimal part of a meter.

1. 8 dm  2. 6 dm  3. 21 dm  4. 567 dm

Write each decimal in word form.

5. 0.9  6. 4.3

7. 1.2  8. 6.8

Compare the fractions. Write >, <, or =.

9. $\frac{7}{10}$ ● $\frac{7}{100}$  10. $\frac{1}{100}$ ● $\frac{2}{100}$

11. $\frac{4}{10}$ ● $\frac{40}{100}$  12. $\frac{3}{10}$ ● $\frac{33}{100}$

## (b) For use with Lesson 2 (pages 246–249)

Write a decimal for each fraction.

13. $\frac{1}{10}$  14. $\frac{6}{10}$  15. $\frac{3}{10}$  16. $\frac{4}{10}$

17. $\frac{9}{10}$  18. $\frac{5}{10}$  19. $\frac{3}{10}$  20. $\frac{2}{10}$

## (c) For use with Lesson 3 (pages 250–255)

Write each fraction as a mixed number.

21. $\frac{21}{10}$  22. $\frac{99}{10}$  23. $\frac{18}{10}$  24. $\frac{54}{10}$

Order from greatest to least.

25. 1.1, 1.5, 2.0, 0  26. 4.5, 4.1, 5, 4.7

27. 3.3, 3, 0.3, 33  28. 1.2, 1.1, 0.9, 1.0

Compare the numbers. Write >, <, or =.

29. 2.3 ● 2.7  30. 0.5 ● 0.9  31. 3 ● 2.9  32. 4 ● 4.6

# Module 4.6 Section B

## a For use with Lesson 4 (pages 256–259)

Write each measurement as a decimal part of a meter.

1. 9 cm
2. 45 cm
3. 235 cm
4. 9 dm
5. 300 dm
6. 325 cm
7. 9 dm 5 cm
8. 4 m 6 dm
9. 8 m 4 cm

Write each fraction as a decimal.

10. $\frac{14}{100}$
11. $\frac{15}{100}$
12. $\frac{55}{100}$
13. $\frac{93}{100}$
14. $\frac{12}{100}$
15. $\frac{21}{100}$
16. $\frac{29}{100}$
17. $\frac{7}{10}$
18. $\frac{7}{100}$

## b For use with Lesson 5 (pages 260–261)

Order each group from least to greatest.

19. 9, 10.9, 9.1, 8.9
20. 6.5, 6.4, 4.6, 5.4
21. 0.9, 0.87, 1.2, 1.0
22. 3.5, 2.9, 2.93, 3.45
23. 5, 5.7, 6.02, 6.2
24. 0.32, 0.3, , 3.0, 3.2
25. 1.2, 2.0, 1, 2.10
26. 7.4, 7.32, 7.5, 7.52

Rounded to the nearest whole number, which numbers round to 2?

27. $2\frac{3}{4}$
28. 1.8
29. 1.2
30. 2.2

Rounded to the nearest ten, which numbers round to 10?

31. 15
32. 11
33. 9
34. 4

# Module 4.6 Section C

## (a) For use with Lesson 6 (pages 264–267)

Compare the decimals. Write $>$, $<$, or $=$.

1. 5.5 ● 5.55
2. 4.4 ● 4
3. 0.45 ● 0.5
4. 3 ● 3.00
5. 0.03 ● 0.33
6. 7.25 ● 7.5
7. 10.1 ● 10.01
8. 1.0 ● 1.000
9. 3.78 ● 3.8
10. 6 ● 6.01
11. 7.7 ● 7.27
12. 2.0 ● 20.2

Find the missing number.

13. $\frac{5}{10} + \frac{1}{10} = n$
14. $\frac{9}{10} - n = \frac{8}{10}$
15. $\frac{3}{10} + n = \frac{6}{10}$
16. $n - \frac{2}{10} = \frac{1}{10}$
17. $\frac{17}{100} + \frac{4}{100} = n$
18. $\frac{31}{100} - \frac{5}{100} = n$

## (b) For use with Lesson 7 (pages 268–269)

Write each amount of money in decimal form.

19. 2 quarters, 1 nickel
20. 1 quarter, 2 dimes, 3 pennies
21. 3 quarters, 1 dime, 1 nickel, 3 pennies
22. 2 dimes, 7 pennies
23. 2 quarters, 1 dime, 3 nickels, 4 pennies
24. 7 nickels, 7 pennies
25. 14 nickels, 18 pennies
26. 11 quarters
27. 20 nickels, 17 pennies
28. 2 fives, 2 ones, 1 quarter, 4 dimes, 3 nickels, 8 pennies
29. 3 quarters, 1 penny
30. 1 one, 1 nickel
31. Which of the above amounts is greatest?
32. Which is the least?

# Module 4.6 Section D

## a For use with Lesson 8 (pages 272–275)

Add to find each sum greater than 1.

1. $\begin{array}{r} 0.3 \\ +0.4 \\ \hline \end{array}$

2. $\begin{array}{r} 1.3 \\ +1.2 \\ \hline \end{array}$

3. $\begin{array}{r} 0.9 \\ +0.6 \\ \hline \end{array}$

4. $\begin{array}{r} 0.5 \\ +0.7 \\ \hline \end{array}$

5. $\begin{array}{r} 1.8 \\ +0.1 \\ \hline \end{array}$

6. $\begin{array}{r} 2.5 \\ +3.5 \\ \hline \end{array}$

7. $\begin{array}{r} 0.2 \\ +0.7 \\ \hline \end{array}$

8. $\begin{array}{r} 2.4 \\ +2.4 \\ \hline \end{array}$

9. $\begin{array}{r} 2.8 \\ +1.3 \\ \hline \end{array}$

10. $\begin{array}{r} 3.9 \\ +6.2 \\ \hline \end{array}$

11. $\begin{array}{r} 8.8 \\ +7.5 \\ \hline \end{array}$

12. $\begin{array}{r} 1.6 \\ +9.4 \\ \hline \end{array}$

## b For use with Lesson 9 (pages 276–278)

Find the missing decimals in these equations.

13. $3.5 + 7.9 = n$
14. $9.3 + 5.1 = n$
15. $n + 7.7 = 10$
16. $6.8 - n = 6.1$
17. $20.5 + n = 23.8$
18. $3 - n = 1.3$
19. $n + 7.8 = 8.7$
20. $5.3 - 3.5 = n$
21. $6.2 + n = 6.2$
22. $n - 16.5 = 1.2$
23. $n + 4 = 4.7$
24. $n - 9.8 = 9.8$

## c For use with Lesson 10 (pages 279–283)

Copy the charts. Find the missing numbers. The sums should be correct across and down.

25.

| | | |
|---|---|---|
| 2.4 | 0.3 | 2.7 |
| 0.9 | | |
| | | 4.8 |

26.

| | | |
|---|---|---|
| 4.01 | 2.27 | 6.28 |
| 0.47 | | 3.97 |
| | | |

# Module 4.7 Section A

## ⓐ For use with Lesson 1 (pages 292–295)

Choose a reasonable capacity for each object.

| | |
|---|---|
| 1. straw | 10,000,000 L |
| 2. bucket | 15 L |
| 3. fish tank | 25 mL |
| 4. pond | 600 mL |
| 5. canteen | 45 L |

Change each measure to milliliters.

6. 20 L 7. 2 L 8. 200 L 9. 2,000 L 10. 0.2 L

Change each measure to liters.

11. 7,000 mL 12. 700 mL 13. 70 mL 14. 7 mL 15. 0.7 mL

## ⓑ For use with Lesson 2 (pages 296–298)

Multiply each number by 5, 10, and 100. Make a table.

16. 8 17. 76 18. 217 19. 6,395 20. 42,524

21. 7 22. 38 23. 744 24. 2,666 25. 70,000

## ⓒ For use with Lesson 3 (pages 299–301)

Divide a, then predict the quotient for b.

26. a. $358 \div 5$
    b. $358 \div 10$

27. a. $71 \div 5$
    b. $71 \div 10$

28. a. $488 \div 10$
    b. $488 \div 5$

29. a. $905 \div 10$
    b. $905 \div 5$

30. a. $68 \div 5$
    b. $68 \div 10$

31. a. $680 \div 10$
    b. $680 \div 5$

32. a. $80 \div 10$
    b. $80 \div 5$

33. a. $579 \div 5$
    b. $579 \div 10$

34. a. $777 \div 5$
    b. $777 \div 10$

# Module 4.7 Section B

## (a) For use with Lesson 4 (pages 302–304)

Find the product. Then write how many sets of 10 are in each.

| | | |
|---|---|---|
| 1. 30 × 74 | 2. 40 × 68 | 3. 70 × 29 |
| 4. 20 × 83 | 5. 50 × 84 | 6. 90 × 34 |
| 7. 40 × 66 | 8. 30 × 33 | 9. 60 × 54 |
| 10. 70 × 45 | 11. 20 × 40 | 12. 50 × 20 |

## (b) For use with Lesson 5 (pages 305–309)

For each multiplication choose the best estimate. Explain your choice.

| | | | |
|---|---|---|---|
| 13. 39 × 61 | 30 × 60 | 40 × 70 | 40 × 60 |
| 14. 56 × 87 | 60 × 90 | 60 × 80 | 50 × 90 |
| 15. 48 × 63 | 40 × 60 | 50 × 60 | 50 × 70 |
| 16. 65 × 95 | 70 × 90 | 60 × 90 | 70 × 100 |
| 17. 179 × 43 | 200 × 40 | 200 × 50 | 100 × 40 |
| 18. 223 × 478 | 200 × 400 | 300 × 500 | 200 × 500 |
| 19. 543 × 786 | 500 × 700 | 500 × 800 | 600 × 800 |
| 20. 904 × 384 | 900 × 400 | 900 × 300 | 1,000 × 400 |

Compare these products. Write $>$, $<$, or $=$.

| | |
|---|---|
| 21. 20 × 30 ● 19 × 29 | 22. 31 × 51 ● 30 × 50 |
| 23. 49 × 89 ● 50 × 90 | 24. 100 × 80 ● 103 × 83 |
| 25. 30 × 40 ● 39 × 27 | 26. 100 × 100 ● 97 × 99 |
| 27. 31 × 40 ● 41 × 30 | 28. 20 × 40 ● 18 × 38 |
| 29. 80 × 50 ● 81 × 52 | 30. 30 × 30 ● 28 × 28 |

# Module 4.7 Section C

## a For use with Lesson 6 (pages 314–317)

Change grams to kilograms and kilograms to grams.

| | | |
|---|---|---|
| 1. 1 g | 2. 1 kg | 3. 10 g |
| 4. 10 kg | 5. 100 g | 6. 100 kg |
| 7. 1,000 g | 8. 1,000 kg | 9. 10,000 g |
| 10. 10,000 kg | 11. 250 g | 12. 25 kg |

## b For use with Lesson 7 (pages 318–321)

Multiply *a* and multiply *b*. Use the products to find the answer to *c*.

| | | |
|---|---|---|
| 13. a. 23 × 40 | b. 23 × 5 | c. 23 × 45 |
| 14. a. 64 × 70 | b. 64 × 8 | c. 64 × 78 |
| 15. a. 37 × 8 | b. 37 × 7 | c. 37 × 15 |
| 16. a. 56 × 10 | b. 56 × 1 | c. 56 × 9 |
| 17. a. 75 × 50 | b. 75 × 3 | c. 75 × 53 |
| 18. a. 25 × 30 | b. 25 × 2 | c. 25 × 32 |
| 19. a. 46 × 20 | b. 46 × 2 | c. 46 × 22 |

Use estimation to tell which number is the correct product.

| | | | | |
|---|---|---|---|---|
| 20. 29 × 18 | 450 | 622 | 522 | 322 |
| 21. 78 × 41 | 3,198 | 2,998 | 2,898 | 4,658 |
| 22. 9 × 58 | 422 | 522 | 622 | 722 |
| 23. 38 × 51 | 1,268 | 2,938 | 3,648 | 1,938 |
| 24. 61 × 77 | 3,697 | 4,697 | 4,987 | 5,987 |

# Module 4.7 Section D

## (a) For use with Lesson 8 (pages 322–327)

Write the number of digits in each quotient.

1. 6,893 ÷ 30
2. 5,613 ÷ 80
3. 876 ÷ 40
4. 9,502 ÷ 60
5. 529 ÷ 70
6. 782 ÷ 20

Write the first digit of the quotient when 4,358 is divided by the following.

7. 40
8. 50
9. 5
10. 30
11. 60
12. 10

Choose the correct quotient.

| | | | |
|---|---|---|---|
| 13. $2\overline{)1{,}460}$ | 73 | 730 | 7,300 |
| 14. $8\overline{)120}$ | 15 | 150 | 1,500 |
| 15. $6\overline{)144}$ | 24 | 240 | 2,400 |
| 16. $3\overline{)2{,}490}$ | 83 | 830 | 8,300 |
| 17. $5\overline{)1{,}500}$ | 3 | 30 | 300 |
| 18. $20\overline{)1{,}080}$ | 54 | 540 | 5,400 |
| 19. $60\overline{)55{,}800}$ | 93 | 930 | 9,300 |

## (b) For use with Lesson 9 (pages 328–329)

Choose the most sensible temperature for the following.

| | | | |
|---|---|---|---|
| 20. freezer | 21. refrigerator | 40°F | 100°F |
| 22. teapot | 23. library | 10°F | 76°F |
| 24. swimming pool | 25. hot tub | 180°F | 69°F |

26. Subtract 0.5 degrees from each temperature that ends with zero.

# Module 4.8 Section A

## a For use with Lesson 1 (pages 340–345)

Write as a ratio.

1. ■ headlights to 1 car
2. ■ eggs to 1 dozen
3. ■ oz to 1 pint
4. ■ players to 1 baseball team
5. 1 yd to ■ ft
6. 1 cm to ■ mm
7. 1 lb to ■ oz
8. 1 gal to ■ qt
9. 1 km to ■ m
10. 1 quarter to ■ pennies
11. 1 m to ■ cm
12. 1 hour to ■ minutes

## b For use with Lesson 2 (pages 346–349)

Write a fraction in simplest form for the following percents.

13. 75%
14. 50%
15. 30%
16. 60%
17. 1%
18. 90%
19. 80%
20. 43%
21. 45%
22. 99%
23. 25%
24. 10%

Write the fractions as percents.

25. $\frac{70}{100}$
26. $\frac{45}{100}$
27. $\frac{48}{100}$
28. $\frac{54}{100}$
29. $\frac{30}{100}$
30. $\frac{95}{100}$
31. $\frac{84}{100}$
32. $\frac{2}{100}$
33. $\frac{5}{100}$
34. $\frac{8}{100}$
35. $\frac{12}{100}$
36. $\frac{50}{100}$

Write the percents as fractions in simplest form.

37. 1%
38. 10%
39. 20%
40. 43%
41. 30%
42. 50%
43. 91%
44. 2%
45. 25%
46. 75%
47. 40%
48. 11%
49. 100%
50. 60%
51. 5%
52. 15%

# Module 4.8 Section B

## a For use with Lesson 3 (pages 350–353)

What is the probability of seeing these items in your school? Write *likely* or *unlikely*.

1. 1 newspaper
2. 4 backpacks
3. 6 rulers
4. 1 horse
5. $87,000
6. 1 exit sign
7. 200 pianos
8. 2 clocks
9. 3 fire alarms
10. 1 notebook
11. 1 ring
12. 1,000 bushels of corn

## b For use with Lesson 4 (pages 354–357)

Write the experimental probability of flipping heads (H) in these coin-flip trials.

13.

| H | III |
|---|---|
| T | II |

14.

| H | 卌 II |
|---|---|
| T | 卌 I |

15.

| H | 卌 卌 |
|---|---|
| T | 卌 III |

16.

| H | 卌 卌 III |
|---|---|
| T | 卌 卌 卌 |

17.

| H | 卌 I |
|---|---|
| T | 卌 卌 I |

18.

| H | 卌 III |
|---|---|
| T | 卌 卌 II |

Write each fraction in simplest form.

19. $\frac{5}{10}$
20. $\frac{2}{6}$
21. $\frac{12}{16}$
22. $\frac{12}{24}$
23. $\frac{2}{8}$
24. $\frac{9}{12}$
25. $\frac{6}{10}$
26. $\frac{8}{10}$
27. $\frac{15}{20}$
28. $\frac{40}{80}$
29. $\frac{6}{16}$
30. $\frac{4}{8}$
31. $\frac{8}{12}$
32. $\frac{2}{24}$
33. $\frac{6}{12}$
34. $\frac{50}{100}$
35. $\frac{10}{20}$
36. $\frac{2}{10}$
37. $\frac{20}{100}$
38. $\frac{25}{100}$
39. $\frac{6}{8}$
40. $\frac{5}{15}$
41. $\frac{25}{30}$
42. $\frac{4}{14}$
43. $\frac{8}{10}$
44. $\frac{9}{18}$
45. $\frac{18}{24}$
46. $\frac{8}{32}$

# Module 4.8 Section C

## ⓐ For use with Lesson 5 (pages 362–365)

Tell whether each probability is closer to 0 or 1.

1. 1 out of 4
2. 2 out of 3
3. 5 out of 9
4. 7 out of 15
5. 3 out of 7
6. 9 out of 20
7. 6 out of 17
8. 51 out of 100
9. 49 out of 100
10. 511 out of 10,000
11. 60 out of 100
12. 999 out of 1,000

## ⓑ For use with Lesson 6 (pages 366–371)

Compare the probability for the two events in each set. Use >, <, or =.

13. toss 3 coins, get 3 heads ● get 3 tails
14. toss 3 coins, get 3 heads ● get 2 heads
15. toss 4 coins, get at least 2 tails ● get at least 3 tails
16. toss 4 coins, get at least 1 head ● get at least 1 tail

Give the probability of these events.

17. toss 3 coins, get 3 heads
18. toss 3 coins, get 3 tails
19. toss 3 coins, get 3 heads or 3 tails
20. toss 3 coins, get 1 tail
21. toss 3 coins, get more heads than tails
22. toss 3 coins, get 0 heads
23. toss 3 coins, get exactly 1 head
24. toss 3 coins, get 2 heads and 1 tail

# Module 4.8 Section D

## a For use with Lesson 7 (pages 372–375)

From a bowl of 6 red, 7 green, 9 yellow, and 10 blue marbles, find the probability of drawing the following.

1. a red marble
2. a green marble
3. a yellow marble
4. a blue marble
5. a red or green marble
6. not a blue marble
7. not a green or yellow marble
8. an orange marble
9. a red or green or yellow or blue marble
10. not a black marble

## b For use with Lesson 8 (pages 376–379)

Find the correct tree diagram. Then write each probability.

**a.**

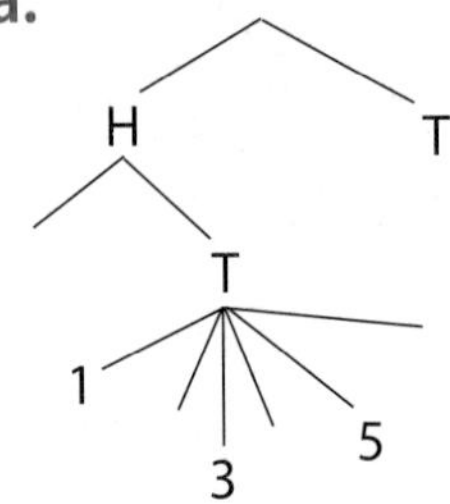


**b.**

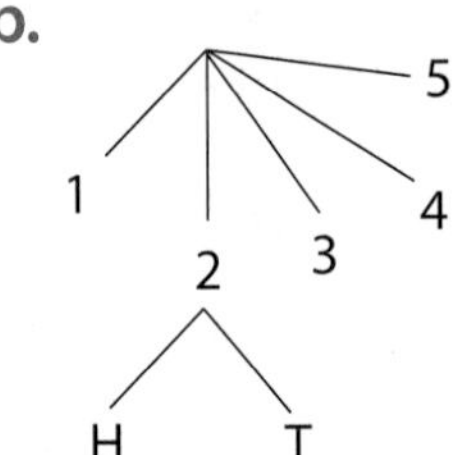


**c.**

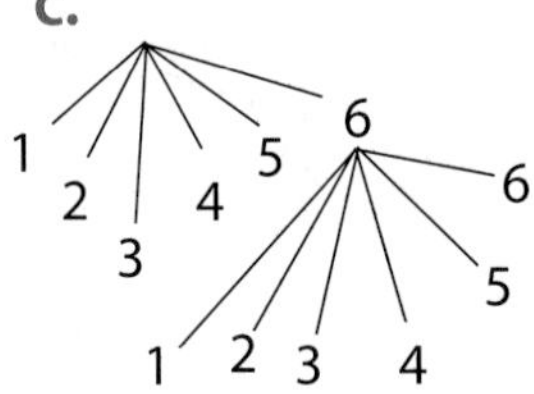


**d.**

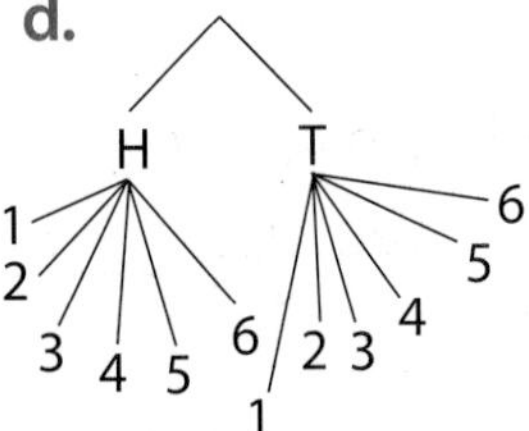


**e.**

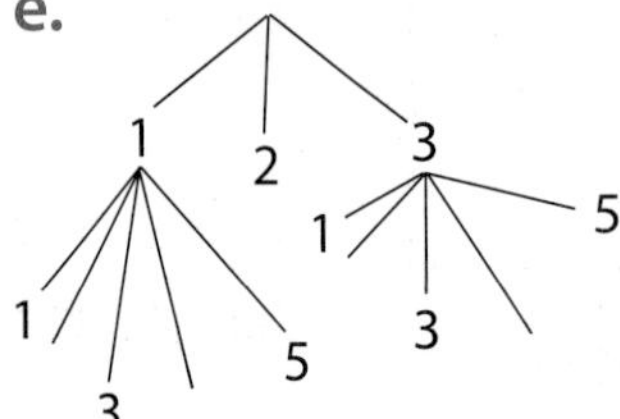


**f.**

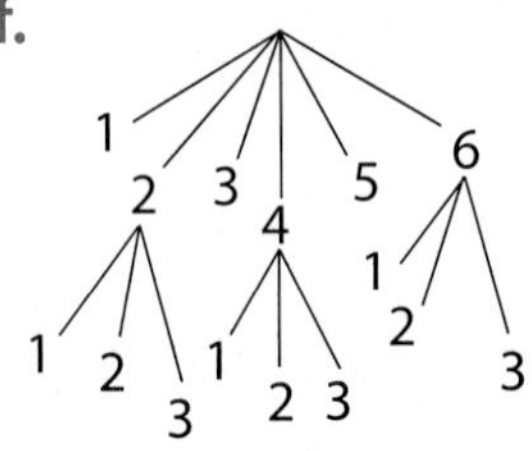


11. heads on a coin, 1 on a number cube
12. even number on a number cube, 1 on a spinner labeled 1–3
13. 2 on a spinner labeled 1–5, heads on a coin
14. 6 on a number cube, 6 on a spinner labeled 1–6
15. heads on a coin, tails on a second coin, odd number on a number cube
16. two odd numbers on spinners labeled 1–3 and 1–5

# Glossary

## A

**acre** (p. 312) A unit of area in the U.S. Customary System. 1 acre = 43,560 square feet or 4,840 square yards

**addends** (p. 272) Numbers being added in addition.

$$\begin{array}{r} 5 \\ +\ 3 \\ \hline 8 \end{array}$$

5, 3 → addends
8 → sum

**angle** (p. 20) Two rays with the same endpoint.

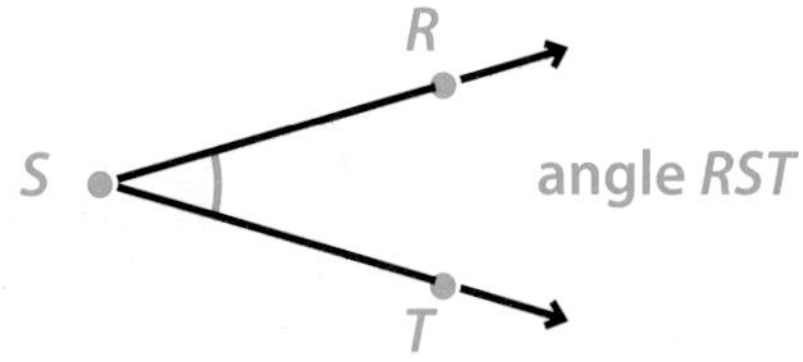


**area** (p. 26) The number of square units in the surface of a shape.

Area is 9 square units.

**array** (p. 72) An arrangement of rows and columns. An egg carton is an example of an array.

**average** (p. 226) A number that stands for a set of numbers. To find an average, divide the sum of a group of numbers by the number of addends. The average of 2, 8, 9, and 21 is 10 because 40 ÷ 4 = 10.

## B

**bar graph** (p. 141) A graph that uses bars to compare data.

## C

**capacity** (p. 164) The amount a container can hold.

**Celsius** (p. 328) The metric temperature scale that has 0 degrees as the freezing point of water and 100 degrees as the boiling point.

**center of a circle** (p. 348) The point that is the same distance from all points on the circle.

**centimeter (cm)** (p. 247) A metric unit for measuring length. 100 cm = 1 meter

**certain event** (p. 363) An event whose probability is 1 because it happens every time.

**circle** (p. 157) A figure, such as this one, made up of points that are all the same distance from the center point.

center

**circle graph** (p. 175) A circle divided into parts to show numbers.

# Glossary

**circumference** (p. 349) The distance around a circle.

**common factor** (p. 134) A number that is a factor of two or more given numbers. The common factors of 8 and 12 are 1, 2, and 4.

**common multiple** (p. 134) A number that is a multiple of two or more numbers. Example: 12 is a common multiple of 2, 3, 4, and 6.

**Commutative Property of Multiplication** (p. 102) Changing the order of the factors does not change the product. Example:

$$5 \times 8 = 40$$
$$8 \times 5 = 40$$
so $5 \times 8 = 8 \times 5$

**compatible numbers** (p. 223) Numbers that divide easily for use in estimating quotients.

**cone** (p. 29) A solid with one circular face and one vertex.

**congruent** (p. 10) Having the same size and shape.

**coordinate grid** (p. 198) A grid in which the points are named by ordered pairs. See *ordered pair* for illustration.

**cube** (p. 29) A solid with six square faces, all the same size.

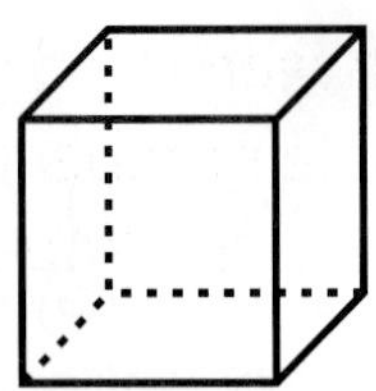

**cubic unit** (p. 40) A unit used to measure the volume of a solid. A cubic centimeter is the volume of a cube with every edge measuring 1 centimeter.

**cup (c)** (p. 164) A unit for measuring capacity in the U.S. Customary System. 2 c = 1 pint

**cylinder** (p. 29) A solid with circular bases and no corners.

## D

**data** (p. 191) Numbers that give information.

**day** (p. 63) The time it takes Earth to make one complete turn.

**decimal** (p. 250) A number that uses the base ten system and a decimal point. Another way to write fractions with denominators of 10, 100, and so on. Examples: 0.2 and 1.76

**decimal fraction** (p. 250) See *decimal.*

**decimal point** (p. 242) The point between the digits that separates the whole number from the fractional part of a number.

**decimeter (dm)** (p. 246) A unit of length in the metric system.
1 dm = 0.1 meter or 10 centimeters

**denominator** (p. 149) The bottom number of a fraction. It shows the total number of equal parts. The denominator in the fraction $\frac{2}{3}$ is 3.

**diagonal** (p. 117) A line segment that joins two vertexes.

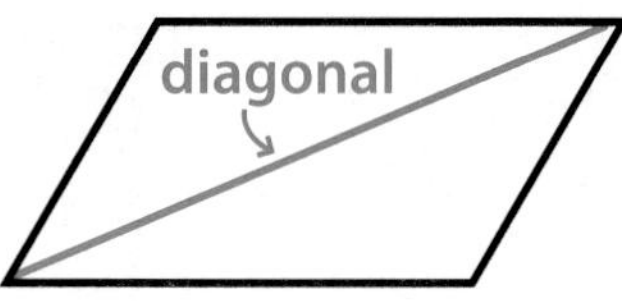


**diameter** (p. 349) A line segment through the center of a circle that has its two endpoints on the circle.

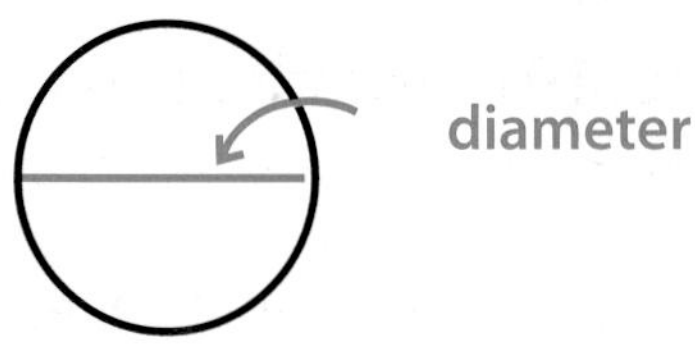


**difference** (p. 88) The answer in subtraction. In the number sentence 15 − 8 = 7, the difference is 7.

**digit** (p. 54) The symbol used to name a number in the place-value system. There are ten digits: 0, 1, 2, 3, 4, 5, 6, 7, 8, 9.

**Distributive Property** (p. 320) The product of a factor and a sum is equal to the sum of the products.
Example:

$$5 \times (3 + 2) = (5 \times 3) + (5 \times 2)$$

**dividend** (p. 218) The number being divided in division. In the number sentence 36 ÷ 4 = 9, the dividend is 36.

**divisor** (p. 218) The number that divides the dividend in division. In the number sentence 30 ÷ 5 = 6, the divisor is 5.

**edge** (p. 31) The line segment formed when two faces of a solid meet.

**endpoints** (p. 16) Points at the ends of a line segment. Also see *line segment.*

**equally likely** (p. 354) Having the same probability. The chances of getting "heads" or "tails" on the toss of a coin are equally likely.

**equivalent fractions** (p. 155) Fractions that name the same number. $\frac{1}{2}$, $\frac{2}{4}$, and $\frac{3}{6}$ are equivalent fractions.

**estimate** (p. 84) An answer that is not exact.

**even number** (p. 53) A number that is a multiple of 2. Examples: 2, 8, 22, 46

**experimental probability** (p. 354) The probability that is found by doing an experiment.

**face** (p. 31) A flat surface of a solid.

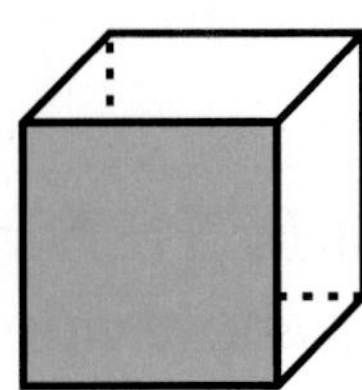

**factor** (p. 101) A number being multiplied to obtain a product. In the number sentence $4 \times 6 = 24$, the factors are 4 and 6.

**Fahrenheit** (p. 328) The temperature scale that has 32 degrees as the freezing point of water and 212 degrees as the boiling point.

**flip** (p. 10) Reflecting a figure about a line.

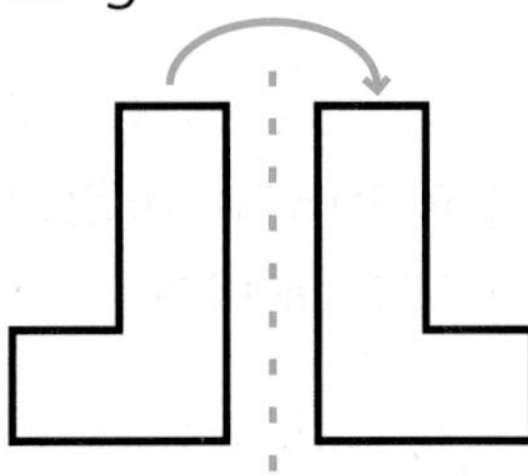

**foot (ft)** (p. 75) A unit of length in the U.S. Customary System. 1 ft = 12 inches

**fraction** (p. 145) A number that shows part of a whole unit. $\frac{1}{2}$, $\frac{4}{5}$, and $\frac{5}{7}$ are fractions.

**fraction greater than one** (p. 158) A fraction in which the numerator is larger than the denominator. A fraction greater than one can be simplified to a mixed number or a whole number. Also called an improper fraction.

**front-end estimation** (p. 84) An estimation strategy in which you use front-end digits first, then adjust if necessary.

## G

**gallon (gal)** (p. 165) A unit for measuring liquids in the U.S. Customary System. 1 gal = 4 quarts

**gram (g)** (p. 315) A metric unit for measuring mass. 1,000 g = 1 kilogram

**grid** (p. 198) Parallel and perpendicular line segments on which points are plotted.

**hexagon** (p. 6) A polygon with 6 sides and 6 angles.

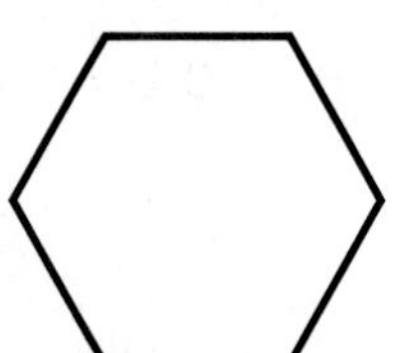

## I

**impossible event** (p. 363) An event that has no chance of happening.

**improper fraction** See *fraction greater than one.*

**inch (in.)** (p. 75) A unit of length in the U.S. Customary System.
12 in. = 1 foot

**intersect** (p. 4) When two or more lines or line segments meet or cross at a common point.

## K

**kilogram (kg)** (p. 314) A metric unit for measuring mass. 1 kg = 1,000 grams

**kilometer (km)** (p. 249) A metric unit for measuring length. 1 km = 1,000 meters

## L

**line** (p. 16) A set of points that extends on and on in both directions.

**line graph** (p. 299) A graph that uses a line to show changes over time.

**line of symmetry** (p. 7) A line that separates a figure into two matching parts.

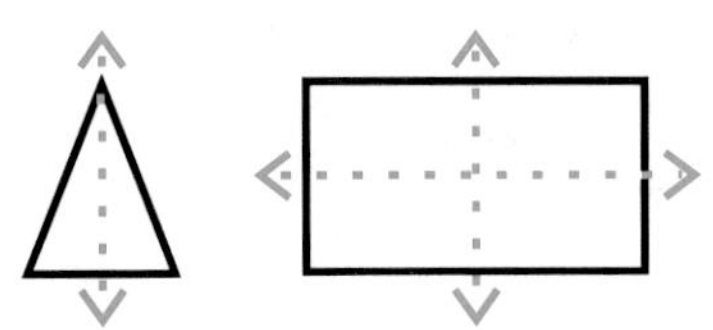

**line segment** (p. 16) A part of a line with two endpoints, named with two letters. The line segment below is named line segment *AB*.

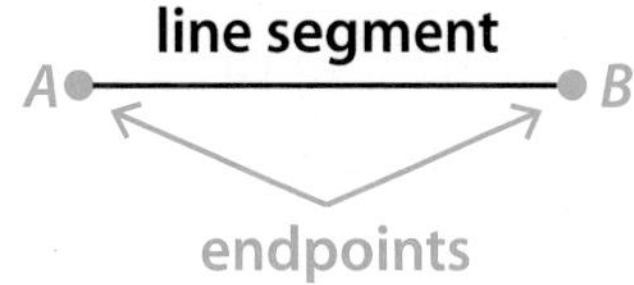


**liter (L)** (p. 292) A metric unit for measuring capacity. 1 L = 1,000 milliliters

**lowest terms** See *simplest form.*

## M

**mean** (p. 293) See *average.*

**median** (p. 293) The middle number in a set of data after the data are arranged in order from least to greatest. If you have five numbers in order, the third is the median.

**meter (m)** (p. 244) A metric unit for measuring length. 1 m = 100 centimeters

**mile (mi)** (p. 51) A unit of length in the U.S. Customary System. 1 mi = 5,280 feet

**milliliter (mL)** (p. 294) A metric unit for measuring capacity. 1,000 mL = 1 liter

**mixed number** (p. 158) A number that has a whole number part and a fraction part, such as $1\frac{1}{2}$.

**mode** (p. 317) The number that appears most often in a set of data.

**multiple** (p. 134) The product of a given number and any whole number. A multiple of 3 is 15.

**Multiplication Property of One** (p. 102) Every factor multiplied by 1 equals the factor. Example:

$$3 \times 1 = 3$$

## N

**net** (p. 33) A pattern of flat, connected shapes. This net can be folded to make a cube.

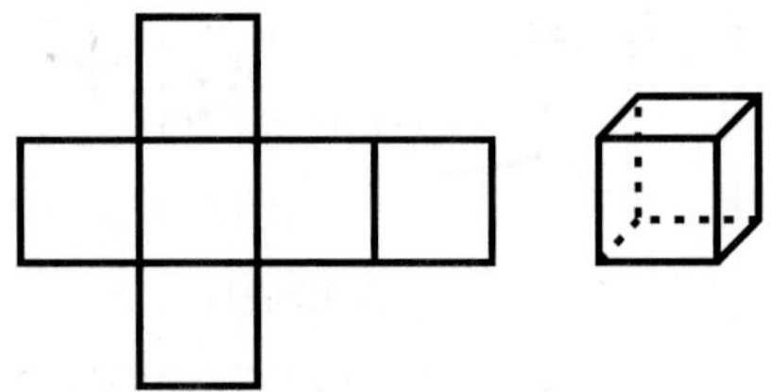

**number sentence** (p. 183) A sentence that shows how numbers are related. Examples: $6 + 2 = 8$, $5 + 3 > 6$

**numerator** (p. 149) The top number of a fraction. It shows the number of parts chosen. The numerator in the fraction $\frac{2}{3}$ is 2.

## O

**octagon** (p. 156) A polygon with eight sides.

**odd number** (p. 53) A number that is not a multiple of 2. Examples: 3, 7, 19, 21

**ordered pair** (p. 198) A pair of numbers that shows the location of a point on a grid. The ordered pair for the point shown on the coordinate grid is (4, 2).

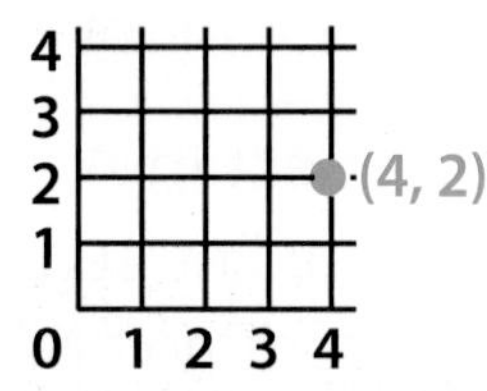


**ounce (oz)** (p. 166) A unit for measuring weight in the U.S. Customary System. 16 oz = 1 pound

**outcome** (p. 356) A possible result. Each number or color on a spinner is a possible outcome.

## P

**parallel lines** (p. 4) Lines that run the same way but never intersect.

**parallelogram** (p. 7) A quadrilateral with opposite sides parallel.

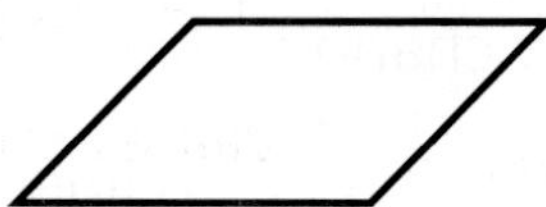

**pentagon** (p. 19) A polygon with five sides.

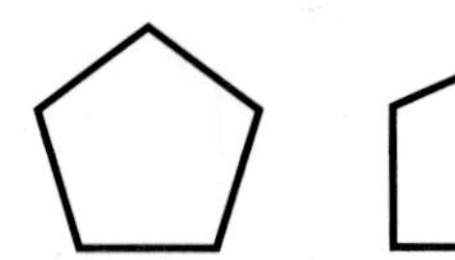

**percent** (p. 346) Hundredths written with a % sign. Example: $0.33 = \frac{33}{100} = 33\%$

**perimeter** (p. 26) The distance around any figure.

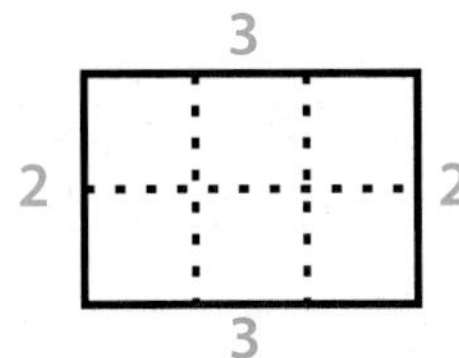


The perimeter is 10 units.

**period** (p. 58) A group of three digits within a whole number, named by starting at the right. The first three periods in a number are ones, thousands, and millions.

| Millions | Thousands | Ones |
|---|---|---|
| 987, | 654, | 321 |

**perpendicular lines** (p. 4) Two lines that meet or cross to form right angles.

**pictograph** (p. 226) A graph that shows data by using pictures that represent a certain number.

**pint (pt)** (p. 164) A unit for measuring capacity in the U.S. Customary System. 1 pt = 2 cups

**place value** (p. 52) A value assigned to a position in a number. The place values for a 3-digit number are shown below.

| Hundreds | Tens | Ones |
|---|---|---|
| 3 | 7 | 6 |

**point** (p. 16) An exact location. Points are usually labeled with capital letters.

**polygon** (p. 6) A closed shape formed by line segments. Squares and triangles are types of polygons.

**pound (lb)** (p. 166) A unit for measuring weight in the U.S. Customary System. 1 lb = 16 ounces

**probability** (p. 350) The chance that something will happen.

**product** (p. 101) The answer in multiplication. In the number sentence $8 \times 6 = 48$, the product is 48.

**pyramid** (p. 29) A solid with a polygon for a base and triangles for faces.

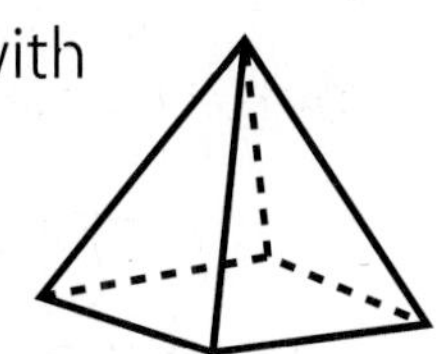

# Q

**quadrilateral** (p. 7) A polygon with four sides. Examples:

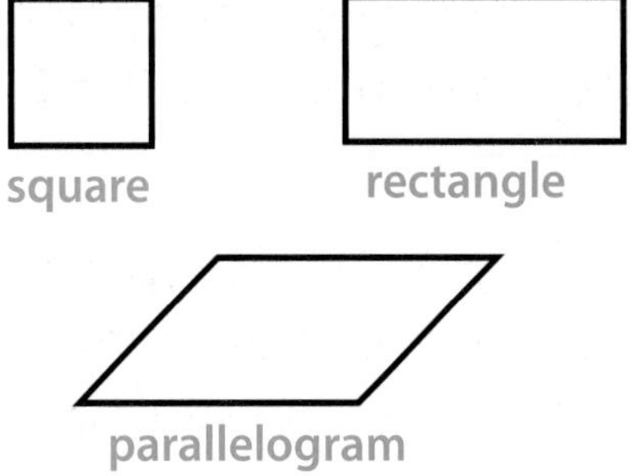


**quart (qt)** (p. 164) A unit for measuring capacity in the U.S. Customary System. 1 qt = 2 pints

**quotient** (p. 301) The answer in division. In the number sentence $56 \div 7 = 8$, the quotient is 8.

# R

**radius** (p. 349) A line segment from the center to a point on a circle.

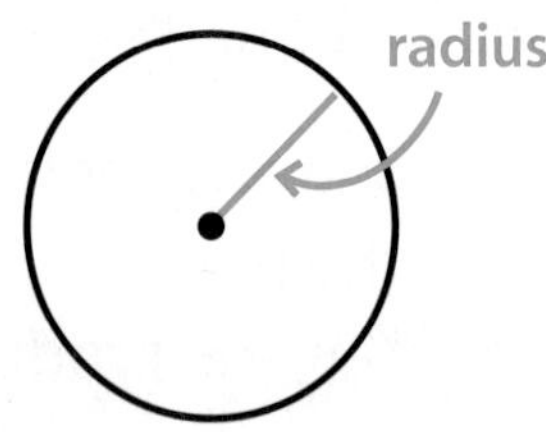


**range** (p. 316) The difference between the greatest and the least numbers of given data.

**ratio** (p. 340) A comparison of two numbers. Example: 2 bicycles to 3 cars = $\frac{2}{3}$ or 2:3 or "two to three."

**ray** (p. 16) A part of a line with one endpoint. A ray goes on and on in one direction.

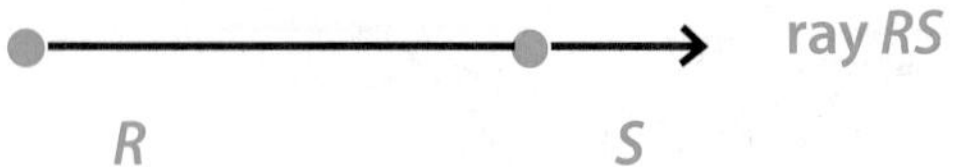


**rectangle** (p. 18) A special kind of parallelogram with all angles right angles.

**rectangular prism** (p. 29) A solid that has six rectangular faces.

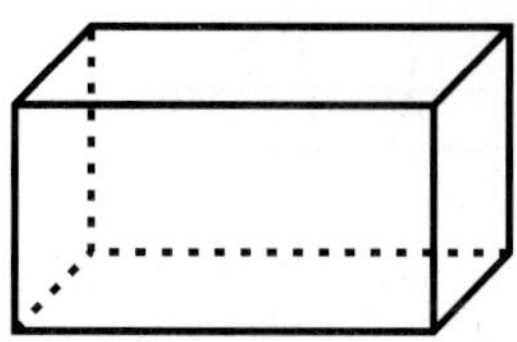

**remainder** (p. 114) The number left over when a division is complete.

**right angle** (p. 4) An angle that measures 90 degrees and makes a square corner.

**Roman numeral** (p. 212) A numeral in the ancient Roman number system. Some Roman numerals are I, V, X, L, and C.

**rounding** (p. 80) Changing a number to the nearest ten or hundred to make it easier to use. Example: 67 rounded to the nearest ten is 70.

# S

**set** (p. 171) A collection or group of objects or numbers.

**sides** (p. 6) The segments that make up a polygon.

**similar figures** (p. 201) Figures that have the same shape. They do not need to have the same size.

**simplest form** (p. 155) When the numerator and denominator are as small as possible. In simplest form, $\frac{6}{12}$ is $\frac{1}{2}$. Also called *lowest terms.*

**slide** (p. 10) Moving a figure in one direction.

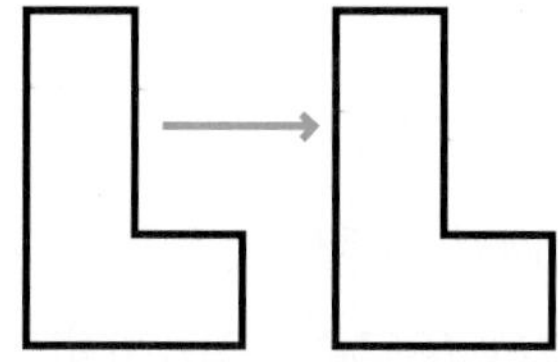

**sphere** (p. 29) A solid that has no flat faces and no vertexes. A ball is a model of a sphere.

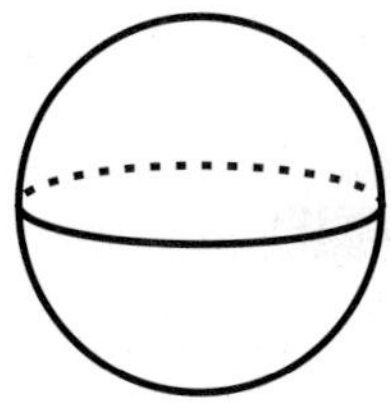

**square** (p. 138) A rectangle with four sides the same length.

**square unit** (p. 26) A unit used to measure area.

**standard form** (p. 52) The simplest way to show a number using digits. The standard form of 3 tens and 6 ones is 36.

**stem-and-leaf plot** (p. 132) A way to show data. Usually, the tens' digits are "stems" and the ones' digits are "leaves." The plot below shows this data: 20, 29, 31, 42, 45, 48.

| stem-and-leaf plot | |
|---|---|
| 2 | 0 9 |
| 3 | 1 |
| 4 | 2 5 8 |

**survey** (p. 174) Information gathered by asking questions and recording answers.

**time log** (p. 67) A record of how time is spent.

**ton (t)** (p. 167) A unit for measuring weight in the U.S. Customary System. 1 t = 2,000 pounds

**tree diagram** (p. 376) A picture used to count the ways things can be combined.

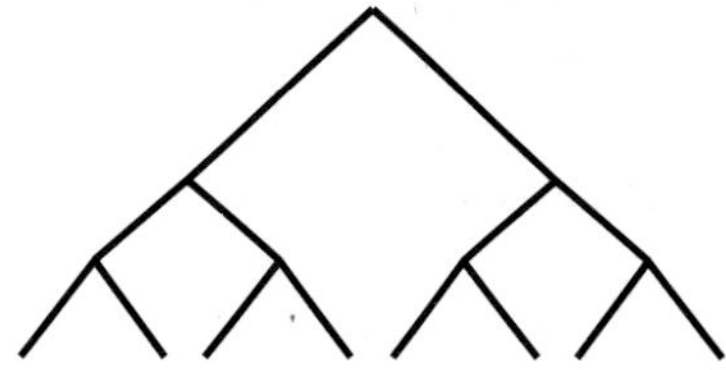

**trial** (p. 356) Each try in a probability experiment, such as one spin of a spinner.

**triangle** (p. 18) A polygon with three sides.

**turn** (p. 10) Rotating a figure about a point.

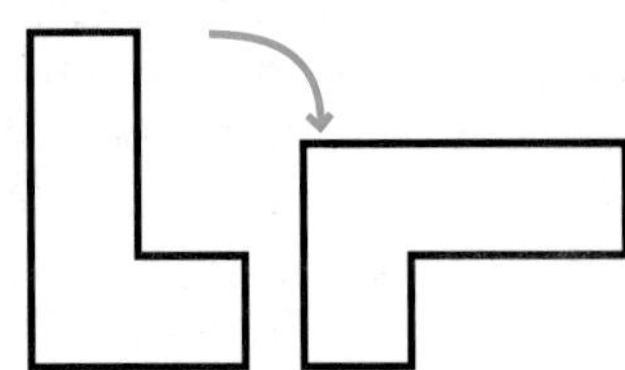

# V

**vertex** (p. 18) The common endpoint of two rays or two segments. Where three or more edges of a solid meet.

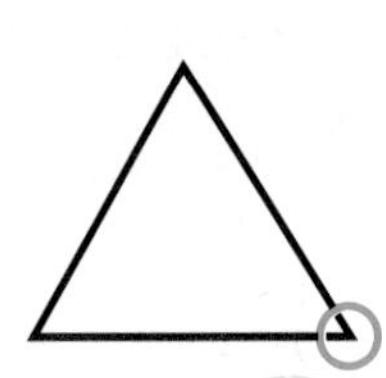

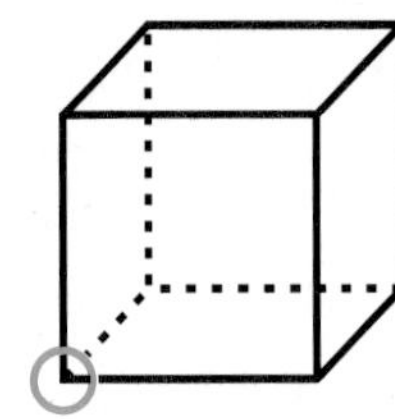

**volume** (p. 40) The amount of space inside a solid shape.

# Y

**yard (yd)** (p. 75) A unit for measuring length in the U.S. Customary System. 1 yd = 3 feet

**year** (p. 51) The time it takes Earth to revolve around the sun.

# Z

**Zero Property of Multiplication** (p. 102) Every factor multiplied by 0 equals 0. Example:

$$6 \times 0 = 0$$

# Index

# E



# F

## G



## H



## I



## J



## K



## L

# Index



## M

# Index

# Q



# R

# Index

## T



## U



## V



## W



## Y



## Z

# Acknowledgments

## Text *(continued from page iv)*

First published in Australia in 1990 by William Collins Pty Ltd., Sydney, in association with Anne Ingram Books. Text and illustrations copyright © 1990 by Rod Clement. Reprinted by arrangement with Gareth Stevens, Inc. **66** "January/Yas Nilt' ees" from *Alice Yazzie's Year,* poems by Ramona Maher. Poems copyright © 1977 by Ramona Maher. Reprinted by permission of the author. **104** From *Ernie and the Mile-Long Muffler,* by Marjorie Lewis. New York: Coward, McCann & Geoghegan, Inc., 1982. **148** From *Ramona the Pest,* by Beverly Cleary. New York: William Morrow and Company, Inc., 1968. **216** From "The Reward from a Sparrow" in *Chinese Folk Tales* by Louise and Yuan-Hsi Kuo. Millbrae, California: Celestial Arts, 1976. **276** From *Golden Girls: The Stories of Olympic Women Stars,* by Carli Laklan. New York: McGraw-Hill Book Company, 1980. **322** From *Just a Dream,* by Chris Van Allsburg. Copyright © 1990 by Chris Van Allsburg. Reprinted by permission of Houghton Mifflin Co. All rights reserved. **362** From "Crossing the River" from *Stories to Solve: Folktales from Around the World,* by George Shannon. New York: William Morrow and Company, Inc., 1985.

## Illustrations

**4** Randy Chewning. **60–61** Tatjana Krizmanic. **110–11** Carl Kock. **122** Richard Waldrep. **230** Phillip Geib. **214–15** Mercedes McDonald. **308–9** Steven Mach. **342–43** Ruta Daugavietis.

## Photography

**Front cover** Allan Landau. **Back cover** Sharon Hoogstraten. **i** Allan Landau. **ii–iii** Allan Landau. **vi** Sharon Hoogstraten. **vii** Michael Holford (tr); Allan Landau (br). **viii** Richard Waldrep (tr); Sharon Hoogstraten (cr); Allan Landau (br). **ix** Sharon Hoogstraten (l); Aric Attas (r); Allan Landau (b). **x** Allan Landau. **xi** Aric Attas. **xii–xiii** Allan Landau. **xiv** Allan Landau. **xv** Sharon Hoogstraten. **xvi** Allan Landau. **1–3** © Peter Pearson/Tony Stone Images. **5** Ralph J. Brunke (l, c, r). **6** Ralph J. Brunke (t, b). **7** Sharon Hoogstraten. **8** Sharon Hoogstraten. **10** © Carol Highsmith. **11** Sharon Hoogstraten. **12** © Robert Frerck/Odyssey (t), Sharon Hoogstraten (b). **13** Ralph J. Brunke (l, c, r). **15** Sharon Hoogstraten. **18–19** Ralph J. Brunke. **20** Sharon Hoogstraten. **22–23** Ralph J. Brunke. **24** © Patti McConville/ Image Bank (inset). **24–25** Sharon Hoogstraten. **25** © Garry Gay/Image Bank (inset). **26** © Georg Gerster/Comstock. **27** Sharon Hoogstraten (t, b). **28** Ralph J. Brunke. **29** Sharon Hoogstraten. **30** Allan Landau (t), Sharon Hoogstraten (b). **31** Allan Landau. **32** Allan Landau. **33** Allan Landau (l, c, r). **34** Ralph J. Brunke (l, r). **35** Sharon Hoogstraten. **38–39** Sharon Hoogstraten. **39** Sharon Hoogstraten (inset). **40** Ralph J. Brunke (l), Sharon Hoogstraten (r). **41** Ralph J. Brunke (c), Sharon Hoogstraten (t, b). **42** Sharon Hoogstraten (t, b). **43** Sharon Hoogstraten (tr, tl, tc, c, bl, br). **45** Sharon Hoogstraten. **46** Allan Landau (inset). **46–47** © Donavon Reese/Tony Stone Images. **47** Sharon Hoogstraten (t), Allan Landau (b). **48** Allan Landau. **49** Sharon Hoogstraten. **50–51** Sharon Hoogstraten. **52** Sharon Hoogstraten. **53** Sharon Hoogstraten. **54** Allan Landau. **57** Sharon Hoogstraten (l, r). **62** Aric Attas. **63** Allan Landau (t, b). **64** Sharon Hoogstraten. **65** Allan Landau. **66** © Larry Ulrich/Tony Stone Images. **67** Sharon Hoogstraten. **70** Sharon Hoogstraten (l), Bettman Archive (r). **71** Allan Landau. **72–73** Michael Holford. **74–75** Allan Landau. **75** Sharon Hoogstraten. **76–77** Sharon Hoogstraten. **78** Sharon Hoogstraten. **79** Allan Landau. **82** Sharon Hoogstraten (t), Allan Landau (bl, br). **83** Allan Landau **86–87** Sharon Hoogstraten. **88** Sharon Hoogstraten. **90** Sharon Hoogstraten. **94** Marsden Hartley, "Vase of Flowers," Nefsky/Art Resource (inset). **94–95** Aric Attas. **96** Allan Landau. **97** Sharon Hoogstraten, Charles Hogg (insets, t, c, b). **98** Charles Hogg (insets t, b,c). **98–99** Charles Hogg. **99** Charles Hogg (insets tl, tr), Sharon Hoogstraten (inset b). **100** Sharon Hoogstraten. **101** Sharon Hoogstraten. **102–3** Sharon Hoogstraten. **104** Aric Attas.**105** Allan Landau. **106** Allan Landau. **107** Sharon Hoogstraten. **108** Aric Attas (b), Allan Landau (c). **108–9** Allan Landau. **112** Sharon Hoogstraten. **113** Chris Walker for the Chicago Tribune (t), Sharon Hoogstraten (b). **114–15** Sharon Hoogstraten. **115** Chris Walker for the Chicago Tribune (inset). **116** Aric Attas (bl). **116–17** Aric Attas. **117** Allan Landau (l, r). **118–19** Sharon Hoogstraten. **123** Allan Landau. **124** Sharon Hoogstraten (tr, tl). **124–25** Allan Landau. **125** Sharon Hoogstraten (t, b). **126** Sharon Hoogstraten. **127** Sharon Hoogstraten. **128** March of Dimes (l, c, r). **129** Sharon Hoogstraten. **130** Allan Landau (t, c), © Scott Camazine/Photo Researchers (b). **131** Allan Landau (t, c), © Scott Camazine/Photo Researchers (b).

**132** Sharon Hoogstraten (l), Allan Landau (insets c, r). **133** Sharon Hoogstraten.**134** Allan Landau. **135** Sharon Hoogstraten. **136** Sharon Hoogstraten. **136–37** Allan Landau. **138** Sharon Hoogstraten. **142–43** Sharon Hoogstraten. **143** Allan Landau (tr). **144** Aric Attas, © Mike Kullen/Picture Cube (inset). **145** Art Wise. **146–47** Aric Attas. **148** Aric Attas.**149** Aric Attas. **151** Allan Landau. **152–53** Aric Attas. **154** Allan Landau. **157** Allan Landau. **160** Allan Landau. **161** Allan Landau (t, c), Aric Attas (b). **162–63** Aric Attas. **166–67** Sharon Hoogstraten. **169** Archive Photos. **171** Aric Attas. **172–73** Allan Landau. **174** Allan Landau. **175** Allan Landau (t, c), Aric Attas (b). **176** Allan Landau (t, b). **177** Aric Attas. **179** Sharon Hoogstraten (t), Allan Landau (b). **180–81** Allan Landau. **182** Allan Landau. **184** Sharon Hoogstraten. **184–85** Aric Attas (b). **185** Aric Attas. **186** © Nicole Katano/Tony Stone Images (t), Allan Landau (b). **187** © Robert E. Daemmrich/Tony Stone Images (l), Aric Attas (r). **190–91** Allan Landau (b). **191** Comstock (t), © Nicole Katano/Tony Stone Images (c). **193** Sharon Hoogstraten, Art Resource (inset).**194** Allan Landau.**195** Aric Attas.**196** © Paul Trummer/The Image Bank. **199** Sharon Hoogstraten. **200–201** Sharon Hoogstraten. **202–3** Aric Attas. **204** The British Museum (t), Aric Attas (b). **205** Susan Andrews (t), Aric Attas (b). **206** Aric Attas (t), Sharon Hoogstraten (b). **207** Allan Landau. **208–9** Sharon Hoogstraten. **210–11** Aric Attas. **212** George Sullivan (t), © Nick Nicholson/The Image Bank (b). **216** Sharon Hoogstraten. **217** Sharon Hoogstraten. **218** Allan Landau. **219** Sharon Hoogstraten. **220** Sharon Hoogstraten. **221** Aric Attas. **222** Aric Attas. **223** Sharon Hoogstraten. **224–25** Sharon Hoogstraten. **227** Aric Attas (t), Field Museum of Natural History CN-86877.8c (b). **228–29** Sharon Hoogstraten. **231** Allan Landau. **232–33** Art Wise. **234** © Duncan S. McNab. **235** Sharon Hoogstraten. **236** Sharon Hoogstraten. **238** Bridgeman/Art Resource. **238–39** Sharon Hoogstraten. **241** Allan Landau. **242–43** Sharon Hoogstraten. **244** Allan Landau (l), Sharon Hoogstraten (r). **245** Allan Landau. **246** Ed Nagel. **247** Sharon Hoogstraten. **248** Ed Nagel. **250** Ed Nagel. **251** Ed Nagel. **252** Aric Attas. **254–55** Sharon Hoogstraten. **256** Aric Attas. **257** Art Wise. **258** Aric Attas (l, r). **258–59** Ed Nagel. **260** Allan Landau. **262** © Jim Pickerell/Tony Stone Images (inset). **262–63** Aric Attas. **270–71** Art Wise. **274** Aric Attas.

**276** Bettmann Archive. **277** Aric Attas. **278–79** Aric Attas. **280–81** Sharon Hoogstraten. **282–83** Art Wise. **286–87** Sharon Hoogstraten. **288** Sharon Hoogstraten. **289** Sharon Hoogstraten. **290–91** Sharon Hoogstraten. **291** Allan Landau (inset). **293** Sharon Hoogstraten. **294** Allan Landau (inset). **294–95** Sharon Hoogstraten. **295** Allan Landau (insets l, r). **296–97** Allan Landau. **297** Aric Attas (r). **298** Aric Attas. **299** Sharon Hoogstraten. **300** Allan Landau (inset). **300–301** Sharon Hoogstraten. **301** Allan Landau (inset). **302–3** Aric Attas. **304** Allan Landau. **305** Allan Landau. **306** Allan Landau. **310** Allan Landau (tc, bc), Sharon Hoogstraten (l, r). **311** Allan Landau (l), Sharon Hoogstraten (r). **312–13** Allan Landau. **313** © Russ Kline/Comstock (inset t), © L.L.T. Rhodes (inset b). **314–15** Aric Attas. **315** Allan Landau (insets tr, tl, br, bl). **316** Sharon Hoogstraten. **317** Allan Landau. **318–19** Allan Landau. **320–21** Sharon Hoogstraten. **322** Sharon Hoogstraten. **323** Sharon Hoogstraten. **324** Sharon Hoogstraten. **325** Aric Attas. **326** Allan Landau. **328** Sharon Hoogstraten. **329** Allan Landau (t), Sharon Hoogstraten (b). **330–31** Sharon Hoogstraten. **334–35** Sharon Hoogstraten. **336** Allan Landau (t, b). **337** Aric Attas. **338–39** Aric Attas. **340** © Steve Gottlieb/FPG International (br), © Sumo/Image Bank (bl). **340–41** Aric Attas. **344** © Tom Mackie/Tony Stone Images (cl), © Barbara Filet/Tony Stone Images (cr). **344–45** Aric Attas. **345** © Jean Francois Causse/Tony Stone Images. **346–47** Sharon Hoogstraten. **347** Allan Landau (inset). **348** Susan Andrews (insets l, c, r). **348–49** Sharon Hoogstraten. **350–51** Sharon Hoogstraten. **352–53** Aric Attas. **354** Allan Landau. **356–57** Sharon Hoogstraten. **358–59** Aric Attas. **360–61** Aric Attas. **363** Sharon Hoogstraten. **364–65** Aric Attas. **366** Susan Andrews. **367** Susan Andrews (t), Aric Attas (b). **368–69** Allan Landau. **370–71** Sharon Hoogstraten. **372–73** Sharon Hoogstraten. **374–75** Aric Attas. **376** Sharon Hoogstraten. **377** Susan Andrews. **378** Susan Andrews (inset). **378–79** Sharon Hoogstraten. **382–83** Aric Attas. **384** Aric Attas. **385** Allan Landau (bl); Aric Attas (r). **386–87** Sharon Hoogstraten. **388** Allan Landau (l); Sharon Hoogstraten (r). **389** Sharon Hoogstraten. **390** Allan Landau (l); Sharon Hoogstraten (r). **396** Allan Landau. **399** Allan Landau. **403** Aric Attas. **404–5** Sharon Hoogstraten. **405** Allan Landau (b). **406–7** Aric Attas.